SPONSORED BY

Katie Shu Sui Pui Charitable Trust

（本系列丛书由舒小佩慈善基金赞助）

|酒店及旅游业管理系列教材|

主编 邱汉琴

Hospitality and Tourism Financial Management

酒店及旅游业财务管理

彭康麟（Kanglin Peng）蔡铭志（Henry Tsai）/著

ZHEJIANG UNIVERSITY PRESS
浙江大学出版社

图书在版编目(CIP)数据

酒店及旅游业财务管理＝Hospitality and Tourism Financial Management：英汉对照 / 彭康麟，蔡铭志著.—杭州：浙江大学出版社，2019.5

ISBN 978-7-308-16286-9

Ⅰ.①酒… Ⅱ.①彭…②蔡… Ⅲ.①饭店—企业管理—双语教学—高等学校—教材—英、汉②旅游企业—财务管理—双语教学—高等学校—教材—英、汉 Ⅳ.①F719.2②F590.66

中国版本图书馆 CIP 数据核字（2016）第 240896 号

酒店及旅游业财务管理

Hospitality and Tourism Financial Management

彭康麟(Kanglin Peng)　蔡铭志(Henry Tsai)　著

责任编辑	樊晓燕
责任校对	袁菁鸿
封面设计	春天书装
出版发行	浙江大学出版社
	（杭州市天目山路 148 号　邮政编码 310007）
	（网址：http://www.zjupress.com）
排　　版	杭州林智广告有限公司
印　　刷	杭州杭新印务有限公司
开　　本	710mm×1000mm　1/16
印　　张	19.75
字　　数	384 千
版 印 次	2019 年 5 月第 1 版　2019 年 5 月第 1 次印刷
书　　号	ISBN 978-7-308-16286-9
定　　价	69.00 元

浙江大学出版社市场运营中心联系方式：(0571) 88925591；http://zjdxcbs.tmall.com

总　序

　　香港理工大学酒店及旅游业管理学院已经有 40 多年的历史。学院致力于引领全球酒店及旅游教育的发展,无论在科研还是教学等方面,都在全球享有较高知名度,尤其是在发表学术研究文献方面,在全球位列第二,在教与学方面,亦处于国际领先地位。学院 65 位教职人员来自 22 个国家和地区,着重教学创新与研究。学员能够在多元文化环境下追随国际知名的学者学习有着良好职业前景的学科。2011 年,香港理工大学的教学及研究酒店——唯港荟正式启用,强化了学院的人才培育工作,以满足香港地区内以至全球酒店及旅游业界对专业人才的殷切需求。

　　"酒店及旅游业管理硕士学位课程"是引进了国际、国内最前沿的教育理念,为从事旅游业研究与实践的业界人士而开设的学历教育课程。该课程自 2000 年与浙江大学合办以来,依托世界一流的香港理工大学和浙江大学的教学资源,已经培养了 600 多位政府各级官员、业界管理人才以及学术界科研精英。课程通过综合的、先进的知识为学生提供了宏观的视野,让学生在具有扎实的工作经验的基础上,提高经营管理的深度,建立超前的意识,发展系统地解决问题的能力。

　　虽然香港理工大学酒店及旅游业管理学院的酒店及旅游业管理硕士学位课程取得了一定的成功,为业界培养了优秀人才,但是在办学的过程中,我们深刻地意识到教材资源的缺乏。因此,香港理工大学具有优秀双语能力的教授等师资人员专门为"酒店及旅游业管理硕士学位课程"设计

Prelude

With more than 40 years' history, the School of Hotel and Tourism Management (SHTM) at The Hong Kong Polytechnic University (PolyU) is positioned to lead the world's hospitality and tourism education in the years to come. It has high reputation in both academic research and teaching. Especially, the School is ranked No. 2 in the world among academic institutions in hospitality and tourism based on research and scholarly activities. In terms of teaching and learning, it is also in a leading position. With a faculty of 65 academic staff members from 22 countries and regions, the School offers innovative teaching and research in a creative learning environment. Students are able to study in a multicultural context and to learn from an internationally renowned faculty whose programmes provide outstanding career opportunities. The official opening of the teaching and research hotel—Hotel ICON in 2011 has further strengthened the School's efforts in nurturing hospitality graduates to address the growing demands of the hospitality and tourism industry in Hong Kong, the region, and around the world.

The MSc in Hotel and Tourism Management is a programme designed for hotel and tourism practitioners, with the aim of introducing latest education concept in Hong Kong and internationally. Since 2000, the programme has been offered collaboratively by the Hong Kong Polytechnic University and Zhejiang University, which has cultivated more than 600 government officials, industry managers, and academic talents. The programme provides students with a macro perspective from the comprehensive and advanced knowledge, improves the ability of management, and establishes advanced awareness, as well as develops systematic problem-solving skills based on solid work experience.

Although the programme of MSc in Hotel and Tourism Management offered by SHTM-PolyU has been highly successful and has cultivated many talents for the industry, we are fully aware of the lack of bilingual teaching and learning resources during the process of delivering these courses. Therefore, professors, who have excellent bilingual competencies from The Hong Kong Polytechnic

了一套中英文对照双语教材——"酒店及旅游业管理系列教材"。本系列教材包括《中国内地酒店及旅游业》《酒店及旅游业人力资源管理》《酒店及旅游业财务管理》《酒店及旅游业研究方法》以及《酒店及旅游业市场营销》。这种双语式的硕士学位课程教材在酒店及旅游业管理专业的研究生教育历史上是具有开创性的,充分体现了我们开办该课程的特色与进一步构建更好的教学交流平台的愿望。该系列教材的开发和推出,将有力地促进香港理工大学与浙江大学的双语课程的持续发展。同时,我们也期待该系列教材可以有助于中国内地日益成熟的旅游管理学硕士(MTA)市场的发展。中国的各行各业已逐渐趋向于国际化,旅游教育更是如此,我们希望这套双语教材的问世将会对内地的旅游教育起到促进作用。

最后,作者要特别感谢舒小佩慈善基金的全力资助,该基金的慷慨资助使得本系列教材得以面世。舒小佩女士寄语并祝福每位读者都能在书中找到自己的"黄金屋",并为响应国家的"一带一路"倡议做出最好的准备。

丛书总编

邱汉琴教授

香港理工大学酒店及旅游业管理学院

University，have designed and developed this bilingual book series for this programme，including *Hospitality and Tourism in Chinese Mainland*，*Hospitality and Tourism Human Resource Management*，*Hospitality and Tourism Financial Management*，*Hospitality and Tourism Research Methods*，and *Hospitality and Tourism Marketing Management*. The uniqueness of this bilingual book series is that it is the first time that such book series were created for a bilingual master degree in hotel and tourism education history，which fully represents the characteristics of this programme and also acts as an interaction platform for students and teachers to interact in order to enhance the teaching and learning experiences. The development and introduction of the bilingual book series is not only to promote the sustainable development of bilingual programme offered by The Hong Kong Polytechnic University and Zhejiang University，but also to look forward to facilitating the development of the increasingly mature market of Master of Tourism Administration（MTA）in Chinese Mainland. Nowadays，various industries in China have been gradually internationalized and we hope that the introduction of the bilingual book series will play a significant role in enhancing tourism education in the Mainland.

Last but not least，the authors wish to express their sincere gratitude to the Katie Shu Sui Pui Charitable Trust for its financial support in making the project of publishing of the Bilingual Hotel and Tourism Management Book Series a reality. They also hereby acknowledge Ms. Shu's wish for each reader to find his/her own dream career by making the best use of the material in the book series in preparation for China's Belt and Road Initiative as a result.

Managing Editor
Hanqin Qiu
Professor
School of Hotel and Tourism Management
The Hong Kong Polytechnic University

$\mathbf{C}$ONTENTS 目 录

C ONTENTS 目 录

绪　论

财务管理是价值创造的过程

　　企业财务管理的主要目标就是公司价值最大化,然而,公司价值却甚难评价。我们所看到的财务绩效与公司股价是一个以古观今、眺望未来的心理预期,唯有在公司价值能给投资人带来希望时,投资人才会进行投资,公司才能持续获得资金,不断地创造公司利害关系人的共有价值。此正向循环就是价值创造的过程,而不断的价值创造则是公司永续经营的动力。本书不仅以传统财务管理的投资政策、融资政策、营运资金政策与红利政策来披露公司价值创造所应关注的细节,而且突破性地叙述了酒店及旅游业服务创新的价值再造。例如,Airbnb 以分享经济、体验经济为理念,公司市值不但高于连锁酒店集团 Marriott,亦是 Expedia 市值的两倍。还有相同概念的 Uber、VizEat 等分别在旅游运输及家居主厨餐饮上不断突破传统餐旅业的价值。

酒店与旅游业财务的创新价值

　　本书要强调的是价值创造过程中的创新因素,诚如彼得·德鲁克所言,是"创新或死亡(innovate or die)"。例如诺基亚没有预料到智能手机的发展,导致其手机在消费市场上销声匿迹。目前市场中的服务创新如 Airbnb 与 Uber 的公司市值已超越全球最大的旅馆与交通营运集团,餐饮服务创新如 VizEat 与 Plate Culture 也通过网络平台逐渐发展全球化的居家主厨服务,传统的旅馆、餐饮与交通产业已察觉到这些餐旅服务创新所带来的威胁,它们积极地投资创新,以求再创价值。

　　在财务评价上,仍可用资本预算、资本结构与资本资产定价模式等章节的方法来评估创新所带来的收入、成本与预期价值,然而,在创新因素的考量

Introduction

Financial Management Is a Process for Value Creation

The main objective of financial management is to maximize the value of a company, however, it is difficult to evaluate the real value of a company. The financial performance and company stock price are the results of investment expectation, which is based on the history to predict a company's financial performance. People invest in a stock when they see the future of the company, then the company can get funding from people's investment to co-create value with stakeholders. This is the process of value creation that drives the sustainable development of a company. This book addresses the details of capital budgeting, financing policy, working capital policy and dividend policy to disclose the value creation of a company in perspectives of aditional financial management. In addition, we describe the value creation from service innovation in hotel and tourism industries. For example, the Airbnb has been the paradigm of share economy and experience economy, its market value is already higher than the biggest hotel chain, Marriott, and is twice of the market value of Expedia. Uber and VizEat, respectively, lead the tide of innovative transportation and dinning services in the hospitality industries.

Hotel and Tourism Financial Value from Service Innovation

Peter Drucker said: "Innovate or die." In this book, we address specially innovation factors in the process of value creation. Nokia did not foresee its fail because of ignoring the development of smartphones. The contemporary innovative services such as Airbnb and Uber's market value has surpassed the world's largest hotel group and transport operator. Food service innovation such as VizEat and Plate Culture also develop the global localized home chef service through internet platforms. Traditional hotels, restaurants and transportation industries have been forced to face these challenges and invested more service innovations in order to create more value.

Financial evaluations of the revenue, cost and expected value of the service innovation can still apply the approaches of capital budgeting, capital structure and capital asset pricing model. In addition to the traditional approaches, service innovation requires additional considerations to the following points for sustainable competiveness in

上需要特别注意下述重点,因为它们在市场竞争中缺一不可。

● 关键成本:创新服务的平均开发成本、个别服务的开发成本、营业额花费在开发新服务上的比例。

● 有效性:每年能开发多少新服务、新服务成功的比例。

● 速度:公司采纳新观念的时间、开发模型的时间、开发模型到投入的时间、服务投入的时间。

我们常用长江后浪推前浪、一代新人换旧人来比喻世代交替,这现象在我们所熟知的产业竞争环境中也屡见不鲜。服务创新造就了餐旅业中的Airbnb、VizEat、Uber 等新兴业态,倍感威胁的星级酒店、高档餐厅、旅游运输等将何去何从,如何以关键成本、有效而快速的创新来正面备战,创造新局,且让我们从财务管理的角度拭目以待。

the dynamic changing market.

● Cost: The average cost of innovative services, developing costs of individual service, the proportion of operational cost for developing new services.

● Effectiveness: How many new services? What is the successful rate among those new services?

● Speed: Time for adapting new concepts, time for developing models, time for manufacturing products, time for providing services.

We often describe alternation of generation by an old saying: a new generation replacing the old one as the waves which come later are stronger and higher. This phenomenon also happens to the industrial competitive environment. Service innovations created new hospitality servies, for example, Airbnb, VizEat, Uber and other emerging companies, which have threatened those existing hotels, restaurants, as well as travel and transportation services. Only by utilizing cost advantege, as well as creating rapid and effective innovations that the traditional hospitality industry can make a breakthrough for comparative advantages. This book is going to outlook the new era of hotel and tourism industries from the perspective of financial management.

第1章　酒店及旅游业财务管理简介

学习目标

- 领会财务管理对酒店及旅游企业的重要性
- 理解会计和财务的差异
- 理解财务管理的范畴
- 理解制定决策的不同观点
- 厘清财务经理的目标
- 了解委托代理关系

1.1　引　言

　　酒店和旅游行业一般被称为"以人为本的行业"。在酒店和旅游业运营的过程中,客人和服务提供者之间产生密切互动。以酒店住宿为例,从客人预订客房,直到入住完成后办理退房,酒店不仅提供硬件设施(如床和浴缸)给客人使用,同时客人需要或者也可能向酒店提出服务要求(例如,客房服务)。这种互动关系对于一个企业的成功(或者失败)或利润底线(或亏损)发挥显著作用。极佳的客房设施或者优秀的服务可以对酒店客房收入做出积极贡献,而陈旧的设施或怠慢的服务员却可以很容易地令客人不再光顾。然而,为了使酒店和旅游企业的里里外外(包括硬件设施和服务)都能达到业主和经理人预期的状态,金融资本的供应、调度和管理是至关重要的。例如,如果没有适当的资本提供,酒店或旅游企业将无法招聘、培训和留住高素质的工作人员向客人提供必需的服务;如果没有仔细规划和调度运营资金,酒店或旅游企业将无法购买牛肉、生产牛排和按时支付供应商欠款。更极端的一个例子是,因为没有合理管理资金,在建中的酒店可能会被迫停工而无法如

Chapter 1　Introduction to Hotel and Tourism Financial Management

Learning Outcomes

- Appreciate the importance of financial management in hotel and tourism businesses
- Understand the differences between accounting and finance
- Understand financial management
- Appreciate perspectives on decision making
- Distinguish the goal for financial managers
- Understand the agency relationship

1.1　Introduction

The hotel and tourism industry is widely known as a "people industry". Close interactions between customers and service providers occur during the course of hotel and tourism operations. In the case of a hotel stay, from the time when a guest makes a reservation to when she or he checks out of the hotel, not only the hotel provides hardware facilities (e.g., bed and bath) for the guest's use but also the guest needs or may request services (e.g., housekeeping services) from the hotel. Such interactions play a significant role in determining a business's success (sometimes, failure) or bottom-line profit (or loss). While excellent guestrooms or staff services could contribute positively to the hotel in terms of, for example, room revenues, run-down facilities or inattentive staff could easily turn customers away. Nevertheless, to make everything (both hardware facilities and services) in hotel and tourism businesses work up to the owner's and operator's performance expectations, the supply, dispatch and management of financial capital is of critical importance. For example, without appropriate supply of capital resources, a hotel or tourism business would not be able to recruit, train, and retain quality staff to provide requisite services to the guests; without careful planning and dispatching of operational capital, a hotel or tourism business would not be able to purchase raw meat, produce steaks and pay the supplier on time. To a further extreme, owing to the lack of due management of financial capital, a hotel under construction may come to a halt and not be completed for operation at all.

6

期完工开业。

　　财务管理是酒店和旅游行业的支柱,无论是业主、管理公司、投资者、债权人,还是员工都应该知道他们所做的直接或间接的决策和行为,都与一个企业的财务管理相关并对其成功与否产生一定的影响。如果酒店或旅游企业从业人员没能对财务管理有适当的体会并掌握相关知识,在执行相对简单的日常运营任务时也会遇到巨大的挑战,并很可能因此导致不愿见到的企业失败——破产。

　　本书将为读者介绍特别针对酒店和旅游企业的与财务管理相关的基本概念和理论以及价值/收入/利润提升的课题,期望读者通过阅读理解这本书之后能对酒店及旅游业财务管理有一个系统性及全面的认识,并能够在他们的企业中运用所学。在此提示,读者没有必要按本书章节顺序阅读学习,可以按自己感兴趣的部分/章节先行阅读。

1.2　会计与财务的差别

　　会计和财务是两个不同的商业功能,但经常被误认为是一个概念。会计的职责主要是记录所有能产生的收入和运营费用,如工资和员工福利等类型的交易。其他货币信息,如现金收支和税费等,都属于会计职责。虽然有各种不同的会计分类,但一般有两种主要形式:财务会计和管理会计。

　　财务会计主要记录财务信息并进行分类。会计循环始于商业交易,经过确认、分析、输入、并过账到相关会计分录,于会计循环结束后进行财务报表编制。主要的财务报表包括资产负债表、损益表以及现金流量表。这些报表在本质上是静态的,因为它们只提供企业在某一时间点的历史财务信息的快照。财务会计着重于过去的交易数据,以期生成和汇总准确和相关的财务资料来为业主和投资者提供评估其投资的数据,为贷款人评估一个公司的借贷能力和其贷款的违约风险,并为政府机构征收企业等各类税款提供信息。例如,一份 20×× 年第二季度的利润表将提供一个企业在所述时间段的经营信息和表现;业主和投资者应该知道该公司在履行其财务义务后是否产生利润。另外,一份 20×× 年 12 月 31 日的年度资产负债表将显示一个企业在上

Financial management is certainly the backbone of hotel and tourism industry and every stakeholder of the industry, whether they are owners, management companies, investors, lenders, or employees, should be aware that their decisions and behaviors are all related to a business's financial management, either directly or indirectly, and have certain impacts on its success. Without adequate knowledge and appreciation on financial management, a hotel or tourism business would find it extremely challenging to perform even simple daily operational functions and very possibly lead to undesirable business failures—bankruptcy.

This book will introduce the readers basic concepts and theories related to financial management, with particular emphasis on hotel and tourism businesses, and topics on value/revenue/profit enhancement, so that after reading through this book, the readers will have a systematic and comprehensive understanding of hotel and tourism financial management and be able to apply what they have learned in this book to their workplace. It should be noted that following the chapter sequence is not necessary; readers could turn to their interested sections/chapters as deemed appropriate.

1.2 Differences between Accounting and Finance

Accounting and finance are two distinct business functions but are frequently mistaken as one concept. The accounting functions mainly deal with ongoing financial record keeping documenting transactions of all types that generate revenues and incur operational expenses such as salaries and employee benefits. Other monetary information such as cash receipts, payments and taxes, among others, all belong to the accounting function. While there are various forms of accounting functions, in general there are two major forms: financial accounting and managerial accounting.

Financial accounting involves recording and classifying financial information. Throughout the accounting cycle, business transactions are identified, analyzed, entered, and posted to relevant entries/journals and at the completion of the accounting cycle, the financial statements are prepared. The financial statements, including mainly the balance sheet, the income statement (or the profit and loss statement), and the statement of cash flows, are static in nature as they provide a snapshot of historical financial information at a certain point in time to the interested parties. The focus of financial accounting is looking at past transaction data and producing and aggregating accurate and relevant financial information for owners and investors to gauge their investment; for lenders to assess a firm's borrow capacity and the default risks of their loans; and for government agencies to levy business and other various types of taxes. For example, a quarterly income statement dated the second quarter of $20 \times \times$ would provide a business' operational information and performance during the said time period; owners and investors shall know whether or not the firm has made any profit after meeting its financial obligations. On the other hand, an annual balance sheet dated 31 December

述日期的总资产、负债和业主权益、利益关系者能借此评估公司的财务状况。因为所编制出的财务信息必须精确，并针对不同时间点和企业能够有对比性，所以企业的财务会计须符合一般公认的会计原则（GAAP）。

正如其名，管理会计允许管理人员应用各种工具在已编制的财务信息基础上再产生新的信息，以便企业制定明智的运营和战略决策。换句话说，管理者应该乐于（或基于职务所需）钻研编制后的财务信息，以评估企业经营绩效并对表现欠佳方面进行改善。例如，管理者可以应用比率分析评估一个企业在某一段时间的库存管理来回答以下的问题：2015 年的存货周转率是多少？相比于 2014 年的数据是改善了还是变差了？是什么原因造成了或高或低的存货周转率？管理者需要深入了解吗？我们餐厅的存货周转率相比我们的竞争对手是高还是低？在适当的比率分析的基础上，管理者应该能够制定可行的、能提高他们库存管理的战略。此外，管理者也可以应用本—量—利（CVP）分析（或称为保本点分析）来解决以下的问题：就一周而言，酒店在以某个平均房价卖房的基础上需销售多少房间才能够保本？也就是说，一个星期的客房收益是否足够支付与出租客房相关的固定成本和变动成本？还可以通过考量概率测算的本—量—利分析设置具有挑战性但合理的管理绩效目标。

值得强调的是，酒店或旅游企业的管理者应该精通会计语言，特别是在管理会计领域的会计语言，这能让他们对所负责运营的部门的里里外外都了若指掌。虽然目前没有一套强制性针对酒店管理会计目的的制度或原则，国际连锁酒店一般会采纳自 1926 年起制定的、目前已是第 11 版的非强制性质的酒店业统一会计制度（USALI），并将其列入酒店管理合同。

而另一方面，财务侧重于购买什么样的资产以及如何支付这些资产。因此，财务涉及一些如股票估值、债券估值、资产多元化、房产估值以及营运资金管理等领域。很明显，可靠和相关的会计信息是财务职责能够发挥得淋漓尽致的必要条件。

人们经常混淆会计和财务的一个可能的原因是，根据酒店或旅游业的组织规模，有可能在组织中只有一个财务总监负责所有与会计和财务相关的职责（可能是小型或独立企业）；而在大型组织中，会计和财务职责一般是分别

20×× would show a firm's total assets, liabilities and owners' equity as of the said date and the stakeholders would be able to assess the financial condition of the firm as a result. As financial information produced ought to be precise and comparable across time and businesses, firms are required to conform to generally accepted accounting principles (GAAP) as far as the financial accounting functions are concerned.

Managerial accounting, as its name might have suggested, allows managers apply various tools to compiled financial information in generating new information to make informed operational and strategic decisions for the business. In other words, managers are interested (or, expected) in digging into compiled accounting records to assess operational performance and pinpoint areas for improvement actions. For example, managers can apply ratio analysis in assessing inventory management of a business during a certain period of time to answer questions like: what is the inventory turnover ratio in 2015? How is it compared to that in 2014? What was the cause of or should the managers be concerned about a high or low inventory turnover ratio? How is our restaurant's inventory turnover compared to our competitors'? On the basis of appropriate ratio analysis, managers should then be able to devise actionable strategies to enhance their inventory management. In addition, managers could also apply the cost-volume-profit (CVP) analysis (or interchangeably called the breakeven analysis) to help answer questions like: on a weekly basis how many rooms should be rented at a certain price in order for the hotel to reach breakeven? That is, can room revenues received in a week cover both fixed and variable costs in association with the room rental? Using CVP analysis it is also possible to set challenging but reasonable management performance targets by taking probability calculation into consideration.

It should be noted that managers of a hotel or tourism business are expected to be proficient in the language of accounting, particularly in the area of managerial accounting, so that they are aware of the ins and outs of their departments where they are held accountable. While no mandatory system or principles are in place for hotel management accounting purposes, the Uniform System of Accounts for the Lodging Industry (USALI) has been in existence since 1926, currently in its 11th edition, and is normally adopted by international hotel chains and written in the management agreements.

Finance, on the other hand, focuses on what kinds of assets to purchase and how they are paid for. Therefore, finance involves a number of areas such as stock valuation, bond valuation, asset diversification, property appraisal and valuation and working capital management, among others. It is rather obvious that, to perform the finance function well, reliable and relevant accounting information is a requisite.

One possible reason why people often mix accounting and finance together is that, depending on the size of a hotel or tourism organization, there may be just one director of finance in charge of all accounting and finance related functions (most likely a small

隶属于不同部门的。此外，在大型组织中，财务相关职责通常是由集团层面承担的，个别酒店承担的更多的是会计相关职责。

1.3　何谓财务管理？

酒店和部分旅游企业需大量固定资产投资，因此，涉及其投资的决策是极为重要的，因为颇小的失误很容易影响全局，造成不当后果。财务管理可以帮助管理者和业主做出包括扩建、改建、地点选择等的明智决定。

简而言之，财务管理是关系到三种主要类型的决策。以酒店开发为例，业主是否有意在中国内地一线城市投资一家由国际连锁酒店集团管理、拥有1000 间客房、不同餐饮和会议设施的五星级酒店，或是在某二线城市投资一家中等规模、由国内连锁酒店集团（或独立酒店管理公司）管理、拥有 800 间客房和一家餐厅的酒店？这样的决定应该是在经过一系列严格的分析，如可行性研究后而提出的，并且这些分析在很大程度上决定了这项投资将如何进行。上述两个酒店投资选项在硬件设施和服务（例如人力资本）的投资规模方面肯定会有所不同。

或者，一间已经建成并经营多年的酒店的管理者希望能翻新其陈旧的客房并改进其形象，以期能够收取更高的房费来增加其客房收入。在这种情况下，酒店经理人会向业主提出改装建议供其考量批准，例如，应该购置什么品牌的电视机或是安装什么档次的地板。这些与资产种类、数量、质量和价格相关的投资决定属于财务管理的第一类决定：投资决策。一般而言，投资决策将决定一个企业的资产结构（即流动资产和固定资产构成），而此结构在本质上是动态的。虽说一个企业的资产结构不会瞬间产生显著变化，然而基于企业运营，其资产组成，例如库存和现金，却可能经常变化。资产结构也是一个企业在市场竞争中的经营基础。从业主的角度来看，他们更希望有一个可产生最大回报的资产结构，否则，他们大可将资金投入其他可以产生更高回报的投资项目。

由于酒店和旅游设施通常需要大额固定资产投资，业主一般不太会单单以现金支付全部投资而没有从商业银行申请贷款来部分地支持发展。在这里我们介绍两种可以被用来支持投资的金融资本：第一种是股权资本；第二

or an independent property); in larger organizations, there will be separate positions for the accounting and finance functions, respectively. Besides, in the latter situation, the finance function is normally handled at the corporate level and financial information taken care of at the individual property level is related more to the accounting function.

1.3   What Is Financial Management?

The hotel and partial tourism businesses are characterized by heavy fixed asset investment and therefore, decisions related to such investment are of paramount importance as small mistakes could easily turn things upside down and result in undesirable outcomes. Financial management helps managers and owners to make informed decisions involving expansion, renovation, choice of location and many others.

In a nutshell, financial management is related to three major types of decision making. Taking hotel development as an example, is the owner interested in investing in a five-star hotel with 1,000 guestrooms, F&B and meeting facilities managed by an international hotel chain in a first-tier city in mainland China or a middle-scale hotel with 800 guestrooms and one F&B outlet managed by a domestic hotel chain (or an independent hotel management company) in a second-tier city? Such decision is made after a series of critical analyses such as feasibility studies and it will largely determine how the investment will proceed. The scale of the investment on hardware facilities and software services (e.g., human capital) of the two aforementioned hotels will certainly be different.

Or, an established hotel may need to renovate its run-down guestrooms in order to revamp its image and be able to charge a higher room rate for increasing its room revenues. In such case, the hotel management will propose and the owner will approve, for example, what brand of television sets to purchase and what grade of flooring to install. These decisions relating to the type, quantity, quality and price of assets to invest belong to the first type of decision in financial management: the investment decision. Generally, the investment decisions will determine the asset structure of a firm (i.e., the composition of current assets and fixed assets) and subsequently the structure is dynamic in nature. While a company's asset structure will not change dramatically overnight, its composition may vary frequently due to changes in, for example, inventory and cash position, as a result of the operations. It is also the asset structure that forms the basis of a company's operations to compete in the marketplace. From the owners' perspective, they would prefer to have an asset structure that can generate the most return; otherwise, they could have put their money elsewhere that generates higher returns for them.

Given the nature of heavy fixed asset investment of hotels and tourism facilities, it is rather unlikely that owners will pay off all the investments in cash without seeking loans from commercial banks to partially support the development. It is proper to introduce

种是债务资本。股权资本是指企业通过出售股票换取对业主来说不需偿还的财政资源。另一方面,债务资本是指企业由商业银行提供贷款所获得的资金;借款人须按与贷款人之间预先约定的时间表偿还贷款给债权人。

因此,有人可能会问,如果业主有足够的钱投资项目发展,为什么他们还会考虑是否向商业银行贷款,并且还得承担利息费用? 然而,贷款决策背后可能有不同的原因。例如,业主可能希望只是把自己的一部分资金投资在某一个项目上,而预留一定的现金在以后投资可能出现的具有更高回报率的其他投资机会。或者,他们可能只是想利用财务杠杆以期获得超高的回报(当然需要承受较高的风险),并且善用利息税盾。虽说如此,因举债过多而陷入财务困境也不是一个好的情况。针对支持投资项目的股权/债务资本发行类型和额度的相关决策,属于财务管理的第二类决定:融资决策。一般来说,融资决策将决定一个企业的资本结构(即债务资本和股权资本的组成)。企业的资本结构与前述的资产结构在本质上都是动态的,它的组成会因为企业为了满足运营需要所产生的融资需求而改变。

通过股权资本、债务资本或两种资本组合所购置的企业资产应该要为业主产生其预期的回报。当酒店或旅游企业在一个会计年度里有所盈余时,如何处理该笔盈余不仅对企业,同时对业主/投资者也至关重要。如果企业正处于成长或扩张阶段,并同时有很多好的项目能够投资,企业可能倾向于保留该笔盈余并用于项目投资。这样做的原因是在投资项目时,以保留盈余作为资金来源比向银行贷款和向业主发行新股要便宜。不过,如果该公司没有好的投资项目,公司董事会可依业主/投资者的持股数分配部分盈余作为红利。

值得注意的是,当董事会在做分配或保留盈余决定的时候,如何评估怎样的投资机会才算是好的项目。如果一家企业手头上有一个可投资项目,其预期收益率是 8%,然而业主要求的回报率是 12%,较简单的做法或许是董事会直接将盈余分配给业主,让他们自行投资以赚取高于 8% 的回报率(最

here that there are basically two forms of financial capitals that can be utilized to support the investment: first the equity capital and second the debt capital. The equity capital refers to financial resources supplied by the owners via the sale of stock and the money raised is not repaid to them. On the other hand, the debt capital is financial resources obtained by taking out a loan from a commercial bank; the loans are to be repaid to the creditors according to a pre-determined payment schedule agreed upon between the borrower and the lender.

So, one might ask that, if the owners have enough money to pay off the development, why do they bother to even consider the option of seeking loans from commercial banks and incurring interest payment? There could be different reasons behind a loan decision. For example, the owners may want to just invest part of their money in one project and keep some cash for other investment opportunities that may arise and earn higher returns in the future. Or, they may just want to capitalize on financial leverage to gain extraordinary returns (of course, by bearing higher risks) and take advantage of interest tax shield. However, it is certainly not a good idea to borrow too much money and get stuck in a situation where financial distress could exist. Decisions related to the issuance, the type and amount of equity/debt capital to support the investment belong to the second type of decision in financial management: the financing decision. Generally, the financing decisions will determine the capital structure of a firm (i.e., the composition of debt capital and equity capital). As with the asset structure, the capital structure of a firm is dynamic in nature as its composition is likely to change as financing needs arise as a result of operational requirements.

Assets of a business supported by equity capital, debt capital or a combination of both are expected to generate required returns for the owners. When a hotel or tourism business has made earnings after a fiscal year, how to deal with the earnings is of critical importance not only to the company but also to the owners/investors. If the company is in the growth or expansion stage and has a number of good projects to pursue, it is likely that the earnings will be retained by the company and used to fund the projects. The rationale behind this is that it is cheaper to fund investments with retained earnings as compared with funds sourced from lenders and equity owners. Nevertheless, if the company doesn't have good projects available, the board of directors of the company could then distribute some of the earnings to the owners/investors in terms of dividends to their shareholdings.

It is worth noting here what a good project means when the board of directors is making a decision on distributing or retaining earnings. If a company has a project at hand that could earn an expected return of, say, eight percent and the owners' required return is 12 percent, it would be better off for the board to simply distribute the earnings back to the owners for their own investment discretion that could possibly earn a return higher than eight percent (or ideally higher than 12 percent). Nevertheless, a project

好是高于 12％）。然而,假设业主要求的回报率低于 8％,这一个可以获得 8％ 回报率的项目就是一个很好的项目。换句话说,评估一个项目是否值得投资的一个准则是看业主的要求回报率。关于是否将盈余以红利的形式分配给业主和分配比例的决定属于财务管理的第三类决定:红利决策。红利决策的重要性在于,在一定程度上它告知投资者的不仅仅是一个企业过去的经营成果同时也包括其未来的盈利能力以及规划和发展潜力。

1.4　制定决策的不同观点

综上所述,财务管理关系到企业制定的三类决策:投资决策、融资决策及红利决策。对于企业而言,虽然并非所有的决策都是财务决策,然而企业做出的决策对企业在财务方面或多或少有一定程度的影响。例如,翻新酒店客房并于客房内安装高科技配备的决策无疑是一个投资决策,而投资决策应该有一个仔细规划和执行的融资决策的支持。酒店的经营成果在某种程度上反映了该装修决策的“回报”,理想的情况是这个回报能带来期望的收益,从而能让董事会在尔后做出红利分配的决策。虽然每个财务管理决策要考虑的因素众多,上述例子显示了一个企业普遍的和具有逻辑的财务管理流程。然而,在现实中不同的利害关系者对某些事情可能会有矛盾的看法,以至于日常运营有时候无法按计划进行。

假设某家有 500 间客房的酒店 2015 年的平均每日房价(ADR)为 450 元(人民币,下同),每间客房的变动成本是 200 元。2015 年的入住率为 80％,客房销售收益是 6570 万元,经营毛利(GOP)为 3650 万元。在制定2016年年度预算时,销售经理希望达到 85％ 的入住率。实现这一目标的方法之一是减少 ADR 至 430 元(每间变动成本保持不变),届时房间的销售收入将有 6670 万元,GOP 有 3568 万元。对于销售经理来说这似乎是个令人鼓舞的预算,因为入住率可以提升 5％,而客房销售收益可增长 100 万元。然而,财务总监很可能会针对这个预算提出质疑,因为酒店 2016 年的经营毛利将会减少。如果销售经理的目标是提升入住率至 88％ 和进一步将每日平均房价降至 410 元,经营毛利会有什么样的变化?(见表 1-1)

earning eight percent of return could still be considered a good project to pursue if the owners' required return is less than eight percent. In other words, one way in assessing whether a project is worthy to be pursued is to look at the owners' required return. Decisions related to whether or not distribute earnings in terms of dividends back to the owners and the proportion of earnings being paid to them belong to the third type of decision in financial management: the dividend decision. The dividend decision is important in that, to a certain extent, it signals to the investors not only about a company's past operating performance but also its future earnings ability and planning and development potential.

1.4 Perspective on Decision Making

As noted above, financial management is about making three types of decisions for a business: the investment, financing and dividend decisions. While not all decisions to be made for a business are financial decisions per se, the decisions made more or less have some implications to the business in a financial way. For example, the decision to renovate hotel guestrooms with installment of high-tech gadgets is undoubtedly an investment decision, which should be supported by a well-planned and executed financing decision. The operational results, somewhat reflecting the "return" of the renovation, should ideally bring about expected earnings, which then allow the board to make a decision on dividends payout. While there are many factors to be considered in the decision making for each of the financial management functions, the example shows a rather general and logical flow of the financial management functions administered in the business. Nevertheless, in reality things might not always go as planned without conflicting viewpoints from various groups of stakeholders.

Suppose the average daily rate (ADR) of a hotel having 500 guestrooms for year 2015 was 450 yuan (RMB, similarly hereinafter) and the variable cost per room was 200 yuan. The occupancy in 2015 was 80%. The room sales revenue was then 65.7 million yuan and the gross operating profit (GOP) 36.5 million yuan. When doing the budget for year 2016, the sales manager aims to achieve 85% occupancy. One way of achieving this goal is by reducing the ADR to 430 yuan (variable cost per room remains unchanged), room sales revenue then becomes 66.7 million yuan and GOP 35.68 million yuan. For the sales manager the budget seems encouraging in that the occupancy is set to increase 5% and the room sales revenue increase 1 million yuan. However, the director of finance is likely to challenge this budget as the GOP for 2016 would deteriorate. What if the sales manager aims an even higher occupancy rate of 88% with a further-reduced budgeted ADR of 410 yuan and how would the GOP change? (See Table 1-1)

表 1-1　客房入住率和经营毛利的关系

平均每日房价(元)	450	430	410
入住率(%)	80	85	88
客房销售间数(间)	146000	155125	160600
客房销售收益(万元)	6570	6670	6585
每间客房变动成本(元)	200	200	200
经营毛利(万元)	3650	3568	3373

如表 1-1 所示,当入住率增加至 88% 时,销售收益会增加 15 万元而 GOP 将进一步降低。换句话说,盲目地以提升入住率为目标会导致不理想的结果。如果财务总监的目标是实现最大可能的经营毛利,其目标会与销售经理实现更高入住率的目标相冲突。为了平衡销售经理和财务总监两者不一致的目标,一个可能的解决方案是设定目标入住率为 84%,平均每日房价为 435 元。也就是说,制定预算销售收益为 6669 万元和经营毛利为 3603 万元。这种妥协将可达成更高的入住率和销售收益,但经营毛利会小幅下降。销售经理可能会认为,若能从竞争对手中争取客户并提高未来的市场份额,所导致的经营毛利小幅下降将是一个很小的代价。或许在一定程度上这样的看法是对的,然而长远来看,酒店应当想出一个能平衡各方冲突的最佳的妥协办法。

1.5　财务经理的目标

会计和财务之间还有一个重要的区别,即会计的目标是利润最大化,而财务的目标是股东财富最大化。

从会计的观点来看,会计准则规定企业应该在发生获取收益及产生费用的交易当下按实记录(亦即应计制会计基础)。管理者经营酒店或旅游企业的最终目标是要能达到他们为某一期间制定的经营和现金预算,并希望通过收益最大化和支出最小化来达到他们盈利最大化的目标。能够达到这样的目标当然就能令管理团队和业主都满意。然而,这个目标忽略了两个问题:一是(现金)回报的时机;二是(现金)回报的不确定性。前者涉及货币的时间价值,后者与风险相关。

例如,参加自由行的张先生及张女士于 2015 年 5 月 5 日在酒店办理退房时以现金支付房费。同一天,一位商务客人迈克尔·陈先生也在同一酒店办理退房,但他的房费记账至其企业账户,企业过几天才能收到酒店寄来的

Table 1 – 1　Relationship between room occupancy rates and operating margins

ADR（RMB yuan）	450	430	410
Occupancy rates（%）	80	85	88
Rooms sold	146,000	155,125	160,600
Sales revenue（RMB million yuan）	65.70	66.70	65.85
Variable cost per room（RMB yuan）	200	200	200
GOP（RMB million yuan）	36.50	35.68	33.73

The above table shows that, when the occupancy percentage increases to 88%, the sales revenue would increase 150,000 yuan and the GOP would decrease further. In other words, blindly aiming at higher occupancy would lead to undesirable outcomes. If the goal of the director of finance is to achieve the highest GOP possible, it will conflict the sales manager's goal in achieving higher occupancy. In balancing the goals of the sales manager and the director of finance, a solution may be to set occupancy rate to 84% with an ADR of 435 yuan. That is, the budgeted sales revenue is then 66.69 million yuan and GOP 36.03 million yuan. Such a compromise would allow for higher occupancy coupled with increased sales revenue with a small drop in gross profit. While the sales manager might argue that this is a small price to pay to steal customers from competitors and increase future market share, which is true to some extent, in the long run better courses of action should be formulated that find the best possible compromise across the conflicting viewpoints.

1.5　Goal for Financial Managers

Last but not the least, one should also note that an important difference between accounting and finance is that, the goal or bottom-line of accounting is profit maximization, while for finance is shareholder wealth maximization.

In the context of accounting, the GAAP dictates that revenues are recorded when they are earned and expenses are recognized when they are incurred (i.e., the accrual accounting basis). The management's ultimate goal in operating a hotel or tourism business is to meet their periodical operations and cash budgets and hopefully maximize their profitability target by maximizing revenues and minimizing expenses. Reaching such a goal will certainly please both the management team and the owners; however, it ignores, first, timing of (cash) returns and second, uncertainty of (cash) returns. The former relates to time value of money and the latter is associated with risk.

For example, on 5th May 2015 Mr. and Mrs. Zhang traveling for leisure purposes checked out of a hotel by paying cash for their room stay. On the same day a business guest, Mr. Michael Chan, of a corporate account also checked out of the same hotel and his room charges was billed to the corporate account and an invoice was later sent to his

发票。从张先生夫妇处赚取的客房收入被记入现金账户借方,并记入客房收入账户贷方;而从那位企业客户处获得的客房收入记入了应收账款借方,并记入客房收入贷方。从两个客房赚取的客房收入贡献了 2015 年 5 月份的部分利润。然而它们之间的区别在于,应收账款的款项有可能会在下一个会计期间才收取(客房收入产生和实际现金收入之间存在时间延迟),或者在更坏的情况下,这笔应收账款可能最后无法收回,而成为呆账(存在坏账的风险);酒店的现金头寸和资金流动性将受到影响。一个更极端但并非不寻常的情况是,从盈利的角度来看一家酒店可能是赚钱的,却有可能因为现金短缺而受到破产的威胁:它可能是因为对应收账款收款时遇到了困难,因此没有足够的现金来支付供应商的欠款。古谚有云"现金为王",它非常适合形容这种情况。

为了帮助股东最大化他们的财富,财务经理的目标应该是企业价值的最大化。一个简单衡量企业价值的指标是一个企业的市值(即股价乘以在外流通股数)。因此,企业价值最大化相当于股价最大化。一个更全面的衡量企业价值的计算公式为市值加上债务、少数股东权益和优先股再减去总现金和现金等价物。这个价值衡量方法被认为能更准确地通过反映债务、少数股东权益和优先股来体现企业价值。然而,问题是股票的股价是怎么决定的?虽然前人曾提出了几个股票估值模型,一般来说股票的价格应相当于当前和未来的股息总和:

$$W_0 = DIV_0 + \sum_{t=1}^{n} V_0(DIV_t)$$

其中:W_0 是股票在当前时间点 0 的价格;DIV_0 是当前的分红派息,DIV_t 是在未来的时间点 t 的分红派息;V_0 为将未来值折现为现值的现值因子。

因此,为了使股东财富最大化,应该重视的是未来红利最大化,特别是分红派息金额、时机和相关的风险。

1.6　委托代理关系

在实现股东财富最大化目标的同时,企业不能忽略委托代理关系的存在及其重要性。Berle 和 Means 于 1932 年首次针对企业所有权和控制权的分离所引起的问题进行评论,之后曾有许多学者也针对股权结构与企业绩效之间的关系进行研究,但对两者之间的关系没有一致的看法。

company. The room revenue earned from the couple was debited to the cash account and credited to the room revenue account while the room revenue earned from the corporate customer was debited to accounts receivable and credited to room revenue. The room revenues earned from both stays contributed partially to the profit in May 2015. The difference between them, however, was that it is possible that the accounts receivable is collected in the next accounting period (a time lag between revenue generation and actual cash receipt) or in a worse case it could turn out to be uncollectible and become bad debt at a later stage (risk of bad debt); the cash position or financial liquidity of the hotel would then be affected. A more extreme however not unusual scenario is that, a hotel may be profitable from the perspective of profit generation but suffers from going bankruptcy because of cash shortage: it could have difficulties in collecting its accounts receivable and thus doesn't have enough cash to pay for its accounts payable to its suppliers. An old saying of "Cash is king" plausibly applies in this situation.

In making efforts to help maximize shareholder wealth, financial managers should aim for firm value maximization. A simple measure of firm value is a firm's market capitalization (i.e., share price multiply by the number of shares outstanding) and therefore, maximizing firm value is equivalent to maximizing share price. A more comprehensive measure of firm value is calculated as market capitalization plus debt, minority interest and preferred shares minus total cash and cash equivalents. This value is considered to more accurately reflect a firm's worth by taking debt, minority interest and preferred shares into consideration. However, a question logically arises is that what determines a stock's share price? While there are several stock valuation models developed, in general a stock's price can be calculated as the sum of present and future dividends as follows:

$$W_0 = \mathrm{DIV}_0 + \sum_{t=1}^{n} V_0(\mathrm{DIV}_t)$$

Where: W_0 is stock price at present time 0; DIV_0 is dividend payout at present time and DIV_t is dividend payout at future time t; V_0 is present value operator bringing future value back to present time.

Therefore, in making efforts to maximize shareholder wealth, more focus should be paid to maximizing future dividends, particularly the amount, the timing and the risk associated with dividend payout.

1.6 The Agency Relationship

In achieving the goal of shareholder wealth maximization, one should not ignore the existence and importance of the agency relationship in corporations. In 1932 Berle and Means first commented on problems caused by the separation of ownership and control in corporations and thereafter many studies have examined the impact of ownership structure on firm performance. However no consensus has been reached.

在委托代理框架中,经理人担任委托人(即业主)的最佳利益代理人。也就是说,总经理和其酒店里的所有下属都属于董事会所聘用的人员,他们以其专业的酒店管理来帮助酒店业主实现他们以财务回报为主的目标,而这些专业努力或作为是不应该受到任何其他利害关系影响的。尽管如此,Jensen认为,由于人是自利的,当他们努力试图合作时,最终仍然会在某些问题上出现利益冲突。当代理人不从委托人的最佳利益出发行事时,会产生由这些冲突导致的代理问题。一些典型的代理问题包括但不限于推卸责任和享受额外的津贴消费。拥有较少企业股份的经理人会比那些拥有更多股份的经理人更容易推卸责任吗? 企业高级经理人是否更容易将企业分配的资源挪为私用? 如果企业有代理问题,股东财富并不太可能最大化,因为业主需要承担监管费用以减少代理问题(称为代理成本)。

值得注意的是,代理关系不仅存在于业主与经理人之间,同时也存在于特许人和加盟商之间以及业主和债权人之间。就特许人和加盟商而言,加盟商是否会实践特许经营协议规定的操作规范? 特许人是否需要密切关注加盟商的运营以防止任何可能损坏特许人的声誉和利益的操作和管理问题的发生? 就业主和债权人来说,业主可以投资于风险较高的项目。如果项目回报好,盈利很大程度上归于股东,否则,债权人将蒙受较大损失(这是使用财务杠杆投资的特别之处)。

In the agency framework, managers acting as agents for the principals (i.e., the owners of a corporation) should strive for the best interest of the principals. That is, the general manager and all his/her subordinates in a hotel are employed by the board of directors to professionally manage the hotel and help hotel owners achieve their goals and objectives, mostly in terms of financial returns, and these endeavors should not be jeopardized whatsoever. Nevertheless, Jensen argues that because people are self-interested in the end, there will be conflicts of interests on certain issues when they attempt to engage in cooperative endeavors. Agency problems, resulting from such conflicts, arise when an agent does not act in the best interest of the principal. Some typical agency problems include, but not limited to, shirking and consumption of perquisites, etc. Will owner-managers having less shares tend to shirk compared to those having more? Is it likely that senior managers will take advantage of company-allotted resources for personal use? If there are agency problems in a corporation, it is unlikely that shareholder wealth can be maximized as there will be expenses incurred on monitoring and minimizing agency problems (termed agency costs).

It should be noted that the agency relationship exists not only between owner and manager but also between franchisor and franchisee and between owner and lender. In the case of franchisor and franchisee, will the franchisee honor and follow the operation standards dictated in the franchising agreement? Will the franchisor need to pay close attention on the franchisee's operation to prevent any operation and management problems from happening that could possibly damage the reputation and interest of the franchisor? In the case of owner and lender, owners could invest in projects of higher risks. If the project pays off, the earnings largely accrue to the shareholders, if otherwise, the loss is greater for the lenders (this is a feature of investing using financial leverage).

第 2 章　酒店及旅游企业基本财务分析

学习目标

- 理解酒店业统一会计制度的精髓
- 能够分析酒店及旅游企业的财务报表
- 能够应用比率分析来分析企业的财务表现及财务状况

2.1　引　言

从运营的角度来看,一家酒店或旅游企业的底线是赚取能够同时满足业主/投资者和管理公司的利润。企业若能在某一会计期间(例如一个季度)有所盈利,则代表它能赚取的收益足以支付同一期间的运营和其他费用。以酒店为例。酒店由不同的利润中心产生收益,例如客房、餐饮、商务中心、水疗等部门,然而,所有部门,包括成本中心,例如人力资源、市场销售等部门,都会有费用产生。除非同属一个集团、一个连锁品牌或一个档次,不同酒店一般会提供不同类型的产品或服务。而就管理会计而言,这些酒店很可能针对收益和费用科目各自有不同的分类和记录方式。由于缺乏一套标准,投资者到最后会因为不同酒店采用不同的管理会计系统而没有办法比较不同酒店的财务表现。也就是说,如何分类和记录会计交易对于管理决策的制定具有重要意义,因为交易的会计处理方式的不同在很大程度上会影响两家酒店运营底线的可比性。能够解决运营结果可比性问题的可行方案是采用酒店业统一会计制度(USALI)。

2.2　USALI 标准

USALI 是以管理会计为目的,针对会计交易处理所制定的一套标准,而

Chapter 2　Analysis of Financial Fundamentals of Hospitality and Tourism Firms

Learning Outcomes

- Understand the essence of the Uniform System of Accounts for the Lodging Industry (USALI)
- Be able to analyze financial statements of hospitality and tourism firms
- Be able to analyze a firm's financial performance and condition using ratio analysis

2.1　Introduction

From an operational perspective, the bottom line of a hotel/tourism business is to make profit to a level that can satisfy not only the owners/investors but also the management company. Being profitable is equivalent to saying that revenues generated during an accounting period, say a quarter, can cover operating and other expenses incurred during the same period. Take hotels as an example. Revenues could be generated from various profit centers such as rooms, food and beverage, business centers, spa and etc. whereas expenses incur in all departments including cost centers such as human resources, sales and marketing and etc. Unless belonging to the same corporation, same chain or same caliber, hotels often differ in their product and service offerings and for management accounting purposes they likely have different ways of classifying and recording revenue and expense line items. At the end of the day, stakeholders cannot be assured of comparability between two hotel businesses that used two different management accounting systems due to lack of a standard. That is, how accounting transactions are classified and recorded for management decision-making matters because variations in accounting treatment on transactions will largely determine how comparable of the bottom lines between the two hotel businesses is. One viable solution to solving the issue of incomparability of operating results is to adopt the *Uniform System of Accounts for the Lodging Industry* (USALI).

2.2　The USALI Standard

The USALI is a standardized form of treating accounting transactions for management accounting purposes, under which industry stakeholders such as owners/investors, creditors and

业主/投资者、债权人和经理人可在此标准下评估并比较酒店表现,同时做出更明智的决策。USALI 最早是由纽约市酒店业协会于 1926 年发布的。1961 年,美国酒店及住宿协会委托美国会计师协会制定了小型酒店和汽车旅馆的统一会计系统。1996 年这两个统一会计系统合并成 USALI 第 9 版。最新第 11 版的 USALI 是由纽约市酒店业协会、美国酒店教育学院及酒店财务和技术专业人员协会协力出版的,并建议酒店业自 2015 年 1 月 1 日起采用。要注意的是 USALI 并非法定的会计制度,而是由酒店业自行发起的,通常会在国际连锁酒店管理合同中约定遵循。

USALI 是以责任会计的概念制定的,此制度允许酒店衡量运营表现(例如经营毛利或 GOP),令新开业的酒店有一套约定俗成的制度可循,同时可以对比不同酒店的表现。不同于财务会计不仅要依据 2007 年新会计准则从宏观的角度来记录业主的会计交易,同时还要符合国家统计及税收要求,USALI 主要用于评估单一酒店的财务和运营表现。换句话说,业主的财务报表并不等同于酒店的财务报表。

虽然本书并非关于 USALI 的专著,但该系统的某些特点还是值得一提的。USALI 的一个主要特点是其基于责任会计原则能揭示三个不同部门层级损益的运营汇总表。该表的第一级显示了如客房、餐饮等部门的收益来源;第二级揭示了运营收益及经营毛利;第三级呈现扣除利息、税项、折旧及摊销前利润(EBITDA)后投资者的盈利收益。第 11 版的 USALI 运营汇总表有两个版本:一个是给管理公司的;另一个给业主。这两个版本从收益科目一直到 EBITDA 都是相同的。然而,管理公司版本(见表 2 - 1)从 EBITDA 扣除了重置储备后可以得知酒店的运营收益;业主版本(见表 2 - 2)则从 EBITDA 中扣除了所有剩余的费用,例如利息、折旧、摊销和所得税后呈现了酒店的净利润。

酒店为了达到其报表标准化和标杆对比的目的,必须遵从第 11 版 USALI 的格式和术语要求。个别酒店可以删除不相关的会计科目。然而,USALI 并不允许酒店自行添加或取代其他收入和费用科目。如有需要,酒店可以制定子账户/表格,然后将其整理后汇入 USALI 指定的相应科目。由于信息技术的显著发展和其在酒店业的普及应用,第 11 版 USALI 新增了第五项未分配运营部门——"信息和通信系统"。

managers will be able to assess and compare hotel operating performance and to make informed decisions. The USALI was first published in 1926 by the Hotel Association of New York City. In 1961 a uniform system of accounts for small hotels and motels was produced by the National Association of Accountants appointed by the American Hotel & Lodging Association. In 1996 the two uniform system books were combined as the USALI in its ninth edition. The most current USALI, a product of joint efforts from the Hotel Association of New York City, American Hotel & Lodging Educational Institute and Hospitality Financial and Technology Professionals, is in its 11th edition that was recommended for adoption since January 1, 2015. It should be noted that the USALI is not statutory but self-initiated by the hotel industry and often stipulated in hotel management contracts particularly within international hotel chains.

The USALI has been designed and established with the concept of responsibility accounting, allowing hotels measure operating performance (e.g., gross operating profit or GOP), new hotel properties start with a turnkey system and different hotels compare and benchmark performance. Different from financial accounting, whose purpose is for recording owners' accounting transactions from a macro perspective with the needs for meeting statistical and taxation requirements based on the new accounting standards implemented in 2007, the USALI is for assessing financial and operating performance of individual hotel properties. In other words, financial statements of owners are not the same as those of hotels.

While this book is not about the USALI, it is worthy of mentioning some features of the system. One major feature of the USALI is a summary operating statement, showing profit and loss at three levels on the principle of responsibility accounting. The first level shows departmental income from revenue sources such as rooms, food and beverage and etc.; the second reveals the operator's income with GOP and; the third presents investors' earnings with earnings before interest, taxes, depreciation and amortization (EBITDA). The 11th edition now has two versions of summary operating statements: one for operators and the other for owners. The two versions are identical from revenues to EBITDA; however, the operator's version (see Table 2 − 1) deducts a replacement reserve from EBITDA to show the operating income of the property and the owner's version (see Table 2 - 2) deducts all remaining expenses such as interest, depreciation, amortization and income taxes from EBITDA to arrive at the net income of the property.

Due to its reporting standardization and benchmarking purposes, the format and terminology of the 11th edition must be followed by hotels. Individual hotel properties may delete irrelevant line items; however, the USALI doesn't allow for addition or substitution of other revenue and expenses line items. If needed, they could develop sub-accounts/sub-schedules and then roll them into the appropriate line items as specified by the USALI. In this edition, "information and telecommunications systems" has been added as a fifth undistributed operating department due to significant advancement and adoption of information technology in the hotel industry.

表 2 − 1　运营汇总表——管理公司版本

Items	Period Of					
	Current Period			Year-To-Date		
	Actual	Forecast/ Budget	Prior Year	Actual	Forecast/ Budget	Prior Year
Rooms Available:						
Rooms Sold:						
Occupancy:						
ADR:						
Rooms Revpar:						
Total Revpar:						

Items	Period Of											
	Current Period						Year-To-Date					
	Actual		Forecast/ Budget		Prior Year		Actual		Forecast/ Budget		Prior Year	
	$	%²	$	%²	$	%²	$	%²	$	%²	$	%²
Operating Revenue												
Rooms												
Food and Beverage												
Other Operated Departments												
Miscellaneous Income												
Total Operating Revenue												
Departmental Expenses												
Rooms												
Food and Beverage												
Other Operated Departments												
Total Departmental Expenses												
Total Departmental Profit												
Undistributed Operating Expenses												
Administrative and General												
Information and Telecommunciations Systems												
Sales and Marketing												
Property Operation and Maintenance												
Utilities												
Total Undistributed Expenses												
Gross Operating Profit												
Management Fees												
Income Before Non-Operating Income and Expenses												
Non-Operating Income and Expenses												
Income												
Rent												
Property and Other Taxes												
Insurance												
Other												
Total Non-Operating Income and Expenses												
Earnings Before Interest, Taxes, Depreciation, and 　　Amortization												
Replacement Reserve												
Ebitda Less Replacement Reserve												

来源：USALI（2015）

　　此外，USALI 中的部分内容还包括便于行业的股份持有者评估酒店财务状况和业绩的财务指标和经营指标，另外也制定了收入和支出科目字典。

　　若在签订管理合同时指定遵循 USALI，无论是业主或是酒店管理公司应该协商遵循的是哪一个版本的 USALI。例如，第 6 版的 USALI 将管理费用作为营业费用处理，而后来的版本修改了此项做法。如果没有指定所遵循

Table 2 – 1   Summary operating statements—operator's version

| Items | PERIOD OF | | | | | |
| | CURRENT PERIOD | | | YEAR-TO-DATE | | |
	ACTUAL	FORECAST/ BUDGET	PRIOR YEAR	ACTUAL	FORECAST/ BUDGET	PRIOR YEAR
ROOMS AVAILABLE:						
ROOMS SOLD:						
OCCUPANCY:						
ADR:						
ROOMS REVPAR:						
TOTAL REVPAR:						

Items	PERIOD OF											
	CURRENT PERIOD						YEAR-TO-DATE					
	ACTUAL		FORECAST/ BUDGET		PRIOR YEAR		ACTUAL		FORECAST/ BUDGET		PRIOR YEAR	
	$	%²	$	%²	$	%²	$	%²	$	%²	$	%²
OPERATING REVENUE												
Rooms												
Food and Beverage												
Other Operated Departments												
Miscellaneous Income												
TOTAL OPERATING REVENUE												
DEPARTMENTAL EXPENSES												
Rooms												
Food and Beverage												
Other Operated Departments												
TOTAL DEPARTMENTAL EXPENSES												
TOTAL DEPARTMENTAL PROFIT												
UNDISTRIBUTED OPERATING EXPENSES												
Administrative and General												
Information and Telecommunciations Systems												
Sales and Marketing												
Property Operation and Maintenance												
Utilities												
TOTAL UNDISTRIBUTED EXPENSES												
GROSS OPERATING PROFIT												
MANAGEMENT FEES												
INCOME BEFORE NON-OPERATING INCOME AND EXPENSES												
NON-OPERATING INCOME AND EXPENSES												
Income												
Rent												
Property and Other Taxes												
Insurance												
Other												
TOTAL NON-OPERATING INCOME AND EXPENSES												
EARNINGS BEFORE INTEREST,TAXES,DEPRECIATION,AND AMORTIZATION												
REPLACEMENT RESERVE												
EBITDA LESS REPLACEMENT RESERVE												

Source：USALI（2015）

Besides，the USALI has a section on financial ratios and operating metrics to allow industry stakeholders in assessing financial condition and performance of hotels and another section of revenue and expense dictionary.

When signing management contracts，if the USALI is to be followed，it is advised that both the owner and the hotel management company specify which edition of the USALI is to be used. For example，in its sixth edition，the USALI treated management

的版本,业主和管理公司可能会针对究竟管理费用应该置于 GOP 之前还是之后产生争议,因为 GOP 不仅是管理绩效的关键指标,同时也是激励管理费的计算基础。如果在管理合同中没有提到具体应遵循的版本,双方应该遵循合同签订时的 USALI 的版本。此外,该合同还应该规定,当有较新版本的 USALI 时是否即时遵循。

表 2 - 2　运营汇总表——业主版本

| Items | PERIOD OF | | | | | |
| | CURRENT PERIOD | | | YEAR-TO-DATE | | |
	ACTUAL	FORECAST/ BUDGET	PRIOR YEAR	ACTUAL	FORECAST/ BUDGET	PRIOR YEAR
ROOMS AVAILABLE: ROOMS SOLD: OCCUPANCY: ADR: ROOMS REVPAR: TOTAL REVPAR:						

Items	PERIOD OF											
	CURRENT PERIOD						YEAR-TO-DATE					
	ACTUAL		FORECAST/ BUDGET		PRIOR YEAR		ACTUAL		FORECAST/ BUDGET		PRIOR YEAR	
	$	%²	$	%²	$	%²	$	%²	$	%²	$	%²
OPERATING REVENUE												
Rooms												
Food and Beverage												
Other Operated Departments												
Miscellaneous Income												
TOTAL OPERATING REVENUE												
DEPARTMENTAL EXPENSES												
Rooms												
Food and Beverage												
Other Operated Departments												
TOTAL DEPARTMENTAL EXPENSES												
TOTAL DEPARTMENTAL PROFIT												
UNDISTRIBUTED OPERATING EXPENSES												
Administrative and General												
Information and Telecommunciations Systems												
Sales and Marketing												
Property Operation and Maintenance												
Utilities												
TOTAL UNDISTRIBUTED EXPENSES												
GROSS OPERATING PROFIT												
MANAGEMENT FEES												
INCOME BEFORE NON-OPERATING INCOME AND EXPENSES												
NON-OPERATING INCOME AND EXPENSES												
Income												
Rent												
Property and Other Taxes												
Insurance												
Other												
TOTAL NON-OPERATING INCOME AND EXPENSES												
EARNINGS BEFORE INTEREST, TAXES, DEPRECIATION, AND AMORTIZATION												
INTERST, DEPRECIATION, AND AMORTIZATION												
INCOME BEFORE INCOME TAXES												
Income Taxes												
NET INCOME												

来源:USALI(2015)

fees as operating expenses while the later edition did otherwise. If not specified，there would be disputes as to whether to account for management fees before or after GOP，because GOP is a critical indicator not only for management performance but also for the incentive part of the management fees. If no specific edition was mentioned in the management contract，both parties should honor and follow the edition of the USALI at the time when the contract was signed. Furthermore，the contract should also stipulate whether to apply a newer edition of the USALI when it is updated.

Table 2 – 2　Summary operating statements—owner's version

Items	Period Of					
	Current Period			Year-To-Date		
	Actual	Forecast/Budget	Prior Year	Actual	Forecast/Budget	Prior Year
Rooms Available: Rooms Sold: Occupancy: ADR: Rooms Revpar: Total Revpar:						

Items	Period Of											
	Current Period						Year-To-Date					
	Actual		Forecast/Budget		Prior Year		Actual		Forecast/Budget		Prior Year	
	$	%²	$	%²	$	%²	$	%²	$	%²	$	%²
Operating Revenue												
Rooms												
Food and Beverage												
Other Operated Departments												
Miscellaneous Income												
Total Operating Revenue												
Departmental Expenses												
Rooms												
Food and Beverage												
Other Operated Departments												
Total Departmental Expenses												
Total Departmental Profit												
Undistributed Operating Expenses												
Administrative and General												
Information and Telecommunciations Systems												
Sales and Marketing												
Property Operation and Maintenance												
Utilities												
Total Undistributed Expenses												
Gross Operating Profit												
Management Fees												
Income Before Non-Operating Income and Expenses												
Non-Operating Income and Expenses												
Income												
Rent												
Property and Other Taxes												
Insurance												
Other												
Total Non-Operating Income and Expenses												
Earnings Before Interest,Taxes,Depreciation,and Amortization												
Interst,Depreciation,and Amortization												
Income Before Income Taxes												
Income Taxes												
Net Income												

Source：USALI（2015）

2.3　财务报表分析——评估

　　虽然财务报表从表面上看只是汇总了酒店或旅游企业过去的会计交易和目前财务状况,但是对财务报表做进一步分析,则更能够显示出企业的整体表现。正如前面提到的,企业有三大主要财务报表——资产负债表、损益表和现金流量表。在本节中,我们将展示如何分析前两种财务报表,以揭示隐藏于财务报表中关于一个酒店或旅游企业的财务绩效信息。由于现金流的变化是其他两种财务报表变化的结果,所以对现金流量表的分析意义不大。

　　我们可以通过横向分析来分析资产负债表和损益表。一个企业 2015 年的资产负债表或损益表可以对比其 2014 年的报表。也就是说,横向分析的结果可以显示公司本年度相对于上年度的表现。为了使分析比较有意义,应同时计算连续两个周期的实际数字和百分比变化。表 2-3 所示是比较资产负债表的示例。

表 2-3　比较资产负债表

项目	2014 年 12 月 31 日	2015 年 12 月 31 日	Δ(金额)	Δ(百分比)
资产				
流动资产				
现金	$85600	$104625	$19025	22.2%
房产与设备				
家具与设备	$2650500	$2617125	$33375	1.3%
……	……	……	……	……
负债				
长期债务				
应付票据	0	$200000	$200000	无意义
……	……	……	……	……
总负债和业主权益	$9987500	$10559510	$572010	5.7%

　　从表 2-3 所示的比较资产负债表中得知,该企业 2014 至 2015 年期间所持现金从 85600 美元增加到 104625 美元,增加了 19025 美元。然而,这些现金的增长可能是显著的也可能是微不足道的,除非我们将此金额与基数进行比较,以评估其变化的显著性。我们可以计算该变化的百分比:

$$\frac{104625-85600}{85600}\times100\%=22.2\%$$

2.3　*Financial Statement Analysis—Assessment*

While financial statements literally summarize past accounting transactions and present financial positions of a hotel or tourism business, further analysis on them will show a bigger picture of how a firm has performed. As noted earlier, there are three major financial statements—the balance sheet, the income statement and the cash flow statement. In this section we will show how to analyze the first two financial statements to help uncover hidden message about a hotel or tourism business' financial performance. Financial statement analysis on cash flow statement generally do not mean much as changes in cash flows are the results of changes in the other two financial statements.

The balance sheet and income statement can be analyzed through a horizontal analysis. A firm's balance sheet or income statement in 2015 can be compared against that in 2014. That is, a horizontal analysis shows how a firm has performed in the current year relative to the previous year. In order to make the comparison meaningful, both dollar and percentage changes should be obtained over two consecutive periods. The following shows an example of an extracted comparative balance sheet of a firm (See Table 2 - 3).

Table 2 - 3　Comparative balance sheet of a firm

items	December 31, 2014	December 31, 2015	Δ (Amount)	Δ (Percentage)
assets				
current assets				
cash	$85,600	$104,625	$19,025	22.2%
property and equipment				
furnishing & equipment	$2,650,500	$2,617,125	($33,375)	(1.3%)
...	...	...	...	...
liabilities				
long-term debt				
notes payable	0	$200,000	$200,000	N.M.
...	...	...	...	...
total liabilities & owners' equity	$9,987,500	$10,559,510	$572,010	5.7%

From the above comparative balance sheet (Table 2 - 3), we can see that the firm increased its cash position for $19,025 from $85,600 to $104,625 between 2014 and 2015. Nevertheless, such addition could be either significant or insignificant; we will not be able to assess its significance unless we compare it against the base number. As a result, percentage change should also be calculated as follows:

$$\frac{104625 - 85600}{85600} \times 100\% = 22.2\%$$

　　该企业在 2014 年 85600 美元现金的基础上增加了 22.2% 的现金,在大多数人的眼中应该算是显著的。所以我们或许可以得出该企业显著增加了其现金头寸的结论。然而,每个企业应该设置实际数字和百分比变化的临界值(例如,同时有±10000 美元的变化和±4% 的变化);当两种变化同时超过该临界值,企业应进一步调查发生该变化的原因。例如,企业不应该针对 2014 年和 2015 年间家具及设备减少 33375 美元或减少 1.3% 进行调查,因为其改变的百分比未大于±4% 的临界值。

　　我们接下来看比较利润表(见表 2-4)。

表 2-4　比较损益表

项目	2014 年 12 月 31 日	2015 年 12 月 31 日	△(金额)	△(百分比)
收益				
客房	$1041200	$1124300	$83100	7.98%
餐饮	$776796	$847248	$70462	9.07%
……	……	……	……	……
费用				
客房	$800000	$820000	$20000	2.5%
餐饮	$500125	$501466	$1341	0.27%
……	……	……	……	……
净利润	$205400	$245860	$40460	19.69%

　　从表 2-4 所示的比较损益表中得知,该企业从 2014 至 2015 年,客房收入由 104.12 万美元增加到 112.43 万美元,增加了 8.31 万美元,客房支出由 80 万美元增加到 82 万美元。尽管如此,在评估这些变化是否显著时,应同时计算变化的百分比。如果使用与前述相同的数字和百分比变化临界值,虽然客房收入和支出变化皆超过 1 万美元,管理层或许应该探讨为什么客房收入会增加(7.98%),而不需要花太多心思理会客房支出的增加(2.5%)。

　　除了横向分析,我们也可以通过纵向分析来分析资产负债表和损益表,针对报表中各科目对总资产占比(资产负债表)或对销售占比(损益表)进行分析。一个企业 2015 年(或某一会计期间)的资产负债表和损益表可以与其 2014 年的报表对比,或是跨企业(或与行业平均水平)同期进行比较。也就是说,纵向分析可以是一个企业当前的表现相比于前一年的表现,或是在同一年或同一会计期间与其他企业的表现比较。表 2-5 所示是共同比资产负债表的一个例子。

We can probably conclude that the firm had significantly increased its cash position. Because based on its 2014 cash amount of \$85,600, the increase was a 22.2%, which would be considered rather significant by most people. Nevertheless, each firm should set a threshold in both dollar change and percentage change (e.g., a ± \$10,000 **AND** a ±4% change); when both changes exceed the threshold, further examination shall be triggered to uncover the cause of such changes. For example, the \$33,375 or -1.3% reduction in furnishing and equipment between 2014 and 2015 should not trigger the firm's effort to look into the changes because the percentage change was not larger than the threshold of ±4%.

We now turn to a comparative income statement(Table 2-4).

Table 2-4　Comparative income statement

items	December 31, 2014	December 31, 2015	Δ (Amount)	Δ (Percentage)
revenue				
rooms	\$1,041,200	\$1,124,300	\$83,100	7.98%
food & beverage	\$776,796	\$847,248	\$70,462	9.07%
...	...	...	...	...
expenses				
rooms	\$800,000	\$820,000	\$20,000	2.5%
food & beverage	\$500,125	\$501,466	\$1,341	0.27%
...	...	...	...	...
net income	\$205,400	\$245,860	\$40,460	19.69%

From the above comparative income statement, we can see that the firm increased its rooms revenue by \$83,100 from \$1,041,200 to \$1,124,300 and its rooms expenses from \$800,000 to \$820,000, respectively, between 2014 and 2015. Nevertheless, in assessing whether or not these changes are significant, percentage changes corresponding to the dollar changes should be calculated. If using the same threshold of dollar and percentage change for further examination, the management probably should look into what had caused the increase in rooms revenue (7.98%) but not expenses (2.5%), although both revenue and expenses changes exceeded \$10,000.

Apart from the horizontal analysis, the balance sheet and income statement can also be analyzed through a vertical analysis which shows each line item as a percentage of total assets (balance sheet) or of sales (income statement). A firm's balance sheet or income statement in 2015 (or in an accounting period) can be compared against that in 2014 or across firms (or with industry average) for the same period. That is, a vertical analysis shows how a firm has performed in the current year relative to the previous year or to other firms in the same year or accounting period. The following shows an example

表 2−5　共同比资产负债表

项目	2014 年 12 月 31 日	2015 年 12 月 31 日	2014 年占总资产比率	2015 年占总资产比率
资产				
流动资产				
现金	$85600	$104625	0.9%	0.9%
……	……	……	……	……
房产与设备				
建筑	$5434200	$5434200	54.4%	51.5%
……	……	……	……	……
总资产	$9987500	$10559510	100%	100%
负债				
长期债务				
应付票据	0	$200000	0	1.9%
……	……	……	……	……
总负债和业主权益	$9987500	$10559510	100%	100%

　　从表 2−5 所示的共同比资产负债表得知,在 2014 和 2015 两个年度里,现金皆占总资产的 0.9%。然而,由 2014 年完全没有应付票据到 2015 年应付票据占总资产的 1.9%,值得管理层关注。管理层或许应该探寻为什么会有这种增加的变化。

　　我们接下来看共同比损益表(见表 2−6)。

表 2−6　共同比损益表

项目	2014 年 12 月 31 日	2015 年 12 月 31 日	2014 年占总收益比率	2015 年占总收益比率
收益				
客房	$1041200	$1124300	51.90%	50.20%
餐饮	$776796	$847248	38.70%	37.81%
……	……	……	……	……
总收益	$2005000	$2240800	100%	100%
费用				
客房	$800000	$820000	39.90%	36.60%
餐饮	$500125	$501466	24.90%	22.40%
……	……	……	……	……
净利润	$205400	$245860	10.24%	11.00%

of an extracted common-size balance sheet of a firm(Table 2 - 5).

Table 2 - 5   Common-size balance sheet

items	December 31, 2014	December 31, 2015	percentage of total assets 2014	percentage of total assets 2015
assets				
current assets				
cash	$85,600	$104,625	0.9%	0.9%
...	...	...	...	...
property and equipment				
buildings	$5,434,200	$5,434200	54.4%	51.5%
...	...	...	...	...
total assets	$9,987,500	$10,559,510	100%	100%
liabilities				
notes payable	0	$200,000	0	1.9%
...	...	...	...	...
total liabilities & owners' equity	$9,987,500	$10,559,510	100%	100%

From the above common-size balance sheet，we can see that cash accounted for 0.9% of total assets in both 2014 and 2015. Nevertheless，what might catch the attention of the management would be notes payable which increased from none in 2014 to accounting for 1.9% of total assets in 2015. Such increase might trigger the management to look into why such change exists.

We now turn to a common-size income statement (Table 2 - 6).

Table 2 - 6   Common-size income statement

items	December 31, 2014	December 31, 2015	percentage of total revenue 2014	percentage of total revenue 2015
revenue				
rooms	$1,041,200	$1,124,300	51.90%	50.20%
food & beverage	$776,796	$847,248	38.70%	37.81%
...	...	...	...	...
total revenue	$2,005,000	$2,240,800	100%	100%
expenses				
rooms	$800,000	$820,000	39.90%	36.60%
food & beverage	$500,125	$501,466	24.90%	22.40%
...	...	...	...	...
net income	$205,400	$245,860	10.24%	11.00%

从表 2-6 所示的共同比损益表得知，相比 2014 年，无论客房还是食品饮料占总收益的比例在 2015 年都减少了。管理层进一步研究潜在原因：是不是消费行为改变了？市场是否有新的竞争对手？难道酒店有比房间和食品饮料更好的收入来源？这个例子另外一个较有意思的点是，客房和餐饮部门的开支占比也变少了，2015 年净利润占总收益的百分比高于 2014 年的百分比。

概括地说，财务报表分析是衡量一个酒店或旅游企业整体表现的第一步。企业应制定数字变化和百分比变化临界值，以便管理层能有依据来决定是否针对数据变化进一步探讨原因。这种类型的财务报表分析可以扩展延伸至以年度、季度、每月甚至每周或每天为分析基础。

2.4　比率分析——标杆对比

相比于财务报表分析，比率分析是利用三大财务报表的信息，在公平的基础上为企业就不同时期或跨企业进行较微观的财务分析。比率分析的目的不仅是帮助财务报表使用者/利害相关者（例如经理人、债权人和投资者）评价酒店或旅游企业财务表现和状况，而且也可以揭露财务报表中隐藏的重要信息。

例如，经理依靠比率分析来监测运营表现和财务状况。另一方面，债权人依靠比率分析评估公司的偿付能力和流动性或失去其贷款的风险。最后，业主/投资者利用比率分析评估企业表现和投资吸引力。

比率只是些数字，除非拿它们与某些基准相比，否则比率本身没有任何意义。一般而言，比率分析有三种基准类型。第一，可以就同一家企业在不同时期的比率进行比较。也就是说，借由比较企业当期与上期的财务比率可以得知运营表现是改善还是恶化。第二，可以就整个行业进行比较。也就是说，可以对比其他企业的财务比率或者行业平均水平。第三，可以对比目标比率。也就是说，可以将实际财务比率对比预算比率，这样的比较对评价管理绩效是很有用的。

财务比率可以以不同的方式归类，一般来说它们可以分为五组：流动比率、偿债能力比率、活动比率、盈利比率和运营比率。流动比率反映了企业支付其短期债务的能力（即它们能否按时支付账单）。偿债能力比率可衡量一

From the above common-size income statement, we can see that both rooms and food and beverage accounted less of total revenue in 2014 and 2015, which might trigger the management to further examine potential causes: were there changes in the consumer behavior? Were there new competitors in the market? Did the hotel have better revenue sources other than rooms and food and beverage? What's interesting in this example is that expenses in the rooms and food and beverage departments also accounted less, and net income as a percentage of total revenue was higher in 2015 than 2014.

In a nutshell, financial statement analysis is performed as a first step in gauging a hotel or tourism firm's performance from a bigger picture. Thresholds in both dollar and percentage changes should be established so that the management has a guideline for further action once a change reaches the threshold. Such financial statement analysis could be extended and applicable to yearly, quarterly, monthly, weekly or even daily basis if deemed appropriate.

2.4 Ratio Analysis—Benchmarking

Compared to financial statement analysis, ratio analysis is a more micro type of financial analysis using information from the three major financial statements and make comparisons over time or across firms on a fair basis. The purpose of conducting ratio analysis is to not only help users/stakeholders (i.e., managers, creditors and investors) evaluate the financial performance and conditions of a hotel or tourism firm against some standards but also reveal important information not obvious in the financial statements.

For example, managers rely on ratio analysis to monitor operating performance and financial conditions. Creditors, on the other hand, evaluate a firm's solvency and liquidity or the risk of losing their loans. Finally, owners/investors assess performance of a firm and attractiveness of investment.

Ratios by themselves are just numbers and they will not be meaningful unless compared against some kinds of benchmarks. Generally speaking, there are three types of benchmarks for ratio analysis. First, ratios can be compared over time for the same firm. That is, one can compare a firm's financial ratios of the current period versus previous period to identify improvement or deterioration. Second, ratio comparisons can be made across the industry. That is, one can compare a firm's financial ratios against another firm's or the industry average. Third, ratios can be compared with target ratios. That is, one can compare actual financial ratios against budgeted ones and such comparison is useful for evaluating management performance.

While there exist other ways of categorizing financial ratios, generally speaking they can be categorized into five groups: liquidity ratios, solvency ratios, activity ratios, profitability ratios and operating ratios. Liquidity ratios reflects a firm's ability to meet its short-term obligations (Can they pay bills on time?). Solvency ratios measures a firm's

个企业的债务使用程度和支付其长期债务的能力。活动比率(也称为效率比率)可评估一个企业如何有效地利用其资源(即资产)产生销售收益。盈利能力比率反映了企业的销售回报(即利润)和业主的投资回报。最后,运营比率可协助分析通常供内部使用的关于经营业绩的信息。

表 2-7 至表 2-9 所示是由谷歌财经抽取的希尔顿酒店控股集团(NYSE:HLT)的样本财务报表,我们将其作为比率分析数据之用。

表 2-7　样本资产负债表

(12 月 31 日)　　　　　　　单位:百万美元(每股数据除外)

年份	2014	2013	2012
现金及现金等价物	566	594	755
现金及短期投资	566	594	755
应收贸易账款	844	731	719
总应收账款	1104	927	838
库存	404	396	415
预付费用	133	148	153
其他流动资产	292	318	666
总流动资产	2499	2383	2827
房产/厂房/设备	9026	9058	9197
商誉	6154	6220	6197
无形资产	6943	7216	7373
长期投资	170	260	291
其他长期资产	2054	596	366
总资产	26125	26562	27066
应付账款	299	319	286
应计费用	980	1099	1097
一年内到期的长期债务/资本租赁	137	52	407
其他流动负债	841	672	559
总流动负债	2257	2142	2349
长期债务	11267	12343	15132
资本租赁	288	328	456
总长期债务	11555	12671	15588

degree of debt use and its ability to meet its long-term obligations. Activity ratios (also called efficiency ratios) assesses how effectively a firm is using its resources (i.e., assets) to generate sales revenue. Profitability ratios reflects a firm's return (i.e., profit) on sales and owners' investments. Lastly, operating ratios assist in analyzing operating results, usually for internal use.

The followings are financial statements sample of Hilton Worldwide Holdings Inc (NYSE: HLT) extracted from Google finance, which we will use for illustration in ratio analysis(see Table 2 - 7 to Table 2 - 9).

Table 2 - 7   Balance sheet

(as of December 31)

in millions of USD (except for per share items)

Year	2014	2013	2012
cash & equivalents	566	594	755
cash and short term investments	566	594	755
accounts receivable—trade, net	844	731	719
total receivables, net	1,104	927	838
total inventory	404	396	415
prepaid expenses	133	148	153
other current assets, total	292	318	666
total current assets	2,499	2,383	2,827
property/plant/equipment, total, net	9,026	9,058	9,197
goodwill, net	6,154	6,220	6,197
intangibles, net	6,943	7,216	7,373
long term investments	170	260	291
other long term assets, total	2,054	596	366
total assets	26,125	26,562	27,066
accounts payable	299	319	286
accrued expenses	980	1,099	1,097
current port. of LT debt/capital leases	137	52	407
other current liabilities, total	841	672	559
total current liabilities	2,257	2,142	2,349
long term debt	11,267	12,343	15,132
capital lease obligations	288	328	456
total long term debt	11,555	12,671	15,588

续　表

年份	2014	2013	2012
总负债	11692	12723	15995
递延所得税	5216	5053	4948
少数股东权益	—38	—87	—146
其他负债	2383	2420	2026
总负债	21373	22199	24765
普通股	10	10	1
资本公积	10028	9948	8452
保留盈余（累计亏损）	—4658	—5331	—5746
其他权益	—628	—264	—406
总权益	4752	4363	2301
总负债和股东权益	26125	26562	27066
在外流通股份数	984.62	984.62	984.62

表 2-8　样本损益表

（12 月 31 日截止前 12 个月）　单位：百万美元（每股数据除外）

年份	2014	2013	2012
收益	10502	9735	9276
总收益	10502	9735	9276
销售成本	4019	3877	3988
销售/一般/行政费用	8201	8030	7572
折旧/摊销	628	603	550
总运营费用	8829	8633	8176
经营收益	1673	1102	1100
利息费用	618	620	569
税前收益	1147	698	573
税后收益	682	460	359
少数股东权益	—9	—45	—7
扣除非经常项目前之净利润	673	415	352
净利润	673	415	352
扣除非经常项目后可分配给普通股股东的利润	673	415	352
包括非经常项目后可分配给普通股股东的利润	673	415	352

continued

Year	2014	2013	2012
total debt	11,692	12,723	15,995
deferred income tax	5,216	5,053	4,948
minority interest	-38	-87	-146
other liabilities，total	2,383	2,420	2,026
total liabilities	21,373	22,199	24,765
common stock，total	10	10	1
additional paid—in capital	10,028	9,948	8,452
retained earnings（accumulated deficit）	$-4,658$	$-5,331$	$-5,746$
other equity，total	-628	-264	-406
total equity	4,752	4,363	2,301
total liabilities & shareholders' equity	26,125	26,562	27,066
total common shares outstanding	984.62	984.62	984.62

Table 2 − 8 Income statement

（12 months ending December 31）

in millions of USD（except for per share items）

Year	2014	2013	2012
revenue	10,502	9,735	9,276
total revenue	10,502	9,735	9,276
cost of revenue	4,019	3,877	3,988
selling/general/admin. expenses，total	8,201	8,030	7,572
depreciation/amortization	628	603	550
total operating expense	8,829	8,633	8,176
operating income	1,673	1,102	1,100
interest expense	618	620	569
income before tax	1,147	698	573
income after tax	682	460	359
minority interest	-9	-45	-7
net income before extra. items	673	415	352
net income	673	415	352
income available to common excl. extra items	673	415	352
income available to common incl. extra items	673	415	352

续　表

年份	2014	2013	2012
摊薄加权平均股数	986	923	984.62
扣除经常项目后之每股盈余	0.68	0.45	0.36
摊薄每股盈余	0.66	0.28	0.38

表 2 - 9　样本现金流量表

（12 月 31 日截止前 12 个月）　单位：百万美元(每股数据除外)

年份	2014	2013	2012
净利润	682	460	359
折旧/折耗	628	603	550
递延所得税	14	65	73
非现金项目	−133	672	72
运营资金变动	175	301	56
由运营活动产生的现金	1366	2101	1110
资本支出	−402	−376	−567
其他投资项目现金	92	−6	9
由投资活动产生的现金	−310	−382	−558
融资现金项目	−9	9	182
发行(回购)股票	13	1243	—
发行(回购)债券	−1074	−3115	−758
由融资活动产生的现金	−1070	−1863	−576
外汇影响	−14	−17	−2
现金变动	−28	−161	−26
现金利息支付,补充	514	535	486
现金所得税支付,补充	429	233	103

1. 流动比率

顾名思义,流动比率说明一个企业的流动资产有怎样的流动性。换句话说,流动比率显示该企业是否有足够的现金或准现金资产来按时支付账单。在这个比率类别中,我们将介绍流动比率、酸性测试比率(或速动比率)、运营现金流相对流动负债比率、应收账款周转率和平均收账期。

continued

Year	2014	2013	2012
diluted weighted average shares	986	923	984.62
diluted eps excluding extraordinary items	0.68	0.45	0.36
diluted normalized eps	0.66	0.28	0.38

Table 2-9 Cash flow statement
(12 months ending December 31)

in millions of USD (except for per share items)

Year	2014	2013	2012
net income	682	460	359
depreciation/depletion	628	603	550
deferred taxes	14	65	73
non-cash items	−133	672	72
changes in working capital	175	301	56
cash from operating activities	1,366	2,101	1,110
capital expenditures	−402	−376	−567
other investing cash flow items, total	92	−6	9
cash from investing activities	−310	−382	−558
financing cash flow items	−9	9	182
issuance (retirement) of stock, net	13	1,243	−
issuance (retirement) of debt, net	−1,074	−3,115	−758
cash from financing activities	−1,070	−1,863	−576
foreign exchange effects	−14	−17	−2
net change in cash	−28	−161	−26
cash interest paid, supplemental	514	535	486
cash taxes paid, supplemental	429	233	103

1. Liquidity ratios

As the name suggests, liquidity ratios tell how "liquid" a firm's current assets are. In other words, liquidity ratios show whether the firm has sufficient cash and near cash assets to pay bills on time. In this ratio category we will introduce the current ratio, the acid test ratio (or quick ratio), the operating cash flow to current liabilities ratio, accounts receivable turnover and average collection period.

（1）流动比率

流动比率（CR）是流动资产与流动负债之比，计算公式如下：

$$CR = \frac{流动资产}{流动负债}$$

流动比率若等于 1，即表示企业拥有的流动资产恰好足够支付其流动负债。因此，酒店或旅游企业应该维持一个大于 1 的流动比率，以满足其能够支付短期债务的要求。以希尔顿酒店的财务数据为例，我们发现它 2014 年的流动比率为 1.1072，2013 年的为 1.1125。换句话说，2013 年希尔顿有 1.1125 美元的流动资产可以用来支付每 1 美元的流动负债，同时提供 0.1125 元的缓冲；然而，2014 年它只有 1.1072 美元的流动资产可用于支付每 1 美元的流动负债，仅提供了 0.1072 美元的缓冲。虽然这两年的流动比率都大于 1，但该酒店或许应该了解一下流动性略为下降的原因。

（2）酸性测试比率

流动资产中包括如库存和预付费用等流动性较低的资产。虽说库存可能会在企业破产时遭变卖以偿还其债务，但企业平时是不会以库存支付供应商的欠款的。因此，相比流动比率更能够严谨地衡量企业流动性的是酸性测试比率（ATR），也称速动比率（QR），它等于速动资产除以流动负债。公式如下：

$$酸性测试比率 = \frac{速动资产}{流动负债}$$

其中：速动资产等于流动资产减去库存和预付费用。

我们发现希尔顿 2014 年的酸性测试比率为 0.8693，2013 年为 0.8585，这显示了 2014 年该公司的流动性明显优于 2013 年，这结果与通过流动比率（CR）比较流动性的结果相异。探讨希尔顿在 2013 年和 2014 年期间的流动性是如何受库存和预付费用的影响应该是很有意思的。

（3）运营现金流相对流动负债比率

运营现金流相对流动负债比率（OCFTCL）反映企业运营活动产生能够支付其账单的现金流的能力，计算公式为

$$运营现金流相对负债比率 = \frac{运营现金流}{平均流动负债}$$

计算这个比率需要同时使用现金流量表和资产负债表的财务数据。希尔顿 2014 年的 OCFTCL 是 0.6211，2013 年是 0.9356。其 OCFTCL 在 2013 年至 2014 年期间的下降相当显著，值得进一步探讨。当现金流的信息不易获得时，可以用 EBITDA 或净运营利润数据代替。

（1）The current ratio

The current ratio（CR）measures the current assets relative to the current liabilities and is calculated as

$$CR = \frac{Current\ assets}{Current\ liabilities}$$

A current ratio of one indicates that for every one dollar of current liabilities, there is one dollar of current assets that can be used to cover it. As a result, a current ratio of larger than one is desired for a hotel or tourism business to stay liquid in meeting its short-term obligations. Using Hilton's financial figures as an example, we find that its current ratio was 1.1072 in 2014 and 1.1125 in 2013. In other words, in 2013 for every one dollar of Hilton's current liabilities, it has $1.1125 current assets available to cover its short-term obligations, providing a $0.1125 cushion, whereas in 2014 for every one dollar of Hilton's current liabilities, it has $1.1072 current assets available to cover its short-term obligations, providing a $0.1072 cushion. While the current ratios for both years were all above one, there was slight decrease in the firm's liquidity that might be looked into.

（2）The acid test ratio

Included in the current assets are some less liquid ones such as inventory and prepaid expenses. While inventories might be liquidated in the event of a firm's bankruptcy to pay its debt obligations, it is unlikely that a firm would pay its bills using its inventory. Therefore, a more stringent measure of a firm's liquidity than the current ratio is the acid test ratio (ATR), also called quick ratio (QR), and is calculated by dividing the quick assets by the current liabilities, where the quick assets is equal to the current assets minus inventory and prepaid expenses：

$$ART = \frac{Quick\ assets}{Current\ liabilities}$$

We now find that Hilton's acid test ratio was 0.8693 in 2014 and 0.8585 in 2013 and the results show that in fact in 2014 the firm's liquidity was better than that in 2013, which contradicts the comparison results obtained by examining the current ratio. It would be interesting to look into how the amount of inventory and prepaid expenses may have affected Hilton's liquidity during 2013 and 2014.

（3）Operating cash flow to current liabilities

Operating cash flow to current liabilities（OCFTCL）reflects a firm's ability of paying its bills by cash flows generated from operations and is calculated as

$$OCFTCL = \frac{Operating\ cash\ flow}{Average\ current\ liabilities}$$

This ratio requires financial figures from not only the cash flow statement but also the balance sheet. The OCFTCL for Hilton was 0.6211 in 2014 and 0.9356 in 2013. The decrease of Hilton's OCFTCL from 2013 to 2014 was rather significant and would deserve further investigation. When cash flow information is not readily available, EBITDA or

（4）应收账款周转率

应收账款周转率（ART）衡量企业收款速度，计算公式如下：

$$应收账款周转率 = \frac{年赊销额}{平均应收账款}$$

由于赊销销售额通常不为外人所知，计算时可以年销售收益代替。然而，应该注意所得的应收账款周转率将被高估。希尔顿 2014 年的应收账款周转率是 13.3359，2013 年的是 13.4276，它们之间的些微差异可以忽略。应收账款周转率为 13.3359 说明了希尔顿每年平均收款 13.3359 次。

企业应该偏好更高还是更低的应收账款周转率呢？较高的应收账款周转率表明企业收账效率较高，然而，这也意味着其给客户的信贷政策相对来说较严格，从而可能会因此失去某些客户。

（5）平均收账期

平均收账期（ACP）是另一个衡量企业收款速度的指标，计算公式如下：

$$平均收账期 = \frac{365\ 天}{应收账款周转率}$$

以上公式说明了由应收账款转换成现金所需的平均天数。希尔顿 2014 年的平均收账期是 27.37 天，2013 年是 27.18 天。

2. 偿债能力比率

偿债能力比率，也称杠杆比率，不仅说明一个企业的负债程度，同时也可衡量其支付长期债务的能力。对于这个比率类别，就负债程度我们将介绍负债比率、债务权益比率和长期债务对总资本比率；就支付长期债务的能力衡量，我们将介绍利息保障倍数和运营现金流对总负债比率。

（1）负债比率

负债比率（DR）应该是一个最直观的用来衡量负债程度的指标，计算如下：

$$负债比率 = \frac{总负债}{总资产}$$

希尔顿 2014 年的负债比率是 0.8181，2013 年的是 0.8357。虽然负债程度仍比较高，但希尔顿在降低债务使用上取得了些许成绩。希尔顿 2014 年的年度报告显示，基于其轻资本的商业模式，希尔顿几乎能够使用所有的自由现金流来预付债务。仅在 2014 年，希尔顿就预付了 10 亿美元债务。

net operating income could serve as a good proxy.

（4）Accounts receivable turnover

Accounts receivable turnover（ART）measures how quickly a firm collects its sales money and is calculated as

$$ART = \frac{\text{Annual credit sales}}{\text{Average accounts receivable}}$$

As credit sales are normally not known to outsiders, annual sales revenue could be used as proxy for credit sales. However, it should be noted that the resultant accounts receivable turnover would then be overstated. The accounts receivable turnover for Hilton was 13.3359 in 2014 and 13.4276 in 2013 and the difference between them was negligible. A 13.3359 accounts receivable turnover indicates that HLT on average collects its sales money 13.3359 times in a year.

Is a high or low accounts receivable turnover ratio preferred? A higher accounts receivable turnover shows that a firm is rather efficient in collecting its sales money; however, it could also mean a more stringent credit policy extended to its customers and might turn the business away.

（5）Average collection period

Average collection period（ACP）is another measure of speed in collecting sales money and is calculated as

$$ACP = \frac{365 \text{ days}}{\text{Accounts receivable turnover}}$$

The above formula shows the number of days needed to convert the average accounts receivable into cash. The average collection period for Hilton was 27.37 days in 2014 versus 27.18 days in 2013.

2. Solvency ratios

Solvency ratios, also called leverage ratios, tell not only a firm's degree of debt use but also its ability to meet the long-term debt obligation. In this ratio category we will introduce, for degree of debt use, the debt ratio, the debt-equity ratio and the long-term debt to total capitalization ratio and for ability to meet long-term debt, number of time interest earned ratio and the operating cash flow to total liability ratio.

（1）The debt ratio

The debt ratio(DR) is likely the most intuitive measure for degree of debt use and is calculated as

$$DR = \frac{\text{Total liabilities}}{\text{Total assets}}$$

Hilton's debt ratio was 0.8181 in 2014 and 0.8357 in 2013. While still rather heavy, it shows Hilton had made some improvement in its debt use by lowering its debt ratio. A peek into Hilton's 2014 Annual Report, with its light capital business model, Hilton was able to use nearly all its free cash flow to prepay debt. In 2014 alone, Hilton prepaid $1

（2）债务权益比率

负债比率的另一个表示方式是用债务权益比率（DER）来衡量总负债相对于总业主权益的比率，计算公式为

$$债务权益比率 = \frac{总负债}{总业主权益}$$

希尔顿 2014 年的债务权益比率是 4.4977，2013 年的是 5.0880。该比率再次表明希尔顿两年之间债务的使用有所下降。

（3）长期债务对总资本比率

长期债务对总资本比率（LTDTC）反映了长期债务占总资本额的百分比，计算公式如下：

$$长期债务对总资本比率 = \frac{长期债务}{总资本}$$

其中：总资本等于所有长期和永久融资来源的总和。

希尔顿 2014 年的长期债务对总资本比率为 0.7086，2013 年为 0.7439，这表明希尔顿 2014 年于其总资本中依赖长期债务的程度比 2013 年要小一些。

（4）利息保障倍数

利息保障倍数（NTIE），也称作利息偿付比率，反映企业以其息税前收益支付利息费用的能力，计算公式如下：

$$利息保障倍数 = \frac{息税前收益}{利息费用}$$

希尔顿 2014 年的利息偿付比率是 2.8560，2013 年的是 2.1258，表明希尔顿的支付利息能力有所提升。深入查看损益表得知，相比 2013 年，希尔顿在 2014 年不仅有较少的利息费用，同时也有较多来自其运营的收益。

（5）运营现金对总负债比率

运营现金对总负债比率（OCFTTL）反映企业以其运营现金流来支付其总负债的能力，计算公式如下：

$$运营现金对总负债比率 = \frac{运营现金流}{平均总负债}$$

计算这个比率需要同时使用现金流量表和资产负债表的财务数据。希尔顿 2014 年的运营现金对总负债比率是 0.0627，2013 年的是 0.0895。该比率减少的主要原因是运营现金流在 2014 年显著减少，这值得进一步研究。与 OCFTCL 的计算类似，当现金流的信息不易获得时，可以用 EBITDA 或净运营利润数据代替。

billion of debt.

（2）The debt-equity ration

A variant of the debt ratio is the debt-equity ratio（DER）which measures the amount of total liabilities relative to that of total equity and is calculated as

$$DER = \frac{Total\ liabilities}{Total\ equity}$$

Hilton's debt-equity ratio was 4.4977 in 2014 and 5.0880 in 2013 and again, the ratios indicate some reduction of debt use between the two years.

（3）The long-term debt to total capitalization ratio

The long-term debt to total capitalization ratio（LTDTC）reflects the use of long-term debt as a percentage of total capitalization and is calculated as

$$LTDTC = \frac{Long\text{-}term\ debt}{Total\ capitalization}$$

Where total capitalization is the sum of all long-term and permanent sources of financing.

Hilton's long-term debt to total capitalization ratio was 0.7086 in 2014 and 0.7439 in 2013, indicating less dependence on long-term debt for its capitalization in 2014 compared to 2013.

（4）The number of time interest earned ratio

The number of time interest earned ratio（NTIE）also called the interest coverage ratio, shows a firm's ability to pay its interest expenses using earnings before interests and taxes and is calculated as

$$NTIE = \frac{EBIT}{Interest\ expenses}$$

Hilton's interest coverage ratio was 2.8560 in 2014 and 2.1258 in 2013, indicating its better ability in meeting its interest expense obligation. A further look into its income statement, not only Hilton had less interest expenses but also higher earnings from its operations in 2014 compared to 2013.

（5）Operating cash flow to total liabilities

Operating cash flow to total liabilities（OCFTTL）reflects a firm's ability in meeting its debt obligation by cash flows generated from operations and is calculated as

$$OCFTTL = \frac{Operating\ cash\ flow}{Average\ total\ liabilities}$$

This ratio requires financial figures from not only the cash flow statement but also the balance sheet. The OCFTTL for Hilton was 0.0627 in 2014 and 0.0895 in 2013. The decrease of Hilton's OCFTTL from 2013 to 2014 was majorly due to a significant reduction of operating cash flow in 2014 and deserves further investigation. Similar to the calculation of OCFTCL, when cash flow information is not readily available, EBITDA or net operating income could serve as a good proxy.

3. 活动比率

活动比率,也称为效率比率,说明企业是如何有效地利用其资产提供产品和服务给客人而产生销售收益的。对于这个比率类别我们将介绍库存周转率、固定资产周转率和资产周转率。

(1) 库存周转率

库存周转率(ITR)说明企业是如何有效地利用其库存生产产品和提供服务的,计算公式如下:

$$库存周转率 = \frac{售货成本}{平均库存额}$$

希尔顿2014年的库存周转率是10.0475,2013年的是9.5610,说明希尔顿2014年能更有效地管理库存。

企业会偏好高还是低的库存周转率?较高的库存周转率意味着企业能相当有效地管理其库存或者维持相对较低的库存水平,然而,它也可能意味着该公司更容易面临缺货问题,顾客有可能因为无法获得所需产品而心生不满。相反,如果企业的库存周转率较低,它可能会面临较高的库存成本,并且食材可能更容易腐坏。

(2) 固定资产周转率

固定资产周转率(FATR)反映企业如何有效利用其物业、厂房和设备来产生销售收益,计算公式如下:

$$固定资产周转率 = \frac{销售收益}{平均固定资产}$$

希尔顿2014年的固定资产周转率是1.1615,2013年的是1.0666,说明希尔顿2014年比起2013年在运用其固定资产来产生销售收益方面有些许进步。换句话说,2013年时希尔顿就其每1美元的固定资产可以产生1.0666美元的销售收益,2014年时有了进步,其每1美元固定资产可以产生1.1615美元的销售收益。然而,在解读这个比率时要小心陷阱。因为这个比率的分母是平均固定资产,而固定资产的累计折旧决定了固定资产的账面价值,进而影响比例的计算。

(3) 资产周转率

资产周转率(ATR)反映企业如何有效利用其总资产来产生销售收益,计算公式如下:

$$资产周转率 = \frac{销售收益}{平均总资产}$$

希尔顿2014年的资产周转率是0.3987,2013年的是0.3631,说明希尔顿2014年比起2013年在运用其总资产来产生销售收益方面有些许进步。换句话说,2013年时希尔顿就其每1美元的总资产可以产生0.3631美元的销售收益,2014年时更进一步,其每1美元总资产可以产生0.3987美元的销

3. Activity ratios

Activity ratios, also called efficiency ratios, tell how efficiently a firm is using its assets to generate sales revenue and provide products and services to its guests. In this ratio category we will introduce the inventory turnover ratio, the fixed asset ratio and the assets turnover ratio.

(1) The inventory turnover ratio

The inventory turnover ratio(ITR) shows how efficiently a firm uses its inventory to produce products and provide services and is calculated as

$$ITR = \frac{Cost\ of\ goods\ sold}{Average\ inventory}$$

Hilton's inventory turnover ratio was 10.0475 in 2014 and 9.5610 in 2013, indicating its slightly more efficient turnover of inventory in 2014 as compared to 2013.

Is a high or low inventory turnover ratio preferred? A higher inventory turnover ratio implies that a firm is rather efficient in using its inventory or maintaining a rather low inventory level; however, it could also mean that the firm may face a stockout problem more easily and might disappoint its customers when orders cannot be fulfilled. On the contrary, if a firm has a lower inventory turnover ratio, it may incur higher inventory cost plus a higher probability that raw materials may become rotten.

(2) The fixed assets turnover ratio

The fixed assets turnover ratio(FATR) reflects how a firm uses its property, plant and equipment in generating sales revenue and is calculated as

$$FATR = \frac{Total\ revenue}{Average\ fixed\ assets}$$

Hilton's fixed assets turnover ratio was 1.1615 in 2014 and 1.0666 in 2013, showing a slightly efficient use of its fixed assets in generating its sales revenue in 2014. In other words, in 2013 Hilton generated $1.0666 in sales revenue for every one dollar of its fixed assets and in 2014 it did better by generating $1.1615. However, there's a pitfall in interpreting this ratio. As the denominator of the ratio is the average fixed assets, the accumulated depreciation of the fixed assets largely determines the book value of the fixed assets, hence affecting the ratio calculation.

(3) The assets turnover ratio

The assets turnover ratio (ATR) measures how a firm uses its total assets in generating sales revenue and is calculate as

$$ATR = \frac{Total\ revenue}{Average\ total\ assets}$$

Hilton's assets turnover ratio was 0.3987 in 2014 and 0.3631 in 2013, showing a slightly efficient use of its total assets in generating its sales revenue in 2014. In other words, in 2013 Hilton generated $0.3631 in sales revenue for every one dollar of its total assets and in 2014 it did better by generating $0.3987. However, similar to the fixed

售收益。然而,与解读固定资产周转率时要小心陷阱类似,这个比率的分母是平均总资产,所以总资产的累计折旧决定了总资产的账面价值,进而影响比例的计算。

4. 盈利比率

盈利比率通过销售、资产或股权来衡量企业盈利。

（1）利润率

就销售而言,利润率(PM)反映了企业可以从每 1 美元的销售额中获取多少利润,计算公式如下:

$$利润率 = \frac{净利润}{总收益}$$

希尔顿 2014 年的利润率是 0.0641,2013 年的是 0.0426,说明其在这两年的盈利有 50% 的增长。其 2014 年的总收益比 2013 年高出约 8%,而 2014年的净利润比 2013 年高出 62%,这表明希尔顿除了增加其销售收益之外还能有效地控制其开支。

（2）运营效率比率

运营效率比率（OER）衡量企业可以从每 1 美元销售额中获取多少运营利润（或扣除固定费用前利润）,计算公式如下:

$$运营效率比率 = \frac{运营利润}{总收益}$$

希尔顿 2014 年的运营效率比率是 0.1593,2013 年的是 0.1132,说明其在这两年里运营效率有 40% 的增长。其 2014 年的总收益比 2013 年高出约8%,而 2014 年的运营利润比 2013 年高出 52%,这表明希尔顿除了增加其销售收益之外还能有效地控制其运营开支。

读者应该注意利润率和运营效率比率之间是有区别的。因为在计算时剔除了不属于管理层控制的固定费用,如利息和折旧费,所以使用运营效率比率来衡量管理绩效是比较合理的。

（3）资产回报率

就资产而言,资产回报率(ROA)反映了企业可以从每 1 美元资产投入中获取多少利润,计算公式如下:

$$资产回报率 = \frac{净利润}{平均总资产}$$

希尔顿 2014 年的资产回报率是 0.0255,2013 年的是 0.0155,说明其在这两年里的资产回报率有 65% 的增长。其 2014 年的平均总资产比 2013 年低

assets turnover ratio there's a pitfall in interpreting this ratio. As the denominator of the ratio is the average total assets, the accumulated depreciation of the fixed assets also affects the book value of the total assets, hence affecting the ratio calculation.

4. Profitability ratios

Profitability ratios measures how profitable a firm is and can be scaled by sales, assets or equity.

(1) Profit margin

In terms of sales, profit margin(PM)reflects how much profit a firm can retain from every one dollar of sales and can be calculated as

$$PM = \frac{\text{Net income}}{\text{Total revenue}}$$

Hilton's profit margin was 0.0641 in 2014 and 0.0426 in 2013, showing 50% improvement in profitability between the two years. While the total revenue in 2014 was about eight percent higher than in 2013, the net income in 2014 was 62% higher than in 2013, indicating Hilton had done a good job in controlling its expenses, in addition to increasing its sales revenue.

(2) Operating efficiency ratio

Operating efficiency ratio(OER)measures how much operating income (or income before fixed charges) a firm can retain from every one dollar of sales and can be calculated as

$$OER = \frac{\text{Operating income}}{\text{Total revenue}}$$

Hilton's operating efficiency ratio was 0.1593 in 2014 and 0.1132 in 2013, showing 40% improvement in profitability between the two years. While the total revenue in 2014 was about eight percent higher than in 2013, the operating income in 2014 was about 52% higher than in 2013, indicating Hilton had done a good job in controlling its operating expenses, in addition to increasing its sales revenue.

One should note the main difference between the profit margin and the operating efficiency ratio. In measuring management performance, using the latter ratio would be more reasonable because fixed charges such as interest and depreciation expenses not under the control of the management is not included in its calculation.

(3) Return on assets

In terms of assets, Return on assets(ROA)reflects how much profit a firm can generate from every one dollar of assets and can be calculated as

$$ROA = \frac{\text{Net income}}{\text{Average total assets}}$$

Hilton's ROA was 0.0255 in 2014 and 0.0155 in 2013, showing a significant 65% improvement between the two years. Although the average total assets in 2014 was slightly lower than in 2013, the net income in 2014 was 62% higher than in 2013,

一些,而 2014 年的净利润比 2013 年高出 62%,说明希尔顿在利用资产来产生盈利这方面取得了进步。然而,虽然还适用于希尔顿这个个案,但一般在解释 ROA 时得格外谨慎,因为作为其分母的平均总资产是受折旧影响的。

(4) 资产毛回报率

资产回报率的另一个表示方式是资产毛回报率(GROA),计算公式如下:

$$资产毛回报率 = \frac{息税前收益}{平均总资产}$$

对比资产回报率,在计算资产毛回报率时是以息税前收益代替净利润以去除融资对衡量盈利造成的影响。希尔顿 2014 年的资产毛回报率是 0.0670,2013 年的是 0.0492,说明其在这两年里资产回报率有 36% 的增长。

(5) 股东回报率

就股权而言,股东回报率(ROE)反映了企业可以从每 1 美元业主权益(包括优先股和普通股)投入中获取多少利润,计算公式如下:

$$股东回报率 = \frac{净利润}{平均股东权益}$$

希尔顿 2014 年的股东回报率是 0.1477,2013 年的是 0.1245,说明其在这两年里股东回报率有些许增长。其 2014 年的平均股东权益较 2013 年增加了近 37%,而 2014 年的净利润比 2013 年高出 62%,这表明 2014 年希尔顿带给股东每 1 美元股权更高的投资回报。

(6) 普通股股东回报率

股东回报率的另一个表示方式是普通股股东回报率(ROCE),计算公式如下:

$$普通股股东回报率 = \frac{普通股股东盈利分配}{平均股东权益(普通股)}$$

对比股东回报率,在计算普通股股东回报率时,普通股股东盈利分配等于净利润减去优先股红利。因为希尔顿并没有优先股,所以其普通股股东回报率等于股东回报率。

值得注意的是财务杠杆对股东回报率可能造成的影响。如表 2-10 所示,假设有两家相同的酒店——酒店 A 和酒店 B,它们之间唯一的区别是资本结构。酒店 A 有较高的债务融资(即 0.8 的负债率);酒店 B 有较低的债务融资(即 0.2 的负债率)。也就是说,酒店 A 具有较高的财务杠杆,而酒店 B 的财务杠杆则较低。当生意好时,它们的息税前收益皆有 5000 万元人民币,然而由于它们须付不同的利息费用,所以酒店 A 的股东回报率为 1.33,而酒店 B 为 0.41。当生意不好时,1200 万元的息税前收益会导致酒店 A 的股东回报率为 0,而酒店 B 的为 0.079。综上所述,我们不难得出高财务杠杆企业

indicating that Hilton was able to better utilize its total assets in generating profit. However, while may not be the case for Hilton, it should be noted that ROA should also be interpreted with caution as its denominator is the average total assets, which is subject to depreciation.

(4) Gross return on assets

Gross return on assets(GROA) is variant of ROA calculated as

$$GROA = \frac{EBIT}{Average\ total\ assets}$$

Compared with ROA, in the calculation of GROA, EBIT is used in lieu of net income to remove the financing effect when measuring profitability. Hilton's GROA was 0.0670 in 2014 and 0.0492 in 2013, also showing a significant 36% improvement between the two years.

(5) Return on equity

In terms of equity, Return on equity (ROE) reflects how much profit a firm can generate from every one dollar of owners' equity (including both preferred and common equity) and can be calculated as

$$ROE = \frac{Net\ income}{Average\ equity}$$

Hilton's ROE was 0.1477 in 2014 and 0.1245 in 2013, showing some improvement between the two years. While the average equity in 2014 increased 36.78% compared to in 2013, the net income in 2014 was 62% higher than in 2013, indicating that in 2014 Hilton was able help bring higher return, in terms of per dollar of equity investment, to its owners.

(6) Return on common equity

Return on common equity(ROCE) is a variant of ROE calculated as

$$ROCE = \frac{Earnings\ avaiable\ for\ comm\ on\ shareholder}{Average\ common\ epuity}$$

Compared with ROE, in the calculation of ROCE, earnings available for common shareholder is used by deducting preferred dividends from net income. As Hilton doesn't have any preferred equity, its ROCE is the same as ROE.

It is worth noting the effect of leverage on ROE as shown in Table 2 - 10. Assuming that there are two identical hotels, Hotel A and Hotel B, and the only difference between them is their capital structure: Hotel A is financed with higher debt than equity capital (i.e., a debt ratio of 0.8) and Hotel B with lower debt than equity capital (i.e., a debt ratio of 0.2). That is, Hotel A is considered to have a higher financial leverage while Hotel B a lower financial leverage. When business is good, they both have an EBIT of 50 million RMB but with different net income amounts due to their different amounts of interest expenses, leading to Hotel A having a 1.33 ROE and Hotel B 0.41 ROE. When business is bad, their lower EBIT of 12 million RMB results in zero ROE for Hotel A and 0.079 ROE for Hotel B. From what is described here, it is not difficult to conclude that,

的股东回报率的变化范围较大,这也就是为什么有较高财务杠杆的企业通常被认为有较高风险。

表 2-10　酒店财务杠杆效应

单位:百万元人民币

项目	酒店 A(高负债/低股权)		酒店 B(低负债/高股权)	
负债	80	80%	20	20%
股东权益	20	20%	80	80%
总资产	100	100%	100	100%
项目	生意好时	生意不好时	生意好时	生意不好时
息税前收益	50	12	50	12
利息费用	-12	-12	-3	-3
税前利润	38	0	47	9
所得税	-11.4	0	-14.1	-2.7
净利润	26.6	0	32.9	6.3
回报率	26.6÷20=1.33	0÷20=0	32.9÷80=0.41	6.3÷80=0.079
备注:年利率=15%;税率=30%				

(7) 每股盈利

每股盈利(EPS)衡量企业基于每 1 股普通股所赚取的盈利,计算如下:

$$每股盈利=\frac{净利润}{加权平均普通股股数}$$

希尔顿 2014 年的每股盈利是 0.6835 美元,2013 年的是 0.4215 美元,说明了其在这两年的每股盈余有 62%的增长。虽然基于一年的时间来计算普通股的加权平均股数更为准确,但为简单起见,我们在计算时使用简单平均数。

(8) 市盈率

市盈率(PE)表示股票市场为企业盈利能力定价。也就是说,市盈率揭示了投资者回收其投资额所需时间(通常以年记)。较高的市盈率说明一只股票的"热度",而超高市盈率可能意味着股票有成为"泡沫"的危险。市盈率计算公式如下:

$$市盈率=\frac{每股股价}{每股盈利}$$

希尔顿股票 2014 年 12 月 31 日和 2013 年 12 月 31 日的收盘价分别为 26.09 美元和 22.25 美元,因此,它 2014 年的市盈率为 38.17,2013 年为 52.79。比较 2014 年和 2013 年两个市盈率,那些于 2013 年购买希尔顿股票的投资者同时实现了资本收益和更高盈利的期望。

the range of ROE is bigger for firms with a higher financial leverage and that is why firms with a higher financial leverage is considered riskier.

Table 2 – 10　The effect of leverage

in million of RMB

Items	Hotel A (high debt / low equity)		Hotel B (low debt / high equity)	
debt	80	80%	20	20%
equity	20	20%	80	80%
total	100	100%	100	100%
Items	in good time	in bad time	in good time	in bad time
EBIT	50	12	50	12
interest expense	− 12	− 12	− 3	− 3
income before tax	38	0	47	9
income tax	− 11.4	0	− 14.1	− 2.7
net income	26.6	0	32.9	6.3
ROE	26.6 ÷ 20 = 1.33	0 ÷ 20 = 0	32.9 ÷ 80 = 0.41	6.3 ÷ 80 = 0.079
Note：interest rate = 15%；tax rate = 30%				

（7）Earnings per share

Earnings per share （EPS） measures how much profit a firm can generate from every one share of common equity and is calculated as

$$EPS = \frac{Net\ income}{Weighted\ average\ shares\ of\ common\ equity}$$

Hilton's EPS was \$0.6835 in 2014 and \$0.4215 in 2013，showing 62.2% growth between the two years. While it would be more accurate by calculating a weighted average shares of common equity during a year's time，for simplicity reasons we used the simple average number in our calculation.

（8）The price to earnings ratio

The price to earnings ratio(PE)shows the price the stock market places on every one dollar of a firm's earnings ability. That is，the PE ratio implies how long （normally in years） it takes for investors to recoup their investment in a stock. A higher PE ratio indicates the "hotness" of a stock and an extremely high PE ratio may imply a risk of the stock being a "bubble". PE is calculated as

$$PE = \frac{Price\ per\ share}{EPS}$$

The closing price of Hilton's stock on December 31，2014 and 2013 was \$26.09 and \$22.25，respectively，and therefore，its PE was 38.17 in 2014 and 52.79 in 2013. Comparing the two PE ratios in 2014 and 2013，it shows that the investors who bought Hilton's stock in 2013 realized not only capital gain but also higher earnings expectations.

5. 运营比率

业主和经理人可以利用运营比率衡量和分析酒店和旅游企业的经营状况。在第 11 版 USALI 中有一部分详细介绍酒店行业利益相关者常用的运营指标。在本节中,我们将介绍一些主要的运营比率。

(1) 销售组合

销售组合反映各个部门对总收益贡献的百分比,计算公式如下:

$$销售组合(某部门)百分比 = \frac{某部门收益}{总收益} \times 100\%$$

(2) 付费住宿率

付费住宿率显示了酒店如何有效利用其主要资源——客房,计算公式如下:

$$付费住宿率 = \frac{付费住宿客房数}{可供出租客房数} \times 100\%$$

另一方面,免付费住宿率显示免费出租客房占已出租客房的比例,计算公式如下:

$$免付费住宿率 = \frac{免费住宿客房数}{可供出租客房数} \times 100\%$$

(3) 平均每间客房入住人数

平均每间客房入住人数反映每间客房的平均客人数,计算公式如下:

$$平均每间客户入住人数 = \frac{住客数量}{销售客房数(付费+免费)}$$

(4) 双人以上住宿率

双人以上住宿率反映出租客房中有两个以上住客占所有出租客房的百分比,计算公式如下:

$$双人以上住宿率 = \frac{有两个以上住客的出租客房数}{销售客房数} \times 100\%$$

(5) 平均每日房价

平均每日房价(ADR)指的是销售客房的实际房价,计算公式如下:

$$平均每日房价 = \frac{客房收益}{付费住宿客房数}$$

(6) 每间可出租客房收益

每间可出租客房收益(RevPAR)显示了可供出租客房的实现房价,计算公式如下:

$$每间可出租客房收益 = \frac{客房收益}{可供出租客房数}$$

5. Operating ratios

Operating ratios allow owners and managers in gauging and analyzing the operations of hotel and tourism businesses. In the 11th edition of the USALI there is a section on operating metrics which details a number of operating ratios commonly used by hotel industry stakeholders. In this section we will introduce some key operating ratios.

(1) Mix of sales percentage

Mix of sales percentage shows the percentage of contribution of various departments to total revenue and is calculated as

$$\text{Mix of sales (department } x \text{) percentage} = \frac{\text{Revenue from department } x}{\text{Total revenue}} \times 100\%$$

(2) Paid occupancy percentage

Paid occupancy percentage shows how efficiently a hotel utilizing its main resources—rooms for business and is calculated as

$$\text{Paid occupancy percentage} = \frac{\text{Paid rooms occupied}}{\text{Available rooms for rent}} \times 100\%$$

On the other hand, complimentary occupancy percentage shows the percentage of rooms occupied that are complimentary and is calculated as

$$\text{Complimentary occupancy percentage} = \frac{\text{Complimentary rooms occupied}}{\text{Available rooms for rent}} \times 100\%$$

(3) Average occupancy per room

Average occupancy per room tells the average number of guests per room and is calculated as

$$\text{Average occupancy per room} = \frac{\text{Number of guests}}{\text{Number of rooms occupied (paid + comp)}}$$

(4) Multiple occupancy

Multiple occupancy tells the percentage of rooms sold that are occupied by more than one guest and is calculated as

$$\text{Multiple occupancy} = \frac{\text{Number of rooms occupied by more than one guest}}{\text{Number of rooms occupied}} \times 100\%$$

(5) Average daily rate

Average daily rate (ADR) tells the achieved room rate from rooms sold and is calculated as

$$\text{ADR} = \frac{\text{Rooms revenue}}{\text{Paid rooms occupied}}$$

(6) Revenue per available room

Revenue per available room (RevPAR) shows the achieved room rate from rooms available for rent and is calculated as

$$\text{RevPAR} = \frac{\text{Rooms revenue}}{\text{Available rooms for rent}}$$

另外,每间可出租客房收益也可以通过平均每日房价乘以付费住房率计算,计算公式如下:

$$每间可出租客房收益 = 平均每日房价 \times 付费住房率$$
$$= \frac{客房收益}{付费住宿客房数} \times \frac{付费住宿客房数}{可供出租客房数}$$

(7) 每位顾客收益

每位顾客收益(RevPAC)显示基于每位顾客的实现收益,计算公式如下:

$$每位顾客收益 = \frac{总收益}{顾客人数}$$

(8) 人均餐饮消费

人均餐饮消费显示每位顾客餐饮平均消费,计算公式如下:

$$人均餐饮消费 = \frac{餐饮收益}{顾客人数}$$

人均餐饮消费还可以进一步分为人均食品消费和人均饮品消费,同时也可按用餐时段计算。

(9) 食品成本比率

食品成本比率衡量已售食品成本占食品销售收益百分比,计算公式如下:

$$食品成本比率 = \frac{已售食品成本}{食品销售收益} \times 100\%$$

(10) 饮品成本比率

饮品成本比率衡量已售饮品成本占饮品销售收益百分比,计算公式如下:

$$饮品成本比率 = \frac{已售饮品成本}{饮品销售收益} \times 100\%$$

(11) 劳动成本比率

劳动成本比率表示包括工资和相关福利的(部门)劳动成本占总(部门)收益的百分比,计算公式如下:

$$部门劳动成本比率 = \frac{部门劳动成本}{部门总收益} \times 100\%$$

(12) 翻桌率

翻桌率为餐厅运营活动的主要指标,计算公式如下:

$$翻桌率 = \frac{某一餐时服务顾客人数}{某一餐时可提供餐位数}$$

(13) 乘坐率

乘坐率为航空公司运营活动的主要指标,计算公式如下:

$$乘坐率 = \frac{某段期间销售座位数}{某段期间可提供座位数}$$

Alternately，RevPAR can be calculated by multiplying ADR by paid occupancy percentage as follows

$$RevPAR = ADR \times Paid\ occupancy\ percentage$$

$$= \frac{Rooms\ revenue}{Paid\ rooms\ occupied} \times \frac{Paid\ rooms\ occupied}{Available\ rooms\ for\ rent}$$

(7) Revenue per available customer

Revenue per available customer（RevPAC）shows the achieved revenue from each customer and is calculated as

$$RevPAC = \frac{Total\ revenue}{Total\ number\ of\ customers}$$

(8) Average check

Average check shows the average amount of food and beverage check per customer and is calculated as

$$Average\ check = \frac{Food\ \&\ beverage\ revenue}{Number\ of\ customers}$$

Average check can also be further separated into average food check and average beverage check and examined by per meal period.

(9) Food cost percentage

Food cost percentage measures the percentage of food cost to food sales and is calculated as

$$Food\ cost\ percentage = \frac{Cost\ of\ food\ sold}{Total\ food\ revenue} \times 100\%$$

(10) Beverage cost percentage

Beverage cost percentage measures the percentage of beverage cost to beverage sales and is calculated as

$$Beverage\ cost\ percentage = \frac{Cost\ of\ beverage\ sold}{Total\ beverage\ revenue} \times 100\%$$

(11) Labor cost percentage

Labor cost percentage shows the percentage of （departmental） labor cost，including payroll and related fringe benefits，to total （departmental） revenue and is calculated as

$$Departmental\ labor\ cost\ percentage = \frac{Labor\ cost\ by\ department}{Total\ departmental\ revenue} \times 100\%$$

(12) Seat turnover

Seat turnover is a major indicator of a restaurant's business activity and is calculated as

$$Seat\ turnover = \frac{Customer\ served\ in\ a\ meal\ period}{Number\ of\ seats\ available\ in\ a\ meal\ period}$$

(13) Load factor

Load factor is a major indicator of an airline's business activity and is calculated as

$$Load\ factor = \frac{Number\ of\ seats\ sold\ in\ a\ period}{Number\ of\ seats\ avaiable\ in\ a\ period}$$

由上可知,运营比率的计算需要使用更多详细的运营数据。更重要的是这些比率对于业主和经理人来说,不仅可用于评估运营表现,还可用于运营规划和控制。

值得注意的是,不同的使用者对于同一个财务比率应该更高还是更低可能有自己的偏好。例如,债权人、业主和经理人会如何从自己的角度来评价一个企业的流动比率? 债权人因为关注企业是否能按时支付他们的债务,所以会偏好更高的流动比率,而另一方面,业主可能不喜欢高流动比率,因为这等同于企业更好地投资其流动资产所导致的机会成本。

6. 比率分析的局限

虽然有不少财务比率可供业主和经理人运用,但它们的使用会受到一定的限制。

第一,比率分析仅有助于显示可能存在的问题。比率本身是没有意义的,且其变动仅能简单地揭示不同的财务和运营结果的比较。使用者应从自身的利益出发,从企业年度报告及相关资料来发现这些变化的真正原因。

第二,当一个企业有多种业务时,企业通常会在它们的财务报告中公布合并财务报表,而不会为每种业务公布该业务详细的财务报表,所以这类企业很难找到一个合适的行业标杆。

第三,由于抽样偏差的关系,所选的行业平均比率水平可能不合适。由于缺乏可比数据,一家企业通常会主观地选择其对比的标杆企业组。如果该标杆组包含了所有表现较好的企业,受比企业虽然自身表现良好,也可能会被评为表现不佳;如果该标杆组包括了一些表现不佳的企业,受比企业虽然表现不好,也可能会被评为表现好于标杆组。

第四,不同的会计惯例可能会影响比率分析和比较。不同企业可能对固定资产采取不同的折旧方法,这肯定会影响到固定资产(和总资产)的账面价值。因此,若涉及固定资产比率的比较,需要格外小心。

第五,季节性可能会影响某些比率。例如,库存周转率和付费住宿率可能会受到季节性因素的影响。

第六,某些比率是可以操控的。如下例所示。

如果一家企业的流动比率为 1.5(例如,150 万美元的流动资产和 100 万美元流动负债)。该企业计划申请新的贷款,但首席财务官认为,在该流动比率下贷款申请不足以通过银行的审批。他可以支付一些流动负债来提高该

As can be seen from above, operating ratios requires more detailed data from operations and they are very important for owners and managers not only for examining operational performance but also for operational planning and control.

It should be noted that users of financial ratios may have their own preference on the same ratio. For example, how would creditors, owners and managers assess the current ratio of a firm from their own perspective? While creditors care more about the firm's ability to pay their debt obligations on time and thus would probably prefer a higher current ratio, owners on the other hand may not like a high current ratio as this represent opportunity cost should there be better ways of investing the firm's current assets.

6. Limitations of ratio analysis

While there exist a number of financial ratios available for use by owners and managers, their uses are subject to a number of limitations.

First, ratio analysis only helps indicate that problems may exist. Ratios by themselves are meaningless and their changes simply reveal the different financial and operational outcomes from comparisons. It is to the users' interest to dig into a firm's annual report or relevant materials to uncover the real cause of those changes.

Second, when a firm has multiple lines of business, it is difficult to find a proper industry benchmark because normally firms will publish consolidated financial statements for their financial reporting and may not have detailed financial statements for each line of their businesses.

Third, industry average ratios can be improper due to sampling bias. Oftentimes due to lack of comparable data firms may be forced to benchmark their financial ratios against a subjectively selected group. If the group includes all better-performing firms, the subject firm, although performs well, may appear underperforming; if the group includes all under-performing firms, the subject firm, although performs badly, may appear superior to the benchmarking group.

Fourth, different accounting practices may affect ratio analysis and comparison. Firms may adopt different depreciation methods in depreciating their fixed assets and this will certainly affect the book values of the fixed assets (and the total assets as well). Therefore, ratio comparisons made involving fixed assets would require extra caution if possible.

Fifth, seasonality may affect some ratios. For example, inventory turnover ratio may be subject to the impact of seasonality, so are paid occupancy percentage and etc.

Sixth, some ratios could be manipulated. See below an example.

If a firm has a current ratio of 1.5 (e.g., $1.5 million in the current assets and $1 million in the current liabilities). The firm plans to apply for a new loan and the chief financial officer feels that the ratio is not impressive enough for the bank to approval the loan request. He may pay off some current liabilities to improve the ratio. How will the ratio change if the firm pays off $0.5 million current liabilities with the current assets? If

比率。如果该企业以流动资产来支付其 50 万美元的流动负债,其流动比率将如何变化? 如果企业现有的流动比率为 0.8(例如,80 万美元流动资产和 100 万美元流动负债)或 1(例如,各有 100 万美元的流动资产和流动负债),支付 50 万美元流动负债后其流动比率会变成多少?

the firm's existing current ratio is 0.8 (e.g., $0.8 million in the current assets and $1 million in the current liability) or one (e.g., $1 million in the current assets and the current liability，respectively)，what would be the new current ratio after paying off the $0.5 million current liabilities?

第3章 成本概念

学习目标

- 能定义成本
- 理解应用于酒店及旅游行业的不同类型的成本
- 知道如何估计混合成本中的固定和变动成本
- 理解成本分摊

3.1 引　言

　　成本是规划、执行和监督酒店及旅游企业运营过程的一个需要考虑的重要问题。如果业主和经理人不懂成本的概念及其与酒店和旅游企业的关联，他们将无法开展业务，更不用说持续经营企业。

　　成本可以定义为购置能为组织带来任何当前和/或未来利益的商品和服务而花费的现金或现金等价物。在核算成本时有时不一定有资产交换的情形产生。以设备采购为例，酒店可以全额现金支付2.5万元人民币的洗碗机，这属于资产的交换（现金→洗碗机）。该酒店在花费了（或牺牲）这2.5万元人民币的流动资产后，期望这次购买可以提升其食品和饮品运营额，并在未来产生相关收益。洗碗机以其购置成本、运费和安装费总和在资产负债表上的固定资产部分列出。随着时间流逝，机器的折旧费用会在损益表上认列。或者，酒店或旅游企业会支付一笔费用给顾问进行餐厅/业务拓展咨询，这类成本或费用并没有资产交换（现金→咨询服务），但计入当期损益。最后，如果有不幸的事件如洪水发生，那些毁于洪水的未投保库存将在损益表上认列损失，因为企业已经无法从这些受损库存中产生未来利益。图3-1描绘了成本、费用和损失之间的关系。

Chapter 3　Cost Concept

📖 Learning Outcomes

- Define cost
- Understand different types of costs applicable to hospitality and tourism business
- Know how to estimate the fixed and variable components of mixed costs
- Understand cost allocation

3.1　Introduction

Cost is an important matter for consideration during the process of planning, executing and monitoring hospitality and tourism operation. Without knowing the cost concept and its relevance to hotel and tourism businesses, owners and managers would not be able to even start the business, not to mention sustaining it as a going concern.

Cost can be generally defined as the cash or cash equivalent value sacrificed for goods and services that are expected to bring either current and/or future benefits to an organization. There may or may not be exchange of assets when it comes to costing. For example, for equipment purchase, a hotel may pay for a dishwater in full with cash, say ¥25,000 and this is an exchange of assets (cash → dishwasher). The hotel spent (or sacrificed) its current assets of ¥25,000 in anticipating that such purchase would improve its food and beverage operations and generate relevant revenues in the future. The dishwasher is listed at the sum of its acquisition cost and any delivery and installation cost under the section of fixed costs on the balance sheet. As time goes by, its depreciation will be expensed and listed on the income statement. Or, a hotel or tourism firm may pay a consultant for a restaurant/business expansion study and such cost, or expense, has no exchange of assets (cash → consulting service) and is recognized in the income statement. Lastly, when unfortunate events such as flood happened, the loss incurred because of uninsured inventory destroyed by flood is recognized on the income statement and considered a cost to the firm as no future benefit can be produced from these destroyed inventory. The relationship between cost, expense and loss can be depicted in Figure 3 – 1.

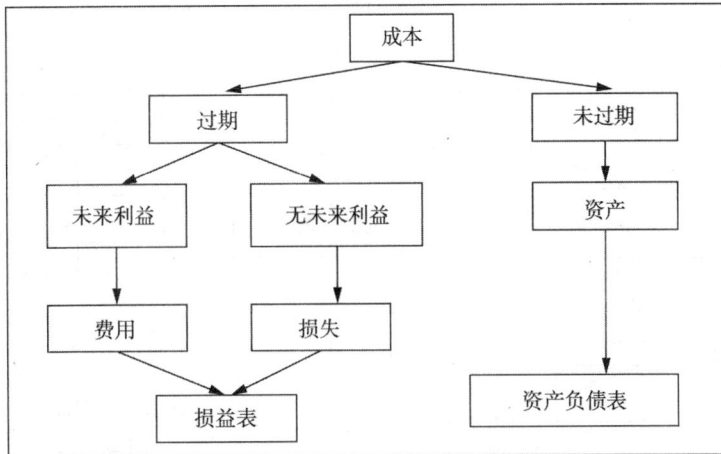

图 3-1　成本、费用和损失之间的关系

3.2　成本的类型

　　了解有关酒店和旅游企业不同类型的运营成本非常重要,因为某些类型的成本不论有无生意都会产生,有些则不会。我们在本节将介绍四种类型的成本,包括固定成本、变动成本、混合成本和总成本。

　　固定成本是指无论产品是否售出或服务是否提供都会产生的成本。无论销售量怎样变化,固定成本在短期内(通常是一年内)不变。固定成本包括租金、保险和折旧费用等。图 3-2 描绘了固定成本和销售量之间的关系。

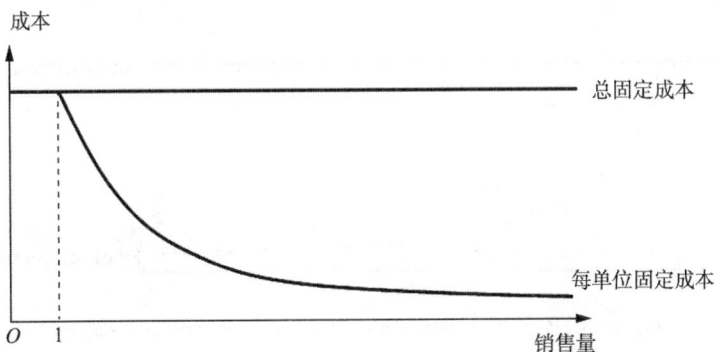

图 3-2　固定成本和销售量之间的关系

　　如图 3-2 所示,总固定成本不会发生改变(至少在短期内)。当酒店出租一间客房时,其平均固定成本,即每单位固定成本,与总固定成本是一样的;当酒店出租两间以上客房时,每单位固定成本开始时将急剧下降,并在卖

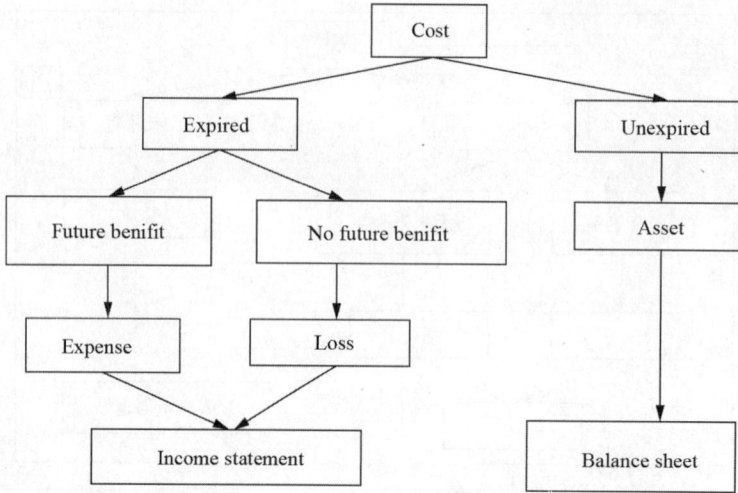

Figure 3 – 1　The relationship between cost, expense and loss

3.2　Different Types of Cost

　　Knowing the different types of costs in relation to hospitality and tourism operation is critical as some type of cost incurs no matter whether there's business or not and some does not incur if there is no business. In this section we will introduce four types of cost including fixed cost, variable cost, mixed cost and total cost.

　　Fixed cost refer to cost that incur whether or not products are sold or services are rendered. Fixed cost remain constant in the short run (generally within one year), regardless of changes in sales volume. Examples of fixed cost are rent, insurance and depreciation expense. The relationship between fixed cost and sales volume is depicted in Figure 3 – 2.

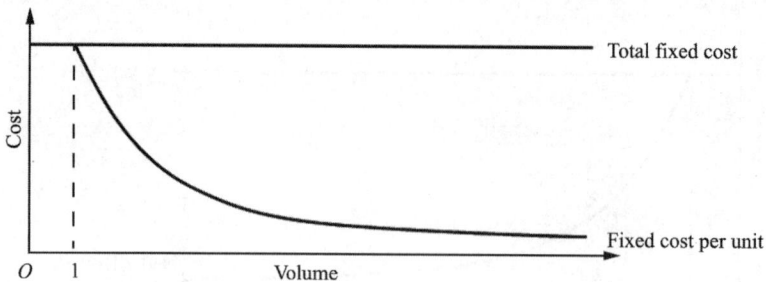

Figure 3 – 2　The relationship between fixed cost and sales

　　As shown in the above figure, the total fixed cost would not change (at least in the short-run). When a hotel rent out a room, the average fixed cost, or fixed cost per unit, remains the same as the total fixed cost; when the hotel rents out two and more rooms, its fixed cost per unit will start to decrease sharply at the beginning and flatten out when more and more rooms are sold. That is, the relationship between the total fixed costs and

出越来越多房间时趋于平缓。也就是说,总固定成本和销售量之间的关系是呈曲线形的。每间客房占的固定成本份额会随着出租房间数增加而变少。

如图 3-3 所示,固定成本可以再分成两种:一种是产能固定成本;另一种是自主固定成本。

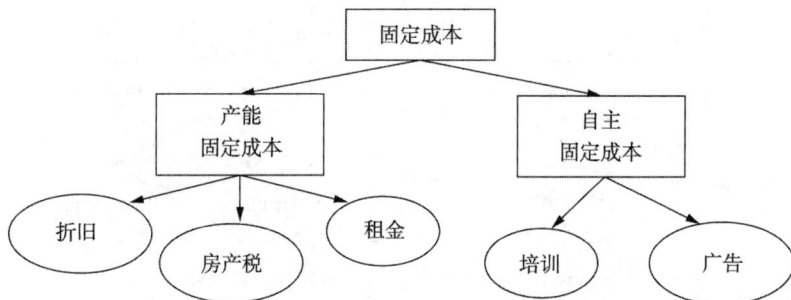

图 3-3　固定成本种类

酒店或旅游企业为了售卖产品及提供服务给顾客,一定会存在如折旧费用、房产税和租金等产能固定成本以维持运营。酒店应位于建筑物内(一般情况下),如果业主拥有业权,则须支付房产税。如果酒店位于出租物业内,业主则须支付租金。另一方面,自主固定成本,如培训和广告费用等,一般由企业自行裁量决定支出。有些企业可能认为花钱培训是值得的,而其他企业可能会认为并非如此。

顾名思义,变动成本是指那些根据销售量的变化而按比例改变的成本。企业如果没有生意就不会有相关的变动成本产生。变动成本的例子包括已售食品成本和在生产过程中使用的物料。销售越多的食品,就会使用越多的原料。图 3-4 描绘了变动成本和销售量之间的关系。

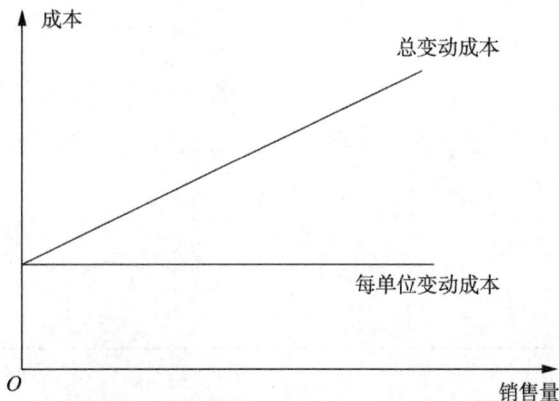

图 3-4　变动成本和销售量之间的关系

sales volume is curvilinear. The more rooms are rent out, the less share of fixed costs each room will have to account for.

Fixed costs can be grouped under two categories: one is capacity fixed costs and the other discretionary fixed costs as shown in Figure 3 - 3.

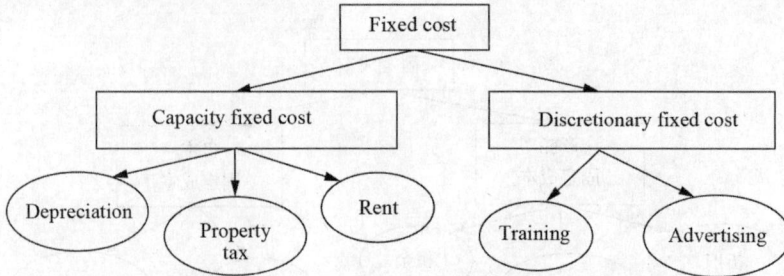

Figure 3 - 3　Different types of fixed cost

Capacity fixed costs ought to exist for a hotel or tourism business to run its operation in selling its products and rendering services to the customers and examples are depreciation expense, property tax and rent. Hotels should be located inside a building (most of the time) and owners are required to pay property tax if the building are owned by them or pay rent if the hotel is in a rental property. Discretionary fixed cost, on the other hand, are normally spent with a firm's own discretionary and justification and examples are training cost and advertising expenditure. Some firms may find it valuable to spend money on training while others may think otherwise.

Variable cost, as the name suggests, refer to those costs that change proportionally to changes in sales volume. If there's no business activity, relevant variable cost would not incur. Examples of variable cost are cost of food sold and supplies used in production. The more foods are sold, the more ingredients would be used. The relationship between variable cost and sales volume is depicted in Figure 3 - 4.

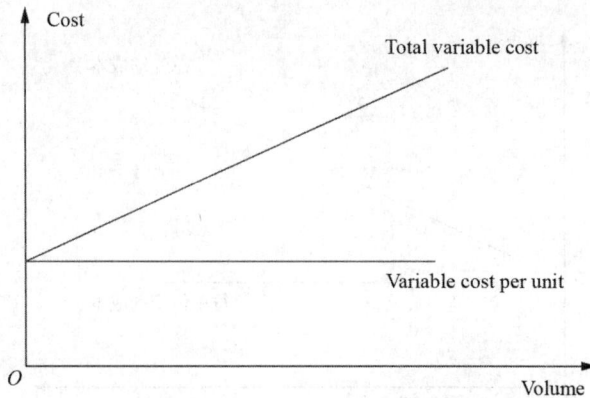

Figure 3 - 4　The relationship between variable cost and sales volume

因为总变动成本和销售量之间的关系呈线性,总变动成本可以按下列公式计算:

$$总变动成本＝单位变动成本×销售量$$

举例来说,客人退房后房务员整理一间客房的成本为 100 元人民币(包括客房用品和房务员的工资),假设有 100 个待整理客房,与客房整理相关的总变动成本为 1 万元人民币。

应该注意的是,单位变动成本可能会受到企业批量采购的影响。例如,如果洗发水订货量为 1000 瓶,单位成本为每瓶 10 元人民币,而如果订货量超过 1000 瓶,每瓶成本则为 9.8 元人民币。计算每间客房变动成本时应该反映批量折扣。

某些类型的成本同时具有固定和变动成本,它们被称为混合成本。混合成本的例子包括销售人员的工资支出和设备的维护成本。对于销售人员,他们的薪酬可能包括具有固定性质的每月工资加上具有变动性质的基于工作表现的销售提成。无论他们表现好坏他们都可获得固定月薪;如果表现好,他们的工资总额将因佣金收入而增加。图 3-5 描绘了混合成本和销售量之间的关系。

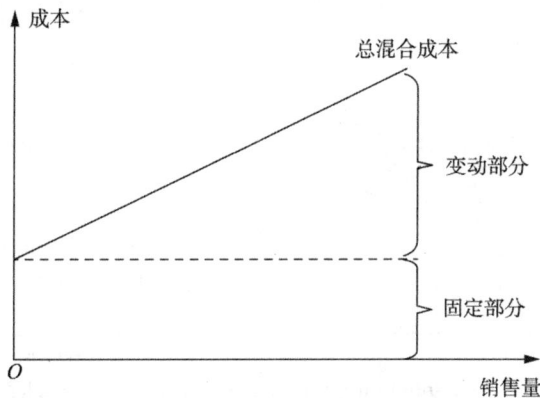

图 3-5 混合成本和销售量之间的关系

混合成本为固定成本和变动成本的加总,如下式所示:

$$混合成本＝固定成本＋(每单位变动成本×销售量)$$

企业如果没有生意,其混合成本将等同于固定成本。因为有变动成本部分,混合成本会随着销售量增加而增加。此外,类似于平均固定成本的概念,平均混合成本或每单位混合成本将随销售量的增加而逐渐减少。如图 3-6 所示,单位混合成本和销售量间呈曲线关系。

Because the relationship between total variable cost and sales volume is linear, total variable cost can be calculated as

Total variable cost = Variable cost per unit × Number of units sold

For example, if it costs ¥100 to turn around a hotel room (including guestroom supplies and housekeeper wage) after a guest checked out and there are 100 rooms to be turned around, the total variable cost associated with the housekeeping tasks will be ¥10,000.

One should note that when there's volume ordering, variable cost per unit may be affected. For example, if the unit cost for shampoo is ¥10 per bottle with an order quantity of 1,000 and ¥9.8 with an order quantity of more than 1,000, the calculation of variable cost per room sold should reflect the reduction of volume discount.

Certain types of cost have both a fixed and a variable component and they are termed mixed cost. Examples of mixed cost are salary expenses for sales personnel and equipment maintenance cost. For sales personnel, their compensation may consist of a fixed component in terms of monthly salary plus a variable component in terms of sales commission conditioned upon their work performance. Whether they perform or not, they will receive fixed monthly salary; if they perform, their total compensation will be higher because of the addition of commission income. The relationship between mixed cost and sales volume is depicted in Figure 3 – 5.

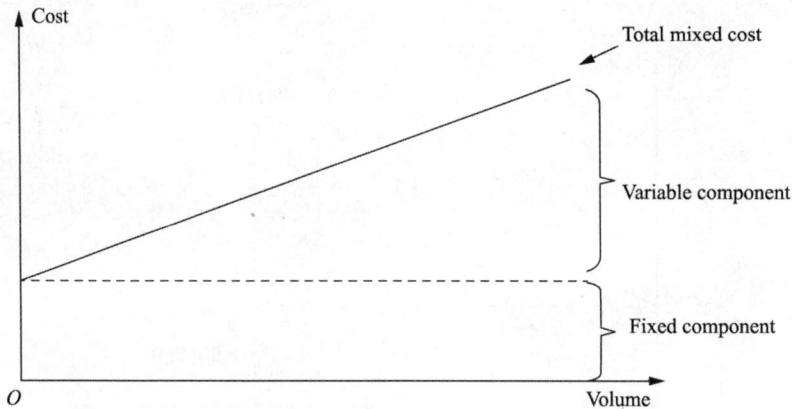

Figure 3 – 5   The relationship between mixed costs and sales volume

Mixed cost can be calculated as the sum of fixed cost and variable cost as

Mixed cost = Fixed cost + (Variable cost per unit × Number of units sold)

If there is no business activity, mixed costs will be of the same amount as fixed cost. Because of the variable component, mixed cost will go up as sales volume increases. Besides, similar to the concept of average fixed cost, the average mixed cost, or mixed cost per unit, will gradually decrease as sales volume increases. The relationship between the total mixed cost and sales volume is curvilinear as depicted in Figure 3 – 6.

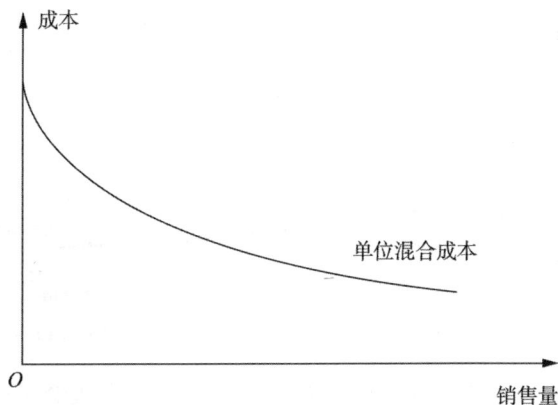

图 3 - 6　单位混合成本和销售量间的关系

在酒店和旅游运营中存在不同类型的固定、变动和混合成本。总成本则包括总固定成本和总变动成本。图 3-7 描绘了总成本和销售量之间的关系。

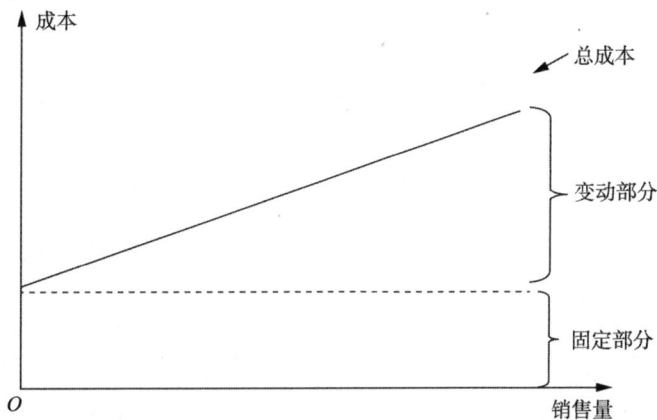

图 3 - 7　总成本和销售量之间的关系

总成本由总固定成本和总变动成本加总得出，如下式所示：

总成本＝总固定成本＋（每单位变动成本×销售量）

企业如果没有生意，其总成本将等同于固定成本。因为有变动成本部分，总成本会随着销售量增加而增加。

3.3　估计混合成本中的固定和变动成本

如前所述，混合成本为固定成本和变动成本的总和，混合成本的多寡则取决于销售量。了解混合成本的组成对管理者来说是非常重要和有用的，因为其不仅可以衡量企业的运营表现，同时也有助于管理者更精确地计划和准备运营预算。也就是说，某些成本信息的提供可以帮助管理者做出更明智的决策（例如，表现分析和预测）。

有三种方法将混合成本细分为固定和变动部分：高/低两点法、散点图法和回归法。

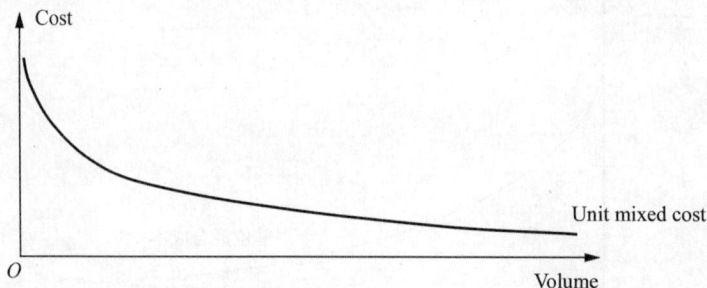

Figure 3 - 6   The relationship between unit mixed cost and sales volume

In hotel and tourism operations, there exist various types of fixed, variable and mixed cost. Total cost consists of total fixed cost and total variable cost and the relationship between total cost and sales volume can be depicted in Figure 3 - 7.

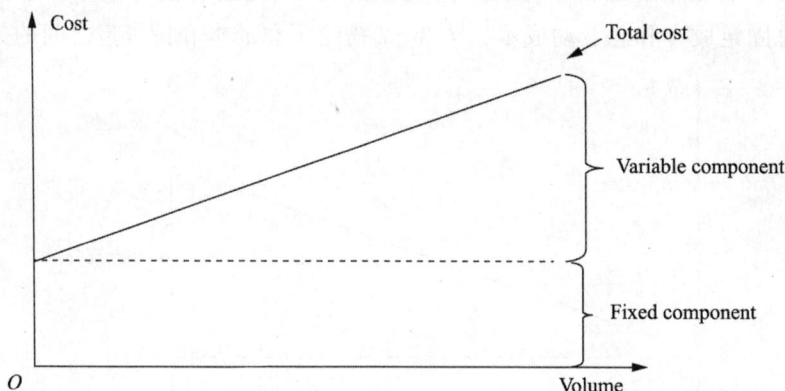

Figure 3 - 7   The relationship between total cost and sales volume

Total cost can be calculated as the sum of total fixed cost and total variable cost as

Total cost = Total fixed cost + (Variable cost per unit × Number of unit sold)

If there is no business activity, total cost will be of the same amount as fixed cost. Because of the variable component, total cost will go up as sales volume increases.

3.3   *Separating Mixed Cost into a Fixed and a Variable Component*

As mentioned earlier, mixed cost is calculated as the sum of fixed cost and variable cost and the amount of mixed cost is dependent upon business volume. Knowing the composition of mixed cost is critical and useful as managers can not only measure their business performance but also plan and prepare their operating budgets more precisely. That is, there is a number of management functions (e.g., performance analysis and forecasting) that can be carried out in making informed decisions if costing information is made available.

There are three ways to separating mixed cost into a fixed and a variable component: the high/low two-point method, the scatter diagram method and the regression method.

1. 高/低两点法

顾名思义,高/低两点法基于两个极端销售活动期间进行估计,以下例说明。假设你是丛林快餐店的经理,想要找出工资成本信息进行运营规划。表3-1显示每月劳动力成本和相对应的每月服务顾客人数信息。

表 3-1　劳动力成本信息

月份	劳动力成本(美元)	服务顾客人数
一月	8000	2250
二月	7800	2120
三月	8800	2300
四月	9200	2550
五月	9300	2600
六月	9000	2400
七月	8200	2200
八月	7500	1850
九月	7200	1750
十月	6800	1700
十一月	6750	1650
十二月	6200	1500
总　数	94750	24870

从上面的信息中,我们首先确定五月份通过服务 2600 名顾客产生了最高的 9300 美元劳动力成本,而十二月份通过服务 1500 名顾客产生了最低的 6200 美元劳动力成本。其次,在计算服务每名顾客所产生的劳动力变动成本时,我们以 9300 美元减去 6200 美元,再将其差异(即 3100 美元)除以两个月服务顾客人数之差(即 1100 名顾客),如下所示:

$$服务每名顾客劳动力变动成本 = \frac{9300 - 6200}{2600 - 1500} = 2.82(美元)$$

这 2.82 美元提供了怎样的成本信息? 这可以解释成通过对比五月和十二月之间的成本信息,每多服务一位顾客,总劳动成本将增加 2.82 美元。同样地,少服务一位顾客,总劳动成本也将减少 2.82 美元。有了服务每位顾客

1. The high/low two-point method

As the name suggests, the high/low two-point method bases estimation on data from two extreme periods of sales activity and can be illustrated using the following example. Suppose that you are the manager of Jungle Restaurant, a quick-service restaurant, and are interested in finding out labor cost information for planning purposes. Table 3 – 1 shows information on monthly labor cost and the number of customers served for the corresponding months.

Table 3 – 1   Labor cost information

Month	Labor cost ($)	Number of customers served
January	8,000	2,250
February	7,800	2,120
March	8,800	2,300
April	9,200	2,550
May	9,300	2,600
June	9,000	2,400
July	8,200	2,200
August	7,500	1,850
September	7,200	1,750
October	6,800	1,700
November	6,750	1,650
December	6,200	1,500
Total	94,750	24,870

From the above information, we first identify that the month of May had the highest amount of labor cost of $9,300 by serving 2,600 customers while the month of December had the lowest amount of labor cost of $6,200 by serving 1,500 customers. Second, we can obtain the amount of variable labor cost per customer served by subtracting $6,200 from $9,300 and divide the resultant difference (i.e., $3,100) by the difference of the number of customers served between the two months (i.e., $1,100) as follows:

$$\text{Variable labor cost per customer served} = \frac{9300 - 6200}{2600 - 1500} = 2.82$$

What does $2.82 tell about costing information? It could be interpreted that, by comparing costing information between the months of May and December, for each additional customer served, total labor cost would be increased by $2.82. Similarly, for one less customer served, total labor cost would be saved by $2.82. With information on

劳动力变动成本信息,我们就可以利用五月份或十二月份的成本信息来估算每月固定成本。假设我们使用五月份的成本信息,将2.82美元乘以2600名顾客,可以得到五月份的总变动成本,再将总变动成本从五月份的总劳动成本中减去,得到五月份的固定成本如下:

$$五月份固定成本＝9300－(2.82×2600)＝1968(美元)$$

正如前面提到的,固定成本应保持不变(至少在短期内),因此,其他月份的每月固定成本应该是接近五月的。现在如果使用十二月份的成本信息,算出的变动成本为4230美元而固定成本是1970美元。五月份和十二月份的每月固定成本仅相差2元,这是可以忽略的,因为我们只在两个月数据的基础上估计固定和变动成本。

以高/低两点法来估算混合成本中的固定和变动成本的构成有其优缺点。该方法相当简单而且易于使用,可以帮助管理者快速得知成本信息。然而,须权衡的是,该方法仅考虑我们例子中12个数据点中的2个,精确度可能会受影响,因为大部分成本信息未在估算中使用。

2. 散点图法

散点图法因为使用了所有的数据点来估计混合成本中的固定和变动成本,在估计精确度上要比高/低两点法高些。使用同一个丛林快餐店的例子,所有每月劳动力成本信息绘制如图3-8所示,Y轴代表混合成本而X轴表示相应成本所服务顾客的人数。

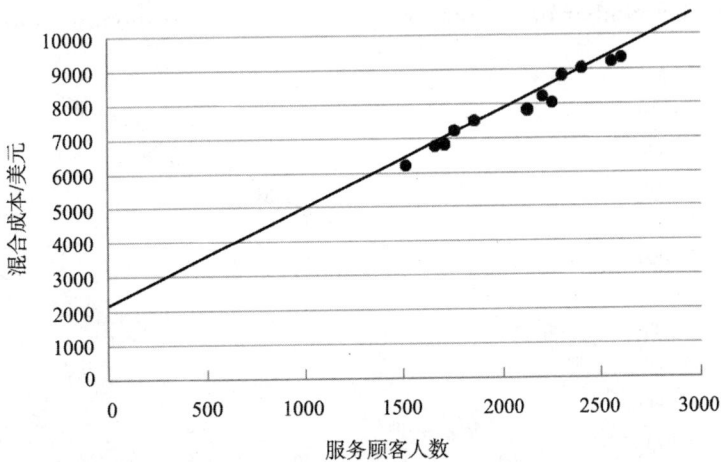

图 3-8　劳动力成本信息的散点图

variable labor cost per customer served of $2.82, we can then estimate the amount of monthly fixed cost by using either the May or December costing information. Using the May costing information, the amount of total variable cost can be obtained by multiplying 2,600 customers by $2.82, and the resultant amount can be subtracted from total labor cost in May to derive the fixed cost for May as follows:

$$\text{Fixed cost for May} = 9300 - (2.82 \times 2600) = 1968$$

As mentioned earlier, the fixed cost amount should remain constant (at least in the short run) and therefore, the monthly fixed cost amount for other months should be close to that for May. Now, if using the December costing information, variable labor cost are calculated as $4,230 and fixed cost are then $1,970. The difference on the monthly fixed cost amount between May and December is only $2, which could be neglected as we were estimating both the fixed and variable cost only on the basis of two months' data.

There are pros and cons of using the high/low two-point method in estimating the fixed and variable cost components of mixed cost. The method is rather straightforward and easy to apply, which could serve as quick reference for managers. However, the trade-off is that, the method only considers two out of 12 data points in our example, which could lack preciseness as the majority of costing information is not used in the estimation.

2. The scatter diagram method

The scatter diagram method is an improvement over the high/low two-point method, which includes all data points in the estimation of fixed and variable cost of mixed cost and arguably should be more precise in the estimation. Using the same example of Jungle Restaurant, as shown in Figure 3 – 8 all monthly labor cost information is plotted on the diagram with the Y-axis representing mixed cost amount while the X-axis indicating the number of customers served for the corresponding month.

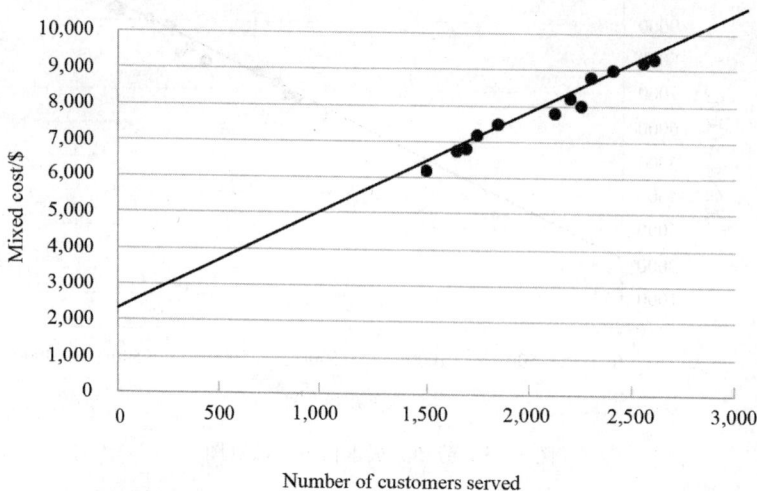

Figure 3 – 8　Scatter diagram of labor cost information

然后绘制一条尽可能接近到所有点的趋势线。也就是说,这条趋势线代表的是所有的数据点和线之间距离总和最小的一条直线。趋势线延伸并与 Y 轴相交的截距即为估计的每月固定成本金额(约 2300 美元)。每年的固定成本金额可由每月 2300 美元乘以 12 个月得知,或者

$$每年固定成本金额=每月 2300 美元 \times 12 个月=27600 美元$$

然后从每年混合成本金额中减去 2.76 万美元后即可得知每年变动成本金额,或者

$$每年变动成本金额=94750 美元-27600 美元=67150 美元$$

然后将 6.715 万美元除以服务顾客人数即可得知服务每名顾客所产生的劳动力变动成本,或者

$$服务每名顾客劳动力变动成本=67150 美元 \div 24870=2.7 美元$$

虽说此法在估计时会利用到所有的数据点,但要正确地使用散点图法还要绘制一个能相对精确地估计每月固定成本金额的截距。

3. 回归法

回归法在概念上类似于散点图法,其做法是估计一条能尽量通过所有的数据点的线。相对于其他无数可能画出的线,这条特定的线与所有数据点的垂直距离平方和是最小的。回归法和散点图法之间的主要区别是后者是通过手绘而前者是使用统计方法绘制而成的。回归方法也称为最小平方法(OLS),因为它能找出一条数据点和线之间具有最小平方距离的线。回归线的估计用以下等式表示:

$$\hat{y}=a+bx$$

式中:$\hat{y}$ 为混合成本;a 为估计的固定成本;b 为估计的每单位变动成本;x 为销售量。

b 和 a 可以分别计算如下:

$$b=\frac{\sum_{i=1}^{n}(x_i-\bar{x})(y_i-\bar{y})}{\sum_{i=1}^{n}(x_i-\bar{x})^2}$$

$$a=\bar{y}-b\bar{x}$$

使用同一个丛林快餐店的例子。我们可以估计其成本方程式如下:

$$\hat{y}=2201.8+2.7474x$$

每月固定成本金额是 2201.8 美元,而每服务一名顾客所产生的变动成本为 2.7474 美元。

A trend line is then drawn that is as close as possible to all the dots. That is, the trend line is a line that minimizes the sum of the distances between all the dots and the line. The intercept, where the trend line extends and intersects with the Y-axis, is then estimated as the monthly fixed cost amount (about $2,300). Yearly fixed cost amount can be obtained by multiplying $2,300 per month by 12 months, or

$$\text{Yearly fixed cost} = 2300 \text{ per month} \times 12 \text{ months} = 27600$$

$27,600 is then subtracted from the amount of yearly mixed cost to derive the amount of yearly variable cost, or

$$\text{Yearly variable cost} = 94750 - 27600 = 67150$$

Variable cost per customer served can then be obtained by dividing $67,150 by total number of customers served, or

$$\text{Variable cost per customer served} = 67150 \div 24870 = 2.7$$

While all data points are used in the estimation, the key to properly utilize the scatter diagram method is relatively precise drawing of the diagram so as to derive an accurate estimation of an intercept of the monthly fixed cost amount.

3. The regression method

The regression method estimates a line going through all the points such that the sum of the squared vertical distance to the line from all the points will be the smallest among all possible lines drawn through the points, which is conceptually similar to the scatter diagram. The major difference between the regression method and the scatter diagram method is that the latter is performed manually while the former by using statistical method. The regression method is also termed ordinary least square (OLS) method because it identifies a line with the least squared distance between the data points and the line. The estimated regression line is represented by the equation below:

$$\hat{y} = a + bx$$

Where, $\hat{y}$ = mixed costs, a = estimated fixed costs, b = estimated unit variable costs and x = sales volume. b and a can be calculated respectively as follows:

$$b = \frac{\sum_{i=1}^{n}(x_i - \bar{x})(y_i - \bar{y})}{\sum_{i=1}^{n}(x_i - \bar{x})^2}$$

$$a = \bar{y} - b\bar{x}$$

Using the same example of Jungle Restaurant, a cost equation is estimated as

$$\hat{y} = 2201.8 + 2.7474x$$

The monthly fixed cost is $2,201.8 and the variable cost per customer served is $2.7474.

我们可以比较以三种不同的方法估计混合成本中的固定和变动成本的结果(见表 3-2)。

表 3-2 三种方法结果比较

方 法	每月固定成本(美元)	服务每位顾客变动成本(美元)
高/低两点法	1968	2.82
散点图法	2300	2.70
回归法	2201.8	2.75

因为使用的估计方法不同,所以每月固定成本金额和服务每位顾客的变动成本金额有所差异并不令人意外。三种方法各有利弊。使用哪种方法取决于履行管理职能所需时间、精度和目的。如果时间紧迫且可以接受粗略的信息,采用高/低两点法应该足够。但如果要求的精度较高,就一定要采用回归法了。

3.4 成本分摊

成本分摊是责任会计制度要求下成本会计的核心。决定一个部门的盈利或产品及服务表现时能够追溯的相应费用称为直接成本。例如,在确定某一个餐饮菜单选项的盈利时,配料成本被认为是直接成本;或者,前台员工的工资和福利待遇是估算客房部门利润时应该考虑的部门直接成本。直接成本是相当容易认定的。一些难以追溯但用来支持产生运营收入的费用称为间接成本。这些费用来自行政、销售和市场营销、信息技术和公共区域的水电使用等。可以利用一些虽说主观但合理的方法来分摊间接成本。

例如,酒店公共区域的水电费用可以基于面积或收益金额分配到不同的利润中心。假设六月份某一酒店公共区域的水电费用为 5 万元人民币,酒店只有两个运营部门,一个是客房部,另一个是餐饮部。此外,客房和餐饮部门的面积分别为 2000 平方米和 500 平方米。5 万元人民币的公共区域水电费

We now can take a look and compare the results of separation of mixed costs into a fixed and variable component using the three different methods as Table 3 – 2 shows.

Table 3 – 2　Comparsion of three methods

Method	Monthly fixed cost(US dollar)	Variable cost per customer served(US dollar)
high/low two-point	1,968	2.82
scatter diagram	2,300	2.70
regression	2,201.8	2.75

Because of the different methods used in the estimation, it is not surprising to note the different results of monthly fixed cost and variable cost per customer served derived. The three different methods have their own pros and cons. The adoption of a method to be used depends on the purpose of and time and accuracy required for carrying out the managerial functions. If time is of essence and approximate information is acceptable, probably the high/low two-point method would suffice. On the other hand, if accuracy is required, definitely the regression method should be adopted.

3.4　Cost Allocation

Cost allocation is the center of cost accounting and required in a responsibility accounting system. Expenses that can be traced to a product, service, or department are direct costs to be accounted for in determining profitability or performance of the corresponding subject. For example, when determining the profitability of a food & beverage menu item, the cost of ingredients is considered a direct cost; or, when determining departmental income for the rooms department, salaries, wages and fringe benefits for front office agents are considered direct cost of the department. Direct cost is rather straightforward and easily identified. Nevertheless, some expenses that are more difficult to trace and incurred in support of generating operating revenues are considered indirect cost; examples are expenses from the administrative and general functions, sales and marketing, information technology functions or utility in public areas. Some rationale, nevertheless subjective, could be developed in allocating indirect cost.

For example, utility expenses in public areas of a hotel can be allocated to different profit centers on the basis of, say, area or revenue amount. Suppose the utility expenses for public areas in a hotel in the month of June were 50,000 RMB and the hotel only had two operating departments: one was rooms and the other food and beverage. Furthermore, the areas of the rooms and food and beverage departments were 2,000 square-meter and 500 square-meter, respectively. The 50,000 RMB utility expenses in public areas could be allocated on the basis of departmental area to the two departments

用可按部门面积分配给两个部门：

$$分配给客房部的水电费用 = 50000 \times \left(\frac{2000}{2000 + 500} \right) = 40000(元)$$

因此,分配给餐饮部门的水电费用为 1 万元。或者,假设客房和餐饮部门分别产生了 48 万元和 30 万元的收益。公共区域 5 万元的水电费用可按收益金额分配给两个部门：

$$分配给客房部的水电费用 = 50000 \times \left(\frac{480000}{480000 + 300000} \right) = 30769(元)$$

因此,分配到餐饮部门的水电费用为 19231 元。

as follows:

$$\text{Utility expenses to rooms} = 50000 \times \left(\frac{2000}{2000 + 500}\right) = ¥40000$$

and therefore, utility expenses to the food and beverage departments were ¥10,000. Or, suppose that the rooms and food and beverage departments generated ¥480,000 and ¥300,000 in revenues, respectively. The ¥50,000 utility expenses in public areas could be allocated on the basis of revenue generated to the two departments as follows:

$$\text{Utility expenses to rooms} = 50000 \times \left(\frac{480000}{480000 + 300000}\right) = ¥30769$$

and therefore, utility expenses to the food and beverage department were then ¥19,231.

第4章 本—量—利分析

![学习目标图标] **学习目标**

- 理解本—量—利分析的概念
- 能描述关于本—量—利分析的假设与局限
- 能针对单一产品应用本—量—利分析
- 能进行敏感度分析
- 了解边际贡献和边际贡献率
- 能针对多元产品应用本—量—利分析
- 理解运营杠杆的概念

4.1 引 言

虽然财务经理的目标是股东财富最大化,但如果运营没有盈利,这样的目标是难以达成的。管理者经营酒店或旅游企业最终的目标是满足他们定期的运营和现金预算,并希望通过收入最大化和费用最小化来最大限度地提升他们的盈利。当收入超过费用时可以产生利润;反之则会有损失。有很多原因可能影响收入的产生和费用的波动而导致运营结果变化。因此,在酒店和旅游企业运营的背景下,成本、销售量和利润之间的交互作用值得仔细检验,它们的关系如图4-1所示。

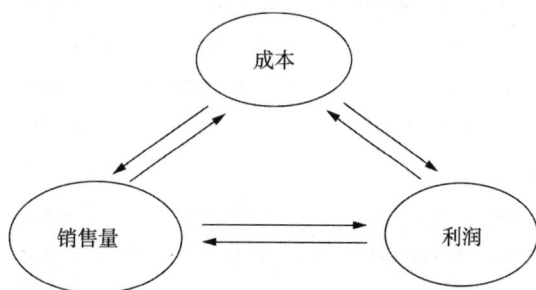

图4-1 成本、销售量和利润之间的关系

本—量—利分析是一种用于分析固定成本、变动成本、销售量和利润之间关系的管理工具。本—量—利分析可以应用于解决许多管理和运营问题,

Chapter 4　Cost-volume-profit Analysis

Learning Outcomes

- Understand the concept of cost-volume-profit analysis
- Be able to describe assumptions and limitations associated with cost-volume-profit analysis
- Be able to perform cost-volume-profit analysis for single product
- Be able to conduct sensitivity analysis
- Understand the concept of contribution margin and contribution margin ratio
- Be able to perform cost-volume-profit analysis for multiple-service operations
- Understand the concept of operating leverage

4.1　Introduction

While the goal for financial managers is shareholder wealth maximization, such goal cannot be reached if profitable operation is not achieved. The manager's ultimate goal in operating a hotel or tourism business is to meet their periodical operations and cash budgets and hopefully maximize their profitability by maximizing revenues and minimizing expenses. When revenues exceed expenses, profits are generated; otherwise, loss will incur. There

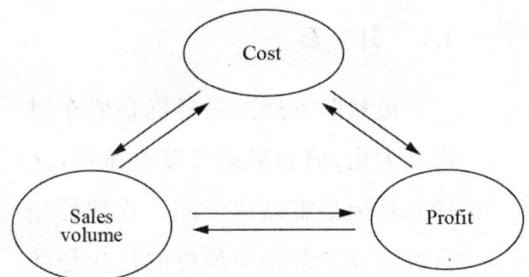

Figure 4 – 1　The relationship among cost,
volume and profit

are many factors that may affect revenue generation and expense fluctuation, leading to variation of operating results. Therefore, in the context of hospitality and tourism operation, there exists inter-correlations among cost, sales volume and profit, which deserves careful examination, and their relationships can be depicted in Figure 4 – 1.

Cost-volume-profit (CVP) analysis is a management tool that analyzes the relationship among fixed cost, variable cost, sales volume and profit. CVP analysis can be applied to solve many management and operational problems and to allow managers make informed decisions to maximize operating profit. For example, CVP analysis can

并帮助管理者做出明智的决定来最大限度地提高运营利润。例如,本—量—利分析可以回答以下问题:

- 估算要达到要求利润所需要的收益水平;
- 运营的保本点是多少?
- 过了保本点之后达到某一水平住宿率时的利润是多少?
- 增加广告费用会对保本点销售额产生什么影响?
- 为了能支付广告费用同时达到所需利润需要增加多少客房销售量?
- 房价、变动成本或固定成本的增加会对利润产生什么影响?

通过理解和运用本—量—利分析还可以回答更多管理和运营的“假设”的问题。不过,许多管理者最想问和最应该问的第一个问题是:运营的保本点是多少? 管理者需要了解并努力至少能达到保本点才不会产生运营亏损。此外,管理者还能因为运营表现不仅达到而且超过保本点而受到表扬。保本点是使利润(即税前利润或简称 I_b)为零时的销售金额或量。换句话说,当收益等于总成本时就能实现保本,同时该企业没有税前利润也没有所得税责任。因此保本点可以看作是本—量—利分析的一个特例。更多关于保本点的计算将在后面说明。

4.2　关于本—量—利分析的假设与局限

在应用本—量—利对酒店或旅游企业的运营进行分析时,管理者需要知道一些基本假设,这样才能够确保其运营条件能适当地应用本—量—利分析。如果没有满足这些假设,本—量—利分析的结果和后续的管理决策将是不可靠且可疑的。本—量—利分析应用的假设如下说明。

第一个假设是固定成本应保持不变。正如在第三章中提到的,固定成本在短期内应保持不变(通常在一年以内),而这个假设应是合理的。第二个假设是,总变动成本会随销售量按比例或线性增加,也就是说,每单位变动成本保持不变。这样的假设在短期内也是合理的。第三个假设是,销售收益应该随销售量按比例增加,也就是说,一个产品的价格在短期内保持不变,这个假设在一定程度上也是合理的。第四个假设是,混合成本可以区分成固定和变动部分,在第三章我们已介绍过如何操作。第五个假设是,所有成本可以分摊给个别运营部门(即利润中心)。当违反上述假设时,做出某些调整后仍然

answer the following questions:

- Determine the revenue required for achieving desired profit;
- What is the breakeven-point (BEP) of operation?
- What is the profit at a given occupancy percentage above the BEP?
- What will be the effect on the sales BEP if we increase advertising cost?
- What increase in room sales is needed to cover advertising cost and still reach desired profit?
- What will be the effect on profit if the price, variable cost, or fixed cost increase?

There are many more management and operational "what-if" questions that can be answered by comprehending and applying CVP analysis. Nevertheless, most likely the first question that many managers want to and should ask is: what is the BEP of operation? Managers want to know and work on meeting at least the BEP so that operating loss doesn't happen. Besides, their performance would be praised if operating results can not only beat the BEP but also exceed it. BEP is the level of sales, in terms of sales amount or quantity, at which the profit (income before taxes or I_b for short) is zero. In other words, BEP is achieved when revenue equals total costs and the firm has zero I_b with no income tax liability. BEP can thus be viewed as a special case in CVP analysis. More on BEP calculation will be explained later.

4.2 *Assumptions and Limitations Associated with CVP*

In applying CVP analysis to hospitality or tourism operations, there are some basic assumptions to be aware of so that managers can ensure that their operational parameters would allow CVP analysis to be applied appropriately. Without meeting these assumptions, the results of CVP analysis and subsequent management decisions made could be unreliable and suspicious. The assumptions for applying CVP analysis are described below.

The first assumption is that fixed cost should remain constant. As mentioned in Chapter Three, fixed cost shall remain constant during the short term (normally within one year) and such an assumption is considered to be reasonable. The second assumption is that total variable costs increase proportionally or linearly to sales volume; that is, variable cost per unit remains constant. Such an assumption is considered to be reasonable during the short term. The third assumption is that sales revenue generated should increase proportionally to sales volume; that is, the price of a product remains constant during the short term, which to some extent is also reasonable. The fourth assumption is that mixed costs can be separated into their fixed and variable elements and in Chapter Three we introduced how this can be done. The fifth assumption is that all costs can be assigned to individual operated departments (i.e., profit centers). When the above-mentioned assumptions are violated, adjustments should be made so that CVP analysis could still be applied and the results could be trusted. For example, when total variable

可以应用本—量—利分析并信任分析结果。例如,可能由于客房用品批量折扣的关系,当总变动成本不随销售量增加而按比例增加时,分析应考虑按不同销售水平进行。

满足所有的假设条件之后,可以应用本—量—利分析来帮助解决管理问题。尽管如此,本—量—利分析仅仅是一种管理工具,它并不能解决运营的每一个问题。管理者若要能解释和明智地使用分析结果也应该注意其局限性。首先,本—量—利分析只考虑定量因素而忽略了定性因素。虽然运营结果在一定程度上反映了管理层经营酒店/旅游企业的能力,但本—量—利分析考虑的仅仅是运营的定量结果。其次,本—量—利分析的结果只适用于相关范围,也就是说,分析结果和随后的应用仅仅在某一存在特定的成本和销售量关系的销售范围之内有效。

4.3　单一产品的本—量—利分析

最容易理解本—量—利分析的方法是从分析单一产品开始。由于本—量—利分析关注的是成本、销售量和利润之间的关系,我们可以一步步勾画它们之间的关系如下。首先,如图 4-2 所示,销售收益和销售量之间应该是呈线性关系的,销售量越大,销售收益越高。

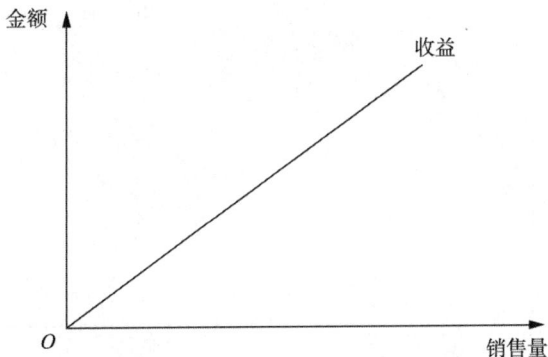

图 4-2　销售收益和销售量之间的关系

第二,如图 4-3 所示,总成本和销售量之间的关系也是线性的,截距表示固定成本;销售量越多,总成本就越高。

第三,图 4-2 和图 4-3 结合之后的图 4-4 呈现了成本、销售量和利润之间的关系。收益和总成本的交叉点是保本点,也就是产生的收益等于支出的总成本。此外,当产生的收益足以支付总成本后,收益大于总成本的区域

cost do not increase proportionally to sales volume increases possible due to volume discounts applied to room supplies, the analysis should be done by taking different levels of sales volume into consideration.

With all the assumptions met, CVP analysis can then be proceeded for helping solve management problems. Nevertheless, CVP analysis is only one of the management tools available and cannot solve every single problem related to operations. Managers should also be aware of its limitations so as to interpret and use the results wisely. First, CVP analysis only considers quantitative factors and ignores qualitative factors. While operating results to a certain extent reflect the management's ability in operating a hotel/tourism business, what is considered in CVP analysis is only quantitative outcome of operation. Second, CVP analysis results are only applicable under the relevant range; that is, the results and subsequent applications are only valid under a band of sales volume where a specific relationship between cost and volume exists.

4.3 CVP Analysis for Single Product

CVP analysis is best understood by starting with analyzing a single product. As CVP analysis is concerned about the inter-correlations among cost, sales volume and profit, we can delineate their relationships step by step as follows. First, the relationship between sales revenue and volume should be linear as shown in Figure 4 - 2; the more the sales volume, the higher the sales revenue.

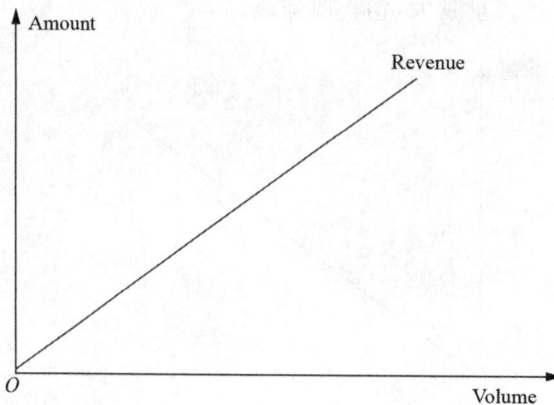

Figure 4 - 2   The relationship between sales revenue and volume

Second, the relationship between total cost and sales volume is also linear, with an intercept representing fixed cost, as shown in the following Figure 4 - 3; the more the sales volume, the higher the total cost.

Third, the relationship among cost, volume and profit is shown in Figure 4 - 4 by combining Figure 4 - 2 and Figure 4 - 3. The intersection between revenue and total cost is the BEP, where revenue generated equals to total cost incurred. Besides, the area where revenue is greater than total cost is the amount of profit (or I_b) retained after

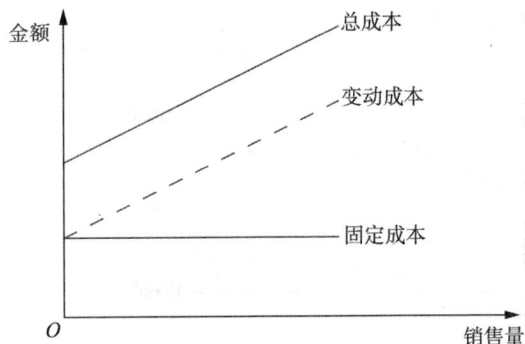

图 4-3　总成本和销售量之间的关系

即为利润(或 I_b)。另一方面,当产生的收益不足以支付总成本,收益小于总成本的区域即为亏损。

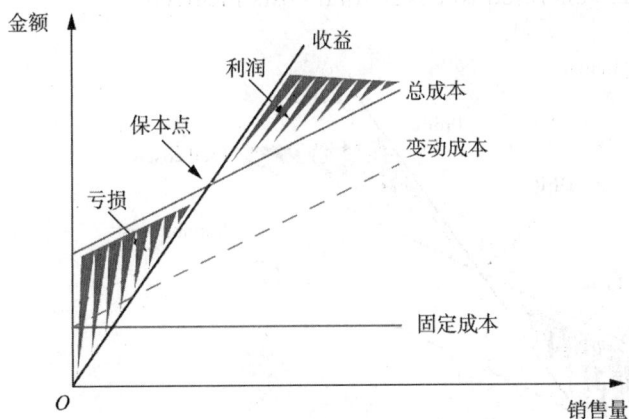

图 4-4　成本、销售量和利润之间的关系

简单地说,利润(或 I_b)、收益与成本之间的关系描述如下。

设 P=价格,V=单位变动成本,Q=数量或者销售量,F=固定成本,I_b=税前利润,R=总收益,C=总成本,由于税前利润等于总收益减去总成本,我们列出以下公式:

$$I_b = R - C = PQ - (V \times Q + F) = PQ - VQ - F = (P - V)Q - F$$

因此,单一产品或服务运营的基本关系式为

$$I_b = (P - V)Q - F$$

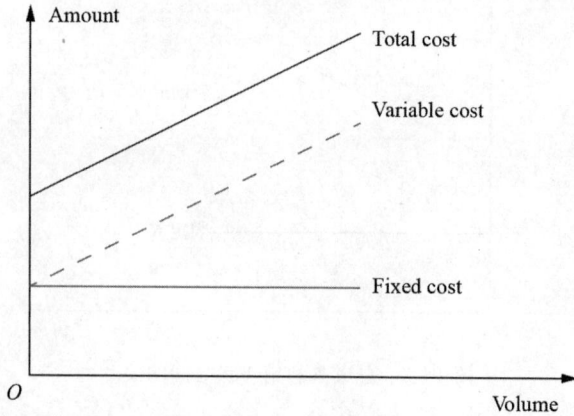

Figure 4 – 3　The relationship between total cost and volume

total cost incurred are covered by the amount of revenue generated. On the other hand, the area where revenue is less than total cost is the amount of loss incurred due to insufficient revenue generated to cover total costs incurred.

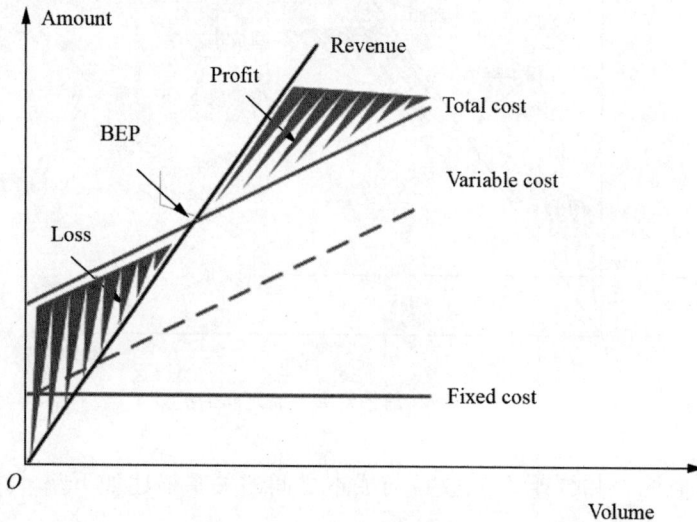

Figure 4 – 4　The relationship among cost, volume and profit

In a nutshell, the relationship between profit (or I_b), revenue and cost can be described as follows.

Let P = price, V = unit variable cost, Q = quantity or sales volume, F = fixed cost, I_b = income before taxes, R = total revenue and C = total cost. Because income before taxes is equal to total revenue minus total cost, we have the following equation:

$$I_b = R - C = PQ - (V \times Q + F) = PQ - VQ - F = (P - V)Q - F$$

Therefore, the basic relationship equation for a single product/service operation is then:

$$I_b = (P - V)Q - F$$

在保本点时产生的总收益等于总成本，我们得知：

$$I_b = (P - V)Q_{BEP} - F = 0$$

而 Q_{BEP} 为保本点时的销售量。所以

$$Q_{BEP} = \frac{F}{(P - V)}$$

让我们来看看计算保本点的例子。迈克尔酒店是一个有 30 间客房的经济型酒店。其每年固定成本为 187500 美元；平均房价为 40 美元，每间房变动成本为 15 美元。试测算：（1）酒店要达到保本点须售卖多少间客房；（2）保本点时的住房率。

首先，我们根据测算 Q_{BEP} 的公式将每年固定成本 187500 美元除以平均房价和每间出售客房变动成本之差。所以，酒店要达到保本点须售卖的客房数为

$$Q_{BEP} = \frac{187500}{40 - 15} = 7500 (间)$$

应该如何解读这 7500 间客房？迈克尔酒店不论有没有生意或客房出售，其每年都得支付固定成本 187500 美元。酒店每出售一间客房就会有 25 元的盈利可以用以支付固定成本，因此，酒店需要出售 7500 间客房来支付全数的固定成本。

其次，只要我们知道为了达到保本点所须出售的客房数（即 7500 间房），就可以测算达到保本点时的住宿率如下：

$$住宿率_{保本点} = \frac{7500}{30\ 间 \times 365\ 天} \times 100\% = 68.49\%$$

解读达到保本点时的住宿率相当简单：迈克尔酒店在一年之间需要达到平均 68.49% 的住宿率才能足够支付其固定成本并保本。

上述测算可以用图 4-5 进行图解。按年计算，迈克尔酒店在还未售出 7500 间客房前，它还未保本而且产生了运营亏损；过了保本点之后，它开始产生盈利，也就是 I_b。

必须注意的是，在一年之内只要酒店能出售 7500 间客房或达到 68.49% 的平均住宿率，酒店即可放心，因为它们并不会产生运营亏损（除非有不可预期的事故发生）。因为，超过保本点的那一部分的销售（基于金额或是数量），称为安全边际，计算结果见表 4-1。

At BEP where revenue generated equals to total cost incurred, we should have

$$I_b = (P - V)Q_{BEP} - F = 0$$

where, Q_{BEP} is the quantity sold at BEP. Therefore,

$$Q_{BEP} = \frac{F}{(P - V)}$$

Let's look at an example for BEP calculation. Michael Hotel is a 30-room budget hotel. Its annual fixed cost is \$187,500; the average room rate is \$40 with a variable cost per room sold of \$15. Determine: (1) the number of rooms sold required for the hotel to break-even and (2) the occupancy percentage at the BEP.

First, according to the formula of calculating Q_{BEP}, we can divide the annual fixed cost of \$187,500 by the difference of the average room rate and the variable cost per room sold. Therefore, the number of rooms sold required for the hotel to break-even is

$$Q_{BEP} = \frac{187500}{(40 - 15)} = 7500(\text{rooms})$$

How can this quantity of 7,500 rooms be interpreted? On an annual basis, Michael Hotel will have fixed cost of \$187,500 to cover, whether or not there's any business activity or room sold. Therefore, for every one room sold, the hotel will have a profit of \$25 to help recover the fixed cost; it will then require the hotel to sell at least 7,500 rooms to recover the whole amount of fixed cost.

Second, as long as we know how many rooms to be sold in order to reach the BEP (i.e., 7,500 rooms), we can calculate the occupancy percentage at the BEP as follows:

$$\text{Occupancy}_{BEP} = \frac{7500}{30 \text{ rooms} \times 365 \text{ days}} \times 100\% = 68.49\%$$

It is rather straightforward to interpret the occupancy percentage at the BEP: Michael Hotel will have to achieve an average occupancy of 68.49% throughout the year in order to cover its fixed cost and be break-even.

The above calculation can also be illustrated using the graph below in Figure 4-5. On an annual basis, before 7,500 rooms are sold, Michael Hotel will not reach its BEP and still incurs operating loss; after the BEP, it will start to earn profit, which is I_b.

It should be noted that, throughout the year as long as 7,500 rooms have been sold, or an average 68.49% occupancy percentage has been reached, the hotel can rest assured that they are "safe" because they would not incur operating loss (unless something unexpected happens). Therefore, a margin of safety, representing the part of sales (either in terms of dollar amount or volume) that exceeds the BEP, can be calculated as Table 4-1.

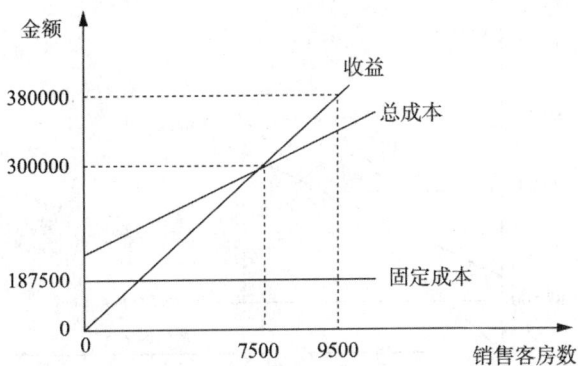

图 4 - 5 迈克尔酒店本—量—利分析图解

表 4 - 1 安全边际计算

项目	保本点	5 万美元盈利	安全边际
客房收益(万美元)	30	3.8	8
客房销售量	7500	9500	2000

如图 4 - 5 所示,迈克尔酒店多出售超过 7500 间客房销售保本点的那 2000 间（或者在相关范围内的任何数目）表示了其酒店的安全边际。换句话说,该酒店需要产生 380000 元的客房收益来达到相同水平的安全边际。

管理者应该尽可能地扩大安全边际（当然客房数须在相关范围内）以达到良好的运营结果。这要如何做到呢？很明显,根据定义,管理者可以通过增加销售量或是降低 Q_{BEP} 来增加安全边际。此外,也可以进行敏感度分析。我们往回看计算保本点的公式:

$$Q_{BEP} = \frac{F}{P - V}$$

其他因素保持不变,假设固定成本增加,保本点会提高;假设价格增加,保本点会降低;假设每单位变动成本增加,保本点也会提高。我们再回看迈克尔酒店的例子。假设迈克尔酒店的固定成本增加了 2.5 万美元,它得多售出多少间客房来赚取 5 万美元的净利润?

之前我们测算要赚取 5 万美元的净利润（假设没有所得税）需要销售的客房数为

$$Q_{\$50000I_b} = \frac{187500 + 50000}{40 - 15} = 9500(间)$$

现在增加了 2.5 万美元的固定成本后,要赚取 5 万美元净利润所需的销售量变成

$$Q_{\$50000I_b} = \frac{187500 + 50000 + 25000}{40 - 15} = 10500(间)$$

因此,在增加了 2.5 万美元的固定成本之后,迈克尔酒店得多售出 1000 间客房,这不只是为了支付修正后的 21 万美元固定成本,同时还要维持 5 万美

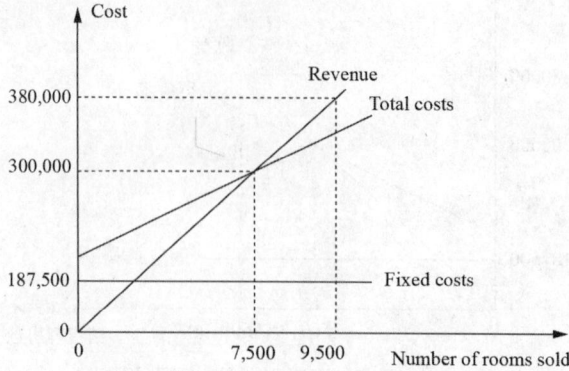

Figure 4 – 5   Graph illustration for the CVP analysis of Michael Hotel

Table 4 – 1   Margin of Safty

Items	Break-even	Profit of $50,000	Margin of safety
Room revenue	$300,000	$380,000	$80,000
Number of rooms sold	7,500	9,500	2,000

As shown in Figure 4 – 5, the 2,000 (or any other number that is within a relevant range) more rooms sold above the BEP of 7,500 rooms represents a margin of safety for Michael Hotel. In other words, the hotel will have to generate an amount of $380,000 in room sales to maintain the same level of margin of safety.

In order to achieve favorable operating results, managers should enlarge the margin of safety as much as possible (of course within a relevant range in terms of number of rooms). How can this be achieved? Obviously by definition managers can either increase sales or lower the Q_{BEP} to increase the margin of safety. Besides, sensitivity analysis could also be performed. Let's refer back to the formula for calculating the BEP:

$$Q_{BEP} = \frac{F}{P - V}$$

Other things being held constant, if the fixed costs are increased, then the BEP will increase; if the price is increased, then the BEP will drop; and, if the variable cost per unit sold is increased, then the BEP will also increase. Let's refer back to the example of Michael Hotel. If Michael Hotel's fixed cost was increased by $25,000, how many more rooms must be sold in order to get $50,000 net income?

Previously, the sales volume required for earning $50,000 net income (assuming no income tax):

$$Q_{50,000I_b} = \frac{185000 + 50000}{40 - 15} = 9500(\text{rooms})$$

Now, if there was an increase of fixed cost of $25,000, the sales volume required for earning the same $50,000 net income becomes

$$Q_{50,000I_b} = \frac{185000 + 50000 + 25000}{40 - 15} = 10500(\text{rooms})$$

Therefore, with an increase of $25,000 in fixed cost, Michael Hotel will have to sell 1,000 more rooms in order to not only cover the revised fixed cost of $210,000 but

元的净利润。或者,这多售出的 1000 间客房可以由所增加的 2.5 万美元固定成本除以 25 美元计算出来。

4.4 边际贡献与边际贡献率

从我们针对单一产品进行的本—量—利分析得知,如果企业想盈利或至少能保本的话,单位价格和每单位变动成本之间的差异要是能大到可以更早支付固定成本是最好不过的。这个差异或($P-V$)称作边际贡献(CM),或每单位边际贡献。这个差异之所以被称作边际贡献是因为这个差异在保本点之前是用以支付固定成本的,而在保本点之后则贡献给税前利润。再看迈克尔酒店的例子,40 美元房价和 15 美元单位变动成本之间的差异 25 美元即是边际贡献。

对于只销售单一产品的企业来说,解释这 25 美元的边际贡献是相当容易的。然而,若企业销售多于一种产品,而且其价格不一,情况会相对复杂,某产品的 25 美元边际贡献解释意义不大。客房部的 25 美元边际贡献和商务中心的 300 元边际贡献要如何诠释呢?如果没有将边际贡献按某种基准以比例表示,就无法得知哪一种产品或服务对企业贡献较大。因此,我们可以测算边际贡献率(CMR)来确定一项产品或服务的贡献比率:

$$边际贡献率 = \frac{价格 - 变动成本}{价格}$$

使用迈克尔酒店的例子,其客房销售的边际贡献率为

$$\frac{40-15}{40} = 0.625$$

这 0.625 应该如何诠释?(1-0.625)又该如何解释呢?0.625 可以解释为就每 1 美元的客房销售,在支付了每间客房变动成本后,剩下的 0.625 美元用于在保本点之前支付固定成本或在保本点之后保留为 I_b。也就是说,每 1 美元的客房销售中的 0.375 美元用来支付每间客房的变动成本。

理解边际贡献率对拥有多元产品或服务的企业在应用本—量—利分析是重要的,因为边际贡献率表示了每一美元的销售收益中有多少比率用来支付固定成本或贡献盈利。所以只要有边际贡献率,我们就可以测算达到保本点所需的销售收益:

$$保本点销售收益 = \frac{固定资本}{边际贡献率}$$

我们可以利用上面公式将 187500 美元除以 0.625,得知迈克尔酒店的保本点销售收益为 300000 美元。

4.5 针对多元产品的本—量—利分析

现实中,大多数企业向顾客提供多于一种的产品或服务。例如,一家酒店可能不只提供顾客客房住宿,同时还提供餐饮。在应用本—量—利分析此类情况时,我们应该使用加权平均边际贡献率来反映每一运营部门的相对贡献。

also retain $50,000 in net income. Alternatively, the 1,000 more rooms can be derived by dividing the increased $25,000 fixed cost by $25.

4.4 Contribution Margin and Contribution Margin Ratio

In our illustration of CVP analysis for a single product, we learn that in order for a business to earn any profit or at least be break-even, it would be better if the difference between the unit price and the variable cost per unit sold is large enough so as to recover the fixed cost sooner; such difference, or $(P - V)$, is termed as contribution margin (CM), or *contribution margin per unit*. It is called CM because the difference contributes to the coverage of the fixed cost before the BEP and to I_b after the BEP. Going back to the example of Michael Hotel, the difference between the room rate $40 and the unit variable costs $15 is the contribution margin of $25.

For businesses with only one product for sale, it is rather straightforward to interpret a CM of $25; however, it becomes complicated and rather meaningless when there are more than one types of products, if of various pricing levels, for sale. How will one interpret a CM of $25 from room sales and a CM of $300 from some business center service? Without scaling a CM, one could not determine which types of products/services better contribute to the business. Therefore, we can determine the rate of contribution of products/services by calculating a contribution margin ratio (CMR) as follows:

$$CMR = \frac{P - V}{P}$$

Using the Michael Hotel example, the CMR for its room sales is

$$\frac{40 - 15}{40} = 0.625$$

How can one interpret this 0.625? And how about $(1 - 0.625)$? 0.625 can be interpreted as that, for every one dollar of room sales, after covering the variable cost per room sold, there are 0.625 dollars left to recover the fixed cost before the BEP or to retain as I_b after the BEP. That is, $0.375 out of every one dollar of room sales is used to cover the part of unit variable cost.

Knowing CMR is critical for businesses with multiple products/services in conducting CVP analysis as one can know the percentage of every dollar of sales revenue contributing to the fixed cost and/or profit. Therefore, with CMR, we will be able to determine sales revenue needed at the BEP as

$$\text{Sales revenue}_{BEP} = \frac{\text{Fixed cost}}{\text{CMR}}$$

Using the above equation, we can derive the sales revenue needed at BEP for Michael Hotel by dividing $187,500 by 0.625, which is $300,000.

4.5 CVP Analysis for Multiple-service Operations

In reality, most businesses would have more than one product/service for their customers. For example, a hotel may have not only rooms for rent but also restaurants to provide food and beverage options to customers. In applying CVP analysis to such a context with multiple products/services, we shall use a weighted average contribution margin ratio (CMRw) to reflect relative contribution of individual operated departments.

假设迈克尔酒店有客房部和酒吧餐厅两个运营部门,它们的年运营结果见表4-2。

表4-2 客房部和酒吧餐厅的年运营结果

部门	收益(万美元)	变动成本(万美元)	边际贡献(万美元)
客房	60.00	22.25	37.75
酒吧餐厅	15.00	11.50	3.50
合计	75.00	33.75	41.25

加权平均边际贡献率可以按下列公式测算:

$$加权平均边际贡献率=权重_1×边际贡献率_1+权重_2×边际贡献率_2$$

此处的权重$_1$为第一个运营部门的销售组合占比,而权重$_2$为第二个运营部门的销售组合占比。因此,迈克尔酒店的加权平均边际贡献率可以测算如下:

$$加权平均边际贡献率=\frac{600000}{750000}×\frac{377500}{600000}+\frac{150000}{750000}×\frac{35000}{150000}$$

$$=0.8×0.629+0.2×0.233≈0.55$$

或者,它的加权平均边际贡献率也可以这么测算:

$$加权平均边际贡献率=\frac{总收益-总变动成本}{总收益}$$

$$=\frac{750000-337500}{750000}=0.55$$

那么,这0.55的加权平均边际贡献率是什么意思? 它可以诠释为当企业有多于一种产品或服务时,对企业整体来说每1美元的销售收益,不论这1美元是哪一个部门赚取的,其中的0.55美元即为边际贡献。基于推论及数学测算,加权平均边际贡献率一定是介于各个部门的边际贡献率之间的,同时,测算出来的值会向有较高销售组合百分比的部门(也就是有较高的销售权重的部门)的边际贡献率靠拢。

有了加权平均边际贡献率的概念,我们来看看一个有多元服务企业的税前利润、销售收益、加权平均边际贡献率和固定成本之间的基本关系:

$$税前利润=销售收益×加权平均边际贡献率-固定成本$$

因此,我们可以得知在保本点销售的收益如下:

$$保本点销售收益=\frac{固定成本}{加权平均边际贡献率}$$

以同一家有两个运营部门的迈克尔酒店为例,测算保本点销售收益及赚取50000美元盈利所需的总收益。使用上面的公式,我们可以通过将固定成本187500美元除以0.55的加权平均边际贡献率而得出保本点销售收益

Suppose that Michael Hotel has two operated departments: rooms and a lounge and bar restaurant and the following are their annual operating results as Table 4 – 2.

Table 4 – 2   Annual operating results of departments

Department	Revenue（$）	Variable cost（$）	Contribution margin（$）
rooms	600,000	222,500	377,500
lounge & bar	150,000	115,000	35,000
total	750,000	337,500	412,500

The CMRw can be calculated using the following formula:

$$CMRw = weight_1 \times CMR_1 + weight_2 \times CMR_2$$

Where, $weight_1$ is the sales mix percentage of the first operated department and $weight_2$ is the sales mix percentage of the second operated department. Therefore, Michael Hotel's CMRw is derived as follows:

$$CMRw = \frac{600000}{750000} \times \frac{377500}{600000} + \frac{150000}{750000} \times \frac{35000}{150000}$$

$$= 0.8 \times 0.629 + 0.2 \times 0.233 \approx 0.55$$

Or alternatively, its CMRw can also be calculated as:

$$CMRw = \frac{Total\ revenue - Total\ variable\ cost}{Total\ revenue}$$

$$= \frac{750000 - 337500}{750000} = 0.55$$

So, what does this CMRw of 0.55 mean? It could be interpreted as that, when there are more than one type of products/services, to the business as a whole for every one dollar of sales revenue, $0.55 is the contribution margin no matter which department generated such sales. Based on reasoning and mathematical calculation, the CMRw calculated should always be in between the CMR of the individual departments and, the calculated figure will be more close to the CMR of the department with higher sales mix percentage (i.e, higher sales weight).

With the concept of CMRw in mind, we shall be able to take a look at the basic relationship between I_b, sales revenue R, CMRw and the fixed cost F for a multiple-service property as follows:

$$I_b = R \times CMRw - F$$

Therefore, we can determine the sales revenue at the BEP as follows:

$$R_{BEP} = \frac{F}{CMRw}$$

Using the same Michael Hotel example that has two operated departments, determine the break-even sales revenue and total revenue required when $50,000 profit is desired. Using the formula above, we can derive the break-even sales revenue by dividing the fixed cost of $187,500 by the CMRw of 0.55, which results in $340,909. In

340909 美元。为了赚取 50000 美元的盈利,所需的总收益可以由固定成本 187500 美元与所需的 50000 美元盈利之和除以 0.55 的加权平均边际贡献率而得出 431818.18 美元。

现在,如果房价上升了 20％而销售客房数保持不变,客房部的边际贡献率会变化吗? 当然! 客房部修订后的边际贡献率为

$$边际贡献率 = \frac{价格 \times 120\% - 单位变动成本}{价格 \times 120\%}$$

设 P 是客房部门收益,而 V 可以通过 P 乘以(1－原始的客房边际贡献率)得出,也就是 $0.371P$。因此,客房部修订后的边际贡献率为

$$边际贡献率 = \frac{1.2P - 0.371P}{1.2P} = 0.69$$

我们可以看到,如果其他因素不变,只需增加 20％的房费,客房部的边际贡献率就从 0.629 提高到了 0.69。有了修改后的客房边际贡献率,我们就可以测算迈克尔酒店修订后的加权平均边际贡献率如下:

$$加权平均边际贡献率 = \frac{1.2P}{1.2P + 0.25P} \times 0.69 + \frac{0.25P}{1.2P + 0.25P} \times 0.233$$
$$= 0.8276 \times 0.69 + 0.1724 \times 0.233 \approx 0.6112$$

有了修订后的加权平均边际贡献率,我们可以推导出到达保本点时所需的收益如下:

$$保本销售收益 = \frac{187500}{0.6112} = 306773.56(美元)$$

相比于原来的保本点销售收益 340909 美元,房费增加了 20％后,修正后的保本点收益变成 306773.56 美元。此外,计算要达到 50000 美元盈利所需的收益可将固定成本 187500 美元与所需盈利 50000 美元之和除以修订后的加权平均边际贡献率 0.6112 而得出 388579.84 美元。

现在,如果不仅房间价格提高了 20％,同时酒吧的定价也增加了 10％,其他条件皆保持不变,加权平均边际贡献率会有什么样的变化? 正如前面计算的,修订后的客房边际贡献率仍然是 0.69,而酒吧的边际贡献率将修正如下:

$$修正后酒吧的边际贡献率 = \frac{0.25 \times 价格 \times 110\% - 单位变动成本}{0.25 \times 价格 \times 110\%}$$

而单位变动成本可以通过 $0.25P$ 乘以(1－原始的酒吧边际贡献率)计算得出,即 $0.1918P$。因此,酒吧部门修正后的边际贡献率为

$$修正后酒吧的边际贡献率 = \frac{0.275 \times 价格 - 0.1918 \times 价格}{0.275 \times 价格} = 0.3025$$

我们可以看到,其他条件不变,同时将房价和酒吧价格各提升 20％和 10％之后,客房部修正后的边际贡献率由 0.629 增加至 0.69;酒吧部门修正

order to earn \$50,000 profit, total revenue required can be derived by dividing the summation of the fixed cost of \$187,500 and the desired profit of \$50,000 by the CMRw of 0.55, which then results in \$431,818.18.

Now, if room price is increased by 20% and the number of rooms sold remains the same, will the CMR for the rooms department change? Certainly! The revised CMR for the rooms department is now

$$\text{CMRw} = \frac{P \times 120\% - V}{P \times 120\%}$$

Where P is rooms departmental revenue and V can be derived by multiplying P by $(1 - \text{original CMR}_{\text{rooms}})$, which is $0.371P$. Therefore, the revised CMR for the rooms department is

$$\text{CMR} = \frac{1.2P - 0.371P}{1.2P} = 0.69$$

We can see that, other things being held constant, simply by increasing room rate by 20%, the $\text{CMR}_{\text{rooms}}$ increased from 0.629 to 0.69. With this revised $\text{CMR}_{\text{rooms}}$, we can then calculate a revised CMRw for Michael Hotel as follows:

$$\text{CMRw} = \frac{1.2P}{1.2P + 0.25P} \times 0.69 + \frac{0.25P}{1.2P + 0.25P} \times 0.233$$
$$= 0.8276 \times 0.69 + 0.1724 \times 0.233 \approx 0.6112$$

With this revised CMRw, we can derive the revenue required at the BEP as follows:

$$R_{\text{BEP}} = \frac{187500}{0.6112} = 306773.56$$

With the increased room rate of 20%, the revised revenue at the BEP is now \$306,773.56 as compared to the original \$340,909. Besides, the revised revenue required when \$50,000 profit is earned is then dividing the summation of the fixed cost of \$187,500 and the desired profit of \$50,000 by the revised CMRw of 0.6112, which then results in \$388,579.84 as compared to the original \$431,818.18.

Now, if not only room price is increased by 20% and the number of rooms sold remains the same but also pricing for the lounge and bar is also increased by 10% and the sales volume remains unchanged, other things being held constant, what will happen to the CMRw? The revised CMR for rooms as calculated earlier is still 0.69 and the revised CMR for lounge and bar will change as follows:

$$\text{CMR}_{\text{lounge\_bar}} = \frac{0.25P \times 110\% - V}{0.25P \times 110\%}$$

and V can be derived by multiplying $0.25P$ by $(1 - \text{original CMR}_{\text{lounge\_bar}})$, which is $0.1918P$. Therefore, the revised CMR for the lounge and bar department is

$$\text{CMR}_{\text{lounge\_bar}} = \frac{0.275P - 0.1918P}{0.275P} = 0.3025$$

We can see that, other things being held constant, by increasing both room rate by 20% and lounge and bar pricing by 10%, the $\text{CMR}_{\text{rooms}}$ increased from 0.629 to 0.69 and

后的边际贡献率从 0.233 上升到 0.3025。有了客房部和酒吧部修正后的边际贡献率,我们就可以测算出迈克尔酒店修正后的加权平均边际贡献率如下:

修正后加权平均边际贡献率

$$=\frac{1.2\times 价格}{1.2\times 价格+0.275\times 价格}\times 0.69+\frac{0.275\times 价格}{1.2\times 价格+0.275\times 价格}\times 0.3025$$

$$=0.8136\times 0.69+0.1864\times 0.3025\approx 0.6177$$

由于酒吧的定价在房费提价 20% 的基础上也提价了 10%,修正后的加权平均边际贡献率进一步从 0.6112 上升至 0.6177。有了这个修正后的加权平均边际贡献率,我们可以推导出达到保本点所需的收益如下:

$$保本点收益=\frac{187500}{0.6177}=303545.41(美元)$$

随着客房和酒吧价格各提价 20% 和 10%,相对于原来的保本点收益 340909 美元,修正之后的保本点收益为 303545.41 美元。此外,相比原来为达 50000 美元盈利所需的 431818.18 美元收益,修订后所需的收益可由固定成本 187500 美元与所需 50000 美元盈利之和除以修正后的加权平均边际贡献率 0.6177 而得出 384490.85 美元。

通过上述用加权平均边际贡献率来测算保本点或所需盈利的收益示例得知,理解和在运营中应用加权平均边际贡献率的概念的重要性是显而易见的。为了实现赚取期望盈利的目标,管理者通常会希望有较高的加权平均边际贡献率,以尽早达到保本点。从等式"税前利润=收益×加权平均边际贡献率-固定成本"得知,如果要增加税前利润,第一,管理者可以通过提价、营销活动或其他方式来提高收益。提价虽然可能有助于提高销售收入,但是,使用这种策略时应该谨慎考虑宏观经济环境和市场条件,避免吓跑客户。正如在前面的章节中指出的,营销费用被认为是一种自主固定成本,一般事先预算大约占总收入的百分之三到五。如果营销费用能明智和有效地支出,应当有助于提高销售收入,否则就会浪费。然而,我们是否应该花费或花费多少自主固定成本来提升税前利润?可以支出多少营销、推广和培训的费用?可以支付多少奖金作为奖励管理绩效?这些问题的答案可以通过评估额外固定成本对税前利润的影响或税前利润的变化(ΔI_b)来决定。也就是说,如果固定成本支出所造成的 ΔI_b 大于零的话,则该笔开销是合理的;如果小于零,那么该笔支出就是没有道理的。如果固定成本支出所造成的 ΔI_b 等于零,该笔花费的决定将是无关紧要的。

例如,一家加权平均边际贡献率为 0.25 的酒店花了 10000 美元做市场营销活动。如果 $\Delta_{收益}$=50000 美元,此营销支出对 I_b 的影响为何?

the CMR_{lounge_bar} increased from 0.233 to 0.3025. With this revised CMR_{rooms} and CMR_{lounge_bar}, we can then calculate a revised CMRw for Michael Hotel as follows:

$$CMRw = \frac{1.2P}{1.2P + 0.275P} \times 0.69 + \frac{0.275P}{1.2P + 0.275P} \times 0.3025$$
$$= 0.8136 \times 0.69 + 0.1864 \times 0.3025 \approx 0.6177$$

The revised CMRw is further increased to 0.6177 from 0.6112 because of a 10% increase in pricing of lounge and bar business in addition to 20% increase in room rate. With this revised CMRw, we can derive the revenue required at the BEP as follows:

$$R_{BEP} = \frac{187500}{0.6177} = 303545.41$$

With the increased room rate of 20% and pricing of lounge and bar of 10%, the revised revenue at the BEP is now \$303,545.41 as compared to the original \$340,909. Besides, the revised revenue required when \$50,000 profit is earned is then dividing the summation of the fixed cost of \$187,500 and the desired profit of \$50,000 by the revised CMRw of 0.6177, which then results in \$384,490.85.

Having gone through the above CMRw examples on deriving amount of revenues required for the BEP or with a desired level of I_b, the importance of understanding and being able to apply the concept of CMRw to the operation is obvious: managers would likely want a higher CMRw than otherwise in order to achieve the BEP sooner in order to earn a desired level of profit. From the equation $I_b = R \times CMRw - F$, in order to increase I_b, managers could, first, work on increasing R through price hike, marketing efforts or other means. Price hike might help boost sales revenue; however, this tactic should be employed with caution by considering the macro economic environment and market condition so that customers would not be scared away for other choices.

As noted in the previous chapter, marketing expenses are considered as a type of discretionary fixed cost and they will have to be budgeted well in advance, normally at three to five percent of total revenues. If marketing expenses are spent wisely and effectively, they shall help boost sales revenue; otherwise, they would turn out to be wasted. Nevertheless, whether or how much should/can we spend on discretionary fixed cost so as to raise I_b? How much marketing, promotion or training expenses could be spent? How much bonus could be paid out for rewarding management performance? The answers to these queries could be determined by examining the effect of additional fixed cost on I_b, or changes in I_b (or ΔI_b). That is, if ΔI_b is greater than zero as a result of an increase in discretionary fixed cost, then the spending is justifiable; if smaller than zero then the spending is not justified. The decision to spend would be indifferent if ΔI_b is equal to zero.

For example, a hotel having a CMRw of 0.25 has spent \$10,000 for a marketing campaign. If $\Delta R = \$50,000$, what is the impact of such marketing expenditure on I_b?

由于

$$\Delta_{税前利润} = \Delta_{收益} \times 加权平均边际贡献率 - \Delta_{固定成本}$$

则

$$\Delta_{税前利润} = 50000 \times 0.25 - 10000 = 2500（美元）$$

也就是说，$\Delta_{税前利润}$ 的 2500 美元是来自营销活动 10000 美元的额外支出，表明该营销活动对税前利润似乎有积极的影响，未来酒店可以复制或聚焦类似的活动。然而，是否有关于活动开支门槛或必须增加多少收益才足够支持活动开支的信息？换句话说，收益 R 须增加多少才能使 $\Delta_{税前利润}$ 至少为零？用同样的公式：

$$\Delta_{税前利润} = \Delta_{收益} \times 加权平均边际贡献率 - \Delta_{固定成本}$$

令 $\Delta_{税前利润}$ 等于零，我们得知

$$0 = \Delta_{收益} \times 0.25 - 10000$$

解出　　　　$$\Delta_{收益} = 40000（美元）$$

而这 40000 美元要如何解释？为了这 10000 美元的营销活动支出，酒店必须产生额外的 40000 美元收益以保本。

第二，降低固定成本水平也可以增加税前利润。固定成本有两种——产能固定成本和自主固定成本。然而，管理者（甚至是业主）必须评估企业为了增加税前利润而削减某些固定成本的做法是否可行，特别是在经济低迷时期。例如，很多酒店/旅游企业在经济低迷时期往往会削减已预算的广告开支，因为他们相信在这个时期消费者可自由支配于休闲活动的收入会减少，支出广告预算很可能会造成浪费。减少人力或暂停某些服务/产品也有助于降低工资等方面的固定成本。然而，减少这些产能固定成本将对销售收入带来负面影响，需要谨慎施行。

第三，税前利润可以通过提高加权平均边际贡献率而增加。有许多方法可以提高加权平均边际贡献率的水平，换句话说就是降低变动成本占总成本的比例。例如，购置额外的设备或培训员工以提高他们的生产率。我们来看一个使用培训手段帮助提高员工的生产力和工作效率，从而提高加权平均边际贡献率水平的例子。假设一个酒店每月固定成本为 50000 美元，其加权平均边际贡献率为 0.5。酒店在考虑对员工进行一个花费 5000 美元的一系列的培训课程，并预计训练后其加权平均边际贡献率可以提高到 0.6。酒店应该进行培训或其培训费用能收回吗？对这类问题的决策很大程度上取决于酒店现有的收益水平。

Since

$$\Delta I_b = \Delta R \times CMRw - \Delta F$$

then

$$\Delta I_b = 50000 \times 0.25 - 10000 = 2500$$

That is, with an additional spending of \$10,000 on the marketing campaign, ΔI_b will be \$2,500, which indicates that this marketing campaign appears to have a positive impact on I_b and the hotel probably may replicate or focus similar types of campaigns in the future. Nevertheless, would there be a threshold for the campaign or by how much must revenue increase to justify the campaign expenditure? In other words, what is the required increase in R so that ΔI_b is at least zero? Using the same equation

$$\Delta I_b = \Delta R \times CMRw - \Delta F$$

and letting ΔI_b equals zero, we have

$$0 = \Delta R \times 0.25 - 10000$$

and solve for

$$\Delta R = 40000$$

How would this \$40,000 be interpreted? In order to justify the spending of \$10,000 on this marketing campaign, a hotel will have to generate additional \$40,000 in revenue so as to be break-even.

Secondly, I_b could also be increased with a reduced level of F. While there are two major types of fixed costs: capacity and discretionary, it will be up to managers (or even owners) to determine whether it is feasible to cut certain fixed cost in an attempt to enhance I_b, particularly at times of economic downturn. For example, while debatable, many hotel/tourism businesses would tend to cut advertising expenditure, although budgeted in advance, during bad economic times because they believe consumers would have less discretionary income for leisure activities; spending budgeted advertising money would likely turn out to be wasteful. Reducing manpower or shutting down certain services/products would help reduce fixed cost in terms of salaries and so on; however, reducing such capacity fixed cost would likely bring negative impacts on sales revenue, which needs to be employed with greater caution.

Thirdly, I_b could be increased with an enhanced level of CMRw. There could be a number of ways to help enhance level of CMRw, or in other words reduce the percentage of variable cost to total costs. For example, additional equipments could be acquired so that operations could be run in a more efficient manner or training could be provided to employees so that their productivity could be enhanced. Let's look at an example of using training as a means to help improve employees' productivity and work efficiency so as to increase the level of CMRw. Suppose that a hotel's monthly fixed cost is \$50,000 and its CMRw is 0.5. The hotel is considering holding a series of training sessions for its employees at a cost of \$5,000 and it is expected that the CMRw could be enhanced to 0.6 after training. Should the hotel conducting the training, or would expenditure on training pay off? The decision to such question largely depends on the hotel's existing revenue level.

首先,我们找一个进行培训与否对酒店的税前利润都没影响的无差别收益点,如下:

$$税前利润(无培训)＝税前利润(有培训)$$

$$无差别收益点×0.5－50000＝无差别收益点×0.6－(50000＋5000)$$

我们发现无差别收益点为 50000 美元。这 50000 美元可以解释为,在这个特定的收益水平,无论有无花费 5000 美元的额外培训费用对酒店都是没有影响的。在无培训和 0.5 的加权平均边际贡献率的情况下,酒店的税前利润为－25000 美元(亏损 25000 美元);通过培训,其税前利润依然是－25000美元。

其次,如果酒店当前的收益金额不是 50000 美元呢? 如果当前的收益为 50100 美元而没有培训,其税前利润将是 $50100×0.5－50000＝－24950$(美元);有培训的话,其税前利润将是 $50100×0.6－55000＝－24940$(美元)。虽然训练与否对于税前利润只产生 10 美元的差别(这可能是我们这里使用的数据导致的),我们还是可以推断,在当前收益比无差别收益金额大的情况下,进行训练将令酒店提高其税前利润。另一方面,如果当前的收益为 49900 美元,无培训的税前利润是 $49900×0.5－50000＝－25025$(美元);有培训时其税前利润将是 $49900×0.6－55000＝－25060$(美元)。虽然进行培训对税前利润的影响点是多亏损 10 美元,我们还是可以推断,在当前收入水平低于无差别收入金额时,若进行培训可能会给酒店造成更大的损失。简单地说,当销售强劲时(高于无差别收益点),企业可以在培训上花钱以达到更高的税前利润;当销售疲软时(低于无差别收益点),即使培训可能有助于提高员工的工作效率,公司也应谨慎看待额外花费培训的钱。

4.6　运营杠杆的概念

如前面提到的,一个企业的总成本可被划分成固定成本和变动成本;某些企业可能有较高比例的固定成本,而另一些可能有较高比例的变动成本。企业的固定成本在其总成本中的占比称为运营杠杆,有公式:

$$运营杠杆＝\frac{固定成本}{总成本}$$

因此,有较高固定成本占比的企业有较高的运营杠杆;有较高变动成本占比的企业有较低的运营杠杆。相较而言,有较高运营杠杆的企业可能有较高的边际贡献率而那些具有低运营杠杆的企业有较低的边际贡献率。运营杠杆水平表示与企业运营相关的风险水平。让我们来看看下面的两个酒店的月度损益信息(见表 4-3)。

First, we can find the indifference revenue $\hat{R}$, where having training or not makes no difference to the hotel's I_b as follows:

$$I_b(\text{without training}) = I_b(\text{with training})$$

$$\hat{R} \times 0.5 - 50000 = \hat{R} \times 0.6 - (50000 + 5000)$$

We then find that $\hat{R}$ is $50,000. This $50,000 can be interpreted as that, at this very level of revenue, whether spending an extra amount of $5,000 on training would be indifferent to the hotel. Without training and a CMRẇ of 0.5, the hotel will be expecting an I_b of $-$25,000 (or a loss of $25,000); with training, its I_b will still be $-$25,000.

Second, what if the hotel's exiting revenue amount is not $50,000? If the current revenue is $50,100 without training, its I_b will be $50,100 \times 0.5 - $50,00 = $-$24,950; with training its I_b will be $50,100 \times 0.61 - $55,000 = $-$24,940. Although the difference on I_b as a result of training is only $10 in savings (most likely due to the number we used here), we can infer that in the case where the existing level of revenue is greater than the indifference revenue amount, with training, the hotel could likely improve its I_b. On the other hand, if the current revenue is $49,900, without training its I_b will be $49,900 \times 0.5 - $50,000 = $$-$25,050; with training its I_b will be $49,900 \times 0.6 - $55,000 = $$-$25,060. Although the difference on I_b as a result of training is again only $10 more in loss, we can also infer that in the case where the existing level of revenue is less than the indifference revenue amount, with training, the hotel is likely incur greater loss. In a nutshell, when sales are strong (above the indifference level), a company can be more flexible on spending money on training to achieve a better I_b; when sales are weak (below the indifference level), the company should be cautious about spending extra money on training even though it may help improve employee efficiency.

4.6 The Concept of Operating Leverage

As mentioned previously, the total costs of a firm can be partitioned into the fixed and variable components; some firms may have a higher percentage of fixed cost than variable cost while others may have more variable cost than fixed cost. The ratio of a firm's fixed cost to its total cost is termed the operating leverage:

$$\text{Operating Leverage} = \frac{\text{Fixed cost}}{\text{Total cost}}$$

Therefore, for firms having a higher percentage of fixed cost than variable cost, it is said that they have a high operating leverage; for those having a higher percentage of variable cost than fixed cost, they have a low operating leverage. Comparatively speaking, firms having a high operating leverage will likely have a high CMR while those having a low operating leverage will likely have a low CMR. The level of operating leverage signifies the level of risk associated with a firm's operation. Let's look at the monthly profit and loss information of two hotel properties (see Table 4 - 3).

表 4 - 3　两个酒店的月度损益信息

项目	A 酒店		B 酒店	
	金额	占比	金额	占比
收益（万美元）	50	100%	50	100%
变动成本（万美元）	30	60%	20	40%
固定成本（万美元）	20	40%	30	60%
净利润（万美元）	0	0	0	0

A 酒店和 B 酒店都具有相同的 50 万美元收益和 50 万美元的总成本，因此净利润为 0 元。然而，这两家酒店损益之间唯一的区别是它们的运营杠杆。在这个例子中，A 酒店的运营杠杆比 B 酒店的低。我们可以绘制出两家酒店的成本信息，如图 4 - 6 所示。

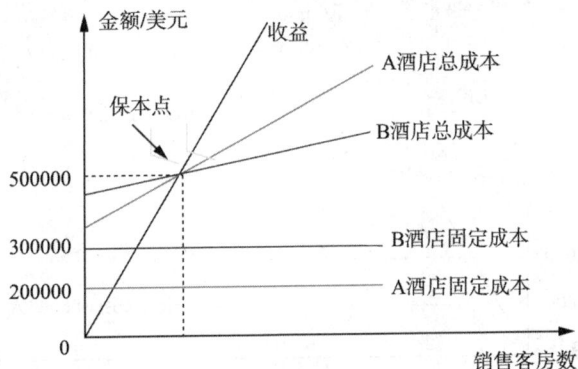

图 4 - 6　酒店营运分析

从图 4 - 6 得知，在保本点之前销售任意客房数的情况下，B 酒店的亏损（即总成本减去收益）都比 A 酒店的亏损要大。另一方面，在保本点之后销售任意客房数的情况下，B 酒店的盈利（即收益减去总成本）也都比 A 酒店的盈利要多。换句话说，在保本点之前销售任意客房数的情况下，高运营杠杆的酒店的亏损范围更大，在保本点之后销售任意客房数的情况下，高运营杠杆的酒店的盈利范围也更大。简而言之，具有高运营杠杆（或边际贡献率）的酒店在运营上会面临较高的风险。

Table 4 - 3 Monthly profit and loss information of two hotels

Items	Hotel A		Hotel B	
	$	%	$	%
revenue	500,000	100	500,000	100
variable cost	300,000	60	200,000	40
fixed cost	200,000	40	300,000	60
net income	0	0	0	0

Both hotel A and hotel B had the same amount of revenue of $500,000, total cost of $500,000 and hence net income of $0. However, the only difference between the two hotels' profit and loss is their operating leverage. In this case, hotel A is said to have a lower operating leverage than hotel B. We can plot the two hotels' cost information in the Figure 4 - 6。

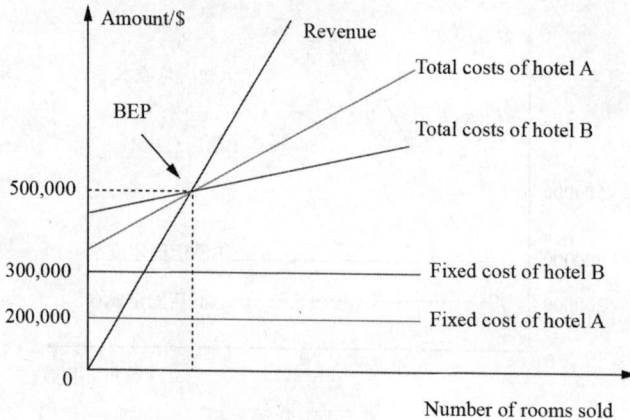

Figure 4 - 6 Hotels' operations analysis

From Figure 4 - 6, we can see that before the BEP at any particular number of rooms sold, the loss for hotel B (i.e., total costs minus revenue) are larger than that for hotel A. On the other hand, after the BEP at any particular number of rooms sold, the profit for hotel B (i.e., revenue minus total cost) are also larger than that for hotel A. In other words, at any particular number of rooms sold, the range of loss is greater for hotels with a higher operating leverage before the BEP and at the same time the range of profit is also greater after the BEP. In a nutshell, those properties having a higher operating leverage (or CMR) is facing higher risk in their operation.

第 5 章　基于成本的定价

学习目标

- 理解定价的重要性
- 了解非正式的定价方法
- 领悟传统的基于成本的定价方法
- 了解并能应用赫伯特公式定价

5.1　引　言

定价是管理层须频繁做的最直接也最重要的商业决策之一。有了适当的定价决策,企业将不仅能够吸引并留住顾客,同时也能产生能满足其利润最大化运营目标的应有的收益。如果酒店客房或餐饮的价格太高,客户可能无法感到物有所值,因而投向其他住宿和餐饮选择。在这种情况下,酒店客房可能租不出去或食物无法售出,但相关的固定费用仍须支出。另一方面,如果酒店客房或餐饮的价格太低,虽然可吸引顾客住宿酒店或在餐厅用餐,但是,酒店或餐厅可能发现其盈利达不到预期水平,无法满足其运营预算或业主的要求。在最坏的情况下,酒店或餐馆可能会产生运营亏损,如果这种不利的局面持续一段时间,则会面临破产的危险。

如上述所示,定价像一把双刃刀剑。一方面,定价不仅直接影响一个企业的顶线(即收益)同时也影响其底线(即净利润);另一方面,价格也反映企业如何定位其产品和服务,因此,它会影响顾客如何看待企业的产品和服务。位于中国一个三线城市的经济型酒店内,一份价格为 120 元的早餐可能被视为漫天要价,而同样价格的早餐在一家地处一线城市的四星级酒店可能会被视为物有所值。我们将在以下几节介绍现实中其他影响企业定价决策的因素。

Chapter 5   Cost-based Pricing

Learning Outcomes

- Understand the importance of pricing
- Understand informal pricing approaches
- Comprehend traditional cost-based pricing methods
- Understand and be able to apply the Hubbart formula to pricing

5.1   Introduction

Pricing is one of the most direct and critical business decisions that the management has to frequently make. With proper pricing decisions, a business will be able to not only attract and retain customers but also generate due revenues for meeting its operational goal of profit maximization. If a hotel room or meal is priced too high, customers may not perceive value for the money to be spent and be turned away for other accommodation or food options. In this case, the hotel rooms may be left unrented or food items are left unsold albeit the associated fixed expenses are still accounted for. On the other hand, if a hotel room or meal is priced too low, while customers may be lured for staying in the hotel property or eating at the restaurant, the hotel or the restaurant may find the level of profitability undesirable and fail to meet their operating budgets or the owner's requirement. In a worst scenario, a hotel or restaurant may incur operating loss and face a risk of going bankrupt if such unfavorable situation continues for some time.

As illustrated above, pricing is like a two-edge sword. On the one hand, pricing directly affects not only the top line (i.e., revenue) but also the bottom line (i.e., net income) of a business. On the other hand, pricing is likely to reflect how a business position its products and services and as a result, it also influences how customers perceive the products and services that a business offers. A RMB 120 breakfast meal at an economy hotel located in a third-tier city in China may be perceived as outrageous while the same price for a breakfast meal at a four-star hotel in a first-tier city is likely to be perceived as valued for money. In reality, there are other factors that may influence a business's pricing decisions and we will introduce them in the following sections.

5.2　非正式定价方法

为了应对多变的酒店和旅游商业环境,管理者需要有效地制定其定价决策,不仅运营有利润,同时也能让顾客满意。因此,他们在日常运营中会采取包括竞争对手、直觉、心理、试误和指导价等非正式的定价策略。

酒店或旅游企业经营者为自己的产品和服务定价的一个最直接的方式是,参考提供相同或相似类型产品和服务给顾客的竞争对手的定价。例如:当隔壁一家四星级酒店收费 750 元一晚含早餐和免费互联网服务时,另一家提供类似住宿和服务的四星级酒店为了保持在价格方面有竞争力将其房价定为 750 元上下(可能更高或更低)并不令人意外;或者另一个三星级酒店为了凸显其吸引力可能将其房价定为 450 元。又如:香港海洋公园收取成人(12 岁及以上)门票 385 港元和儿童门票 193 港元,而香港迪士尼乐园门票收费价格为成人(12～64 岁)539 港元、儿童 385 港元和长者(65 岁及以上)100 港元。虽说香港海洋公园的门票与迪士尼乐园相比要便宜得多,但它们在设定各自门票价格时,除了其他方面的考虑之外,应该也参考了对方的定价方案,以便吸引和保有自己的目标顾客群体,因为它们在香港是两个重要的主题公园。

定价方案也能依由管理层的直觉来制定。对于一家位于中国一线城市中央商业区的四星级商务酒店来说,由于商务客的费用一般是由企业支付的,因此,这些商务客对价格较不敏感,所以管理者可以直观地以较高的价格销售其产品和服务,从而使酒店产生较高水平的收益。另一个例子:人们可能希望暂时摆脱他们的日常生活或在节假日期间与家人出游,航空公司、旅行社等旅游产品/服务提供商可以直观地在节假日期间提价,以迎合这些游客群体,因为价格并不是这些游客的主要考量。在另一方面,即使利润率要小得多,滑雪度假村的经理在淡季即将来临前可以直观地降价,以吸引消费者到其度假村进行其他的活动。

经理们也可能通过运用心理定价法来猜测顾客对不同价格水平的反应。顾客在选择酒店及旅游消费时已越来越精明,而且他们可以仅点击鼠标或智能手机即可选择酒店和获得现成的与旅游相关的产品和服务的信息。例如,

5.2 *Informal Pricing Approaches*

In order to react to changing hospitality and tourism business environments, managers often need to make their pricing decisions in an efficient manner to not only run their businesses profitably but also keep their customers happy. Therefore, there are some informal pricing strategies that they may adopt in daily operations including competitor, intuition, psychological, trial-and-error and guided pricing.

One of the most direct ways for a hotel or tourism operator to price their products and services is to make reference to how much a competitor is charging its customers for the same or similar types of products and services. When a four-star hotel next door is charging ¥750 a night plus breakfast and free Internet services, it would not be surprising for another four-star hotel offering similar types of accommodations and provisions to price its hotel room rate close to ¥750 (could be higher or lower) in order to remain competitive in terms of pricing; or, for another three-star hotel to price its hotel room rate at, say, ¥450, to appear attractive to potential customers. Another example: Ocean Park in Hong Kong charges HKD 385 for adult (aged 12 or above) and HKD 193 for child for admission and Hong Kong Disneyland charges HKD 539 for adult (ages 12~64), HKD 385 for child and HKD 100 for senior (ages 65+). While Ocean Park charges much less for admission as compared to Hong Kong Disneyland, it is likely that when setting their admission pricing, in addition to other considerations both companies should also have made reference to each other's pricing scheme so as to attract and retain their own target customer groups because they are the only two theme parks in Hong Kong.

Pricing scheme could also be determined by management's intuition. For a four-star business hotel located in the CBD in a first-tier city in China, the managers could sell the products and services at higher prices intuitively because it is very likely that their business customers' bills are paid by their companies. Therefore, these business customers should be less price-sensitive and the hotel will be able to generate a higher level of revenues. Another example: knowing that people may want to temporarily get away from their daily routines or have a family vacation with children during holiday seasons, airlines, travel agencies and other tourism product/service providers could intuitively set higher prices during holiday seasons to accommodate these groups of tourists because price may not be of critical concern to them. On the other hand, knowing that the slow season is coming, managers at ski resorts may intuitively drop their prices, even for a much smaller profit margin, in order to lure customers to their resorts for other activities.

Managers will also want to apply psychological pricing approach by guesstimating how customers would react to different levels of price. Customers have become more and more sophisticated when it comes to their choice of hospitality and tourism consumption because there are many options available and information on hospitality and tourism

在为新的菜式制定价格时,餐厅经理可能需要将心比心,从潜在客户的立场来推测顾客接受设定的价格的可能性。如果价格定得太高,顾客会认为菜式过于昂贵而不点该样菜式。另一方面,如果价格设置得太低,而该菜式非常受欢迎,餐厅经理可能会遗憾当初为何不设定更高的价格,而是放弃了原本应有的收益。最坏的情况是客户可能不再光顾该餐厅。

作为与心理定价法相关的定价方法,在评估顾客对不同的价格水平的认知和接受程度时,管理者可能先设置一个最有可能被客户接受的菜单价格。如果顾客的反应是良好的,管理者可以逐步提高价格以进一步评估顾客会如何应对这样的提价。但是,如果提价后客户的反应不好或销售收益减少,这样的提价或许不是一个明智之举,管理者可能需要调整价格至原来的水平。另一个例子:如果一家酒店正在考虑在半年内增加酒店平均房价10%而经理不知道顾客会怎么反应,管理者初期可以将其房价增加5%~8%,如果销售数据显示没有负面影响,酒店可以在第二阶段增加额外2%~5%的提价,再看看市场如何反应。

地方或国家酒店协会或政府有时也会有指导价,虽说这种情况不常见。例如,中国海南省的三亚以其美丽的风景和宜人的气候吸引了许多国内外游客前来度假旅游。不过,也曾经发生游客被不法业者针对客房、餐饮和旅游产品和服务漫天索价的丑闻,从而严重损害了三亚的目的地形象,并影响了游客旅游三亚的意愿。为了对付这些奸商的行为和做法,三亚政府针对特定假期,如在中国春节或黄金周期间,要求酒店和餐馆只能向顾客收取低于指导价的费用。如在2016年春节期间酒店标间的房价不能超过5000元。高端酒店若要收取更高的价格(最高6000元)则需要获得三亚政府物价局的审查批准。同样地,早餐价格不能超过350元,午餐和晚餐的价格不能超过500元。

上述所有非正式定价方法已经实行多年,在某些情况下有的定价方法可以帮助企业创造理想的销售收益,并给予业主必要的回报。然而,当最终的

related products and services is readily available with a click of the mouse or a tap on a smartphone. For example, when setting prices for new menu items, for example, a restaurant manager may need to put him/herself in potential customers' shoes and guesstimate whether the prices set would be deemed acceptable to them. If the price is set too high, customers may perceive the menu item to be too expensive and not order it. On the other hand, if the price is set too low, even if the menu item turns out to be extremely popular, the restaurant manager may feel regret why not setting the price higher at the beginning, thus leaving money on the table. In a worst scenario, customers may be turned away for other restaurants.

As a related pricing approach to the psychological one, in assessing customers' perception or level of acceptance on different price levels, managers may first set the menu price that is most likely to be perceived as reasonable by customers. If the reactions from the customers are rather favorable, the managers may increase the price little by little to further assess how customers react to such price increase. However, if the reactions from the customers are rather unfavorable or there's reduction in sales revenue due to such price increase, it is likely that the price increase was not a sensible move and the managers may want to act accordingly by adjusting the price back to the original level. Another example: if a hotel is thinking about increasing its average hotel room rate by 10% in six months and the hotel manager is not sure how the customers would react or perceive such rate move, the manager can start by increasing its room rate by 5%~8% first and if the sales figures do not show any negative impact compared to the sales figures when there was not rate increase, then the hotel can add additional 2%~5% rate increase in the second stage and see how the market react.

Guided pricing is also implemented, however infrequently, by local or national hotel associations or government. For example, Sanya in Hainan Province of China is famous for its beautiful scenery and pleasant climate and many international and local tourists have visited Sanya for leisure purposes. However, there have been scandals that tourists were charged outrageous prices for hotel rooms, meals and tourism products and services, hence seriously damaging Sanya's destination image and discouraging potential tourists from visiting Sanya. In countering such wicked behaviors and practices, Sanya government provided guided pricing scheme and mandated that hotels and restaurants can only charge their customers under the guided prices during certain holiday seasons such as the Chinese New Year period or the Golden Week period. For example, in 2016 during the Chinese New Year the room rate for a standard room in a hotel cannot be higher than ¥5000; for high-end hotels to charge a higher price (up to ¥6,000), they will need to get an approval with scrutiny from the pricing authority of Sanya government. Similarly, the price for breakfast cannot be higher than ¥350 and for lunch and dinner ¥500.

All the above informal pricing approaches have been in existence for years and some may work quite well in certain situations in generating desirable sales revenues and

结果并未如预期所料时,企业可能会变得无利可图,容易面临意想不到的包括倒闭的结局。上述非正规定价方法的一个明显的局限性在于它们并未考量成本。

5.3　传统基于成本的定价方法

谨慎的经营者和管理者时时记着创造收益和盈利,所以在制定价格时都考虑了成本。酒店和餐饮业有一些传统的基于成本的定价方法。

1. 客房定价

酒店客房定价之"千分之一"法是指基于每间客房项目成本以每 1000 元定价为 1 元。例如,在路凼金光大道上有 360 间客房、耗资成本达 80 亿元澳门币(1 美元＝8 元澳门币)的澳门四季酒店于 2008 年开业,每间客房工程造价大约是 2220 万元澳门币。如果使用"千分之一"法的话,一间客房应该定价 22000 元澳门币或 2750 美元,听起来相当离谱。互联网上搜索显示,2016 年 4 月 1 日该酒店一晚住宿花费为从要价 3000 元澳门币的 55 平方米豪华客房至要价 16000 元澳门币的 213 平方米皇家套房,远远低于计算出的 22000 元澳门币!我们来看另一个例子。有 567 间客房、耗资 15 亿元港币(1 美元＝7.8元港币)的香港沙田凯悦酒店于 2007 年开业,每间客房工程造价约为 265 万元港币。如果使用"千分之一"法的话,酒店客房平均每晚应定价 2650 元港币或 340 美元,似乎还算合理。2016 年 4 月 1 日该酒店一晚住宿花费为从 1100 元港币的 38 平方米标准房至 7100 元港币的 81 平方米摄政套房。可以应用此特定定价法的例子不胜枚举。那么,这"千分之一"定价法有用吗?从以上两个例子可见,计算得出的"房价"只是指标性的,该方法可能不适用于每一个酒店物业,因为该方法既可以高估也可以低估酒店的平均房价。"千分之一"定价法的局限性说明如下。

第一,客房定价纯粹基于过去而非当前产生的建筑成本,因此计算出的房价可能被低估。因为建筑相关费用的显著差异,房价低估的问题对于已开业几十年的酒店来说更为严重。2007 年第四季度香港五星级酒店物业每平方米建筑成本从 19800 元港币到 24100 元港币不等;在 2015 年第三季度时每平方米建筑成本在短短 8 年间由 24100 元港币增加了近 77%,至 42600 元

requisite returns to owners. Nevertheless, when the end results did not turn out to be expected, the business may become unprofitable and vulnerable to unexpected outcome including going out of business. One significant limitation to the above-mentioned informal pricing approaches lies in their ignorance on cost consideration.

5.3 Traditional Cost-based Pricing Methods

Mindful operators and managers have taken cost information into pricing consideration so as to keep in mind generation of not only revenues but also profits from business operations. There are some traditional cost-based pricing methods applicable to both hotel and restaurant businesses.

1. Guestroom pricing

In hotel room pricing, the "$1 per $1,000" approach refers to that rooms are priced at $1 for each $1,000 of project cost per room. For example, Four Seasons Hotel Macao at Cotai Strip with 360 guestrooms costing MOP 8 billion (USD 1 = MOP 8) opened in 2008; the project cost per room for this hotel was around MOP 22.2 million. Using the "$1 per $1,000" approach a hotel room on average should be priced at MOP 22,000 or USD 2,750, which sounds rather outrageous. A search on the Internet shows that a one-night-stay at the hotel checking in on April 1, 2016 will cost from MOP 3,000 for a 55 square meter deluxe room to MOP 16,000 for a 213 square meter Royal Suite, which is way below the calculated MOP 22,000 per night! Let's look at another example. Hyatt Regency at Shatin, Hong Kong with 567 guestrooms costing HKD 1.5 billion (USD 1 = HKD 7.8) opened in 2007; the project cost per room for this hotel was around HKD 2.65 million. Using the "$1 per $1,000" approach the hotel room on average should be sold at HKD 2,650 or USD 340 per night, which appears more reasonable; its room rates on April 1, 2016 range from HKD 1,100 for a 38 square meter standard room to HKD 7,100 for an 81 square meter Regency Suite. There are more examples that can be given to apply this particular pricing method. So, how useful is this "$1 per $1,000" approach in pricing rooms? As seen from the above two examples, the calculated "room rate" is just indicative and may or may not be applicable to every hotel property because the method could either overestimate or underestimate the average room rate for a hotel. The limitations of the $1 per $1,000 pricing method are described below.

First, room rates are priced based purely on construction costs incurred in the past, not the current time period, and therefore the rates calculated may be underestimated. The problem associated with underestimation of room rates could be more serious for hotel properties that have opened for decades because of significant differences in construction-related cost. Construction cost per square meter for a five-star hotel property in Hong Kong ranged from HKD 19,800 to HKD 24,100 at 4th quarter of 2007; the cost range increased from HKD 24,100 to HKD 42,600 at 3rd quarter of 2015,

港币。相对来说没那么严峻的情况显示，北京、上海、广州和深圳建设成本增幅在同一期间为 27%～38%。

第二，这种定价方法只考虑工程成本而没考虑运营成本，因此计算出的房价可能被低估而无法支付所需的运营成本。一般来说，在正常的运营条件、经济环境和谨慎的酒店管理下，酒店可以产生 30%～50% 的运营毛利率。换句话说，典型的酒店运营成本占其销售收入的 50%～70%，这是相当显著的，但却无法保证有利润，更不用说给予业主期望的回报。

第三，因为这种定价方法忽略了需要在制定房价时考虑的所有可能帮助提升顾客体验的服务内容（如超凡的服务质量和友好的服务人员），所以计算出的房价也可能被低估。

第四，特别是对于豪华酒店或提供多元化产品和服务的酒店物业，这种定价方法高估了其房价。如上述的四季酒店例子所示，为了提供必要的形象、设施、标准和与四季酒店品牌相关联的感知，相对于其他较低等级的豪华酒店物业，四季酒店的建筑项目成本将显著增加，从而增加了每间客房的工程成本。

2. 餐饮定价

劳动力成本和食品/饮料的成本为餐饮运营中两个最大的成本支出项。根据市场和餐馆类型的不同，已售食品的成本一般介于 25% 至 35%。为了产生足够的食品和饮料收益来支付已售货品的成本和其他运营费用，从而实现合理的利润，餐饮定价时应考虑期望的成本百分比，如以下步骤所示：

（1）确定一个理想的餐饮成本的百分比；

（2）将 1 除以期望的食品/饮料成本百分比得出价格乘数；

（3）测算烹调食品所需的原料成本；

（4）将烹调食品所需的材料成本乘以价格乘数；

（5）将测算结果进位，同时管理者对价格进行主观调整。

假设一家餐厅希望能持续平稳运营，因此将食品成本百分比控制在 35%，这便是其期望的食物成本百分比。然后将 1 除以 35% 得到价格乘数

representing a 77% increase in just eight years. In a less dramatic case, percentage increase on construction cost in Beijing, Shanghai, Guangzhou and Shenzhen ranged from 27% to 38% during the same eight-year time period.

Second, this pricing method only considers construction cost but not operating cost, and thus, the calculated room rate might be underestimated and fail to cover requisite operating cost. Generally speaking, under normal operating conditions, economic environments and prudent hotel management, hotels could generate a gross operating percentage between 30%~50%. In other words, operating costs account for 50%~70% for typical hotels, which is rather significant, and therefore, profits could not be guaranteed, not to mention producing desirable returns for owners.

Third, the calculated room rate may also be underestimated because this pricing method ignores all the other service provisions that may be able to help enhance guest experience (e.g., extra-ordinary service quality or friendly service staff) that could certainly be priced in room rate.

Fourth, this pricing method can also result in overestimated room rates particularly for luxurious hotels or hotel properties offering diversified products and services. As shown in the above-mentioned Four Seasons Hotel example, in order to offer requisite image, facilities, standard and perception associated with the Four Seasons brand, it is very possible that the construction project costs will be jacked up significantly compared to other less luxurious hotel properties, thus a heightened amount of project cost per room.

2. F&B pricing

In F&B operations, two highest cost items are labor cost and cost of food/beverage sold. Depending on the market and types of restaurants, cost of food sold could range from 25% to 35%. In order to generate enough revenues in food and beverage to cover not only the cost of goods sold but also other operating costs to achieve reasonable profit, F&B pricing could take desirable cost percentage into consideration in the following steps:

(1) Decide a desirable F&B cost percentage;

(2) Determine a price multiple by dividing one by the cost percentage;

(3) Determine the ingredient cost in producing the foot items;

(4) Multiply the cost of F&B item by the price multiple; and,

(5) Round up the calculated amount and make further managerial subjective adjustment to the price.

Suppose a restaurant would like to have its food cost percentage be controlled at 35% so as to remain viable in running the business, this will be its desirable food cost percentage. The price multiple is then derived by dividing one by 35%, which is equal to 2.86. Next, the restaurant ought to conduct a detailed food cost analysis in determining

2.86。接下来,餐厅应该进行详细的食品成本分析,来测算烹调某一菜式所需材料的成本。例如,煮食一客海南鸡饭所需材料及相关成本如表 5 - 1 所示。

表 5 - 1　一客海南鸡饭所需材料及相关成本

材料	单位价格(港元)(a)	净重(b)	金额(港元)($a \times b$)
冰鲜鸡	55	0.35 千克	19.25
调味饭	9.8	0.1 千克	0.98
辣椒酱	12	0.056 千克	0.67
姜蓉	12	0.056 千克	0.67
腌菜沙拉和配菜	1	1 份	1.00
中式菜汤	1.5	1 份	1.50
绿色蔬菜	9.8	0.2 千克	1.96
总计(港元)	—	—	26.03

然后我们将材料成本(即 26.03 港元)乘以价格乘数(即 2.86)得出 74.45 港元的价格。在定价的最后一步,我们先针对计算出的价格无条件进位至 75 港元以满足 35％的食品成本百分比要求,然后根据合理的理由进行必要的价格调整。管理者可以调整所计算的价格到比方说 78 港元,因为就消费者心理层面来讲,75 港元和 78 港元可以说根本没有或只有极小差别。如果 78 港元的价格被顾客接受,那么这代表了每售出一客海南鸡饭产生了额外 3 港元的利润,反之,餐厅可以随时向下调整价格至 75 港元。

我们以上演示的以价格乘数来导出菜品价格的方法是相当简单的。然而,在现实中这个方法的使用取决于餐厅经理希望如何深入地分析食品配料的使用及其费用,计算可以变得非常复杂,但是更精确。例如,有可能在制备过程中蔬菜有所浪费,而这类浪费也应被考虑和计算为成本,从而会增加所计算的食物成本金额。

另一方面,饮料定价更为简单。通常餐馆可以从饮料的销售中赚取较高比例的利润。假设一家餐厅想实现 20％的饮料成本百分比,而且价格乘数 5 是由 1 除以 20％得出。对于一瓶成本为 6.25 港元的啤酒,我们将 6.25 港元乘以 5 可得出 31.25 港元的价格。无条件进位后一瓶啤酒可以定价为 32 港元。

5.4　赫伯特公式定价法

赫伯特公式定价法是一个一开始即考虑所需利润水平来制定酒店房价

how much it costs, in terms of the ingredients required, to produce a certain menu item. For example, the ingredients required and associated costs in producing a set of Hainan chicken rice are as Table 5 - 1.

Table 5 - 1　Cost in producing a set of Hainan chicken rice

Ingredient	Unit-price(HKD) (a)	Net quantity (b)	Amount(HKD)($a \times b$)
chilled chicken	55	0.35kg	19.25
flavored rice	9.8	0.1kg	0.98
chili paste	12	0.056kg	0.67
ginger paste	12	0.056kg	0.67
pickle salad and garnish	1	1portion	1.00
chinese vegetable soup	1.5	1portion	1.50
green vegetables	9.8	0.2kg	1.96
total	—	—	26.03

We then multiply the cost of the ingredients (i.e., HKD 26.03) by the price multiple (i.e., 2.86) to arrive at a price of HKD 74.45. In the last step of pricing this menu item, we will first round up the calculated price to HKD 75 in order to meet the 35% cost percentage requirement and then make any necessary price adjustment based on justifiable reasons. The manager can adjust the calculated price to, for example, HKD 78, because psychological speaking HKD 75 and HKD 78 may make no or very little difference to consumers. If the price of HKD 78 works, then this represent an additional three Hong Kong dollars in profit for every set of Hainan chicken rice sold; if it doesn't, the restaurant can always adjust the price downward back to HKD 75.

What we demonstrated above in deriving food price using a price multiple is rather straightforward; however, in reality, depending how in-depth a restaurant manager would like to analyze food ingredient usage and cost, the calculation could become very complicated however more precisely. For example, there could be wastage on vegetables during the preparation process and this type of wastage cost should also be factored and added in the calculation, hence increasing the calculated food cost amount.

On the other hand, the case of beverage pricing is much simpler and restaurants normally can earn a higher percentage of profit out of beverage sales. Suppose a restaurant would like to achieve a 20% beverage cost percentage, and the price multiple is determined by dividing one by 20%, which is five. For a bottle of beer costing HKD 6.25 we can then multiply HKD 6.25 by 5 to arrive at a price of HKD 31.25. After rounding up the calculated amount a bottle of beer can be priced at HKD 32.

5.4　Hubbart Formula for Pricing

The Hubbart formula is a systematic method to pricing hotel rooms taking a required

的系统性方法。也就是说,该定价方法由期望的利润水平开始算至所要求的客房收益水平,因此被称为由下而上法。赫伯特公式定价法一般分两个阶段完成:第一,确定所要求的客房收益水平;第二,针对不同房型制定不同房价。

第一阶段:确定所要求的客房收益水平

可以按照下面介绍的步骤来确定要求的客房收益水平。

(1)确定整个酒店所需的净利润(NI)。酒店管理的运营目标是产生期望的净利润水平以履行对业主的受托责任,在这一步,我们可以通过将业主的投资(股权)乘以期望的股本回报率(ROE)推导所需的净利润:

$$净利润 = 业主的投资 \times 期望的股本回报率$$

(2)折算净利润至息税前盈利(EBIT)。在酒店管理层帮助业主实现其所需的净利润水平之前,所得税和利息费用都需要支付。息税前盈利可以通过将净利润除以(1-所得税率)后再加上利息开支得到:

$$息税前盈利 = [净利润 \div (1-所得税率)] + 利息开支$$

(3)将包括折旧费、房产税和保险费用的固定费用加上息税前盈利得出扣除未分配运营费用后的利润,即运营毛利(GOP):

$$运营毛利 = 息税前盈利 + 固定费用$$

(4)加上未分配运营费用(例如行政及总务、销售和市场营销、信息技术等)得出所需获得的运营部门利润:

$$所需获得的运营部门利润 = 运营毛利 + 未分配运营费用$$

(5)加上估计的非客房部门亏损或扣除非客房部门的利润推导出客房部所需的部门利润:

$$客房部所需的部门利润 = 所需获得的运营部门利润$$
$$+ 估计非客房部门亏损$$
$$或$$
$$- 估计非客房部门的利润$$

(6)加上客房部直接费用推导出客房部所需的部门收益:

$$所需客房收益 = 客房部所需的部门利润 + 客房部直接费用$$

level of bottom line profit into consideration at the beginning. That is, the pricing method starts with a desired level of profit to determine a required level of room revenue and is thus called a bottom-up approach. The Hubbart formula to pricing is generally completed in two stages: first, determine a required level of room revenue and second, set up different room rates for different types of rooms.

Stage one: determine a required level of room revenue

In determining a required level of room revenue, one can follow the steps described below.

(1) Identify desired net income (NI) for the whole hotel. As the operational goal for hotel management is to generate a desired level of net income to fulfill its fiduciary duty to owners, in this step we can derive required net income by multiplying owners' investment (equity) by desired return on equity (ROE) as follows:

$$NI = Owners'\ investment \times Required\ ROE$$

(2) Convert NI to earnings before income taxes plus interest expenses (EBIT). Before hotel management can help owners achieve their required level of NI, income taxes need to be paid and interest expenses should be taken care of. EBIT can be derived by dividing NI by one minus the tax rate and then add back interest expenses as follows:

$$EBIT = [NI \div (1 - Tax\ rate)] + Interest\ expenses$$

(3) Add fixed charges including depreciation expenses, property tax, and insurance expense to EBIT to derive income after undistributed operating expenses, or gross operating profit (GOP) as follows:

$$GOP = EBIT + Fixed\ charges$$

(4) Add undistributed operating expenses (e.g, administrative & general, sales & marketing, information technology, etc.) to derive a required amount of operating departmental income as follows:

Required operating departmental income = GOP + Undistributed operating expenses

(5) Either add estimated non-rooms departmental losses or deduct estimated non-rooms departmental profits to derive a required amount of rooms departmental income as follows:

Required rooms departmental income
= Required operating departmental income
+ Estimated non-rooms departmental losses
or
− Estimated non-rooms departmental profits

(6) Add direct expenses of rooms department to derive a required amount of rooms departmental revenue as follows:

Required rooms departmental revenue = Required rooms departmental income
+ Direct expenses of rooms department

(7) 计算所需的平均房价(ADR)。有了所需客房收益的金额就可以将其除以一年内估计出售的客房数而测算出所需的平均房价:

$$平均房价 = 所需客房收益 \div 估计出售的客房数$$

从以上的七个步骤可知,如果从损益表底部考虑到顶部(即所谓的由下而上法),将能更容易理解和应用此方法。为了实现期望的净利润水平,酒店应该已经产生足够的客房收益来支付所需的各种费用。

我们在下例中应用赫伯特公式。

似曾相识酒店是一家耗资 400 万美元建设的有 100 间客房的酒店。来自股东权益的资金将有 280 万美元,其余部分将来自利率为 10% 的银行贷款。业主期望有 20% 的股东年回报率。所得税税率为 36%。折旧费用估计为每年 8 万美元。利息和折旧费是酒店的主要固定费用。其他固定费用估计为 4 万美元。未分配运营费用将达到 80 万美元,客房部的直接费用估计为每间出售客房 20 美元。第一年的入住率预计为 70%。该酒店的客房应定价多少元?

按照上面提出的七个步骤,我们可以得到明年所需的 ADR 如下。

(1) 净利润 $= 280 \times 20\% = 56$(万美元)

(2) 息税前盈利 $= [56 \div (1 - 36\%)] + 120 \times 10\%$

$$= 87.5 + 12 = 99.5(万美元)$$

(3) 运营毛利 $= 99.5 + 8 + 4 = 111.5$(万美元)

(4) 所需获得的运营部门利润 $= 111.5 + 80 = 191.5$(万美元)

(5) 这个案例没有其他非客房部门盈利或亏损。

(6) 所需客房收益 $= 191.5 + 0.002 \times (100 \times 365 \times 70\%) = 242.6$(万美元)

其中,预估出售客房数 $= 100 \times 365 \times 70\% = 25500$(间)。

(7) 平均房价 $= 2426000 \div 25500 = 95.14$(美元/间)

应当指出的是,所计算的平均房价 95.14 美元是指标性的,并非不能修正。酒店经理可能需要以自己应有的判断对所计算出的平均房价做出一些调整。此外,酒店可能有不同类型的客房以不同的房价销售,同时还可能遇到由于如季节性或经济环境不明朗等因素造成的需求波动,酒店房间的实际

(7) Calculate required average room rate (i.e., ADR). With a required amount of rooms revenue calculated, one can then calculate a required average room rate by dividing required rooms departmental revenue by estimated number of rooms to be sold in a year as follows:

$$ADR = \text{Required rooms departmental revenue}$$
$$\div \text{Estimated number of rooms to be sold}$$

From the above seven steps, it would be easier to comprehend or apply this method by going through an income statement from the bottom to top (the so-called bottom-up approach). In order to achieve a desired level of net income, a hotel should have already taken care of various required expenses, before which the hotel should have already generated enough room revenue.

Let's apply the Hubbart formula to the following example.

Hotel déjà vu, a 100-room hotel, requires $4,000,000 for construction. Contribution from owners' equity will be $2,800,000 and the rest will be obtained from a bank loan at an interest rate of 10%. The owners desire an annual return of 20% on their equity. The income tax rate is 36%. Depreciation expense is estimated to be $80,000 per year. Interest and depreciation expenses are the major fixed charges for the hotel. Other fixed cost is estimated to be $40,000. Undistributed operating expenses will total $800,000 and the estimated direct expenses of the rooms department is $20 per room sold. The occupancy for the first year of operation is projected to be 70%. How much should guestrooms in Hotel déjà vu be priced?

Following the seven steps suggested above, we can derive a desired ADR for the next year as follows.

(1) $NI = 2800000 \times 20\% = 560000$

(2) $EBIT = [560000 \div (1 - 36\%)] + 1200000 \times 10\%$
$$= 875000 + 120000$$
$$= 995000$$

(3) $GOP = 995000 + 80000 + 40000$
$$= 1115000$$

(4) Required operating departmental income $= 1115000 + 800000 = 1915000$

(5) There's no other departmental income or loss in this case.

(6) Required rooms departmental revenue $= 1915000 + 20 \times (100 \times 365 \times 70\%)$
$$= 2426000$$

Where, Projected number of rooms sold $= (100 \times 365 \times 70\%) = 25500$

(7) $ADR = 2426000 \div 25500 = 95.14$

It should be noted that the ADR of $95.14 calculated is of indicative nature. Hotel managers may need to make some adjustment to this calculated ADR with their due judgments because the $95.14 is not a rate carved in stone. Furthermore, as a hotel could have different room types selling at different rates and may also encounter demand

卖出价格可能会比所计算的平均房价更高或更低。因此,我们现在就来看看如何进一步为不同的房型制定不同的价格。

第二阶段:制定单人房和双人房房价

为了便于说明,假设似曾相识酒店只销售两种房型——单人房和双人房,我们需要估计每天这两种房型出售的数量。假设每天所出售的客房中,单人房占 40%、双人房占 60%。我们进一步假设,双人房比单人房的房价要高 10 美元。

每日单人房出售房间数 $=100\times70\%\times40\%=28$(间)

每日双人房出售房间数 $=70-28=42$(间)

假设单人房的房价为 x 美元,双人房的房价则为 $(x+10)$ 美元。为了达到每天出售 70 间平均房价为 95.14 美元的客房的目标,所需要的每日客房收益将为 95.14 美元$\times70=6659.8$ 美元,这也应该等同于售出单人房和双人房的合并收益,计算如下:

$$95.14\times70=x\times28+(x+10)\times42$$

然后,我们可以解出上述方程式中的 $x=89.14$(美元)。因此在这个例子中,我们知道为了实现每天出售 70 间平均房价为 95.14 美元的客房,单人房应以平均房价 89.14 美元出售,双人房以平均房价 99.14 美元出售。

除了直接加价法,也可以通过单人房房价加上某百分比作为双人房房价。假设酒店经理认为双人房房价应该比单人房房价高 10%,单人房房价为 x 美元,我们可以写出客房收益方程式如下:

$$95.14\times70=x\times28+(x+10\%\times x)\times42$$

然后,我们可以解出上述方程式中的 $x=89.76$(美元)。因此,为了每天能出售 70 间平均房价为 95.14 美元的客房,单人房应以平均房价 89.76 美元出售,双人房经加了 10% 价差后应以平均房价 98.74 美元出售。

从上面的例子可以看出,赫伯特公式定价法应该也可以应用在食品定价或人均消费中。然而,由于食品选择众多和餐厅服务时段不一,同时要考虑例如客户的数量、翻桌率、就餐时间等变量,使用赫伯特定价法来制定食品价格会是一个相当复杂的课题。

fluctuations due to reasons such as seasonality or uncertain economic conditions, actual hotel room rates may be higher or lower than the calculated ADR. Therefore, we will now look at how to further set different room rates for different types of rooms.

Stage two: determine single and double room rates

For illustration purposes, suppose that Hotel déjà vu only sells two types of rooms— single and double and we will need to estimate the number of rooms to be sold between these two room types on a daily basis. Suppose that on a daily basis, single rooms sold accounted for 40% of occupied rooms and double rooms 60%. We further assume that, compared to single rooms, double rooms will be sold with a $10 mark-up.

The number of single rooms sold on a daily basis $= 100 \times 70\% \times 40\% = 28$ (rooms)

The number of double rooms sold on a daily basis $= 70 - 28 = 42$ (rooms)

Assuming single rooms are sold at x dollars, double room rate will then be $(x + 10)$ dollars. In order to achieve an ADR of 95.14 with 70 rooms sold on a daily basis, the daily room revenue required will be $95.14 \times 70 = \$6,659.8$, which should be equivalent to the combined revenues derived from both occupied single and double rooms as follows:

$$95.14 \times 70 = x \times 28 + (x + 10) \times 42$$

We can then solve x in the above equation to derive that $x = \$89.14$. Therefore, in this example, we know that, in achieving an ADR of $95.14 with 70 rooms sold on a daily basis, in particular the occupied single rooms should be sold at an average of $89.14 while double rooms at $99.14.

In addition to the dollar mark-up approach, one can also apply a percentage mark-up approach by adding a certain percentage to the single room rate as the double room rate. Suppose that the hotel manager thinks that double rooms should have a 10% mark-up in room rate over singles, we can write the room revenue equation as follows, assuming the single rooms sell at x dollars:

$$95.14 \times 70 = x \times 28 + (x + 10\% \times x) \times 42$$

We can then solve x in the above equation to derive that $x = \$89.76$. Therefore, using a 10% mark-up percentage, in achieving an ADR of $95.14 with 70 rooms sold on a daily basis, in particular the occupied single rooms should be sold at an average of $89.76 while double rooms at $98.74.

From the above illustration, one can also apply the Hubbart formula to pricing food items or average customer check; however, given a much wider spectrum of food items and service periods available in a restaurant setting, the use of Hubbart formula to pricing food items would be a complicated task as there are more parameters to be considered such as the number of customers, the table turnover ratio, the meal period etc.

第6章 风险与报酬

学习目标

- 了解风险与报酬的关系
- 计算资产或投资组合的报酬率
- 认识风险与多角化降低风险的意义
- 了解并计算资本资产定价模式

6.1 风险与报酬的概念

报酬是证券在一段时间的得失,通常以百分率表示。大部分的投资,不论是个人或企业总是预期今天所投资的钱会在未来产生更多的钱。报酬这个概念为投资者提供了一个呈现其投资上的财务绩效的便利方式。报酬率为每单位投资的报酬,是报酬最为常用的衡量方式,其公式为

$$报酬率 = \frac{回收金额 - 投资金额}{投资金额}$$

影响报酬最主要的因素是风险。风险是财务分析中重要的概念,特别是在影响证券价格与报酬率方面,风险系指无预期事件造成实质报酬小于预期报酬的概率。因此,实质报酬越低于预期报酬,就代表着越高的投资风险。资产的风险可以用两种方式分析:一是在单一的基础上,资产被视为单独隔离;二是在投资组合的基础上,资产被视为一群资产的组合。

在财务上,预期报酬可以由单一报酬与其概率的乘积和计算而得。事件的概率分配系由其所有可能的个别产出与其发生的概率列举而得,事件的概率则定义为事件可能发生的机会。特定事件会发生的概率总和为 1 或 100%,预期报酬率 $E(R_i)$ 则为每一个可能产出与其概率的乘积和,就是各种

Chapter 6　Risk and Return

Learning Outcomes

- Explain the relation of risk and return
- Caculate the return of an asset/protofolio
- Know the types of risk and explain the concept of diversification
- Know and calculate the capital asset pricing model (CAPM)

6.1　Concept of Risk and Return

Returns are the gains or losses from a security in a particular period and are usually quoted as a percentage. For investments, an individual or business spends money today with the expectation of earning even more money in the future. The concept of return provides investors with a convenient way of expressing the financial performance of an investment. Rate of return is the most common measure of return by considering the return in a way of per unit of investment, as follows:

$$\text{Rate of return} = \frac{\text{Amount received} - \text{Amount invested}}{\text{Amount invested}}$$

The main factor influence returns is risk. Risk is an important concept in financial analysis, especially in terms of how it affects security prices and rates of return. Risk refers to the chance that some unfavorable event will occur that is related to the probability of actually earning less than the expected return; thus, the greater the chance of low or negative returns, the riskier the investment. An asset's risk can be analyzed in two ways: (1) on a stand-alone basis, where the asset is considered in isolation, and (2) on a portfolio basis, where the asset is held as number of assets in a portfolio.

In finance, expected returns can be calculated by the summation of each return times its probability. The probability distribution for an event is the listing of all the possible outcomes for the event, with mathematical probabilities assigned to each. An event's probability is defined as the chance that the event will occur. The sum of the probabilities for a particular event must equal 1.0, or 100 percent. The expected rate of return $E(R_i)$ is the sum of the products of each possible outcome times its associated probability—it is a

132

不同的可能产出与其相关加权概率的加权平均,即

$$E(R_i) = \sum_{s=1}^{S} p(s) \times R(s_i)$$

事件的预期报酬率以连续概率计算,有无限可能的产出,越高而窄的概率分布代表实际的产出越近似预期值,反之,则离预期值越远。因此,高而窄的概率分布意味着证券的风险较低。衡量窄度的方法之一为标准差 σ,有公式:

$$\mathrm{Var}(R_i) = \sum_{s=1}^{S} p(s) \times \{[R(s_i) - E(R_i)]^2\}$$

$$\mathrm{Std}(R_i) = \sigma_i = [\mathrm{Var}(R_i)]^{\frac{1}{2}}$$

例　酒店 A 与酒店 B 股票的报酬概率分布如表 6-1 所示,其预期报酬率与标准差是多少?

表 6-1　酒店 A 与酒店 B 股票的报酬概率分布

天气情况	概率	酒店 A 股票报酬率	酒店 B 股票报酬率
很冷	0.1	−15%	35%
冷	0.3	−5%	15%
平均	0.4	10%	5%
热	0.2	30%	−5%

解　令 A 代表酒店 A,B 代表酒店 B,则

$$E(R_A) = 0.1(-0.15) + 0.3(-0.05) + 0.4(0.10) + 0.2(0.30)$$
$$= 7.00\%$$

$$E(R_B) = 0.1(-0.35) + 0.3(0.15) + 0.4(0.05) + 0.2(-0.05)$$
$$= 9.00\%$$

$$\sigma_A = \sqrt{0.1(-0.150-0.07)^2 + 0.3(-0.050-0.07)^2 + 0.4(0.10-0.07)^2 + 0.2(0.30-0.07)^2}$$
$$= 14.18\%$$

$$\sigma_B = \sqrt{0.1(0.350-0.09)^2 + 0.3(0.150-0.09)^2 + 0.4(0.050-0.09)^2 + 0.2(-0.050-0.09)^2}$$
$$= 11.14\%$$

标准差是用来衡量独立风险的。此标准差为预期值的加权平均变异量,可了解离实际值上下波动的程度。

另一个有用的风险衡量方法是变异系数(CV),即标准差除以预期报酬,它表示每单位报酬所承担的风险。当两个预期报酬不同时,CV 提供更有意义的比较基础:

$$CV = \frac{\sigma}{r}$$

weighted average of the various possible outcomes, with the weights being their probabilities of occurrence:

$$E(R_i) = \sum_{s=1}^{S} p(s) \times R(s_i)$$

Where the number of possible outcomes is virtually unlimited, continuous probability distributions are used in determining the expected rate of return of the event.The tighter, or more peaked, the probability distribution, the more likely it is that the actual outcome will be close to the expected value, and, consequently, the less likely it is that the actual return will end up far below the expected return. Thus, the tighter the probability distribution, the lower the risk assigned to a security.One measure for determining the tightness of a distribution is the standard deviation σ, as:

$$\mathrm{Var}(R_i) = \sum_{s=1}^{S} p(s) \times \{[R(s_i) - E(R_i)]^2\}$$

$$\mathrm{Std}(R_i) = \sigma_i = [\mathrm{Var}(R_i)]^{\frac{1}{2}}$$

Example   The stock return probability of hotel A and hotel B is as Table 6 – 1. What is the stocks' expected return and standard deviation of two hotels?

Table 6 – 1   The stock return probability of hotel A and hotel B

State of weather	Probability	Return on hotel A stock	Return on hotel B stock
very cold	0.1	− 15%	35%
cold	0.3	− 5%	15%
average	0.4	10%	5%
hot	0.2	30%	− 5%

Solution   Let A denote the hotel A and B denote the hotel B,then

$E(R_A) = 0.1(-0.15) + 0.3(-0.05) + 0.4(0.10) + 0.2(0.30) = 7.00\%$

$E(R_B) = 0.1(-0.35) + 0.3(0.15) + 0.4(0.05) + 0.2(-0.05) = 9.00\%$

$\sigma_A = \sqrt{0.1(-0.150-0.07)^2 + 0.3(-0.050-0.07)^2 + 0.4(0.10-0.07)^2 + 0.2(0.30-0.07)^2}$
$= 14.18\%$

$\sigma_B = \sqrt{0.1(0.350-0.09)^2 + 0.3(0.150-0.09)^2 + 0.4(0.050-0.09)^2 + 0.2(-0.050-0.09)^2}$
$= 11.14\%$

The standard deviation is a measure of stand-alone risk. The standard deviation is a probability-weighted average deviation from the expected value, and it gives an idea of how far above or below the expected value the actual value is likely to be.

Another useful measure of risk is the coefficient of variation (CV), which is the standard deviation divided by the expected return. It shows the risk per unit of return, and it provides a more meaningful basis for comparison when the expected returns on two alternatives are not the same:

$$CV = \frac{\sigma}{r}$$

　　大部分的投资者属于风险趋避者。这意味着在两个预期报酬率相同的投资选择中,投资者会选择风险较低的。在风险趋避者所主导的市场中,风险较高的证券应比风险较低的证券有较高的报酬率。

　　在投资组合中的一项资产会比该资产单独存在时的风险低,这很重要,因为大部分的金融资产并非单独持有,而是以投资组合中的一部分持有。从投资者的角度而言,重要的是投资组合的报酬与风险,而非特定资产价格的上下波动,因此,个别证券的风险与报酬应该从其影响投资组合的风险与报酬角度进行分析。

　　(1) 投资组合的预期报酬 $E(R_p)$

　　投资组合的预期报酬是投资组合中个别证券的预期报酬的加权平均。个别证券的权重是其在投资组合中所占的比例。以 w_n 表示某种证券在投资组合中的权重,则

$$E(R_p) = \sum_{n=1}^{N} [w_n E(R_n)]$$

　　(2) 投资组合的变异 σ_p

　　与预期报酬的衡量方式不同,投资组合的变异不是单纯个别证券变异量的加权平均,其公式为

$$\sigma_p = \mathrm{Var}(R_p) = w_A^2 \, \mathrm{Var}(R_A) + w_B^2 \, \mathrm{Var}(R_A) + 2w_A w_B \mathrm{Cov}(R_A, R_B)$$

　　投资组合的风险 σ_p 不是个别证券在投资组合中标准差的加权平均,而是比所有资产标准差 σ_s 的加权平均小。资产的风险取决于每只证券的标准差与证券之间的相关性。相关系数 r 衡量两项变数一起变动的趋势。对证券而言,变数就是报酬。如果投资组合的证券具有不同的相关性,投资组合的多角化就可分散风险。在真实的世界中,证券间的相关性通常呈正相关,但 r 小于 1.0,一些,但非全部的风险可被消除。不可能会有完全无风险的多角化证券组合。虽然大量多角化证券组合最后会带来一定量的风险,但此风险不会大于将钱只投资于一只证券的风险,亦即大部分的风险可因合理的完全多角化予以分散。

　　例　预期报酬率与投资组合报酬变异量。

　　在我们先前的例子中有酒店 A 与酒店 B 两只股票,其报酬率与标准差如下:

$$E(R_A) = 7\% \qquad\qquad E(R_B) = 9\%$$

Most investors are risk averse. This means that for two alternatives with the same expected rate of return, investors will choose the one with the lower risk. In a market dominated by risk-averse investors, riskier securities must have higher expected returns, as estimated by the marginal investor, than less risky securities.

An asset held as part of a portfolio is less risky than the same asset held in isolation. This is important, because most financial assets are not held in isolation; rather, they are held as parts of portfolios. From the investor's standpoint, the most important is the return on his or her portfolio, and the portfolio's risk — not the fact that a particular security goes up or down. Thus, the risk and return of an individual security should be analyzed in terms of how it affects the risk and return of the portfolio in which it is held.

(1) Expected return on a portfolio $E(R_p)$

Weighted average of the expected returns on the individual securities in the portfolio, with the weights being the fraction of the total portfolio invested in each asset. Let w_n denote a security's portfolio weight, then

$$E(R_p) = \sum_{n=1}^{N} [w_n E(R_n)]$$

(2) Portfolio variance σ_p

Unlike the measurement of expected return, the variance of a portfolio is not a simple weighted average of the individual security variances, that is

$$\sigma_p = \text{Var}(R_p) = w_A^2 \text{Var}(R_A) + w_B^2 \text{Var}(R_A) + 2 w_A w_B \text{Cov}(R_A, R_B)$$

The riskiness of a portfolio σ_p is generally not a weighted average of the standard deviations of the individual assets in the portfolio; the portfolio's risk will be smaller than the weighted average of the assets' σ_s. The riskiness of a portfolio depends not only on the standard deviations of the individual security, but also on the correlation between the securities. The correlation coefficient r measures the tendency of two variables to move together. With securities, these variables are the individual security returns. Diversification can reduce risk if the portfolio consists of different correlated securities. As a rule, the riskiness of a portfolio will decline as the number of securities in the portfolio increases. In the real world, where the correlations among the individual securities are generally positive but the σ_p is less than 1.0, some, but not all, risk can be eliminated. It is impossible to form completely riskless security portfolios. Even large portfolios stll carrier a substantial amount of risk, it is less riskness than invest the money in only one security. Most of the riskiness can be eliminated if the security is held in a reasonably well-diversified portfolio.

Example Expected return and variance of portfolio returns.

In our earlier example, there are two stocks, the hotel A and the hotel B. We know the following:

$$E(R_A) = 7\% \qquad E(R_B) = 9\%$$
$$\sigma_A = 14.18\% \qquad \sigma_B = 11.14\%$$

$$\sigma_A = 14.18\% \qquad \sigma_B = 11.14\%$$

假设我们将 100 元的预算投资 50 元于酒店 A、50 元于酒店 B,那么我们投资组合的预期报酬率与标准差是多少?

解 我们的投资权重为酒店 A 和酒店 B 各 50%。一般而言,投资组合的预期报酬率为

$$E(R_p) = \sum w_i \times E(r_i) = 0.5(7\%) + 0.5(9\%) = 8\%$$

为了衡量投资组合的风险,我们必须考虑证券如何一起变动。两只股票 X 和 Y 的关系为

$$SD(R_p) = \sqrt{w_X^2 \sigma_X^2 + w_Y^2 \sigma_Y^2 + 2w_X w_Y \mathrm{Cov_{XY}}}$$

式中:w_X 为股票 X 的投资占比;w_Y 为股票 Y 的投资占比。有关系:

$$w_X + w_Y = 1$$
$$\mathrm{Cov_{XY}} = \mathrm{Corr_{XY}} \sigma_X \sigma_Y$$

协方差负得越多,投资组合的风险越小。以前述酒店例子来说,如果把我们的钱各投资 50% 于两股之间,两只股票的相关系数为 -0.9375,$\sigma_A = 14.18\%$,$\sigma_B = 11.14\%$,$w_A = 0.5, w_B = 0.5$,则

$$\mathrm{Cov_{XY}} = \mathrm{Corr_{XY}} \sigma_X \sigma_Y = -0.9374 \times 0.1418 \times 0.1114 = -0.0148$$

$$SD(R_p) = \sqrt{0.5^2 \times 0.1418^2 + 0.5^2 \times 0.1114^2 + 2 \times 0.5 \times 0.5 \times (-0.0148)} = 2.69\%$$

这个答案告诉我们一些非常重要的概念:这两只股票投资组合的风险小于两者本身的风险。在一般情况下,两只股票的相关性愈小两个股票投资组合的风险愈小。

6.2 资本资产定价模型

资本资产定价模型(CAPM)是分析风险与收益率之间关系的重要工具。该模型主张,任何证券的投资收益率等于无风险利率加上风险溢酬,它只反映了多角化后剩余的风险。其主要结论是:股票间的相关性扮演了多角化投资组合风险的主要角色。在投资组合方面,资产的风险可分为两部分:(1)一部分是可分散的风险,可以通过多角化投资分散风险。这种风险是由某个公司的特别事件引起的。(2)另一部分是市场风险,它反映了整体股市的下跌风险,该风险无法通过多角化投资来消除。它可通过某种股票在市场中上下波动的程度来测量。这种风险从系统层面影响大多数公司,如战争、通货膨胀、经济衰退和高利率等(见图 6-1)。

Say we have $100 and invest $50 into A and $50 into B. What can we expect to make on our portfolio?

Solution We have a weight of 50% in A and 50% in B. Generally, expected portfolio return is

$$E(R_p) = \sum w_i \times E(r_i) = 0.5 \ (7\%) + 0.5 \ (9\%) = 8\%$$

To measure the risk of the portfolio, we have to account for how the securities move together. For two stocks X and Y the relation is:

$$SD(R_p) = \sqrt{w_X^2 \sigma_X^2 + w_Y^2 \sigma_Y^2 + 2 \, w_X \, w_Y \, Cov_{XY}}$$

Where: w_X is the proportion of wealth in asset X; w_Y is the proportion of wealth in asset Y. We have

$$w_X + w_Y = 1$$
$$Cov_{XY} = Corr_{XY}\sigma_X\sigma_Y$$

As the covariance gets more negative, the portfolio can be made less risky. In the hotel example mentioned before, say we divide our money 50—50 between the two stocks. The correlation between the two stocks is -0.9375, $\sigma_A = 14.18\%$, $\sigma_B = 11.14\%$, $w_A = 0.5$, $w_B = 0.5$, so

$$Cov_{XY} = Corr_{XY} \, \sigma_X\sigma_Y = -0.9374 \times 0.1418 \times 0.1114 = -0.0148$$
$$SD(R_p) = \sqrt{0.5^2 \times 0.1418^2 + 0.5^2 \times 0.1114^2 + 2 \times 0.5 \times 0.5 \times (-0.0148)} = 2.69\%$$

This answer tells us something very important: the risk of the portfolio of the two stocks is less than the risk of either one by itself. In general, the lower the correlation between the stocks, the lower the risk of the portfolios of both stocks.

6.2 Capital Asset Pricing Model

The capital asset pricing model (CAPM) is an important tool for analyzing the relationship between risk and rates of return. The model is based on the proposition that any security required rate of return is equal to the risk-free rate of return plus a risk premium, which reflects only the risk remaining after diversification. Its primary conclusion is: The relevant riskiness of an individual security is its contribution to the riskiness of a well-diversified portfolio. In a portfolio context, an asset's risk can be divided into two components: (1) a diversifiable risk component, which can be diversified. It is caused by events that are unique to a firm; (2) A market risk component, which reflects the risk of a general security market which cannot be eliminated by diversification. It can be measured by the stock fluctuation of a given security in the market. The market risk systematically affects most firms, such as war, inflation, recessions, and high interest rates(see Figure 6-1).

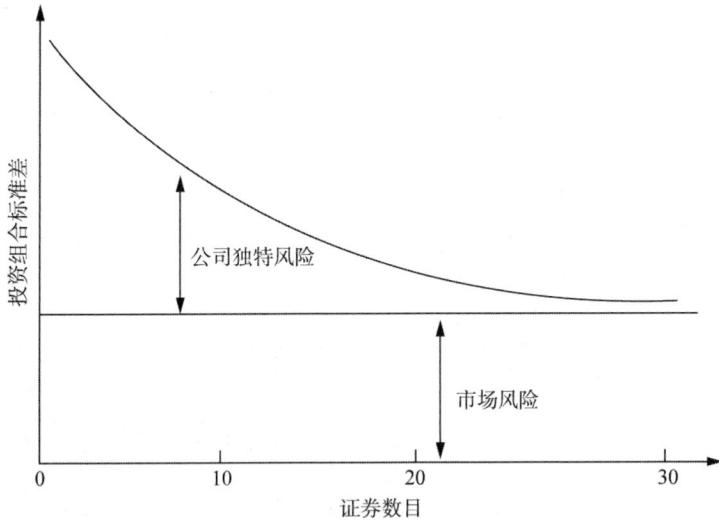

图 6-1　风险组成

$$E(R_i) = R_f + [E(R_M) - R_f]\beta_i$$

β(贝塔系数)反映的是一只证券在整体市场中的相对波动趋势,这是一只证券相对于整体证券的波动性的指标。平均风险证券被定义为一只倾向于与整体市场同步上下波动的证券,据此定义,其 β 值为 1.0。如果一只证券相对于整体市场有两倍的波动,则其 β 值为 2.0;一只证券相对于整体市场仅有一半的波动,则其 β 值为 0.5。由于 β 值可以衡量一只证券对投资组合风险的贡献程度,理论上就可以用 β 正确地衡量证券的风险。证券投资组合的 β 系数是个别证券 β 系数的加权平均值,即

$$\beta_p = \sum_{i=1}^{n} w_i \beta_i$$

由于证券的 β 系数决定了证券如何影响一个多角化的投资组合的风险程度,β 就成了衡量任何证券风险的最佳工具。

资本资产定价模型的例子

假设一个资产的系统性风险是市场组合(平均资产)风险的 1.5 倍。如果由国债利率测得的无风险利率为 5%,市场组合的预期风险溢酬为 8%,那么根据 CAPM,股票的预期收益应为多少?

解　$E(R_i) = R_f + [E(R_M) - R_f]\beta_i = 5\% + (8\% - 5\%)1.5 = 9.5\%$

资本资产定价模型(CAPM)使用 β 的概念衡量某只股票的走势与整体股市走势之间的相关性。CAPM 模型使用 β 的概念并结合投资者厌恶风险

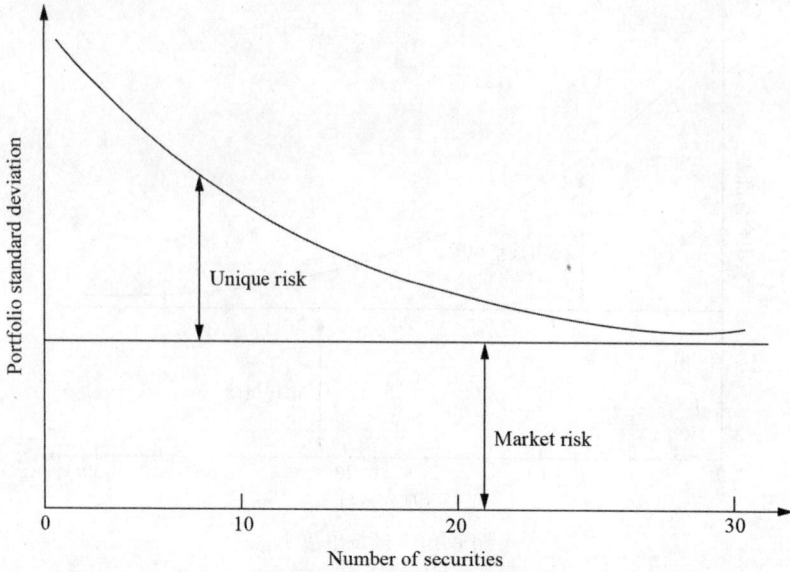

Figure 6 – 1   Risk components

$$E(R_i) = R_f + [E(R_M) - R_f]\beta_i$$

The tendency of a security to move with the market is reflected in its beta coefficient (β), which is a measure of the security's volatility relative to that of an average security. An average-risk security is defined as one that tends to move up and down in step with the whole security market. By definition, it has a beta of 1.0. A security that is twice as volatile as the market will have a beta of 2.0, while a security that is half as volatile as the market will have a beta coefficient of 0.5. Since a security's beta measures its contribution to the riskiness of a portfolio, beta is the best measure of the security's riskiness. The beta coefficient of a portfolio of securities is the weighted average of the individual securities' betas:

$$\beta_p = \sum_{i=1}^{n} w_i \beta_i$$

Since a security's β coefficient determines how the security affects the riskiness of a diversified portfolio, β is the most relevant measure of any security's risk.

Example of using CAPM

Suppose an asset has 1.5 times the systematic risk as the market portfolio (average asset). If the risk-free rate as measured by the Treasury bill rate is 5% and the expected risk premium on the market portfolio is 8%, what is the security's expected return according to the CAPM?

Solution $E(R_i) = R_f + [E(R_M) - R_f]\beta_i = 5\% + (8\% - 5\%)1.5 = 9.5\%$

The Capital Asset Pricing Model (CAPM) employs the concept of beta, which measures risk as the relationship between a particular security's movements and the

的特点,依市场风险和要求报酬率之间的关系,来计算投资者对于特定证券所要求的报酬率。风险和报酬率的关系可以用证券市场线(SML)的图形(见图6-2)予以视觉化。SML 的斜率可以改变,SML 线可向上或向下移动,以反映风险或报酬改变的程度。资本资产定价模型即是据此来反映风险与报酬之间的关系的。

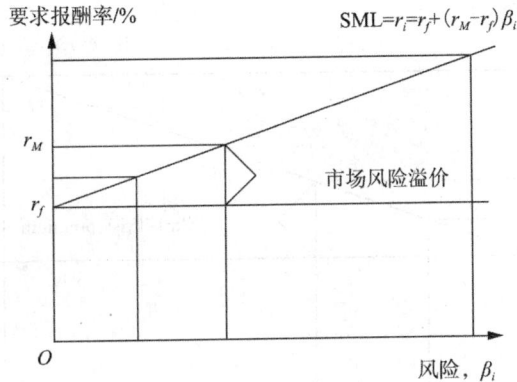

图 6-2　证券市场线(SML)

证券市场线(SML)呈现了个别证券以 β 衡量的风险和必要报酬率之间的关系。该 SML 方程可以找到个别证券的必要报酬率 r_i:

$$r_i = r_f + (r_M - r_f)\beta_i$$

式中:r_f 为对无风险债券的利率;β_i 为第 i 只股票的 β 值;r_M 是市场的整体报酬,或称平均证券;$(r_M - r_f)$ 称为市场风险溢价。它用来补偿投资者承担无风险利率以上的风险的额外收益。

在资本资产定价模型中,市场风险溢价 $(r_M - r_f)$ 与股票的 β 系数相乘确定了无风险利率外的额外报酬,用于补偿投资者投资个别证券的额外风险。这个溢酬可能比整体证券所需的溢酬更大或更小,取决于个别证券相对于整体市场以 β 衡量的相关风险程度。由 $(r_M - r_f)\beta_i$ 计算出的风险溢价加上无风险利率 r_f(国债的报酬率),可确定投资者投资个别证券所要求的报酬率 r_i。SML 的斜率 $(r_M - r_f)$ 显示风险增加一个单位所要求的报酬的增加,它反映了经济体中风险厌恶的程度。

movements of the overall security market. The CAPM use the concept of beta and investors' aversion to risk, specifies the relationship between market risk and the required rate of return to calculate the return that investors require. This relationship can be visualized graphically with the Security Market Line (SML) (see Figure 6 - 2). The slope of the SML can change, or the line can shift upward or downward, in response to changes in risk or required rates of return. The Capital Assets Pricing Model is introduced to form the relationship of risk and return in financial management.

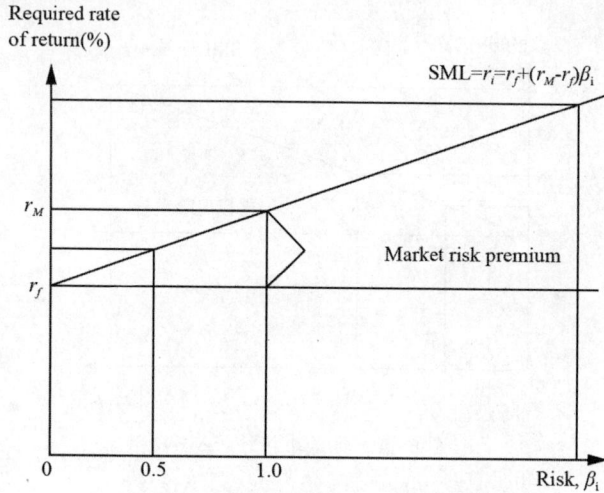

Figure 6 - 2　Security market line

The Security Market Line (SML) shows the relationship between risk as measured by beta and the required rate of return for individual securities. The SML equation can be used to find the required rate of return on security r_i:

$$r_i = r_f + (r_M - r_f)\beta_i$$

Here r_f is the rate of interest on risk free securities; β_i is the ith security's beta; r_M is the return on the market or, alternatively, on an average security; The term $(r_M - r_f)$ is the market risk premium. This is a measure of the additional return over the risk-free rate needed to compensate investors for assuming an average amount of risk.

In the CAPM, the market risk premium$(r_M - r_f)$ is multiplied by the security's beta coefficient to determine the additional premium over the risk-free rate that is required to compensate investors for the risk inherent in a particular security. This premium may be larger or smaller than the premium required on the overall market, depending on the riskiness of that security in relation to the overall market as measured by the security's beta. The risk premium calculated by $(r_M - r_f)\beta_i$ is added to the risk-free rate, r_f (the rate on Treasury securities), to determine the total rate of return required by investors on a particular security, r_i. The slope of the SML, $(r_M - r_f)$, shows the increase in the required rate of return for a one-unit increase in risk. It reflects the degree of risk aversion in the economy.

无风险(又称名义或报价)的利率由两部分组成:(1)无通膨的实质报酬率 r^*;(2)通货膨胀溢价 IP,等于预期通货膨胀率。由于预期通胀率的上升,更高的溢酬必须加上无风险利率来弥补通货膨胀所导致的购买力下降。

风险厌恶程度的增加,反映为 SML 的斜率增加,也反映了相关的风险溢酬。投资者的风险厌恶程度愈大,SML 线的斜率愈大;该证券的风险溢酬越大,所要求的报酬率更高。

许多因素会影响公司的 β。当 β 发生改变时,所要求的必要报酬率也发生变化。一个公司可以通过改变其资产的组成与其所使用的债务来影响其市场风险 β。一个公司的 β 也会受外部因素影响,如同业竞争的加剧、基础专利到期等。

财务管理的主要目标是股价最大化,决定于公司股票的风险程度,以及任何实体资产的相关风险,投资者所看到的亦然。

一些研究提出了对 CAPM 有效性的质疑。Fama 和 French(1992)的研究发现,股票的收益和它们的市场 β 值之间不存在历史关系。他们发现两个变量始终与股票报酬率相关:一是企业的规模;二是市场/账面比率。在调整了其他因素后,他们发现,小企业提供了比较高的报酬,而报酬较高的股票有较低的市场/账面比。在控制了企业规模和市场/账面比后,他们发现了个别股票的 β 和报酬之间没有任何关系。

相较于传统的 CAPM 模型,研究人员和从业者开始将目光转向了一般化多 β 模型,以克服资本资产定价模型的缺点。

在多 β 模型中,市场风险以多项因素衡量,这些因素则取决于影响资产报酬的行为因素,而 CAPM 的风险只取决于整体市场报酬这一单一因素。

多 β 模型的风险因素包含所有无法分散的风险。

The risk-free (also known as the nominal, or quoted) rate of interest consists of two elements: (1) a real inflation-free rate of return, r^*, and (2) an inflation premium, IP, equal to the anticipated rate of inflation. As the expected rate of inflation increases, a higher premium must be added to the real risk-free rate to compensate for the loss of purchasing power that results from inflation.

The level of risk aversion reflects to the risk premium and, the slope of the SML. The greater the investor's aversion to risk, the steeper slope of the line, greater the risk premium for the security, and the higher required rate of return on the security.

Many factors can affect a company's beta. When the beta changes, the required rate of return also changes. A firm can influence its market risk, its beta, through changing the composition of its assets and debt. A company's beta can also change by external factors such as increasing competition in its industry, the expiration of patents.

The goal of financial mangement is to maximize the stock price, which is determined by the riskiness of the firm's security, and the relevant risk of any physical asset assessed by investors.

Some studies have raised concerns about the validity of the CAPM. Fama and French (1992) found there is no historical relationship between stocks' returns and their market betas. They found two variables which are consistently related to stock returns: (1) a firm's size and (2) its market/book ratio. After adjusting for other factors, they found that smaller firms have relatively high returns, and that returns are higher on stocks with low market/book ratios. By contrast, after controlling firm size and market/book ratios, they found no relationship between a stock's beta and its return.

As an alternative to the traditional CAPM, researchers and practitioners have begun to study on the general multi-beta model that challenge the CAPM model.

In the multi-beta model, market risk is measured relative to a set of factors that determine the asset returns, whereas the CAPM measures risk only relative to the market return. The risk factors in the multi-beta model are all nondiversifiable sources of risk.

第7章　资金的时间价值

- 了解利率的意义
- 了解利率的组成要素
- 了解利率的计算
- 计算货币的时间价值

票面上的钱在不同的时间有不同的价值？这意味着我们所见的钱币数额在不同的时间有不同的购买力。货币供给者与需求者以利率为代价进行借贷，以满足在不同时间彼此的需求，因此造成货币在不同时间具有不同价值。本章将逐步介绍利率与其组成要素和计算方法，最后应用货币的时间价值来了解我们日常生活中的投资理财（见图7-1）。

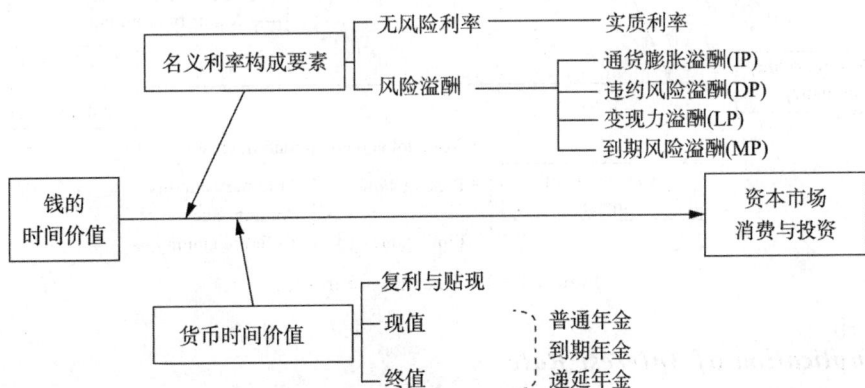

图 7-1　学习架构

7.1　利率的意义

利率是指资金的成本或资金的价格，由资金的供给与需求的函数决定。

Chapter 7　Time Value of Money

Learning Outcomes

- Understand the significance of interest rate
- Understand the components of interest rate
- Realize the calculation of interest rate
- Calculate the time value of money

Nominal money has different value at different times? This means there exists different purchasing power of the same amount of money at different times. Money demand and supply transact at the price of interest rate to meet the needs of borrower and lender at different times which results time value of money. This chapter introduces interest as well as its elements and calculation, followed by the application of the time value of money to investments of our daily life(see Figure 7 - 1).

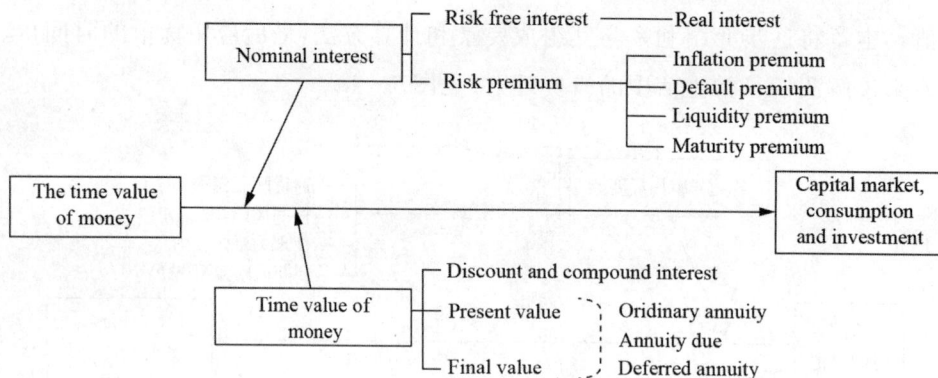

Figure 7 - 1　Learning sturcture

7.1　Implication of Interest Rate

An interest rate is the cost or the price of capital, which is determined by the function of money supply and demand. Interest rate goes high when there is high demand of money, interest rate goes low when money is over-supply. Central Bank of a country has its policy to adjust the interest rate by controlling money supply on the market, so the interest rate affects financial markets significantly.

当利率水准高时,表示资金需求高,当利率水准低时,表明市场上资金较充裕。一国的中央银行往往会对利率作一些政策性的管制和调整,来调节市场上的货币供给,因此利率因素对财务金融市场影响较大。

1. 有效利率

有效利率是以年利率表示借贷时所实现收付的利率。

名义利率会因利率的计算方式(单利计算或复利计算)及计算的时间基础(每天、每月或每年)不同,使得实际收付的利率有所不同,这就是有效利率不同于名义利率的原因。

2. 名义利率

名义利率指一般借贷契约或债券上所载明的利率,为借贷双方或债券发行人据以计算利息的基础。

名义利率与有效利率的差异在于前者是一年利息滚利一次,后者视一年滚利的次数,来决定期末本利和,总和再减掉期初值,就是有效年利率。

有效利率 i 与名义利率 r 的换算公式如下:

$$i = \left(1 + \frac{r}{m}\right)^m - 1$$

式中: m 为一年滚利的次数。

3. 实质利率

名义利率减去通货膨胀率,即为实质利率。其公式为

$$名义利率 = 实质利率 + 物价上涨率$$

一般我们看到的利率(例如银行定存的储蓄率)就是名义利率。换言之,要获得实质利率需要将名义利率扣除物价上涨率。还有:

$$物价上涨率 = \frac{物价指数}{100} - 1$$

举例来说:如果名义利率是 13%,物价指数为 103,那么物价上涨率就是 $\frac{103}{100} - 1 = 0.03$,实质利率就是 $0.13 - 0.03 = 0.1 = 10\%$。

名义利率和实质利率的差别在于:名义利率是随物价涨跌而变化的利率,实质利率则不因物价的波动而变化。

7.2 利率的决定因素

利率的决定因素如下式所示(见图 7-2):

1. Effective interest rate

Effective interest rate expresses as annual interest rate to demonstrate a payment rate of loan.

The nominal interest rate is different from the effective interest rate because of the different way (simple interest or compound interest) and the different duration (daily, monthly, or yearly), these cause the actual payment rates vary. This is the reason why sometimes the nominal interest rate differs from effective interest rate.

2. Nominal interest rate

Nominal interest rate refers to the stated interest rate stated in the loan contract or bond, for lenders and borrowers to caculate the interest.

The difference between nominal interest rate and the effective interest rate comes from the the distinction that the former is a rolling interest return once a year, the latter is determined by the rolling times a year to calculate the final amount of return. The return substract the initial interest rate becomes the effective annual interest rate.

The conversion formulas of effective interest rate i and nominal interest rate r is as follows:

$$i = \left(1 + \frac{r}{m}\right)^m - 1$$

Wherer: m refers to the rolling times a year.

3. Real interest rate

The real interest rate is the nominal interest rate minus the inflation rate. The formula is

$$\text{nominal interest rate} = \text{real interest rate} + \text{inflation rate}$$

In general, the interest rate we saw on a banking billboard is the nominal interest rate (for example, the bank deposit savings rate). In other words, the real interest rate is nominal interest rate deduct the inflation rate. The formula is

$$\text{inflation rate} = \frac{\text{price index}}{100} - 1$$

For example: Nominal interest rate is 13%, price index is 103, then the price inflation is $(103/100) - 1 = 0.03$, the real interest rate is $0.13 - 0.03 = 0.1 = 10\%$.

The difference between real interest rate and nominal interest rate is that the nominal interest rate is the interest rate rises or falls with the price index, the real interest rate does not change along with the fluctuation of the price index.

7.2 *Factors of Interest Rate*

The factors of interest rate have the formula like this(see figure 7 - 2):

名义利率(R)＝实质无风险利率(r')＋通货膨胀溢酬(IP)

$\qquad$＋违约风险溢酬(DP)＋流动性溢酬(LP)＋到期风险溢酬(MP)

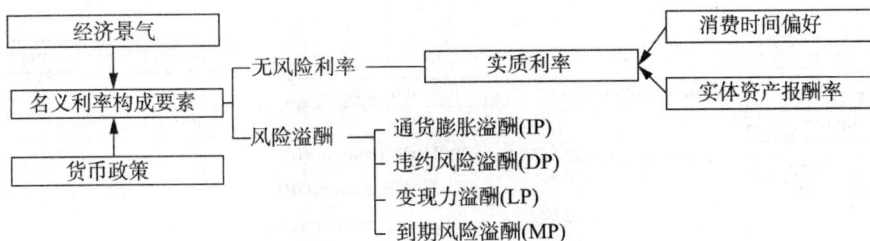

图 7 - 2　利率的决定因素

1. 实质无风险利率

在无通货膨胀预期下,存在无风险证券利率(r')。无风险利率指完全没有风险的利率,即没有违约风险、到期风险、流动风险及通货膨胀的风险。因为现实中并不存在无风险证券,所以无法观察到真实的无风险利率。然而,有一种证券近似无风险证券,即美国国库券。通常政府债券没有违约、流动和到期风险。

2. 名义无风险利率

名义无风险利率(R)为实质无风险利率(r')加上预期通货膨胀溢酬。

3. 通货膨胀溢酬

由于通货膨胀会降低货币的实质购买力和投资的真实报酬率,故资金供给者会要求通货膨胀溢酬(IP)作为补偿。

在计算名义利率时,一般采用的是未来的预期通货膨胀率,而非过去已发生的实际通货膨胀率。计算公式:

$$IP = \frac{CPI_t - CPI_{t-1}}{CPI_{t-1}}$$

式中:CPI 表示消费价格指数。

4. 预期报酬率与风险溢酬

预期报酬率指对于任一投资商品或投资组合,所预期或估计的在未来某一段时间之内所能获取的报酬率。

风险溢酬为预期报酬率减掉无风险利率后的差(代表承担风险可以得到

$$\text{Nominal interest rate}(R) = \text{Risk-free interest rate}(r') + \text{Inflation premium}(\text{IP})$$
$$+ \text{The default premium}(\text{DP})$$
$$+ \text{Liquidity premium}(\text{LP}) + \text{Maturity premium }(\text{MP})$$

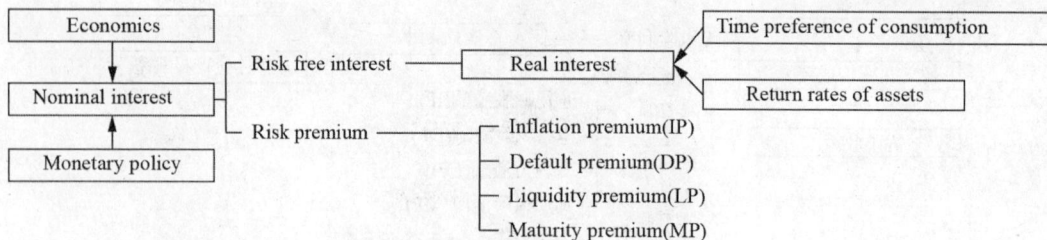

Figure 7 – 2　Factors of interest rate

1. Real risk-free interest rate

The a risk-free interest rate r' is an interest rate without the expectation of inflation. Risk-free interest rate is interest rate without any risk. There is no default risk, maturity risk, liquidity risk and inflation risk in the risk-free interest rate. However, there is no risk-free security. It is impossible to get the real risk-free rate. There is a security which is almost a risk-free security, it is United States Treasury bills. There is no default, liquidity, and maturity risks on the US government bond.

2. Nominal risk-free rate

Nominal risk-free rate(R) equals r' adds expect inflation premium (IP).

3. Inflation premium

Inflation would reduce the real purchasing power of currency and the real rate of return on investment, thus money supplier will ask inflation premium (IP) as risk compensation.

When calculating the nominal interest rate, we use the expected inflation rate rather than the actual inflation rate that has occurred in the past.

$$\text{IP} = \frac{\text{CPI}_t - \text{CPI}_{t-1}}{\text{CPI}_{t-1}}$$

Where, CPI is Consumer price index.

4. Expected rate of return and risk premium

Expected rate of return means that the rate of return will happen within a certain period of time in the future on the investment or portfolio.

The risk premium refers to the amount of the expected rate of return minus the risk-free interest rate (compensation on risk).

For example, you have a set of portfolios, you estimate the expected rate of return

的补偿）。

预期报酬率与风险溢酬的相互关系如下：例如你有一组投资组合，且估计出它的预期报酬率为 10％；而你在投资时当下的定存利率为 2％（即不用冒任何风险即可得到的报酬为"无风险利率"），所以风险溢酬即为 10％－2％＝8％，也就是你愿意承担投资组合的风险所换来的报酬。

5. 违约风险溢酬

借款人不能按时支付贷款的利息或本金，叫作违约，而投资人所必须承担的此种风险称为违约风险。违约风险溢酬指到期日、变现力和其他特性相同的公司债与国库券彼此之间利率的差距。公司倒闭概率愈高，其债券等级愈低，违约风险溢酬就愈高。

违约风险指不付利息与本金的风险。借款人对贷款的违约风险，也会影响证券的市场利率。违约风险愈高，贷款者所要求的利率也愈高。美国政府公债由于没有违约风险，所以其利率在所有可课税证券中最低。对公司债而言，债券等级愈高则违约风险愈低，一般而言其利率也较低。与政府公债有相同到期日及流动性的公司债券，它们和政府公债的利率差距，就是所谓的"违约风险溢酬"。可将违约风险理解为借款人可能无法如期支付本息的风险。而投资人对可能的违约风险所要求的补偿，称为违约风险溢酬。

例如卡债，如果借款人未能按时支付贷款的利息或本金，这时对银行来说就会有违约风险。违约风险溢酬的估算方式：

违约风险溢酬（DP）＋流动性溢酬（LP）＝公司债利率－政府公债利率

案例 ▶▶▶▶▶▶

2008 年，由于中国内地紧缩赴澳门的许可，去澳门旅游的人士锐减，因此澳门的博彩控股有限公司（以下简称澳博）面临着客人数量下降、竞争激烈、收入减少的局面。此外，美国的次级按揭贷款问题亦影响到澳门银行对澳博的融资，澳博的流动资产因而减少，所以其股票发行上市后股价不断下滑。虽然到当年 12 月时新葡京开幕，吸引了部分市民投资，澳博的股票价格升到约 2 元的价位，但是市民仍惧怕次贷风暴的影响，所以投资的股民大多要求较高的违约风险溢酬。金莎赌场结束营业更导致澳门的娱乐博彩业进入紧张的状态，许多银行对澳博的融资重新做出评估，这一情况对澳门博彩控股有限公司的影响更大，因为投资者对博彩业市场欠缺投资信心和动力，投资者对未来的不明朗因素采取保守的态度，投资者觉得投资这一类市场的

for 10% and the present deposit rates at 2% (that is risk-free interest rate), the risk premium is 10% ~ 2% = 8%. That is the risk premium for your risk.

5. The default risk premium

Default is caused when a borrower fails to pay the interest or principal of a loan. Investors take this risk as default risk.

Default risk premium means the difference between corporate bond and treasury bills with the same maturity, liquidity and other properties.The higher probability of a company collapse, the lower its bond rating, the higher the default risk premium.

Default risk refers to the risk of unpaid interest and principal payments. The interest rates of capital market will be influenced by risk of borrower's default.The higher the interest rate required by lenders if the default risk is higher. The lowest rates on all taxable securities is the United States Government bonds because there is no default risk. The higher rating, the lower risk of default for corporate bonds.In general,the interest rate is lower. The default risk premium can be treated as the difference between corporate bond and government bonds with the same maturity and liquidity. This can be understood that default risk is the compensation required by investors if the borrower may not be able to pay the principal and interest on time. The compensation can be treated as the premium of default risk.

Take Credit card debt as an example, the default risk of a bank happens when a borrower can not pay the interest or principal of his/her loan. The formula is as follows:

The default risk premium (DP) + Liquidity premium (LP)

= Corporate bond interest rates − government bonds interest rate

Case ▶▶▶▶▶▶

The amount of tourists to Macau drop sharply because Chinese Mainland tightened the policy of travelling to Macau. This lead that SJM faced a decline in the number of customers. Less revenue, more competition, and the subprime loan problem in the United States affected the bank financing of SJM. SJM's current assets reduced that lead the company's stock price continued to drop. Although the grand opening of the new Grand Lisboa attracted some investments to raise its stock price to 2. The investors were still worry about the effect of the subprime mortgage crisis, such that most of the investors required a higher default risk premium. The close of business of Ferrero Rocher Casino lead Macau entertainment gambting industry into a tension situation. Many banks in Macau re-assessed all financing of gambling listed company. SJM holding limited was effected more because investors lack of investment confidence and motivation on gambling industry. Investors take conservative attitude in the future because of uncertainty factors. Investors thought that investment risk was increasing, so investors required higher returns/interest rate on SJM's stock/bonds. Investors thought that the case of Ferrero Rocher Casino might happen to SJM one day. The case of Ferrero

风险增加了,所以这时投资者对与澳博相关的股票/债券等都会要求较高的利率报酬,他们生怕澳博旗下的其他赌场或其他公司的赌场会有一天步上金莎赌场的后尘。因为在金莎赌场这一例子中,投资澳博等公司的永续债券无法兑成有用的资产或现金,而现时以澳博的情况亦只能接受投资者的要求来筹集资金,作为违约风险溢酬。·

6. 变现力溢酬(流动性溢酬)

任何资产若能在短期间内就被卖成现金,且变卖价格至少和原始买进价格相去不远,则该资产具有高度的变现力或流动性。对于一些变现力不高的证券,投资人会要求变现力溢酬作为补偿。

所谓高度变现力的资产,是指变现价格可预期的资产,因此,它可以在短期内转换为一定数额的现金以支付各项费用。对于政府公债、股票及公司债而言,流动性较高,而小公司证券的流动性较低。假如证券缺乏变现力,则投资人在估计证券的市场利率时,会加上变现力溢酬(LP)。

案例 ▶▶▶▶▶▶

澳门博彩娱乐公司(澳门博彩控股有限公司)的财务报表如图7-3所示。从资料内容来看,公司的现金与负债(长期负债+短期负债)对于应付短期负债的问题资金来说仍相当充裕,所以在短期内的流动性高。而从流动比率来看,公司仍有能力偿还短期的债务,因此投资者对其股票所要求的溢酬会降低。

澳门博彩控股有限公司(0880.H.K)

最新资料		会计资料		盈利	
52周最高	3210	每股账面值	NA	边际利润率	4.77%
52周最低	1200	每股盈利	0.408900		
		短期负债	134.0M	其他比率	
股票相关资料		长期负债	5303.0M	资产回报	8.50%
市值	8150000000	现金	6683.0M	股东权益回报	24.09%
已发行股数	5000.0M			流动比率	127%
		估值比率		长期负债/股东权益	83.32%
股息资料		股价/账面值	NA	债项/股东权益	85.42%
股息	NA	市盈率	3.99		
股息率	NA%	派息比率	NA%		
		损益表资料			
		纯利	1534.0M		
		销售额	321147.0M		

图7-3 澳门博彩控股有限公司财务报表截图

Rocher Casino caused perpetual bonds of the gmbling industry hard to cash into current assets or cash，SJM can only accepted the demand of investors to pay default risk premium for fundraising.

6. Liquidity premium

The liquidity of an asset means that the asset can be sold for cash in a short period，and the bids price is closed to the offers price.Investors would ask for liquidity premium as compensation of low liquidity of securities.

High liquidity assets refers to the assets realization prices can be expected，so it can be cashed into a certain amount of cash in a short time to cover required expenses. Government bonds，stocks and corporate bonds have high liquidity. Liquidity of small company securities is low. Investors will add the liquidity premium if the securities lack of liquidity.

Case ▷▷▷▷▷▷

SJM's financial statements was shown in Figure 7 - 3. The company's cash and debt（long-term debt + short-term debt）from the statements show high liquidity in the short term to cope with short-term debt，and the current ratio the company still has the ability to repay short-term debt，thus the premium of its stock required by investors lower.

SJM(0880.H.K)					
Newest Data		Accounting Data		Earnings	
Highest-52 weeks	3,210	Book value per share	NA	Profit margins	4.77%
Lowest-52 weeks	1,200	EPS	0.4089		
		Short-term debts	134.0M	Other ratios	
Stock Data		Long-term debts	5,303.0M	ROA	8.50%
Market value	8, 150,000,000	Cash	6,683.0M	ROE	24.09%
Issued shares	5,000.0M			Current ratio	127%
		Value ratios		Long debts/Equity	83.32%
Dividend Data		P/B ratio	NA	Liabilities/Equity	85.42%
Dividends	NA	P/E ratio	3.99		
Dividend ratio	NA%	Dividend ratio	NA%		
		Income statement data			
		Net profit	1,534.0M		
		Sales	32,1147.0M		

Figure 7 - 3　Financial statements of SJM

7. 到期风险溢酬

利率风险指由于利率上升而使购买长期债券的投资人遭受损失的风险。到期风险溢酬就是对投资人负担利率风险的一种补偿。

美国财政部发行证券没有违约风险,因为可确定联邦政府会对它所发行的公债支付利息,而且到期时会赎回,因此,政府债券的违约风险溢酬必为零。此外,政府债券有活络的交易市场,所以变现力溢酬也接近于零。至于到期风险则会因债券到期日的不同而不同。

对于长期债券,到期风险指利率风险。由于利率与债券价格呈反向变动,即若利率上升,则债券价格下跌。所谓利率风险指利率上升造成债券价格下跌的损失。一般而言,债券到期日愈长,利率风险愈高,所以,到期风险溢酬必须包括在必要报酬率中,以反映由于到期日增加而产生的利率风险。如果我们比较期间不同但票面利率相同的债券价格对利率变动的敏感性,可发现期间越长的债券,对利率变动的敏感性越高,此时投资人要面对较高的利率变动风险。

对于短期债券,到期风险指再投资风险,即当短期票券到期,所回收之资金须再投资的反复操作,故随着利率的下降,将迫使回收资金以较低的利息再投资,导致利息所得下降。票面利率高的债券比起票面利率低的债券有较高的再投资风险。

7.3　资金时间价值

"货币的时间价值"用以表示时间和货币之间的关系,例如:今天的一元钱和明天的一元钱并不相同,因为今天投资这一元钱可从这项投资中获取明天可得的一元加上利息。现在的货币由于可以作为投资孳息之用,故其价值大于未来等额的货币。从这种意义上可以说:货币只有进入生产周转过程才能实现增值,才具有时间价值。货币若没有随时间的推移而实现增值,即意味着机会成本的损失或货币的贬值。

财务经理必须协助管理部门对这种因不同时间点所产生的金钱价值的差异做出比较,才可能使决策者制定出合理的投资决策、融资政策以及红利支付等,以求最大化公司未来营运的盈余利润,及最小化所负担的风险。

1. 利息的性质

利息即使用货币所支付的代价,亦即收得或偿还的现金超过原始借出或

7. Maturity risk premium

Interest rate risk refers to the loss that price of a long-term bond goes down because of the raise of interest rates. The risk premium is the compensation of investors'risk of interest rate.

The United States treasury security has no risk of default because the Federal Government will pay interest on its debt, and redeem the bond at maturity, therefore the default risk premium of government bonds will be zero. In addition, the government bonds have active trading market, so the maturity risk premium is close to zero as well.

The maturity risk of bond varies with different maturities of the bonds: Long-term debt exposes to the interest rate risk. Reverse changes happen between interest rate and bond price. Interest rate rises, bond price falls. The interest rate risk refers to the falling of bond price due to the rise of interest rate. In general, the longer maturity, the higher risk of a bond. Maturity risk premium must be included in the required rate of return to reflect the higher risk because of the longer maturity. Comparing bonds with different maturity with the same coupon rate, we can find the longer maturity, the higher price sensitivity, investors expose to higher risk of changes in interest rate.

Short-term debt expose to the re-investment risk. When a short-term bill due, we want to reinvest the money after redeeming from a bill. If interest rate falls, the income from interest will reduce because of a reinvestment. A higher coupon rate of bill has a higher reinvestment risk than a lower coupon rate of bill.

7.3 Time Value of Money

"Time value of money" is used to express the relationship between time and money. For example: One dollar has different value in different time because we can invest one dollar to gain interest from this investment. Current money can be invested to gain investment yields, so its value is greater than the same amount of money in the future. This imply that the money need to invest into the production process to gain value, which is the time value of money. Money without gaining value over time means the loss of the cost of opportunity or the depreciation of money.

A financial manager shall assist the company to compute the monetary value at different times for decision makers to work out reasonable investment decision, financing policy as well as the dividend payment. Only by doing so that the company can maximize the company's future operating earnings and minimize the operating risk.

1. The nature of the interest

Interest is the price of using money. That is the return amount exceeds the original

借入的金额部分。而利息的计算取决于本金、利率和时间三个变数。本金指借款或投资金额；利率指流通在外的本金的某一个百分比；时间指流通在外本金的年数或不足一年的期间。其公式为

$$利息＝本金×利率×期间$$

2. 利率的组成要素

如何选定适当的利率？通常会考量下列三项因素。

(1) 纯利率

纯利率(r')指在没有违约风险且预期没有通货膨胀的情形下出借人所要求的代价。

(2) 预期通货膨胀率

预期通货膨胀率为实质利率与通货膨胀溢酬之和($r'＋IP$)。出借人认为处于通货膨胀下，未来所收回货币之价值必然较低，因此必须提高利率以弥补购买力的损失。

(3) 信用风险率

信用风险率定义为

$$信用风险率＝r'＋IP＋DP＋LP＋MP$$

政府公债没有任何信用风险，但私人企业则依其财务稳定性、获利能力等因素而有不同程度的信用风险。

3. 单利

单利指仅依据本金金额来计算利息，利息不滚入本金再生利息（如果利息滚入本金再生利息，则为复利）。

令 P 为本金，i 为利率，n 为期间，假设 $P＝10000$ 元，$i＝12\%$，$n＝3$ 年，则三年的利息总共为 $10000×12\%×3＝3600$(元)(见图 7-4)。

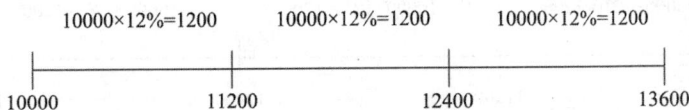

图 7-4　单利计算

例 7-1　设 $i＝15\%$，借入 1000 元，借款期间为 3 年，则三年共计支付多少利息？

解　$1000×15\%×3＝450$(元)

amount of a loan. Calculation of interest depends on the following three variables. Principle: amount of a loan or an investment. Interest: percentage of circulating principle. Time: time of circulating principle. Then we have

$$\text{Interest} = \text{Principal} \times \text{Interest rate} \times \text{During}$$

2. Elements of interest rate

How to select an appropriate rate? We usually take into account the following three factors.

(1) Real interest rate

Real interest rate (r') is the cost required by lenders without default risk and expected inflation.

(2) Expected inflation rate

Expected inflation rate = r' + IP. Lenders believe that inflation cause the less return of their lending money, thus they require for the loss of purchasing power because of inflation.

(3) Credit risk rate

$$\text{Credit risk rate} = r' + \text{IP} + \text{DP} + \text{LP} + \text{MP}$$

There is no credit risk of government bond, but private company has various credit risk according to its financial stability, profitability and other factors of credit risk.

3. Simple interest

Simple interest calculates interest based only on the principal amount, interest is not rolled into the principal to regenerate interest (it is the compound interest if interests rolled into the principal).

Let P is the principal, i is the interest rate, n is the period, assuming $P = 10,000$, $i = 12\%$, $n = 3$ years, A total interest for three years is $10,000 \times 12\% \times 3 = 3,600$ (see Figure 7 - 4).

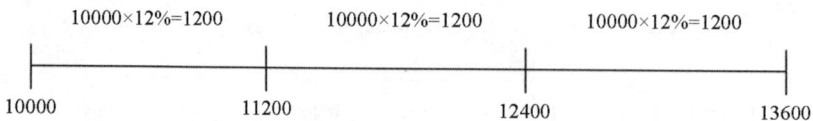

Figure 7 - 4   Calculation of simple interest

Example 7 - 1   If $i = 15\%$, principle = 1,000, loan periods are 3 years, then the total interest payment for three years is

Solution $1,000 \times 15\% \times 3 = 450$

例 7 - 2　设 $i=15\%$，借入 1000 元，借款期间为 3 个月，则三个月共计支付多少利息？

解　$1000 \times 15\% \times 3/12 = 37.5$（元）

单利法通常应用于一年或一年以下的短期投资及债券。

4. 复利

（1）复利的定义和计算

复利指每年利息的计算以原始本金为基础，加上利息继续滚入本金再生利息。复利有如下的特性：期间在两期之上；本金在本期所衍生的利息会加入本金继续于次期衍生新的利息。

令 P 为本金，i 为利率，n 为期间，则

$$利息 = 到期值 - P = P \times (1+i)^n - P = P[(1+i)^n - 1]$$

例 7 - 3　假设 P 为 10000 元，i 为 12%，期间 n 为三年，每年复利一次，如图 7 - 5 所示，有

$$利息 = 1200 + 1344 + 1505 = 4049（元）$$

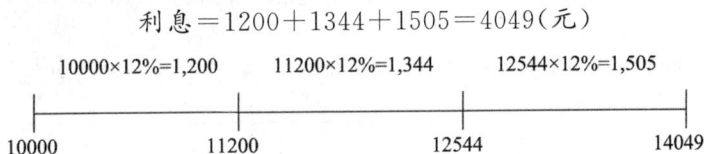

图 7 - 5　复利计算

复利的有效（年）利率为

$$\frac{P[(1+i)^n - 1]}{Pn} = \frac{(1+i)^n - 1}{n}$$

当 i 为 12%，n 为三年时，复利的有效（年）利率大于 12%。

（2）复利的频率

复利的频率不同，则有效利率与名义利率亦有所不同。

$$有效利率（effective\ yield） = (1+i)^n - 1$$

例 7 - 4　设票面利率为 8%，假设每年复利一次，计算其有效利率。

解　有效利率 $= (1+8\%)^1 - 1 = 8\%$

例 7 - 5　设票面利率为 8%，假设每季度复利一次，计算其有效利率。

解　有效利率 $= [1+(8\%/4)]^4 - 1 = 8.24\%$

由上面的例子可知，每年的复利期数若超过一次，则有效利率会大于名义利率。

（3）复利的终值

复利的终值指将某特定时点的金钱价值复利成为未来特定时点的金钱价值（复利就是将今天的价值转换成为终值的过程），即指货币在未来特定时点的价值，包括了货币的时间价值。

假设现在存入一笔本金，按复利计息，经过数期之后，其本金与利息之和即为复利终值（简称 FV）。若现在存入 10000 元利率 8% 的 3 年期定期存款，

Example 7 - 2 If $i = 15\%$, principle $= 1,000$, loan periods are 3 yuan months, then the total interest payment for three months is

- **Solution** $1000 \times 15\% \times 3/12 = 37.5$

Simple interest method should normally be used for 1 year or or less than 1 year of short-term investments and bonds.

4. Compound interest

(1) Definition and calculation of compound interest

Compound interest is the calculation of annual interest based on the original principal, interest continues to roll into the new principal to generate interest.

Let P is the principal, i is the interest rate, n is the period, then

Compound interest $=$ Maturity value $- P = P \times (1+i)^n - P = P[(1+i)^n - 1]$

Example 7 - 3 Let principal(P) is 10,000 yuan, interest rate(i) is 12%, period (n) is three years. Assume compounded once a year, we have (see Figure 7 - 5):

Interest $= 1,200 + 1,344 + 1,505 = 4,049$(yuan)

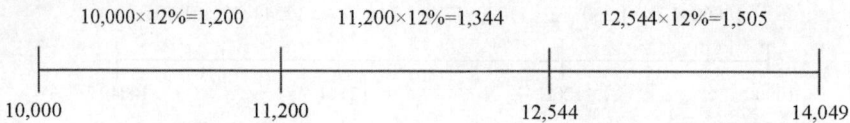

Figure 7 - 5   Calculation of compound interest

$$\text{effective(years)interest rate} = \frac{P[(1+i)^n - 1]}{Pn} = \frac{(1+i)^n - 1}{n} > 12\%$$

(2) The frequency of compounding interest

Frequency of compounding is different, the effective interest rate and the nominal interest rate are also different.

Nominal interest rate (stated interest rate or bank interest rate) $= i$

Effective interest rate (effective yield) $= (1+i)^n - 1$

Example 7 - 4 Coupon rate 8%, if compounded once a year, its effective rate is:

Solution $(1 + 8\%)^1 - 1 = 8\%$

Example 7 - 5 Coupon rate 8%, if compounded once a quarter, its effective rate is:

Solution $[1 + (8\%/4)]^4 - 1 = 8.24\%$

From the foregoing examples, the effective interest rate is greater than the nominal interest rate if the number of compounding periods are more than once in a year.

(3) Compound interest final value(future value)

Compound interest final value is the future monetary value of compound interest from a particular time to the future specific time (compound interest is the process to transform today's money value to future's final value). Final value (FV) refers to the value of the currency in the future at a specific time, including the time value of money.

Assume we deposit an amount of principal at this moment, according to compound interest, the FV is the sum of the compound value of principal and interest after some

则 3 年后的终值为 12597.12 元。

现值转换成终值的过程称为复利计算。

$$终值期数＝现值×(1＋利率)$$

即
$$FV＝P×FVIF_{i,n}$$

$$FVIF_{i,n}(复利终值因子)＝(1＋i)^n$$

由上面的公式我们可知,终值和本金、利率、期数都呈正比关系(见图 7-6)。

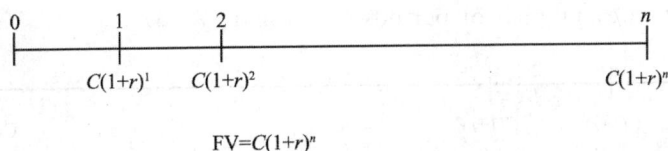

$$FV＝C(1＋r)^n$$

图 7-6 终值和本金、利率、期数的关系

例 7-6 假设第一年初存入 10000 元,每年计息一次,年息 12％,期限三年,则其终值为多少?若改为半年计息一次则终值为多少?

解 每年计息:
$$终值＝10000×FVIF_{12％,3}＝14049(元)$$

半年计息:
$$终值＝10000×FVIF_{6％,6}＝14850(元)$$

(4)复利的现值

复利的现值是在某特定时点(过去或未来)的金钱价值折合成目前的金钱价值,而"折现"就是将复利的概念反推,求得过去某时点上实际的金钱价值。

假设目前存入一笔本金,按复利计息,经过数期之后,其本金与利息之和折算至目前的价值即为复利现值(简称 PV)。其定义如图 7-7 所示,公式如下:

$$PV＝P×PVIF_{i,n}$$

$$PVIF_{i,n}(复利现值因子)＝\frac{1}{(1＋i)^n}$$

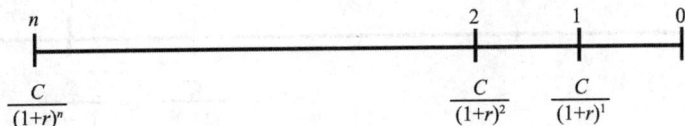

$$PV＝\frac{C}{(1＋r)^n}$$

图 7-7 复利现值定义

例 7-7 假设第一年初存入一笔本金,每年计息一次,年息 12％,期限

periods of time. Deposit 10,000 at the present, interest rate is 8%, 3-year term deposits, the final value is 12,597.12 after 3 years.

Present value converted to the final value is called compound interest calculation.

$$\text{Final value} = \text{Present value} \times (1 + \text{Interest rate})$$

That is

$$FV = P \times FVIF_{i,n}$$

$$FVIF_{i,n} \text{ (final value interest factor)} = (1 + i)^n$$

From the formula above, we can see that the final value is proportional to the principal, interest rate, number of periods (see Figure 7 – 6).

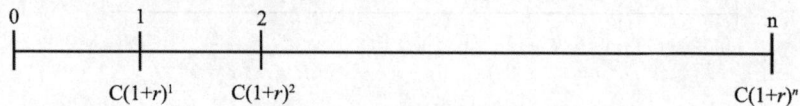

$$FV = C(1+r)^n$$

Figure 7 – 6　Calculation of final value

Example 7 – 6　Assume the deposit 10,000 in the first year, interest on an annual basis, annual interest rate is 12%, and period is three years. What is the final value? If interest on six months, what is the final value?

Solution　Interest on annual basis:

the final value $= 10000 \times FVIF_{12\%,3} = 14049$

Interest on six months:

the future value $= 10000 \times FVIF_{6\%,6} = 14850$

(4) Present value of compound interest (present value)

Present value is the present monetary value converted from an amount of money in a specific time (past or future). Discounted cash is the monetary value in the present that is the reverse perspective of compound interest final value.

Assume we deposit an amount of principal according to compound interest, after several periods, the sum of the principal and interest converted to the present value is the present value (PV) of compound interest (see Figure 7 – 7).

$$PV = P \times PVIF_{i,n}$$

$$PVIF_{i,n} \text{ (present value interest factor)} = \frac{1}{(1 + i)^n}$$

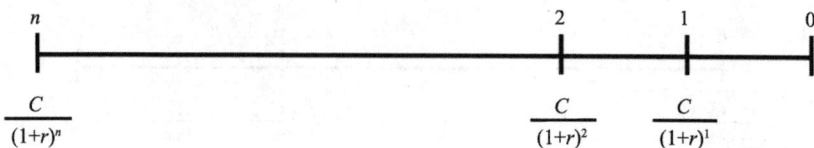

$$PV = \frac{C}{(1+r)^n}$$

Figure 7 – 7　Calculation of present value

Example 7 – 7　Assume we deposit an amount of principal in the first year, interest on an annual basis, annual interest rate is 12%, and the final value is 10,000 after a

三年后本利和为 10000 元,请问第一年初存入之本金为多少?

解　现值 $=10000 \times \text{PVIF}_{12\%,3} = 7118$(元)

例 7-8　求算期数 n。假设有效利率为 $i = 10\%$,目前存入一笔款项为 47811 元,待累积到 70000 元时用以购买机器设备,试问该笔资金须存入几年?

解　(1) 终值法

$$47811 \times \text{FVIF}_{10\%,n} = 70000$$

$$\text{FVIF}_{10\%,n} = \frac{70000}{47811} = 1.46410$$

经查复利终值表得知须存入 4 年。

(2) 现值法

$$70000 \times \text{PVIF}_{10\%,n} = 47811$$

$$\text{PVIF}_{10\%,n} = \frac{47811}{70000} = 0.68301$$

经查复利现值表得知须存入 4 年。

例 7-9　求算利率(插补法的运用)。若存款 2000 元,每年计息 2 次,10 年后本利和为 5000 元,试求存款利率。

解

$$2000 = 5000 \times \text{PVIF}_{i,20}$$

则　$PVIF_{i,20} = \dfrac{2000}{5000} = 0.4$

经查复利现值表,期数为 20 期时,并未找到现值因子刚好为 0.4 的利率,故利用插补法求算,找到现值因子介于利率 $4.5\% \sim 5\%$($\text{PVIF}_{4\%,20} = 0.4564$ 与 $\text{PVIF}_{5\%,20} = 0.376889$),则

$$\frac{i - 0.04}{0.05 - 0.04} = \frac{0.4 - 0.4564}{0.376889 - 0.4564}$$

$$\Rightarrow \frac{i - 0.04}{0.01} = \frac{0.0564}{0.0795}$$

$$\Rightarrow i = 0.0469$$

实际利率为 9.38%(0.0469×2),因为是半年计息一次,上式得出的 4.69% 为半年期的利率,所以应再将其还原为年利率。

5. 年金

所谓年金指连续定期支付(或收取)定额的给付。每期相隔的时间相等,

period of three years. What is the amount of principal in the first year?

Solution   present value $= 10000 \times \mathrm{PVIF}_{12\%,3} = 7118(\mathrm{yuan})$

Example 7 - 8   Solving unknown periods(n).

Assuming effective interest rate $i = 10\%$, we deposit a principal 47,811 yuan now, we will purchase machinery and equipment when the principal and interest accumulate to 70,000 yuan. How many years should be the principal deposited?

Solution   (1) Final value method

$$47,811 \times \mathrm{FVIF}_{10\%,n} = 70000$$

$$\mathrm{FVIF}_{10\%,n} = \frac{70000}{47811} = 1.46410$$

It need 4 years to accumulate to this amount after we check the compound interest table.

(2) Present value method

$$70000 \times \mathrm{PVIF}_{10\%,n} = 47811$$

$$\mathrm{PVIF}_{10\%,n} = \frac{47811}{70000} = 0.68301$$

It needs 4 years to discount to this amount after we check the compound interest table.

Example 7 - 9   Solving unknown calculate interest rate (application of the interpolation method).

If we deposit 2,000 yuan, interest paid twice a year, the amount is 5,000 yuan after ten years. What is the interest rate?

$$2000 = 5000 \times \mathrm{PVIF}_{i,20}$$

then

$$\mathrm{PVIF}_{i,20} = \frac{2000}{5000} = 0.4$$

Check the compound interest table, we failed to find the interest of the present value factor is 0.4 for periods of 20. So we use the interpolation method to do the calculation. We found that the interest rate is between $4.5\% \sim 5\%$ ($\mathrm{PVIF}_{4\%,20} = 0.4564$ and $\mathrm{PVIF}_{5\%,20} = 0.376889$), then

$$\frac{i - 0.04}{0.05 - 0.04} = \frac{0.4 - 0.4564}{0.376889 - 0.4564}$$

$$\Rightarrow \frac{i - 0.04}{0.01} = \frac{0.0564}{0.0795}$$

$$\Rightarrow i = 0.0469$$

Real interest rate is $9.38\%(0.0469 \times 2)$ because we can calculate the annual interest rate based on interest paid every six months for 4.69%.

5. Annuity

Annuity means continuous periodic payment (or charge). Each period of time is equal, the amount of the payment is also equal. Three conditions are essential for the

支付的金额也相等。依年金的定义,必须符合三项条件:(1)每期所支付或收取的金额相同;(2)各次支付或收款所隔的时间固定;(3)每次支付或收款时计算复利一次。

年金按其各期支付的情况不同可分为普通年金、期初年金及递延年金等三种。

(1) 普通年金的终值

普通年金的终值指一项年金各期支付金额的复利终值总和,即将每一期支付的金额,均按复利计算至最后一期期末的终值,各期复利终值之和即为该年金的终值。普通年金终值的计算公式为

$$FVA_n = PMT(1+i)^{n-1} + PMT(1+i)^{n-2} + PMT(1+i)^{n-3} + \cdots + PMT(1+i)^0$$

$$= PMT\sum_{t=1}^{n}(1+i)^{n-t}$$

式中:FVA 代表普通年金终值;PMT 代表年金每期的"支付额";i 代表复利利率;n 代表年金的期数。

下式表示每期支付 1 元,连续支付 n 期,按利率 i 复利计算的年金终值:

$$FVIFA_{i,n} = \frac{(1+i)^n - 1}{i}$$

故若每期支付年金为 PMT,则该年金的终值 FV 可用下式计算:

$$FV = PMT \times FVIFA_{i,n}$$

上述普通年金终值的概念可以用图 7-8 所示的时间线来表示。

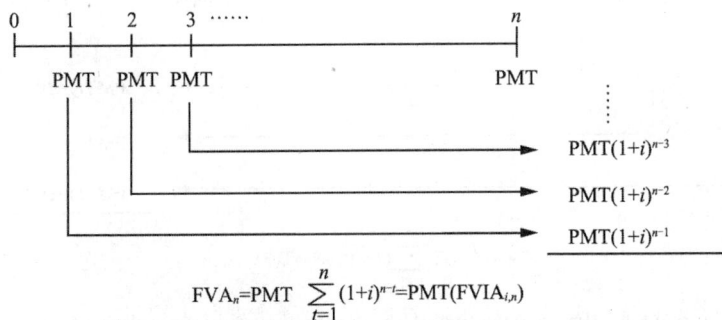

$$FVA_n = PMT\sum_{t=1}^{n}(1+i)^{n-t} = PMT(FVIA_{i,n})$$

图 7-8 普通年金终值的概念

例 7-10 假设甲公司决定在往后三年,以六个月为一期,每期期末存入

definition of an annuity: (1) Each amount of payment or charge is equal. (2) The payment or collection time (interval) is fixed. (3) Calculating compound interest once for each payment or charge.

Annuities can be divided into ordinary annuities, annuity due and deferred annuity according to their payment conditions:

(1) Amount of an Ordinary Annuity

The amount of an ordinary annuity is the sum of the final value of compound interest payments at each phase. The payment at each phase are compounded to the last end to get final value.The sum of final value at each phase is the final value of ordinary annuity.

The formula of ordinary annuity is as follows:

$$FVA_n = PMT(1+i)^{n-1} + PMT(1+i)^{n-2} + PMT(1+i)^{n-3} + \cdots + PMT(1+i)^0$$

$$= PMT \sum_{t=1}^{n} (1+i)^{n-t}$$

Where FVA is the final value of an annuity, PMT represents a payment per period, i is compounded interest rate, n represents the number of periods for an annuity.

The following formula represents payment of 1 yuan per period, continuous payments are last for n periods. The amount of an annuity is then calculated compound interest rate i to the final value of ordinary annuity.

$$FVIFA_{i,n} = \frac{(1+i)^n - 1}{i}$$

If every payment of the annuity is PMT, the future value of an annuity FV can be calculated from the equation:

$$FV = PMT \times FVIFA_{i,n}$$

The perspective of the final ualue of an ordinary annuity can be represented by the timeline (see Figure 7 - 8).

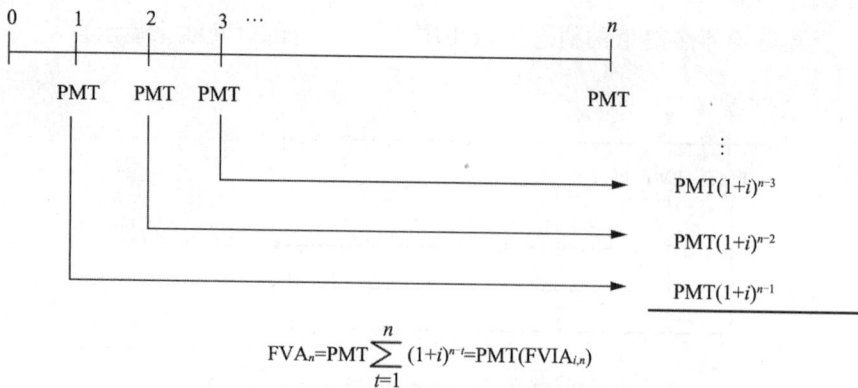

$$FVA_n = PMT \sum_{t=1}^{n} (1+i)^{n-t} = PMT(FVIA_{i,n})$$

Figure 7 - 8　The perspective of the final value of of an ordinary annuity

Example 7 - 10　If a company decides to accumulate sufficient funds to pay the debts with maturity of three years, the company is going to deposit annuity for the following 3

80000 元,以累积足够款项偿付三年后到期的债务。若年利率为 12%,计算第三年年底的存款余额。

解

$$FV = 80000 \times FVIFA_{6\%,6} = 80000 \times 6.975319$$
$$= 558026$$

例 7-11 观澜湖高尔夫球会的会员籍分为特许钻石会籍、钻石会籍、金卡会籍、绿宝石会籍和红宝石会籍,会员卡价格为 26.8 万~168 万元,不同的会籍满足不同的客户需求,从而使得客人在加入会籍时有了更多的选择。下面以红宝石会籍为例,进行分析计算。红宝石会籍的会员卡价格为 26.8 万,它要求会员要先付首期 10%,其余分 10 年期偿还,每期每月的金额为 2000元,试计算本例的利率(假设通货膨胀指数为零,以普通年金现值计算)。

解 先把要交的会费减去首期的 10%:

$$26.8 - 26.8 \times 10\% = 24.12(万元)$$

因为每个月有 2000 元的分期付款,则有关系:

$$2000 \times (FVIFA_{x\%,120}) = 241200(元)$$
$$FVIFA_{x\%,120} = 120.6 \quad 即 \quad [(1+x)120-1]/x = 120.6$$
$$x\% = 1.04\%(每期每月的利率)$$

(2)普通年金现值

普通年金的现值指一项年金各期支付金额,按复利折算至该年金第一期期初现值的总和。普通年金现值的计算公式为

$$PVA_n = PMT(1+i)^{-1} + PMT(1+i)^{-2} + \cdots + PMT(1+i)^{-n}$$
$$= PMT \sum_{t=1}^{n} (1+i)^{-t}$$

式中:PVA 代表普通年金现值;PMT 代表年金每期的"支付额";i 代表复利利率;n 代表年金的期数。

下式表示每期支付 1 元,连续支付 n 期,按利率 i 折算至第一年年初的年金现值:

$$PVIFA_{i,n} = \frac{1 - \dfrac{1}{(1+i)^n}}{i}$$

若每期支付的金额为 PMT,则该年金的现值 PV 可以用下式计算:

$$PV = PMT \times PVIFA_{i,n}$$

例 7-12 乙公司发行面值为 100000 元的公司债,票面利率 10%,10 年

years, each period is six months, each term deposits 80,000, if the annual interest rate is 12%. What is the balance in the end of the third year?

Solution

$$FV = 80000 \times FVIFA_{6\%,6} = 80000 \times 6.975319$$
$$= 558026$$

Example 7 – 11   Hills Golf Club membership has divided into the distinguish diamond membership, diamond membership, golden card membership, emerald membership, and ruby membership. Membership prices range from 268,000 to 1,680,000 yuan. Different memberships customized to different customers, such that customers have choices when joining membership.For example, ruby membership can be evaluated with its value of 268,000 yuan, which is required to pay 10% of down payment, and a mortization of amount 2,000 yuan per month for 10 years.What is the interest rate in this case? (Calculate the present value of ordinary annuity. Assume inflation is zero.)

Solution   First the total fee of membership minus 10% of the down payment:

$$268000 - 268000 \times 10\% = 241200(\text{yuan})$$

2,000 of installments each month:

$$2000 \times (FVIFA_{x\%,120}) = 241200(\text{yuan})$$
$$FVIFA_{x\%,120} = 120.6 \text{ namely } [(1+x)120 - 1]/x = 120.6$$
$$x\% = 1.04\% (\text{each issue / month of interest rate})$$

(2) Present Value of an Ordinary Annuity

The present value of an ordinary annuity refers to the sum of the present value of compound interest payments at each period.

The formula of the present value of an ordinary annuity is presented following.

$$PVA_n = PMT(1+i)^{-1} + PMT(1+i)^{-2} + \cdots + PMT(1+i)^{-n}$$
$$= PMT \sum_{t=1}^{n} (1+i)^{-t}$$

Where PVA depicts the present value of an ordinary annuity, PMT represents an annuity "payments" per period, i is the compounded interest rate, n represents the number of periods for an annuity.

The following formula represents the present value of an ordinary annuity, assume the payment is 1 per period, continuous payments of n periods, interest rate i:

$$PVIFA_{i,n} = \frac{1 - \dfrac{1}{(1+i)^n}}{i}$$

If the payment is PMT per period, the present value of an annuity PV can be calculated from the equation:

$$PV = PMT \times PVIFA_{i,n}$$

Example 7 – 12   Company B issued 100,000 yuan corporate bond, the coupon rate is 10%, maturity is ten years, interest is paid every six months, if market interest rate is

到期,每半年付息一次,若市场利率为 12%,计算该公司债的公平价值。

解　债券现在价值＝每一期利息和＋债券现值

面值为 100000 元,公司债每半年的利息为

$$100000 \times 10\% \times 1/2 = 5000(元)$$

$$5000 \times \text{PVIFA}_{6\%,20} + 100000 \times \text{PVIFA}_{6\%,20}$$

$$= 5000 \times 11.469921 + 100000 \times 0.311805$$

$$= 88530(元)$$

此为折价债券。

(3)期初年金终值

期初年金指每期期初支付的年金。若每年存入 PMT,期数为 n 期,有效利率为 i,则期初年金终值为

$$\text{PMT} \times \text{FVIFA}_{i,n+1} - \text{PMT} = \text{PMT} \times (\text{FVIFA}_{i,n+1} - 1)$$

另外,期初年金终值亦等于普通年金终值乘上 $(1+i)$,即

$$\text{FVIFA}'_{i,n} = \text{FVIFA}_{i,n} \times (1+i)$$

上述期初年金终值的概念可以用图 7-9 所示的时间线来表示。

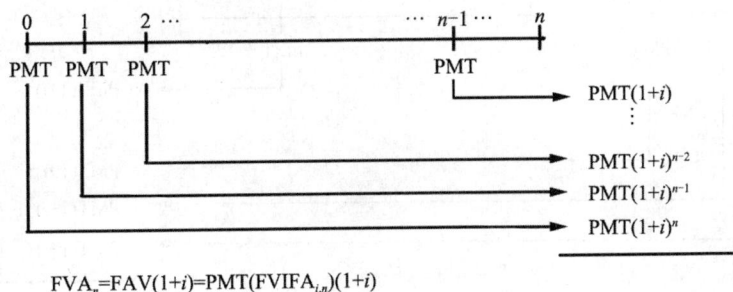

$$\text{FVA}_n = \text{FAV}(1+i) = \text{PMT}(\text{FVIFA}_{i,n})(1+i)$$

图 7-9　期初年金终值的概念

例题 7-13　假设每年年初存款 10000 元,利率 12%,则第 10 年年底的本利和为多少?

解　方法一:

$$10000 \times (\text{FVIFA}_{12\%,11} - 1) = 10000 \times (20.654583 - 1)$$

$$= 196546(元)$$

方法二:

$$10000 \times \text{FVIFA}_{12\%,10} \times (1+12\%) = 10000 \times 17.548735 \times 1.12$$

$$= 196546(元)$$

(4)期初年金现值

普通年金的最后一期收付额是按总期数来折现的,而期初年金的折现数

12%, calculate the fair value of the corporate bond.

Solution the present value of a bond

= the sum of of interest + the present value of a bond

Face value is 100,000 yuan, the interest on the corporate bond every six months is calculated as

$$100000 \times 10\% \times 1/2 = 5000(\text{yuan})$$

$$5000 \times \text{PVIFA}_{6\%,20} + 100000 \times \text{PVIFA}_{6\%,20}$$

$$= 5000 \times 11.469921 + 100000 \times 0.311805$$

$$= 88530(\text{yuan})$$

This is a discount bond.

(3) Amount of annuity due

Annuity due is paid at the beginning of each period, if the pay ment is PMT per year, the periods are n, effective interest rate is i, then the final value of annuity due is

$$\text{PMT} \times \text{FVIFA}_{i,n+1} - \text{PMT} = \text{PMT} \times (\text{FVIFA}_{i,n+1} - 1)$$

In addition, the amount of annuity due is also the final value of ordinary annuity multiple $(1+i)$, namely:

$$\text{FVIFA}'_{i,n} = \text{FVIFA}_{i,n} \times (1+i)$$

The concept of an amount of annuity due can be represented with the timeline (see Figure 7 - 9).

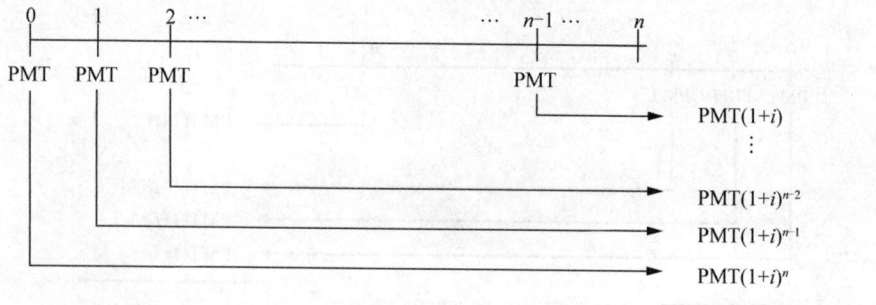

$$\text{FVA}_n = \text{FAV}(1+i) = \text{PMT}(\text{FVIFA}_{i,n})(1+i)$$

Figure 7 - 9   The concept of amount of annuity due

Example 7 - 13   10,000 yuan is deposited at the beginning of each period, interest rate is 12%. What is the amount of annuity due at the end of the tenth year?

Solution   Method one:

$$10000 \times (\text{FVIFA}_{12\%,11} - 1) = 10000 \times (20.654583 - 1)$$

$$= 196546(\text{yuan})$$

Method two:

$$10000 \times \text{FVIFA}_{12\%,10} \times (1 + 12\%) = 10000 \times 17.548735 \times 1.12$$

$$= 196546(\text{yuan})$$

(4) Present value of annuity due

For ordinary annuity, the payment of the last period is discounted based on the total number of periods. For annuity due, the payment of the last period is discounted one period less of the total number of periods. The cash flows of the annuity due earlier than

比收付期数少了一期。亦即,到期年金的现金流量比普通年金提早一期,也就是期初年金的现值因子等于普通年金的现值因子乘以(1+利率),即

$$PVIFA'_{i,n} = PVIFA_{i,n} \times (1+i)$$

或可以应用期初年金终值的概念,即若每年年初存入 PMT,期数为 n 期,有效利率为 i,则到期年金现值为

$$PMT \times PVIFA_{i,n-1} + PMT = PMT(PVIFA_{i,n-1} + 1)$$

上述期初年金现值的概念可以用图 7-10 所示的时间线来表示。

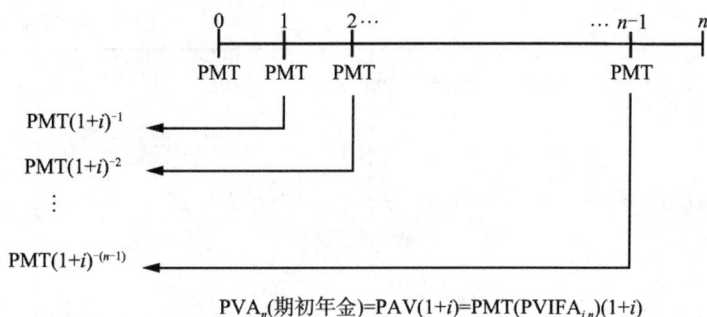

$$PVA_n(期初年金) = PAV(1+i) = PMT(PVIFA_{i,n})(1+i)$$

图 7-10　期初年金现值的概念

例 7-14　假设 A 公司租用设备,每年年初支付租金 50000 元,租期为 5 年,市场利率为 10%,则该设备之现值为多少?

解　方法一:

$$50000 \times (PVIFA_{10\%,4} + 1) = 50000 \times (3.169865 + 1) = 208493(元)$$

方法二:

$$50000 \times PVIFA_{10\%,5} \times (1+10\%) = 50000 \times 4.169865 = 208493(元)$$

(5)递延年金终值

递延年金指若干期后才开始发生收付的年金,亦即于第二期或多期之后才开始收付的年金。递延年金终值的计算方式与普通年金终值或到期年金终值的计算方式相同,只是选用的期数应以开始有年金流动的年度至期末为准。

例 7-15　假如你现在 20 岁,有一家人寿保险公司向你推销保险,条件为你每年缴纳 1 万元保费,连续缴纳 20 年,到你 40 岁时,可以领回 20 万元,以后每 5 年均领回 20 万元,直到你 65 岁,共领取 6 次,总计 120 万元,则事

an ordinary annuity. That is, the present value factor of annuity due is equal to the present value factor of an ordinary annuity multiple $(1 + \text{interest})$. That is

$$\text{PVIFA}'_{i,n} = \text{PVIFA}_{i,n} \times (1 + i)$$

Or we can apply the concept of discounting the final value of annuity due, that is, if we deposited PMT at the beginning of each year, the number of periods is n, the effective interest rate is i. The present value of an annuity due is

$$PMT \times \text{PVIFA}_{i,n-1} + PMT = PMT(\text{PVIFA}_{i,n-1} + 1)$$

The concept of the present value of an annuity due can be represented with the timeline (see Figure 7 - 10).

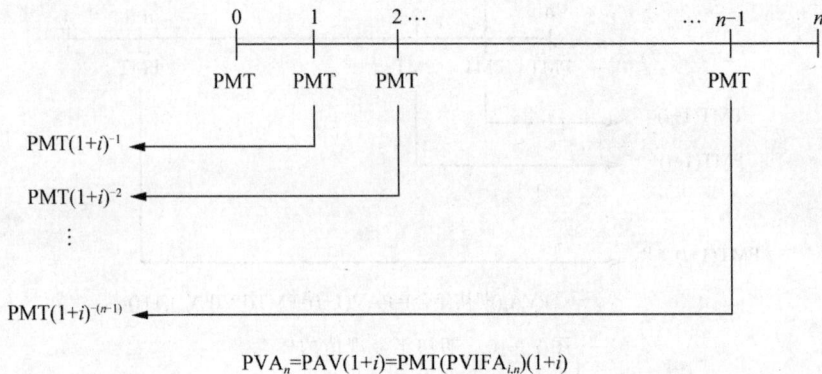

$$\text{PVA}_n = \text{PAV}(1+i) = PMT(\text{PVIFA}_{i,n})(1+i)$$

Figure 7 - 10   The concept of the present value of an annuity due

Example 7 - 14   Assume a company rented an equipment, the company paid the rent of 50,000 yuan at the beginning of each year, and rented the equipment for a period of five years, market interest rate is 10%. What is the present value of the equipment?

Solution   Method one:

$$50000 \times (\text{PVIFA}_{10\%,4} + 1) = 50000 \times (3.169865 + 1) = 208,493(\text{yuan})$$

Method two:

$$50000 \times \text{PVIFA}_{10\%,5} \times (1 + 10\%) = 50000 \times 4.169865 = 208,493(\text{yuan})$$

(5) Future value of a deferred annuity

The deferred annuity refers to the annuity payment occurs after some periods of time. That is the payment starts at the second phase or more phases later. The future value of a deferred annuity is calculated as the future value of an ordinary annuity or annuity due, but the calculation of annual installments should start from the first flow of the annuity to the last period.

Example 7 - 15   If you're twenty, there is a life insurance company to solicit insurance to you, the content is that you pay an annual premium of 10,000 yuan for 20 years. You can get back each installment of 200000 yuan every other 5 years, 6 times of installments, from 40 years old to 65 years old. You can receive total amount of

实上保险公司净赚了多少元?

解 利率以10％计算,过程如图7-11所示。

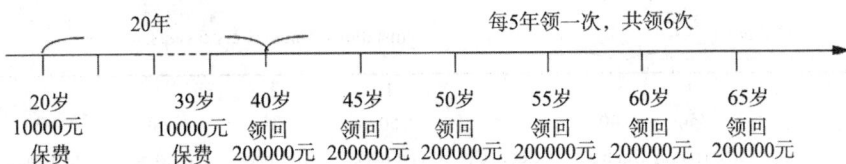

图7-11 例7-15计算过程示例

缴纳的保费价值如下:

复利至40岁时的年金终值为

$$10000 \times \text{FVIFA}_{10\%,20}(1+10\%)=630025(元)$$

将此年金终值再复利至65岁时的终值(非年金)为

$$630025 \times \text{FVIF}_{10\%,25}=6826320(元)$$

领回部分:

重新计算有效利率(因为每5年领回一次),有

$$i=(1+10\%)^5-1=0.61051$$

故每5年领回20万元至65岁时其终值为

$$200000 \times \text{FVIFA}_{0.61051,5} \times 1.61051+200000(末笔)=5388741(元)$$

因此,以65岁时的价值来看,所缴纳的保费共计值6826320元,而领回部分在65岁时的价值为5388741元,故保险公司净赚为

$$6826320-5388741=1437580(元)$$

(6)递延年金现值

递延年金现值的计算有两种方法:一是先求出数期后的年金现值,再计算至目前的复利现值;二是运用普通年金或到期年金的现值而求得,即先假设年金并无递延情况,计算全部期数的年金现值,再计算前面递延期数的年金现值,二者相减即为递延年金的现值。

例7-16 假设小水母公司的职员小香菇预计于第五年年底退休,退休后小水母公司每年年底将给他50000元的退休金,为期10年。小水母公司拟于现在存入银行一笔钱,按年息10％复利,刚好足够支付小香菇的退休金,则小水母公司现在应存入多少钱?

1,200,000 yuan. How much is the insurance company earns?

Solution Figure 7 – 11 shows the calculation of this example (with interest rate of 10%).

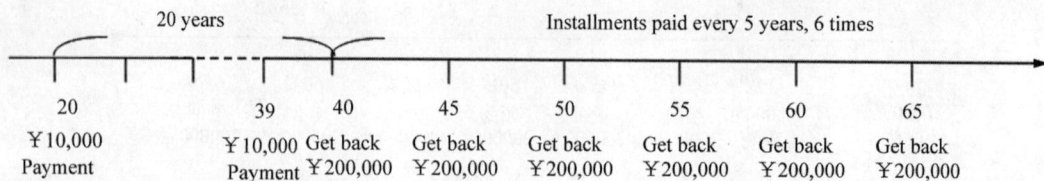

Figure 7 – 11 The calculation of example 7 – 15

The value of insurance payment:

Amount of annuity due compounded to 40-years old is

$$10000 \times FVIFA_{10\%,20}(1+10\%) = 630025(yuan)$$

The final value of the amount of annuity due calculated above compounded to 65-years old is

$$630025 \times FVIF_{10\%,25} = 6826320(yuan)$$

Get back amount:

Calculate the effective interest rate(compounded every other 5 years):

$$i = (1+10\%)^5 - 1 = 0.61051$$

Get back ¥200,000 every other 5 years. The final value of deferred annuity at 65 years old is

$$200000 \times FVIFA_{0.61051,5} \times 1.61051 + 200000 = 5388741 \text{ yuan}$$

Thus at the age of 65, the value of you pay a insurance premium is 6,826,320 yuan, and get back installments amount 5,388,741 yuan. The insurance company get net profit is:

$$6826320 - 5388741 = 1437580(yuan)$$

(6) Present Value of a Deferred Annuity

There are two methods to calculate the present value of a deferred annuity. First, calculate the present value of an annuity for number of periods, then calculate the present value of compound interest annuity. Second, use the perspective of the present value of an ordinary annuity or an annuity due. Assume an annuity is not deferred, calculate the present value of an annuity, then calculate the present value of an annuity of the deferred periods. The present value of the deferred annuity can be calculated by subtracting the two annuities mentioned above.

Examples 7 – 16 Assume a staff Little Mushroom of the Small Jellyfish company is planning to retire at the end of the fifth year, the company will give her pension amout of ¥50,000 each year at the end of the year for ten years. The Small Jellyfish company intends to deposit an amount of money at 10%, compounded annually in the bank to pay the pension.What is the amount of deposit of the company?

解

$$50000 \times \mathrm{PVIFA}_{10,10\%} \times \mathrm{PVIF}_{5,10\%}$$
$$= 50000 \times 6.144567 \times 0.6139 = 188641(元)$$

表 7 – 1 所示为利率计算的公式汇总。

表 7 – 1　利率计算的公式汇总

项目	终值	现值
复利	$\mathrm{FVIF}_{i,n} = (1+i)^n$	$\mathrm{PFIF}_{i,n} = \dfrac{1}{(1+i)^n}$
普通年金	$\mathrm{FVIFA}_{i,n} = \dfrac{(1+i)^n - 1}{i}$	$\mathrm{PVIFA}_{i,n} = \dfrac{1 - \dfrac{1}{(1+i)^n}}{i}$
到期年金	$\mathrm{FVIFA}'_{i,n} = \mathrm{F}_{i,n+1} - 1$ $= \mathrm{F}_{i,n} \times (1+i)$	$\mathrm{PVIFA}'_{i,n} = \mathrm{PVIFA}_{i,n-1} + 1$ $= \mathrm{PVIFA}_{i,n} \times (1+i)$

Solution

$$50000 \times \text{PVIFA}_{10,10\%} \times \text{PVIF}_{5,10\%}$$
$$= 50000 \times 6.144567 \times 0.6139 = 188641(\text{yuan})$$

Table 7 - 1 shows the summary formula of interest calculation.

Table 7 - 1　Summary formula of interest calculation

Items	Future Value	Present Value
Compound Interest	$\text{FVIF}_{i,n} = (1+i)^n$	$\text{PFIF}_{i,n} = \dfrac{1}{(1+i)^n}$
Annuity	$\text{FVIFA}_{i,n} = \dfrac{(1+i)^n - 1}{i}$	$\text{PVIFA}_{i,n} = \dfrac{1 - \dfrac{1}{(1+i)^n}}{i}$
Annuity Due	$\text{FVIFA}'_{i,n} = F_{i,n+1} - 1 = F_{i,n} \times (1+i)$	$\text{PVIFA}'_{i,n} = \text{PVIFA}_{i,n-1} + 1$ $= \text{PVIFA}_{i,n} \times (1+i)$

第8章　资金成本

学习目标

- 了解资金成本的意义
- 理解资金成本的组成
- 计算资金成本

资金成本指公司为实现投资计划所融通的资金来源的成本。公司的资金来源包括银行负债、公司债、普通股、特别股、保留盈余等项目成本。

8.1　加权平均资金成本

由于资金来源广泛,因此资金成本必须涵盖所有来源,故加权平均资金成本 WACC(weighted average cost of capital)的计算公式如下:

$$\text{WACC} = K_a = W_d K_d (1-t) + W_p K_p + W_s K_s + W_e K_e$$

式中:K_d 为负债资金成本;W_d 为负债资金成本比重;K_p 为特别股资金成本;W_p 为特别股资金成本比重;K_s 为保留盈余资金成本;W_s 为保留盈余资金成本比重;K_e 为普通股资金成本;W_e 为普通股资金成本比重;t 为公司税。

简单地说,WACC 就是根据目标资本结构,各资本要素成本依资本要素所占比例加权而得的公司整体资金成本。

1. WACC 的逻辑

(1)资金成本应反映各种不同来源的资金。

(2)资金成本应取决于资金的使用面,而非资金的来源面。

(3)WACC 需要在公司长期目标资本结构及红利政策既定的前提下使用。

Chapter 8   Cost of Capital

📖 Learning Outcomes

- ■ Understand the significance of cost of capital
- ■ Understand the composition of capital cost
- ■ Calculate the cost of capital

Cost of capital is the cost of financing sources for a company's investment plans. Financing sources including bank debt, corporate bonds, common stock, preferred stock, retained earnings and other fundings.

8.1   Weighted Average Cost of Capital (WACC)

Costs must cover all sources of funding to calculate weighted average cost of capital. The calculation is as follows:

$$\text{WACC} = K_a = W_d K_d (1 - t) + W_p K_p + W_s K_s + W_e K_e$$

Where K_d is cost of debt; W_d is proportion of debt; K_p is cost of perferred stock; W_p is proportion of perferred stock; K_s is cost of retained earnings; W_s is proportion of retained earnings; K_e is cost of common stock; W_e is proportion of common stock; t is company's tax.

WACC is the company's overall cost that derived from the weighted average of different costs times their proportions based on the target capital structure.

1. The logic of WACC

(1) Cost of capital should reflect the different sources of funding.

(2) Capital costs should be decided on the applications of funds, rather than the source perspectives.

(3) WACC is applied when a company set up its long-term target capital structure and dividend policy.

2. WACC 的功能

（1）降低成本

通过分析各部门与整体企业的资金成本，使管理部门能估算出整体资金成本，将资金来源的平均成本降至最低，以制定出最有利的融资政策。

（2）有效投资

在做资本预算决策时，公司必须先算出 WACC。资本预算技术评估计划案是否具有可行性，须以 WACC 为折现率，将项目现金流量折现以计算现值评估投资计划。

案例 ▶▶▶▶▶

乌山头地区休闲度假会馆 BOT 财务可行性评估

乌山头地区休闲度假会馆 BOT 财务可行性评估的折现率即平均加权资金成本。假设公司只有负债资金及普通股两种资金来源，负债比例为 60％，贷款利率为 5％，公司税率为 25％，自有资金成本为 10％，故折现率（WACC）计算如下：

WACC＝负债比例×贷款利率×（1－所得税率）＋权益资金比例×自有资金成本＝0.6 × 0.05 ×（1－0.25）＋ 0.4 × 0.1＝6.25％

公司会在做资本预算决策时先算出加权平均资金成本（WACC），再以 WACC 当作折现率。

3. WACC 的限制

（1）WACC 假设项目的风险类似公司风险，因此新投资项目与公司现有风险明显不同时，可能会导致公司做出错误的资本预算决策。

（2）若公司仅利用单一的 WACC 来评断部门项目以决定投资资金的流向，将可能导致错误的决策。

案例 ▶▶▶▶▶

东方明珠

东方明珠公司拥有东方明珠电视塔、上海国际会议中心等上海市标志性的景区和旅游服务设施。公司投资 220 亿元的商业地产项目从 2016 年开始确认盈余，投资项目具有地段优越、购地价格低等特点，投资风险小。同时，公司持有的 1.596 亿元海通证券股权也从 2010 年年底开始解禁，这将成为

2. Functions of WACC

(1) Cost down

A company can estimate the overall cost of capital by analyzing the cost from various departments of enterprises, and to make the most effective financing policies by minizing the average cost of capital.

(2) Effective investment

WACC is essential for capital budgeting. WACC is treated as discount rate to calculate the present value of cash flow of each period in capital budgeting, such that a company can make effective investment decisions.

Case ▶▶▶▶▶▶

Financial feasibility assessment of Black Hills leisure resort BOT

The discount rate or the WACC is for financial feasibility assessment of Black Hills leisure resort BOT. This project assumes that the company only have two sources of funding from debt and common stock, the portion of debt is 60%, the interest rate of loan is 5%, the company tax rate is 25%, and the cost of common stock is 10%. The discount rate (WACC) is calculated as follows:

WACC = debt ratio × loan interest rates × (1 − income tax rate) + equity ratio × cost of own funds = 0.6 × 0.05 × (1 − 0.25) + 0.4 × 0.1 = 6.25%

In principle, a company will calculate the weighted average cost of capital (WACC) as the discount rate of capital budgeting.

3. Limitations of WACC

(1) WACC assume the project risk is similar to company's risk, which might cause the company to make wrong capital budget decisions when the risk of new project is different from the company's existing risk.

(2) If a company's WACC is apptied to different departments, it may lead to wrong decision making of capital budgeting.

Case ▶▶▶▶▶▶

The Oriental Pearl

The Orient Pearl owns the Oriental Pearl TV Tower, Shanghai International Convention Center, other scenic spots and tourism service facilities in Shanghai City. The Orient Pearl began to have surplus from investing of 22 billion yuan in commercial real estate projects from 2010. Investment risks was low because projects were in great locations, purchased at low cost level. In the meantime, the 159,6 millions yuan of Hai Tong stocks that held by the company can circulate in the market which is helpful for corporate operations. The Orient Pearl's

公司业绩波动的平滑剂。其 WACC＝10.78％,在永续增长率＝2％的假设下,通过折算现金流计算得到公司合理价值为 6.65 元。由此得知,通常在估计公司价值时,不会仅利用 WACC 来评断,而会加入其他的假设来避免制定错误的决策。

4. WACC 为税后成本

在所有资金来源中只有负债的利息支出可当作费用,可从纯利润中扣除,从而减少公司的所得税,故负债成本采用税后成本,即

$$负债成本＝K_b(1-t)$$

式中：t 是公司的边际税率。

5. WACC 为新增成本

资金成本指用于投资计划所必须新增资金的成本,而不是指以往的资金成本。以往已投入资金,因属沉没成本(为已发生或已确定发生的支出)而与新计划无关。

6. WACC 不考虑短期负债成本

企业融资原则为短期投资以短期资金支应,长期投资由长期资金支应(以短支短,以长支长),而企业的投资计划多属长期投资,故计算投资计划的资金成本时,不考虑短期资金成本。

案例 ▶▶▶▶▶

剑湖山度假村

剑湖山度假村各开发阶段对休闲酒店开发计划影响显著的因子关系如图 8-1 所示。

图 8-1 中的休闲酒店开发计划分为开发前、开发中及开发后三大阶段。虽然就整体而言,此资本预算应属长期投资,应以长期资金支应,然而开发前与开发后所需的费用属于短期费用项目,故应以短期负债予以支应。

WACC is 10.78%，if the perpetual growth rate is 2%,the company's stock price is 6.65 yuan by discounted cash flow formula. In this case，we can understand that when estimating the company's value，we use not only WACC，but also other criteria to avoid making wrong decisions.

4. WACC is an after-tax cost

A debt cost is after-tax cost because that debt interest payment can be treated as expense from all sources of funding to be deducted from net profit to reduce the corporate income tax. That is

$$\text{Cost of debt} = K_b(1-t)$$

where t is the marginal tax rate of the company.

5. WACC is an additional cost

Cost of capital is an adding capital for a new project without concerning about the past investment. A funding that has been invested in the past is a sunk cost，which means the expenditure has paid，unrelated to a new project.

6. WACC doesn't consider the short-term debt

Principles of corporate finance are short-term investments covered by short-term funds，long-term investments covered by long-term capital. Capital budgeting is a long-term investment process，which needs to use long-term capital，regardless of short-term debts.

Case ▶▶▶▶▶▶

Janfusun Resorts

New developing project of Janfusun Resorts can be divided to three stages. The significant factors of the developing project are as Figure 8-1.

Figure 8-1 shows that the stages of developing project can be divided into three stages. In general，this capital budgeting belongs to long-term investment that is suppose to be covered by long-term capital. However，the first and the last stages of developing project is suggested to be covered by short-term capital because of the short-term expenses.

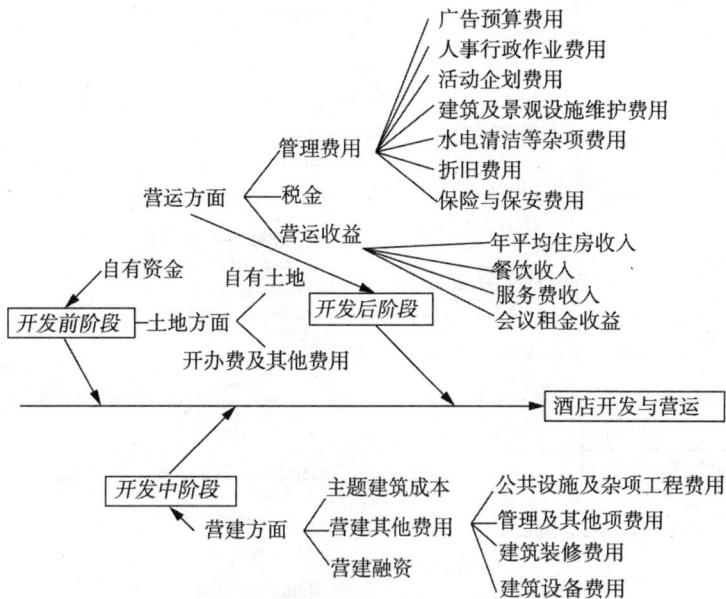

图 8-1　资本预算各阶段的费用项目

7. 假设资金成本计算存在最适资本结构

最适资本结构指存在使资金成本达到最低(公司价值最大)的长期负债与股东权益的比率。公司在评估投资计划时,假设每一投资计划在融资时均考量在公司最适资本结构下进行。

例 8-1　若 ABC 公司的资产负债及股东权益市场价值可以用表 8-1 表示。

表 8-1　**ABC 公司资产负债及股东权益市场价值**

资产	负债及股东权益
V_L: 1000 万元	B: 400 万元
	E: 600 万元

如果债务预期报酬率(K_b)和股东权益预期报酬率(K_e)分别为 8%以及15%,公司税率为 25%,计算 ABC 公司的加权平均资本成本(K_{WACC})。

解　$K_{WACC} = \dfrac{400}{1000} \times 8\%(1-25\%) + \dfrac{600}{1000} \times 15\% = 11.4\%$

8.2　资金成本的重要性

资本结构会影响资金成本,另外,租赁、债券偿还、营运资金等决策均与资金成本有关。资本预算对公司有重大影响,而只有正确的资金成本才能做出正确的投资决策(资本预算)。资本成本系资本预算的折现率。例如,资本预算计算 NPV 时会以 WACC 为折现率来选择使公司价值增加的方案,公式如下:

$$\text{NPV} = -I + \sum_{t=1}^{n} \frac{\text{CF}_t}{(1+\text{WACC})^t}$$

(1) 当新投资方案报酬率>资金成本,公司价值增加。

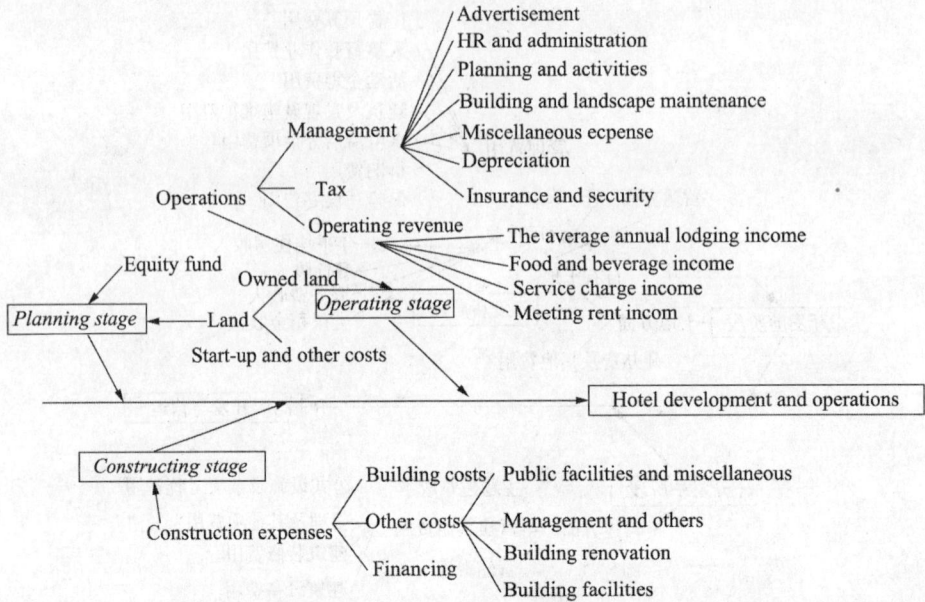

Figure 8 – 1   The items of capital budging at different stages

7. Calculation of WACC assume there exist the target capital structure of a company

The target capital structure, the ratio of long-term debt and equity, exists there the lowest cost of capital (the maximum value of the company). When assess a capital budgeting, we assume that each financing of the investment project is considered based on the target capital structure.

Example 8 – 1   If ABC company's market value of assets as well as liabilities and equity can be expressed in Table 8 – 1.

Table 8 – 1   ABC company's simplify balance sheet

Assets	Liabilities and equity
V_L: ¥10,000,000	B: ¥4,000,000
	E: ¥6,000,000

If the expected rate of debt (K_b) and the expected rate of equity (K_e) are respectively 8% and 15%, the company tax rate is 25%. What is the the weighted average cost of capital of ABC company (K_{WACC})?

Solution

$$K_{WACC} = \frac{400}{1000} \times 8\%(1 - 25\%) + \frac{600}{1000} \times 15\% = 11.4\%$$

8.2   The Importance of Cost of Capital

Capital structure will affect the cost of capital, in addition, leasing, debt repayment, working capital and other decisions are associated with the cost of capital. Capital budgeting had a significant impact to the company. Only a good cost of capital can assure a good investment decision (capital budgeting). The cost of capital is the discount rate of capital budgeting. For example, a company will choose value-added projects by calculating NPV that use WACC as discount rate.

$$NPV = -I + \sum_{t=1}^{n} \frac{CF_t}{(1 + WACC)^t}$$

(1) When rate of return > cost of capital on new investment program, corporate

（2）当新投资方案报酬率＝资金成本，公司价值不变。

（3）当新投资方案报酬率＜资金成本，公司价值减少。

案例 ▶▶▶▶▶

国宾大饭店

国宾大饭店于 1999 年 7 月 30 日与新光三越百货公司签订租赁契约，主要内容为新竹国宾大饭店百货商场的部分约 32500 平方米出租给它经营，而且平均每年依保证营业额计算基本租金收入 13200 万元；超过保证营业额部分依 5％至 8％计算变动租金收入。租赁期间自 2001 年 1 月 1 日起至 2030 年 12 月 31 日止。在这个案例中，显然新竹国宾大饭店认为这项投资的报酬率会大于资金成本从而使公司价值增加，所以才与新光三越百货公司签订租赁契约。

8.3　各项资金成本计算

公司资金来源有两大部分：一是负债，包括银行长期借款、公司债（外部资金来源）；二是股东权益，包括特别股、普通股、保留盈余（内部自有资金）。

1. 长期负债成本

由于负债成本（K_b）即为公司举新债所必须支付的利息，而非旧债的成本，因此我们可以从债券市场上直接观察到此利率。此外，若我们已知公司目前的债信评等，我们可借着找出与公司同等级债券利率或观察具有相同风险的类似公司的债券利率来当作公司的负债成本。

银行长期借款利率或公司债有效利率具有合理避税效果，由于负债的利息支出列为费用，可从课税所得中扣除，因此考虑此合理避税效果，负债成本应做税率调整如下：

$$税后资金成本＝K_b(1-t)$$

式中：t 为公司税率。

例 8 - 2　台北酒店发行票面利率为 14％的债券，并以某价格卖给投资人，于此价格下投资人可获得 16％的收益率，假设公司税率为 30％，请计算台北酒店的税后负债成本。

解　税后资金成本＝16％×（1－30％）＝11.2％

value increases.

(2) When rate of return = cost of capital on new investment program, corporate value unchanges.

(3) When rate of return < cost of capital on new investment program, corporate value reduces.

Case ▶▶▶▶▶▶

The Ambassador Hotel

The Ambassador hotel signed a lease contract with Shin Kong Mitsukoshi (SKM) department store on 30 July in 1999. The main contract is that SKM rented out 9,820 square feet to the Hsinchu Ambassador hotel for operations. The average annual rental income is 132,000,000 on a guaranteed revenue base; 5% to 8% of amount of extra from guaranteed revenue was variable rental income from SKM.Lease period is from 1st January, 2001 to 31 December, 2030. In this case, the reason that Hsinchu Ambassador hotel signed the contract with the SKM is because the return on investment would be greater than the cost of capital.

8.3 Calculating of the Cost of Capital

Company's funding sources including two parts. 1. Debt: long-term bank debts, corporate bonds (external sources of capital). 2. Shareholder's equity: preferred stock, common stock, retained earnings (internal sources of capital). The details of costs are as follows.

1. Cost of long-term debt (K_b)

We can observe K_b directly from the interest rates of bond market because the cost of debt is the interest on a new debt, rather than an old debt. In addition, a company's cost of debt can be evaluated from the company's current credit rating, or be observed from the interest rate of a similar corporate bond with the same corporate risk.

An interest rate of a long-term bank debt or an effective interest rate of a corporate bond has the effect of tax shield, because interest payment on debt is an expense which will be deducted from revenue.The cost of debt is ought to adjust based on corporate tax:

$$\text{After-tax cost of capital} = K_b(1-t)$$

Where: t is tax rate.

Example 8 – 2　The Taipei hotel issued a corporate bond with coupon rate of 14%. The bond was sold to investors.Investors can get earning yield of 16%. The corporate tax rate is 30%. Calculate the after-tax cost of debt of the Taipei hotell.

Solution　　　after-tax cost of capital = 16% × (1 − 30%) = 11.2%

案例 ▶▶▶▶▶▶

中国新城镇发行 13 亿 3 年期人民币债券

中国新城镇发展有限公司——中国综合性新型城镇未来蓝图规划师及领军开发商(香港交易所股份编号:1278.HK;新加坡交易所股份编号:D4N.SI)宣布公司成功于境外完成人民币债券融资交易,发行规模130亿元,为2015年香港市场最大的人民币债券发行主体之一,期限 3 年,利率为5.5%。此次发行的人民币债券已于 4 月 28 日成功结束认购簿记,公司以初始指导利率5.8%宣布开簿,半小时内即获得主力投资者大规模订单支援,最终以多倍认购完美收盘,发行利率为 5.5%,发行规模确定为 13 亿元。本次融资所募集的资金将用于公司业务开发,相信它将有利于加速公司开发已落地项目及投资更多优质的新项目。通过丰富项目组合,公司可建立起更具吸引力、具备稳定投资回报的新业务模式。

2. 权益资金成本

公司的权益资金包括特别股、保留盈余、新发行普通股。

(1) 特别股

特别股股息非公司债务,股息由盈余分配,如果没有盈余可以不发放。特别股有优先权,在没有支付股息前,不能发放普通股股息。特别股无到期日,有发行成本。公司发行特别股时,通常会承诺向投资人每期(年)发放固定红利,所以特别股实际上是一个永续年金,特别股的成本就等于特别股红利除以特别股净发行价格。净发行价格是指扣除发行成本后,公司所收到的每股股价。故其资金成本如下:

$$K_p = \frac{D_p}{P_0(1-f)}$$

式中:D_p 为红利发放率;P_0 为特别股市价;f 为发行成本。

由于特别股股息系由盈余分配,与负债利息可当费用处理不同,故不须做税率调整。

例 8 - 3 万豪酒店发行每股面值 100 元且红利支付率为 12% 的特别股,发行成本为每股市价的 8%。目前万豪酒店特别股每股市价为 98.25 元,求万豪酒店新特别股成本。

解

$$K_p = \frac{100 \times 12\%}{98.25(1-8\%)} = 13.28\%$$

Case ▶▶▶▶▶

China New Town Development Corporation issue 3-year of 13 billion RMB bonds

China New Town Development Corporation (CNTDC) is a new town planner and a lead developer (HKEX stock code: 1278.HK; Singapore Stock Exchange stock code: D4N.SI). CNTDC announced a successful financing transactions completed in offshore RMB bond market, the amount is 13 billion RMB. It was the largest issuance of RMB bonds in Hong Kong in 2015, the period was 3 years, the interest rate was 5.5%. The issuance of RMB debt was finished on 28 Apr. 2015. CNTDC announced open account with initial interest rate of 5.8%. Key Investors had large scale of investments within half an hour, the issue interest rate is 5.5% at the end to the amount of 13 billions RMB. Funds raised from this financing will be used for business development, managers believe this fund helps speed up company's development in new projects to increase profit. The company was able to establish more attractive new business models to have a stable return on investment through portfolios.

2. Cost of equity capital

Equity capital of the company including: preferred stock, initial public offering common stock, retained earnings.

(1) Preferred Stock

Dividends of preferred stocks are not as interest of debt. They are from allocation of surplus. There is no dividend if there is no surplus. A preferred stock has priority than common stock. The dividends of a common stock can not be paid if the dividends of a preferred stock are not paid. A preferred stock has no maturity, but it has issue cost. When a company issues preferred stocks, the company will promise to investors to pay fixed dividends each period (year). Actually, a preferred stock is a perpetuity, the cost of a preferred stock is equal to its dividends divided by the net issue price. The net issue price is the price received after the deduction of issue cost. So the cost of capital of a preferred stock is as follows:

$$K_p = \frac{D_p}{P_0(1-f)}$$

Where: D_p is the payout rate of dividend, P_0 is the price, f is the issue cost.

There is no tax shield for preferred stock because the dividends are paid by earning surplus, other than paid by interest as debt.

Example 8-3 Marriott issues preferred stocks with face value of 100 per share. The dividend payout ratio is 12%. The cost of issue is 8% of the stock price. Currently, Marriott's preferred stock price is 98.25. What is Marriott's cost of preferred stock?

Solution

$$K_p = \frac{100 \times 12\%}{98.25(1-8\%)} = 13.28\%$$

例 8-4　剑湖山世界发行每股面值 10 元且红利支付为 8% 的特别股，发行成本为每股市价的 10%。目前剑湖山世界发行的特别股每股市价为 17.5 元，求剑湖山世界新特别股成本。

解

$$K_p = \frac{10 \times 8\%}{17.5(1-10\%)} = 5\%$$

（2）新发行普通股成本

当保留盈余无法支应企业成长时，企业应考虑发行新股。一般而言，在企业的筹资方式中，资金成本最高的是"发行普通股"，发行新普通股就是寻求外部权益资金，以达成股东预期的必要报酬率。而普通股发行会有发行成本，使取得资金减少，资金成本增加，故其资金较保留盈余成本高。有公式：

$$K_s = \frac{D_1}{P_0(1-f)} + g$$

例 8-5　北江酒店是由大量的地区性连锁酒店合并而成的酒店集团，它希望与国家级的酒店相竞争。公司为了扩大规模而筹措资金，办理现金增资，每股认购价格为 20 元，其承销费用为 3%。北江公司最近一次发放每股 2 元的红利，其成长率为 8%。请计算北江酒店新增普通股的资金成本。

解

$$K_s = \frac{2(1+8\%)}{20(1-3\%)} + 8\%$$

3. 资本资产定价模式法（CAPM）

（1）CAPM 的基本方法

根据资本资产定价模式，在证券市场均衡时，投资人可据此决定普通股必要报酬率：

$$K_s = R_f + (R_m - R_f)\beta_i$$

运用 CAPM 决定普通股必要报酬率时，必须对模式中的三个变数进行估计，即无风险利率、β 系数、市场投资组合的预期报酬率。

（2）CAPM 模式的优缺点

优点：可因风险而调整，对非红利稳定成长的公司也适用。

Example 8 – 4　Janfusun Fancy World issue preferred stocks of face value 10 yuan per share, the dividend payout rate is 8%, the issue cost is 10% of the market price, and the market price is 17.5 yuan per share. What is the preferred cost of Janfusun Fancy World?

Solution

$$K_p = \frac{10 \times 8\%}{17.5(1 - 10\%)} = 5\%$$

(2) The cost of initial public offering

When retained earnings are not enough for business growth, companies should consider issuing new shares. In general, in corporate financing, the highest cost of capital is "common stocks", the issue of new common stocks is to seek external equity capital, shareholders have expectations of getting the required rate of return. The common stocks have issue costs, reduce the capital amount increased the cost of capital, so the cost of capital is higher than the retention.

$$K_s = \frac{D_1}{P_0(1 - f)} + g$$

Example 8 – 5　Beijiang company's cost of capital analysis. Beijiang Hotel, intends to compete with the national level of hotels, is a hotel group merged from a large number of regional hotel chain. In order to expand the scale of hotel group, Beijiang hotel issues initial public offering. The exercise price is 20 yuan per share, the underwriting allowance is 3% of the exercise price, the didvidends is 2 yuan per share that is paid recently, its growth rate is 8%. What is the cost of capital of Beijiang hotel's common stock?

Solution

$$K_s = \frac{2(1 + 8\%)}{20(1 - 3\%)} + 8\%$$

3. The capital asset pricing model (CAPM)

(1) CAPM

According to the capital asset pricing model, investors can decide expected return of a common stock in an equilibrium stock market.

$$K_s = R_f + (R_m - R_f)\beta_i$$

Three variables shall be estimated in CAPM when decide the expected return of a common stock, which are risk-free interest rate; beta; expected rate of return for a market portfolio.

(2) Pros and cons of CAPM

Advantages: Risk can be adjusted which can be applied to those companies without steady growth of dividends.

缺点：CAPM 必须估计两个值，即市场风险溢酬和 β 系数，若估计不正确，则普通股的必要报酬率也不准确。此外，CAPM 运用历史资料预估未来，当未来经济情况转变时，则历史资料的可运用性将降低。如果公司的股东未进行多角化投资，则他们重视的是公司的个别风险而非市场风险。在此情况下，公司真实的投资风险将无法借由 β 值来测量。

（3）保留盈余的成本

保留盈余之所以会有成本，系从机会成本考量，因为盈余发放给股东，作为股东提供资金的报酬，股东可自行投资，但若公司盈余没有发放给股东而由公司保留下来供将来投资之用，此时保留盈余转投资的报酬率应大于股东自行投资所要求的报酬率，否则应将盈余分配给股东，由股东自行投资。然而，公司应发放红利还是将盈余留下来再投资呢？由于红利和资本利得两者的税率并不相同，对大部分股东而言，长期利得的税率较红利税率为低，这使得公司倾向于不发放红利，而将盈余保留下来再投资让股东赚取资本利得，即

$$K_r = \frac{D_1}{P_0} + g$$

例 8 - 6　乔山旅行社的股东权益及公司股票的情形如表 8 - 2 所示。

表 8 - 2　乔山旅行社股东权益及公司股票情形

年份	2012 年	2013 年	2014 年	2015 年
股东红利（千股）	2100	2100	2846	3102
当年度税后净利（千元）	574545	762003	1253338	1718654
股票发行开盘价（元）	69	73	66	155
流通在外股数（百万股）	84	105	126.5	155
每股股票红利（元）	1.81	1.93	2.01	2.00
年成长率	3.88%	4.02%	3.99%	4.00%

请计算乔山旅行社的保留盈余成本。

解　乔山旅行社保留盈余成本为（以 2015 年来看）：

$$K_r = \frac{2(1+4\%)}{155} + 4\%$$

Disadvantages: CAPM estimates two variables, which are market risk premium and beta. The common stock required return is inaccurate if the estimates of the two variables incorrect. In addition, CAPM use historical data to estimate the future, the historical data is inappropriate when the future economic conditions are changing. If the shareholders of the company don't diversify their investments, they focus on the company's individual risk rather than market risk. In this case, the risk of investment can't be able to measure by beta.

(3) The cost of retained earnings

Retained earnings has cost on the perspective of cost of opportunity, which means the retain earnings is rewards to stockholders. Stockers can use the rewards to invest other stocks by themselves. If a company keep retained earnings for future investment, the investment returns should be greater than returns of stockholders' self-investment. Otherwise, the company should distribute dividends to stockholders for their self-investment. Should a company distribute divedends or keep retained earnings for re-investment? It depends on the tax rates which are different between dividends and capital gains. Tax rate of capital gains is lower than dividends for most shareholders that make companies tend to keep retained earnings for companies' re-investments rather than distributing dividends to stockers, that is

$$K_r = \frac{D_1}{P_0} \times g$$

Example 8 - 6 Johnson's cost of retained earnings is shown in Table 8 - 2.

Table 8 - 2   Stocks of Johnson travel agent

Year	2012	2013	2014	2015
Dividends (thousand shares)	2,100	2,100	2,846	3,102
After-tax net income (thousands yuan)	574,545	762,003	1,253,338	1,718,654
IPO price (yuan)	69	73	66	155
Outstanding Shares (million shares)	84	105	126.5	155
Dividends per share (yuan)	1.81	1.93	2.01	2.00
Growth rate	3.88%	4.02%	3.99%	4.00%

What is the cost or retained earnings of Johnson (2015)?

Solution

$$K_r = \frac{2(1 + 4\%)}{155} + 4\%$$

8.4　融资顺位

　　若公司预计未来营运状况变好,那么最佳策略为使用保留盈余(当有足够流动资产时)来进行融资;次佳方案为举债;最差方案才是发行新的权益证券。由于保留盈余以及举债融资会被市场解读为公司对未来看好,因此采用不需稀释股权的融资方案,将使股价上升,现有股东价值最大化。

　　由此可得融资顺位:(1)保留盈余;(2)举债[①];(3)发行新股。

案例 ▶▶▶▶▶▶

台中旅运公司的资本理论策略

　　(1)公司偏好融资顺位为:①内部资金＞②负债＞③发行新股。

　　(2)上述融资顺位的含义:公司没有目标资本结构;公司获利力与负债成反比。

　　1)公司以"债务换回股权"的股价日的报酬率

　　以负债取代股权宣告日的股价上涨,代表投资人认同公司的融资决策(见图 8-2)。

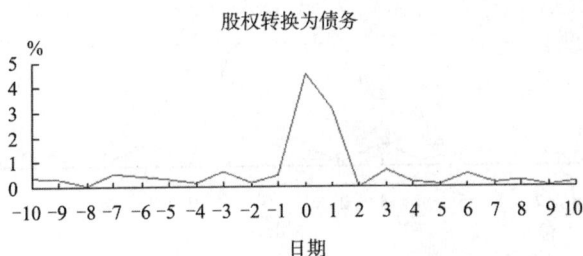

图 8-2　股权转换为债务宣告日前后股价变化

　　以股权取代负债宣告日的股价下跌,代表投资人不认同公司的融资决策(见图 8-3)。

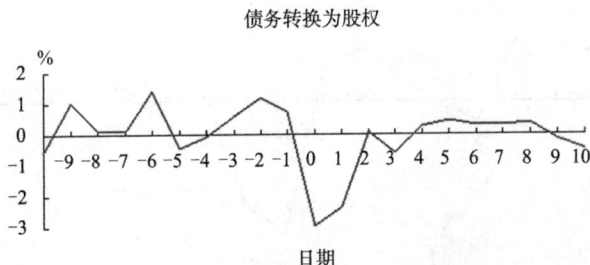

图 8-3　债务转换为股权宣告日前后股价变化

---

①　因为债权人得偿顺位第一,所以利息较低。

8.4 *The Pecking Order*

When a company's operation is getting better than expectation, the best strategy of capital budgeting is to use retained earnings, which means there is sufficient liquid assets. The second-best solution is to use debt; the worst is to issue new equity securities for captal budgeting. Investors interpret that a company is running well if a company raises funding by retained earnings and debt without dilution of equity.Thus the stock price will rise to maximize the value of existing shareholders.

The pecking order is: (1) retained earnings, (2) debt[①], and (3) IPO.

Case ▶▶▶▶▶▶

Capital strategy of Taichung travel transportation company (TTTC)

(1) Company's preference pecking order: ①retained earnings ＞②liabilities ＞③IPO.

(2) Implications: ①There is no target capital structure for the company, ②there is inverse relation between the profit and debt ratio of the company.

1) the return on stock of company's "converting equity into debt"

The stock price was raised when an announcement of converting equity into debt that means investors agreed with the company's financing decision (see Figure 8 – 2).

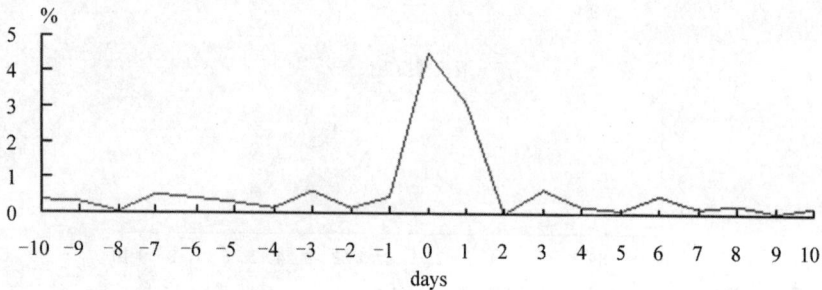

Figure 8 – 2   Change of stock price when converting equity into debt

The stock price was down when an announcement of converting debt into equity that means investors disagreed with the company's financing decision (see Figure 8 – 3).

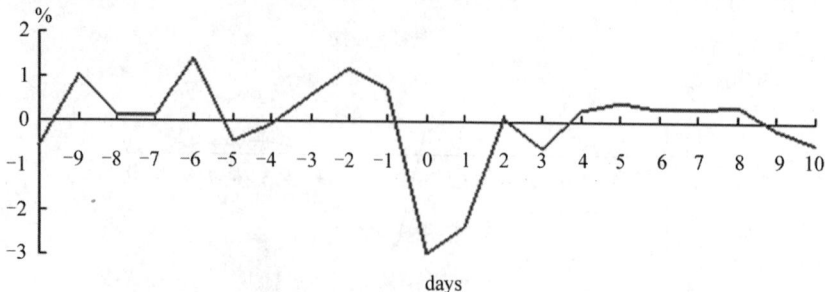

Figure 8 – 3   Change of stock price when converting debt into equity

---

① Creditors get the first default, so the interest is low.

2）公司以"股权换回债务"的股价日的报酬率

由表 8-3 可知,此公司对于内部资金盈余没有明确的规划,但有足够保留盈余可以提供给公司作资本预算,我们认为台中旅运公司会先使用内部融资再对外融资,而外部融资时,应优先使用成本较低的负债,接着才是成本较高的股票。

表 8-3　台中旅运公司举债前后的营运绩效变化

项目	举债前			举债后		
景气阶段	衰退	一般	繁荣	衰退	一般	繁荣
EBIT	$400	$800	$1200	$400	$800	$1200
利息支出	$0	$0	$0	$400	$400	$400
营业净利	$400	$800	$1200	$0	$400	$800
股东权益报酬率	4%	8%	12%	0%	4%	8%
每股盈余	2	4	6	0	4	8

例 8-7　若在 A 酒店的目标资本结构中,负债占 40%、特别股占 10%、普通股占 50%,且 $K_b = 12\%$、$K_p = 15\%$、$K_s = 20\%$,而公司税率 $t = 25\%$。计算 A 酒店的 WACC。

解

$$
\begin{aligned}
WACC &= W_b K_b (1-T) + W_p K_p + W_s K_s \\
&= 0.4 \times 12\% \times (1-0.25) + 0.1 \times 15\% + 0.5 \times 20\% \\
&= 3.6\% + 1.5\% + 10\% \\
&= 15.1\%
\end{aligned}
$$

2）The return on stock of company's "converting debt into equity"

Table 8 - 3 shows that TTTC didn't have explicit plans for retained earnings. TTTC had enough retained earnings for capital budgeting, so we believe that TTTC will use internal financing first, then use external financing. According to Fig.8 - 2, Fig.8 - 3 and Table 8 - 2, we found that TTTC used low-cost debt first, then used high-cost stock for financing.

Table 8 - 3　The performance change of TTTC before and after debt

Items	Before debt			After debt		
Stages	Recession	Normal	Prosperity	Recession	Normal	Prosperity
EBIT	$400	$800	$1,200	$400	$800	$1,200
Interest expense	$0	$0	$0	$400	$400	$400
Net income	$400	$800	$1,200	$0	$400	$800
ROE	4%	8%	12%	0%	4%	8%
EPS	2	4	6	0	4	8

Example 8 - 7　If hotel A has target capital structure of debt for 40%, preferred stock for 10%, and common stock for 50%. The $K_b = 12\%$, $K_p = 15\%$, $K_s = 20\%$, while corporate tax rate $t = 25\%$. What is the WACC of hotel A?

Solution

$$WACC = W_b K_b (1 - T) + W_p K_p + W_s K_s$$
$$= 0.4 \times 12\% \times (1 - 0.25) + 0.1 \times 15\% + 0.5 \times 20\%$$
$$= 3.6\% + 1.5\% + 10\%$$
$$= 15.1\%$$

第9章　资本结构

学习目标

- 了解资本结构的概念
- 描述资本结构理论
- 知道决定资本结构的实际考虑因素

9.1　引　言

酒店和旅游行业是由各种规模（例如,不同销售收益或投资额）和运营模式（例如,连锁、特许经营、独立等）的企业所组成的。不管大企业还是小企业或它们的运营模式如何,企业,或者更确切地说是业主,将需要向各种资本提供者包括银行和投资者寻求财政支持,进行为维持或拓展业务所须做的资产收购和投资。然而,企业怎样去向可能的资本提供者寻求支持？获得来自不同类型资本提供者支持的利弊为何？企业最好向银行借钱还是从股市集资？企业从资本市场寻求资金支持时需要承担什么样的后果和风险？企业决定向谁寻求必要资本支持或是应借款或集资多少资本是关于资本结构概念的议题。

一个企业的资本结构是其长期资金的来源,包括长期债务、优先股和普通股权益（也称为资本额）的价值比例,以长期债务对长期债务与股东权益之和占比反映:

$$长期债务对资本额比率 = \frac{长期债务}{(长期债务 + 股东权益)}$$

换句话说,资本结构反映一家企业使用长期债务资本和股权资本以支持它们购置资产和投资的财务杠杆使用情况。例如,酒店企业因为其巨额固定资产投资而通常被认为是资本密集型投资。相对于股权资本,长期债务资本

Chapter 9 Capital Structure

- Understand the concept of capital structure
- Describe capital structure theories
- Know practical considerations in determining capital structure

9.1 Introduction

The hotel and tourism industries are composed of businesses of various sizes (e.g., in terms of sales revenue or amount of assets invested) and operating modes (e.g., chain, franchised, independent, etc). Regardless of how large or small businesses are or of what their modes of operations belong to, from time to time the businesses, or more precisely the owners, will need to seek financial support from various capital providers including banks and investors for asset purchase and investments to either sustain or grow their businesses. However, how do businesses go about seeking financial support from available capital providers? What are the pros and cons of obtain support from different types of capital providers? Is it better off for a firm to borrow money from a bank or raise it in the equity market? What consequences or risks do businesses bear when seeking financial support from the capital market? The decisions to be made by the businesses as to from whom they should seek support for their requisite capital and how much they should borrow or attract are issues related to the concept of capital structure.

A firm's capital structure is the value proportion of a firm's long-term sources of funding including long-term debt, preferred stock and common equity (also called capitalization) and is reflected as the ratio of long-term debt to the sum of long-term debt and owners' equity:

$$\text{Long-term debt to total capitalization} = \frac{\text{Long-term debt}}{(\text{Long-term debt} + \text{Owners'equity})}$$

In other words, capital structure reflects a firm's usage of leverage from long-term debt capital versus equity capital in supporting their assets purchase and investment. For example, hotels are generally considered capital-intensive investments because of their significant fixed asset investments. Long-term debt capitals often account for a larger

通常占酒店企业资金来源的较大部分。餐馆的财务杠杆一般较小。例如,希尔顿酒店以及温德姆酒店 2014 年 12 月 31 日的长期债务与资本额的百分比分别为 70.86% 和 79.25%。另一方面,达登餐饮截至 2015 年 12 月 31 日的同一个百分比为 38.36%,而麦当劳 2014 年 12 月 31 日的同一个百分比为 53.84%。

然而,在中国,通常酒店企业的资本结构里股权资本多于长期债务资本。例如,2015 年 9 月 30 日金陵饭店的长期债务对资本额的百分比为 25.67%,首旅集团酒店和华天酒店也显示了较少比例的长期债务的使用,百分比分别为 33.47% 和 45.07%。就餐饮业而言,2015 年全聚德集团的资本结构中甚至没有长期债务。而旅游业的黄山旅游发展的这个百分比也只有 0.08%。造成在长期债务和股权资本之间融资偏好差异的一个重要原因是企业筹集股本比债务资本的花费相对较低。

要注意的是,在决定一个企业的资本结构时一般不包括短期债务。在评估企业资产的所有财政支持来源时,总债务和总权益之间的比例被称为财务结构。

了解资本结构本质的重要性在于,每家酒店和旅游企业都应该有一个考虑了本章后述的众多因素且最适合其运营环境的目标资本结构。有了目标资本结构,企业才能够以适当的权重估算其加权平均资本成本。

9.2　资本结构理论

被称为莫迪利亚尼—米勒定理的资本结构理论最初于 1958 年由弗兰科·莫迪利亚尼和默顿·米勒提出。该定理指出,在一个没有交易成本、破产成本和不存在税收的完美资本市场中,企业融资方式与它的价值无关。换句话说,一个企业的价值是独立于它的资本结构并通过它的盈利能力和它的标的资产的风险所决定的。此外,他们认为,有财务杠杆企业的股权成本等于无财务杠杆企业的股权成本加上一些财务风险溢价。该定理通常被视为过于理论化,因为它忽略了很多在现实世界中企业于资产融资的过程中应该要考虑的因素和不确定性。一些资本结构理论在放宽了莫迪利亚尼—米勒定理的假设之后被提出。

资本结构的权衡理论在 1973 年由克劳斯和利岑贝格尔提出,该理论指的是一个企业通过平衡与此类融资决策相关的成本和效益来决定借多少债

portion of hotel firms' capital sources as opposed to equity capital while restaurants are generally of lighter leverage. For example, Hilton Hotel and Wyndham Hotel showed 70.86% and 79.25%, respectively, in their long-term debt to total capitalization percentages as of December 31, 2014. On the other hand, Darden Restaurants showed a percentage of 38.36% as of December 31, 2015 and McDonald's 53.84% as of December 31, 2014.

However, in China normally the capital structure of hotels shows more usage of equity capital than long-term debt capital. For example, as of September 30, 2015 Jinling Hotel showed a 25.67% of long-term debt to total capitalization percentage, BTG Hotels and Huatian Hotel also showed less long-term debt usage with percentages of 33.47% and 45.07%, respectively. For the restaurant industry, Quanjude Group in 2015 did not even have long-term debt in its capital structure and for the tourism industry, Huangshan Tourism Development had a percentage of only 0.08%. One major reason for causing such difference in financing preference between long-term debt and equity capital is the relatively lower expenses for firms to raise equity capital than debt capital in China.

It should be noted here that short-term debt is generally not considered in determining a firm's capital structure; if it is to be accounted for in determining total financial support from all capital sources for a firm's assets, the structure or the proportions between total debts and total equity is termed financial structure.

The importance of understanding the essence of capital structure is that, for each hotel and tourism business, they should probably have a target capital structure most suitable for their own operational environment by considering a number of factors that we will explain later in the chapter. With a target capital structure, a firm will be able to estimate the weighted average cost of capital with the proper weights.

9.2 Capital Structure Theories

The capital structure theory was originally proposed by Franco Modigliani and Merton Miller in 1958, termed the Modigliani-Miller theorem. The theorem states that in a perfect capital market where no transaction costs, bankruptcy costs and no taxes exist, how a firm is financed is irrelevant to its value. In other words, the value of a firm is independent of its capital structure and is determined by its earning power and the risk of its underlying assets. Besides, they argued that the cost of equity for a leveraged firm is the same as that of an unleveraged firm plus some added premium for financial risk. The theorem is normally viewed as too theoretical as it ignores many factors and uncertainties a firm ought to consider in the process of financing its asset investments in the real world. In relaxing the assumptions of the Modigliani-Miller theorem, a few theories of capital structure were advanced.

The trade-off theory of capital structure was proposed by Kraus and Litzenberger in 1973 and refers to that a firm determines how much debt to borrow and how much equity

务或发行多少股权。因为与债务融资相关的利息费用可以抵税，企业可以利用债务融资享受避税或利息税盾带来的好处而降低它的债务成本。换句话说，一个善用债务融资的企业能够享受更多的利息税盾。然而，当企业需要更多资金用于资产购买和投资时是否可以持续使用债务融资？答案是否定的。采用债务融资除了明显的利息支出成本，同时还须承担如破产费用和财务困境成本等额外费用。当企业负债水平提高时，债权人会对企业未来的借款要求较高利率，以补偿其所承担的违约风险。如此一来，该企业不仅有产生足够的现金流以履行其偿债义务（即，支付本金和利息）的压力，同时还有受债权人密切监察的压力。也就是说，当财务杠杆水平持续提高时，进一步利用债务融资的边际收益会下降。因此，企业应注重债务和使用股权融资之间的权衡，以优化企业价值。因此，公司应该有一个最优财务杠杆。

　　资本结构的啄食顺序理论可以追溯到1961年唐纳森对企业融资行为的研究，而后该理论由迈尔斯提出。该理论提出企业的融资偏好应该有优先顺序：内部融资优先于外部融资，如果需要外部融资的话，债务融资优先于股权融资。换句话说，当出现资金需求时，企业应首先寻求最廉价的内部资金来源，也就是留存收益，其次是寻求债务融资，最后才发行需要昂贵的发行成本的新股。在信息不对称的假设之下，投资者认为管理人员拥有公众所没有的关键信息。因此，当企业通过发行新股而不是从内部资源寻求资金时，投资者会认为这样的融资行为暗示该企业可能没能做好产生足够留存收益的工作，所以该企业需要向外部寻求资金。投资者也可能会觉得发行新股暗示着企业价值被高估，经理人只想利用这个态势来圈钱，因此对企业价值产生负面影响。不像权衡理论，在资本结构的啄食顺序理论下并没有目标杠杆比率。

　　选择不同的融资方案时也应关注代理成本。为了减轻债权人所承担的企业违约风险和保证有足够的运营现金流来支付债务，债权人合理地从规避风险的角度可能会制定限制性的债务契约。不过，企业效率和生产力可能因此受到限制而无法发挥其最大潜力来创造利润和提升价值。此外，随着债务

to issue by balancing the benefits and costs associated with such financing decisions. As interest expenses associated with debt financing is tax deductible，firms utilizing debt financing are able to enjoy a tax shelter or interest tax shield as a benefit because its cost of debt is reduced. In other words，the more debt financing a firm is utilizing，the higher interest tax shield it is enjoying. Nevertheless，can a firm keep using debt financing when it needs additional funds for its asset purchase and investments? The answer is No! The costs of using debt financing，besides the obvious interest expense，are the additional costs borne such as the bankruptcy cost and the financial distress cost. When firms are increasingly leveraged，their future debt may be financed with heightened interest rates to compensate debtors for bearing higher default risk. As a result，the firms will be not only stressed for producing due cash flows in meeting their debt obligations (i.e.，making principal and interest payments) but also monitored more closely by debtors. That is，the marginal benefit of further utilizing debt financing declines as the leverage level increases. Therefore，in optimizing firm value，firms shall be focusing on the trade-off between the usage of debt and equity financing. Thus，there would be an optimal debt leverage for a firm.

The pecking order theory of capital structure dates back to Donaldson's study on firms' financing practices in 1961 and was advanced by Myers. The theory states that firms shall adopt a hierarchical order of financing preferences：internal financing is preferred over external financing and debt financing is preferred over equity financing if external funding is needed. In other words，when financial needs arise，firms shall first seek for the most inexpensive source of funding internally，that is，retained earnings. Then，debt financing will be sought after，before issuance of new equity which requires expensive issuance costs. Under the assumption of asymmetric information，investors think that managers would possess critical information not made available to the public. Therefore，when a firm seeks funding by issuing new equity instead of from internal sources，investors would perceive such financing behavior as a signal that the firm has not been doing a good job by producing enough retained earnings，so that the firm needs to go outside of the firm for funds. The investors might also perceive new equity issuance as a signal that the firm is over-valued and that firm managers just try to take advantage of this over-valuation，therefore causing negative impact on firm value. Unlike the trade-off theory，there is no target leverage ratio under the pecking order theory of capital structure.

Agency costs should also be concerned among the choice of different financing options. To mitigate a firm's default risk borne by a debtor and to better secure cash flow from operations to pay for debt obligations，there could be restrictive debt covenants mandated by the debtor，which is reasonable from a risk aversion perspective. However，firm efficiency and productivity may hence be limited that prevent a firm from maximizing its most potential in profit generation and value enhancement. Besides，

融资程度的加深,监控和合同成本也会同时增大。

1. 财务杠杆相关的财务风险

与债务融资相关的另一种代理成本形式为当财务杠杆高的时候,业主往往倾向于投资高风险的项目(使用更多的债权人资金):当项目回报好时,业主往往能坐享其利;当项目的成果不如预期,不利的结果很可能会影响到债权人。来看下面的例子,说明不同的财务杠杆如何影响业主的股本回报率。

假设一家旅行社有 100 万美元总资产,如表 9-1 所示,它可以以 4 种不同的方式进行融资:100% 的股权融资,如方案 1;20%、45% 和 70% 的财务杠杆如方案 2、3 和 4。进一步假设借款利率为每年 10%,所得税税率为 25%。假设明年在正常的经济条件下它的息税前利润预测为 6 万美元(情况 A)。与这个息税前利润相关的不同的财务杠杆水平将如何影响业主的回报?

由表 9-1 可知,在不同的财务杠杆水平下,业主若没有财务杠杆时可能获得4.5% 的股本回报率,而在 70% 财务杠杆时的股本回报率为 -3.33%。由这个情况我们可以得知旅行社如何融资会影响业主的实际回报。另外,假设明年在乐观的经济条件下它的息税前利润预测为 12 万美元(情况 B),业主若没有财务杠杆时可能获得 9% 的股本回报率,而在 70% 财务杠杆时的股本回报率为12.5%。所以在较好的经济情况下,我们可以看到,随着财务杠杆水平的提高,业主可以实现更高的股本回报率。然而,假设明年在悲观的经济条件下它的息税前利润预测为 2 万美元(情况 C),业主若没有财务杠杆时只能获得1.5% 的股本回报率,而在 70% 财务杠杆时的股本回报率更低至 -16.67%。也就是说,当企业表现不好时,具有较高的财务杠杆的企业比那些低财务杠杆企业更容易受影响。

此外,我们还可以看到,在不同的融资方案中股本回报率的变动范围也不相同。方案 1 在不同的息税前利润情况下其股本回报率的变动范围是最小的(即 1.5% ～ 9%),而方案 4 的股本回报率的变动范围最大(即 -3.33% ～ -16.67%)。股本回报率的变动意味着不确定性和风险。换句话说,我们可以推论财务杠杆的增加会令企业的股本回报率或每股收益的波动增加而使得企业的风险增高。因此,有较高融资水平的企业不仅其财务风险较高,而且需要更好的息税前利润水平以求保本。这不仅对经理在创造更好的经营业绩方面施加了压力,同时也使企业的运营增加了较高的不确定性。企业一般会尽量避免与高财务杠杆相关的财务风险,以降低所需的息税前利润水平。

monitoring costs and contractual costs are expected to be increased as the level of debt financing increases.

1. Financial risk associated with financial leverage

Another form of agency costs associated with debt financing is that, when financial leverage is high, owners tend to undertake risky projects (using more debtor's fund): when projects pay off, the favorable results accrue to the owners; when the results of the projects don't turn out as expected, the unfavorable outcome would likely affect the debtors. Look at the following example showing how different financial leverage would impact return on equity for owners.

Suppose that one travel agency has total assets of $1,000,000, as shown in Table 9 - 1, and it could be financed in four different ways: 100% financed by equity as shown in scenario 1; 20%, 45% and 70% financial leverage respectively shown in scenarios 2, 3 and 4. Further assume that the loan interest rate is 10% per annum and the income tax rate is 25%. Suppose that it is forecasted in the next year it can have an EBIT equaling to $60,000 (Case A) under the normal economic condition. How would this level of EBIT associated with different financial leverage levels affect the owners' return? It can be seen in Table 9 - 1 that, with different financial leverage levels, the owners could obtain a ROE of 4.5% when there's zero financial leverage to − 3.33% when there's 70% financial leverage. In this case, how the travel agency is financed affects the actual return for the owners. Alternatively, in the case where EBIT is forecasted to be $120,000 (Case B) under an optimistic economic condition, owners' ROEs range from 9% under no financial leverage to 12.5% under a 70% financial leverage. In the case of a better economic condition, we can see that the owners could realize higher ROEs as the financial leverage level increases. Nevertheless, when EBIT is forecasted to be at the $20,000 level (Case C) under a pessimistic economic condition, owners' ROEs deteriorated from 1.5% under no financial leverage to − 16.67% with a 70% financial leverage. That is, when the business doesn't perform well, businesses with higher financial leverage suffer more than those with lower financial leverage.

Besides, we can also see that the range of ROEs of each financing scenario varies. Scenario 1 has the least variation of ROEs under different EBIT levels (i.e., between 1.5% ∼9%) where scenario 4 has the most variation of ROEs (i.e., − 3.33% ∼ − 16.67%). Variations of ROEs signify uncertainty and risk. In other words, we can infer that financial leverage increases a firm's risk because of increasing variability of a firm's return on equity or the variability of its earnings per share. As a result, a firm with a higher level of debt financing not only has a higher level of financial risk but also needs a better level of EBIT in order to just break-even; this not only creates pressure for the management to produce better operational results but also adds higher uncertainty to a firm's operations. A firm will generally try to avoid financial risk associated with high financial leverage to reduce the requisite level of EBIT.

表 9 - 1　旅行社的融资方式

方　案	1	2	3	4
总资产	$1000000	$1000000	$1000000	$1000000
负债	0	200000	450000	700000
权益	1000000	800000	550000	300000
财务杠杆	0％	20％	45％	70％
息税前利润(情况 A)	$60000	$60000	$60000	$60000
利息费用（10％）	0	(20000)	(45000)	(70000)
税前利润	60000	40000	15000	(10000)
税费（25％）	(15000)	(10000)	(12500)	0
净利润	$45000	$30000	$2500	($10000)
股本回报率	4.5％	3.75％	0.45％	(3.33％)
息税前利润(情况 B)	$120000	$120000	$120000	$120000
利息费用（10％）	0	(20000)	(45000)	(70000)
税前利润	120000	100000	75000	50000
税费（25％）	(30000)	(25000)	(18750)	(12500)
净利润	$90000	$75000	$56250	$37500
股本回报率	9％	9.38％	10.23％	12.5％
息税前利润(情况 C)	$20000	$20000	$20000	$20000
利息费用（10％）	0	(20000)	(45000)	(70000)
税前利润	20000	0	(25000)	(50000)
税费（25％）	(5000)	0	0	0
净利润	$15000	($20000)	($25000)	($50000)
股本回报率	1.5％	(2.5％)	(4.55％)	(16.67％)

注：括号代表负数。

2. 最佳资本结构

我们从上面了解到,在决定企业的融资组合和资本成本时,就债务成本 K_D 而言,企业将在债务融资初期享受利息税盾的好处,之后由于财务困境成本和破产成本增加, K_D 会以较高的速度增加(如图 9 - 1 中所示)。股权融资成本 K_E 会比债务融资的成本要高,同时随着财务杠杆的增加而增高。加权平均资本成本 K_A 是由在资本结构中债务融资占比 W_D 和股权融资占比 W_E 来决定如下:

Table 9 - 1   Financing cases of travel agent

Scenario	1	2	3	4
Total assets	$1,000,000	$1,000,000	$1,000,000	$1,000,000
Debt	0	200,000	450,000	700,000
Equity	1,000,000	800,000	550,000	300,000
Financial leverage	0%	20%	45%	70%
EBIT-Case A	$60,000	$60,000	$60,000	$60,000
Interest expense (10%)	0	(20,000)	(45,000)	(70,000)
EBT	60,000	40,000	15,000	(10,000)
Tax expense (25%)	(15,000)	(10,000)	(12,500)	0
Net income	$45,000	$30,000	$2,500	($10,000)
ROE	4.5%	3.75%	0.45%	(3.33%)
EBIT-Case B	$120,000	$120,000	$120,000	$120,000
Interest expense (10%)	0	(20,000)	(45,000)	(70,000)
EBT	120,000	100,000	75,000	50,000
Tax expense (25%)	(30,000)	(25,000)	(18,750)	(12,500)
Net income	$90,000	$75,000	$56,250	$37,500
ROE	9%	9.38%	10.23%	12.5%
EBIT-Case C	$20,000	$20,000	$20,000	$20,000
Interest expense (10%)	0	(20,000)	(45,000)	(70,000)
EBT	20,000	0	(25,000)	(50,000)
Tax expense (25%)	(5,000)	0	0	0
Net income	$15,000	($20,000)	($25,000)	($50,000)
ROE	1.5%	(2.5%)	(4.55%)	(16.67%)

Note: Bracket represents negative amount.

2. Optimal capital structure

From the above, we learned that in determining a firm's financing mix and its cost of capital, for the cost of debt K_D a firm will enjoy interest tax shield benefit at the beginning of debt financing and later K_D will increase at a higher rate due to added financial distress cost and bankruptcy cost, as depicted in the Figure 9 - 1. The cost of equity financing K_E will be higher than that of debt financing and increases as financial leverage increases. The weighted average cost of capital K_A is determined by the relative proportion of debt financing W_D and equity financing W_E in the capital structure and can be expressed as

$$加权平均资本成本＝债务融资占比×债务融资成本$$

$$＋股权融资占比×股权融资成本$$

我们可从图 9-1 中看到,由于在资本结构中引入债务融资,K_A 一开始会下降,直到某个水平,此时财务困境成本和破产成本超过了利息税盾带来的好处,此时 K_A 会是最低的。这种特定的杠杆比率被称为最佳资本结构。当达到这个最佳资本结构时,企业最能够平衡与债务融资相关的成本和效益,并让业主使用财务杠杆的力量获取自己的财务回报。

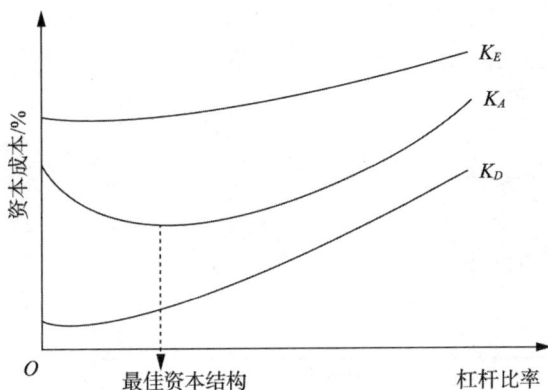

图 9-1　最佳资本结构

然而,在现实中是否任何一家企业都可以找到其最佳资本结构?虽然理论上最佳资本结构是存在的,但寻找该结构一直是研究人员努力尝试的一个非常复杂的任务。目前有着太多的融资产品可供选择,这使得寻找最佳资本结构的任务变得更加复杂。与其寻找最佳资本结构,或许寻找一个最佳资本结构的范围是比较可能实现的任务。

9.3　资本结构的实际考虑

如果一个企业能达到其最佳资本结构,其加权平均资本成本会处于最低水平。在现实中,虽然有许多因素需要考虑和关注,企业应尽其所能考虑最多的实际因素来寻找一个最适合自身的资本结构范围,使其加权平均资本成本在实际上达到能提升企业价值的低水平。涉及寻找最佳资本结构的一些实际问题讨论如下。

$$K_A = W_D K_D + W_E K_E$$

As we can see from the Figure $9-1$, K_A will first decline due to introduction of debt financing into the capital structure until some point where the costs of financial distress and bankruptcy outweigh that the benefit of the interest tax shield and K_A is at its lowest. This particular leverage ratio is called the optimal capital structure. When achieving this optimal capital structure, a firm can most balance the cost and benefit associated with debt financing and allow owners in reaching their financial return using the power of financial leverage.

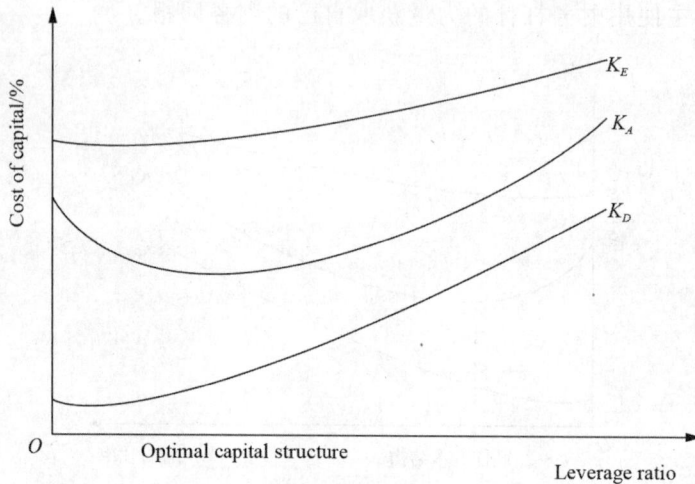

Figure $9-1$ Optimal capital structure

However, in reality can an optimal capital structure for any firm be found? While theoretically an optimal capital structure exists, finding it in an empirical setting is a very complicated task that researchers have been working on; the problem of finding an optimal capital structure is further complicated with the many financing options and products available nowadays. Instead of finding an optimal capital structure point, probably an optimal capital structure range is a more feasible task to achieve.

9.3   *Practical Considerations in Capital Structure*

If a firm could reach its optimal capital structure, its weighted average cost of capital is at the lowest level. In reality, while there are many factors to be considered and of concern, firms should try to identify a band of target capital structure most suitable for them by considering as many practical factors as possible so that the resultant weighted average cost of capital would be at a practically low level for the benefit of enhancing firm value. Some practical considerations related to approaching an optimal capital structure are discussed below.

1. 行业标准

受到如季节性、经济状况、消费者行为和偏好等因素的影响,酒店和旅游业的表现高度波动。因此,经营者在赚取能满足其偿债要求的运营现金流方面面临着很大的不确定性。换句话说,酒店和旅游业经营者可能会面临不同程度的基于自身营商环境的商业风险。如果一个企业有着相对较低的商业风险且具有更稳定的息税前利润,它或许可以借由这样的优势来利用财务杠杆的力量产生更高的利润。相反地,如果一个企业面临较高的商业风险且具有不太稳定的息税前利润,在寻求债务融资时要更加谨慎,因为这会对经营者产生赚取能满足其偿债要求的现金流的压力。因此,在确定融资组合时酒店和旅游企业应该考虑它们自身的商业风险。实证表明,个别企业的资本结构趋于向行业平均水平靠拢。

2. 债权人要求和信贷机构评级

根据企业的财务杠杆水平和过去的信贷记录,债权人可能以契约限制企业贷款用途和未来可借款的债务总额,以降低其违约的可能性。然而,企业是否愿意接受债权人施加的各种类型和约束的债务条款?这种限制性条款会如何影响企业的战略方向和运营而最终影响企业的盈利底线和价值?此外,为了能够灵活地面对未来的投资机会,并增加从债权人成功借款的可能性,企业可能希望通过保持低水平的杠杆比率以维持其借贷能力,并期望能以财政健全的姿态成功获得低息贷款。将运营盈利进行再投资应该可以降低企业在资本结构中的债务使用水平。现在的问题是,杠杆率应该维持在多低的水平才能使得企业不仅可以享有债务融资的税盾利益同时还保持财政健全的姿态呢?尽管这个问题可能没有明确答案,但企业除了产生持续不断的现金流令债权人安心,其杠杆比率也最好不要偏离行业平均水平太多。

3. 管理人员规避风险的态度

管理者可能会比投资者更偏好较低债务融资,从而承担较低的财务风

1. Industry standard

The performance of the hotel and tourism industries is highly fluctuating due to many reasons such as seasonality, economic condition, consumer behavior and preference, among others and therefore, there exists great uncertainty faced by the operators in relation to generating requisite operating cash flows in meeting various financial obligations. In other words, hotel and tourism operators may face different levels of business risks depending on their individual situations such as their business and operating environments. If a firm faces a relatively low business risk and has more stable EBIT, it can probably capitalize on such operating advantage in utilizing the power of financial leverage in generating a higher level of profit. On the contrary, if a firm faces a relatively high business risk and has less stable EBIT, it probably should be more prudent in seeking financial support from debt financing as this would press the operators for generating requisite cash flows in meeting debt obligations. Therefore, hotel and tourism firms should consider their individual business risks when determining their financing mix. Empirical evidence shows that individual firms' capital structure tends to move toward the industry average level.

2. Creditor requirements and credit agency rating

Depending on the level of financial leverage a firm may have had and its past credit history, a debtor may impose restrictive covenants in restricting the usage of the loan extended and the total amount of future debt the firm can borrow for the purpose of reducing the possibility of a default. However, will firms be willing to accept the types and terms of debt constraints imposed by debtors? How might such restrictive covenants affect the strategic directions and operations of the firm and ultimately the bottom line profit and value of the firm? Besides, in order to possess flexibility in reacting to future investment possibilities and increase the chance of successfully borrowing money from creditors, firms may want to maintain their borrowing capacity by keeping their leverage ratio low and appear financially strong to potential creditors to not only secure loans but also be granted low interest rates. Reinvestment of the earnings from operations shall reduce the use of debt in a firm's capital structure. Now the question is that, how low a leverage ratio should a firm maintain not only to enjoy the benefit of debt financing's tax shield but also to appear financially healthy? While there may not be definitive answers to this question, it probably would be wise that a firm's leverage ratio does not deviate too much from industry averages, in addition to assuring debtors' confidence by showing an ability to generating constant cash flows.

3. Managerial risk aversion

Managers possibly prefer lower financial risk characterized by less debt financing

险,因为管理者在面对较低的财务风险时,他们所承担的产生能满足偿债要求的运营结果或至少能达到保本点销售额的压力会较小。如果资本结构中有着较高的杠杆水平,虽然利息费用在损益表中是列在运营毛利之下的,假设运营结果不如预期的话,企业仍然可能产生亏损。

4. 公司控制和治理

在确定企业融资组合时,一个关键的考虑因素是对企业的控制和治理。业主有动诱因从银行借长期债务或发行固定收益证券,包括企业债券和/或优先股,从而利用财务杠杆的力量来达到较高的投资回报。业主另外一个利用债务融资的动机是保持他们对企业的所有权和控制权。如果要发行新股,此举除了将摊薄股份之外,更相当于邀请外人加入业主俱乐部而给企业的未来带来不确定性。有可能有一些拥有相当数量股票的新股东进入董事会(如债权人董事),但他们缺乏必要的行业经验和知识来与其他董事一起为企业做出战略指导。特别是大股东或控股股东可能会要求发出不授予投票权受限制的普通股以维持自己的控制权。最后,但是同样重要的是,有很少或根本没有财务杠杆的企业通常被认为是极佳的被并购目标。换句话说,债务已被目标企业用来作为反收购的防御工具。

than is desired by investors，because with lower financial risk they would be less pressed for generating higher operating results to satisfy debt obligations or at least meet the break-even point sales requirement. With a higher level of leverage in the capital structure，if the operating result is not impressive enough，it is possible that the firm may incur net loss，albeit interest expenses is below the line of gross operating profit on the profit and loss statement.

4. Corporate control and governance

In determining financing mix of a firm，one critical consideration is on corporate control and governance. Owners have an incentive to utilize the power of financial leverage in terms of borrowing long-term debt from banks or issuing fixed-income securities including corporate bonds and/or preferred stocks in accruing higher returns for their investment. Besides，another incentive for capitalizing on debt financing is to maintain their ownership position and controlling power over the firm. If new equity issuance is to be carried out，besides the concern on share dilution，issuing new equity is equivalent to inviting outsiders to join the owners' club and this action comes with uncertainty related to the firm's future. It is possible that some new entrants with sizable amount of shares may be elected to the board of directors (such as creditor-director) but they lack requisite industry experience and knowledge to join force with others in making firm strategic directions. In particular，block shareholders or controlling owners may desire to issue restricted common stocks that don't grant voting rights so as to maintain their controlling power. Last but not the least，firms with little or no financial leverage are often considered excellent candidates for corporate takeover. In other words，debt has been used as a defensive tool for a target firm against takeover.

第 10 章 资本预算与现金流估算

学习目标

- 了解资本预算的意义
- 计算资本预算中的现金流量
- 理解资本预算中特殊情形的现金流量估算

10.1 资本预算

资本预算主要是探讨公司在固定资产上所做的投资决策。企业的投资活动分为两类：一是维持日常营运的经常性投资，又称为营运资金；二是为实现长期策略规划所进行的资本投资。通过分析投资方案，即对不同投资计划进行评估与选择，可以更有效地利用公司资金，进而增加股东的财富。公司利用资本预算制定投资决策时，应该考虑下列几个原则：

(1) 投资方案必须考虑所有的现金流量。

(2) 所选择的投资方案必须能达成股东财富最大化的目标。

(3) 现金流量折现法所采用的折现率为资金机会成本。

(4) 若公司所从事的投资方案之间彼此系互相独立，则公司的价值等于各方案价值的总和，此称为价值附加性原则。根据此原则，在选择最佳投资方案时可以单独考虑某一方案，而不须顾虑方案之间彼此的互动性。

10.2 现金流量估算

在资本预算中，我们估计的是计划在未来产生现金流量的净现值。所有现金流量的估计都是具有前瞻性的。其公式为

现金流量＝税后净利＋折旧－资本支出－净营运资金的变动

Chapter 10　Capital Budgeting and Cash Flows

Learning Outcomes

- Understand the concept of capital budgeting
- Estimate cash flows of capital budgeting
- Understand special cases of cash flows of capital budgeting

10.1　Capital Budgeting

Capital budgeting is to discuss the company's investment decisions made in fixed assets. Company's investment activities are divided into two categories: one is to maintain a regular daily operations of investment, also known as working capital; one is capital investment to achieve long-term strategic planning. By analyzing the investment program, evaluating and selecting from the different investment plans, a company can use capital effectively, thereby increasing shareholders' wealth. When companies use capital budgeting to make investment decision, the following principles should be considered:

(1) The investment program must take into account all the cash flows.

(2) The selected investment programs must be able to reach the goal of maximizing shareholder wealth.

(3) The discount rate of discounted cash flow method should adopt opportunity cost.

(4) If the investment programs of a company are independent from each other, the value of the company is equal to the value sum of the programs, which is called the value-added principle.According to the value-added principle, the best investment program can be considered as an individual program, without being worry about correlating with other programs.

10.2　Cash Flow Estimation

In capital budgeting, we estimate the NPV of the cash flows that a project is expected to produce in the future. All of the cash flow estimates are forward-looking. We have

cash flow = net income + depreciation − capital expenditures − net working capital

1. 增量税后自由现金流量

在净现值分析时我们所折算的现金流是增量税后的现金流量。事实上当计划被采用后,公司的税后总自由现金流量将会有所改变,即有

$$FCF_{计划} = FCF_{公司采用计划} - FCF_{公司无计划}$$

自由现金流量一词指的是,该公司可以免费将这些现金流量自由发放给债权人和股东,因为这些现金流量是完成营运资金及长期资产等必要投资后所剩余的现金流量。该 FCF 的计算变量如表 10-1 所示。

表 10-1　现金流量的计算

计算		变量		解释
	收益		Revenue	公司现金收入的变化,不包括利息支出。
−	营业支出	−	Op Ex	
	息前、税前、折旧前盈余		EBDIT	
−	折旧与摊销	−	D&A	
	营业盈余		EBIT	
	(1−公司边际税率)		(1−t)	
	税后净营业盈余		NOPAT	
+	折旧与摊销	+	D&A	折旧、摊销和投资对 FCF 的影响调整。
	营业现金流量		CF Opns	
−	资本支出	−	Cap Exp	
−	营运资金	−	Add WC	
	自由现金流量		FCF	

自由现金流量(FCF)等于公司投资计划的现金收入的变化,其不计利息费用,加上折旧及摊销项目,减去所有必要的资本支出和营运资金投资。FCF 也等于从投资计划营运后上缴了增量税后的现金流中减去资本支出和营运资金。

$$FCF = [(Revenue - Op\ Exp - D\&A) \times (1-t)]$$
$$+ D\&A - Cap\ Ex - Add\ WC$$

我们首先计算运营增量现金流量(CF Opns),这是该计划预期产生的所有营运费用和相关税负已经支付后的现金流量。

然后,我们减去增量资本支出(Cap Exp)和增量营运资金(Add WC)项目,以获得计划所需的自由现金流量。

1. Incremental after-tax free cash flows

The cash flows we discount in an NPV analysis are the incremental after-tax free cash flows, which refers to the fact that these cash flows reflect the amount by which the firm's total after-tax free cash flows will change if the project is adopted. That is

$$FCF_{Project} = FCF_{Firm\ with\ project} - FCF_{Firm\ without\ project}$$

The term free cash flows (FCF) refers to the fact that the firm is free to distribute these cash flows to creditors and stockholders because these are the cash flows that are left over after a firm has made necessary investments in working capital and long-term assets. The FCF calculation is shown as Table 10-1.

Table 10-1 The free cash flow calculation

	Calculation		Formula	Explanation
	Revenue		Revenue	
−	Case operating expense	−	Op Ex	
	Earnings before interest, taxes, depreciation, and amortization		EBDIT	The change in the firm's cash income, excluding interest expense, resulting from the project.
−	Depreciation, and amortization	−	D&A	
	Operating profit		EBIT	
×	(1 − Firm's marginal tax rate)	×	(1 − t)	
	Net operating profit after tax		NOPAT	
+	Depreciation and amortization	+	D&A	
	Cash flow from operations		CF Opns	Adjustments of the impact of depreciation and amortization and investments on FCF.
−	Capital expenditures	−	Cap Exp	
−	Additions to working capital	−	Add WC	
	Free cash flow		FCF	

The FCF equals the change in the firm's cash income, excluding interest expense, that the project is response for, plus depreciation and amortization for the project, minus all required capital expenditures and investments in working capital. FCF also equals to the incremental after-tax cash flow from operations minus the capital expenditures and investments in working capital required for the project.

$$FCF = \left[(Revenue - Op\ Exp - D\&A) \times (1 - t)\right] + D\&A - Cap\ Ex - Add\ WC$$

We first compute the incremental cash flow from operations (CF Opns), which is the cash flow that the project is expected to generate after all operating expenses and taxes have been paid.

We then subtract the incremental capital expenditures (Cap Exp) and incremental additions to working capital (Add WC) required for the project to obtain FCF.

因此,FCF 就成了任何必要的投资项目中衡量运营所需的税后现金流量的指标。我们以一个独立计划的方式评估公司的现金流量的概念被称为独立原则,也就是说,我们可以把一项计划当成一个独立的公司,其有自己的收入、支出和投资需求,可方便对计划进行评估。

营运的增量现金流量(CF Opns)等于增加的税后净营运利润(NOPAT)加上与计划相关的增量折旧及摊销(D&A)。计算税后净营业利润时,因为一项计划的融资成本反映在 NPV 计算中使用的折现率,我们排除了利息费用。我们使用公司的边际税率(t),因为该计划所产生的利润被视为公司利润的增量。我们计算增量营运现金流量时,将增量折旧及摊销计入其中,因为在现金流量的会计报表中,D&A 表示的非现金费用可降低企业的税赋。然而,由于 D&A 是一种非现金费用,我们必须加回税后净营业利润至 NOPAT,以获得正确的现金流量。

一旦我们完成对 CF Opns 的估计,我们可以简单地减去投资所需的相关的现金流量,以得到一个计划在一个特定时期的 FCF。投资可以根据需要去购买长期的有形资产和无形资产,或投资流动资产。

2. 实际资本预算中估计现金流量

增量现金流的计算有五个一般性的规则:(1)在计算中只包含现金流量。不包括分摊的成本或费用,除非它们与现金流量有关。(2)包括其他计划项目对该计划现金流量的影响。如果其他计划预计将减少或增加该计划的产品销量,我们必须计入其他计划对该计划现金流量的影响。(3)包括所有的机会成本。机会成本的意思是投资该计划所放弃其他计划的成本。(4)忘掉沉没成本。沉没成本是已经产生的费用,且当你在某个特定时间点评估一个项目时是与其有关的,但重要的是当你在一个特定的时间点评估一项计划时,你会预期有多少资金可以投资于未来与所期望得到的报酬;这意味着过去的投资是不相关的。(5)只包括税后现金的计算。公司投资者在一个计划中所获得的税后现金流量增量只一定程度地与税前盈余有关。

例 10 - 1　有一个连锁平价酒店规划在一个新址开设新的分店,预期服务销售额为每年 400 万元,估计这些销售额中有 75 万元是酒店集团中其他酒店的现有客户贡献的。什么是新酒店在资本预算决策中应使用的正确增量收入?上面提到的新酒店拥有一栋建筑物,目前尚未提供服务。建筑物的原始成本是 700 万元,其目前的市场价值为 1200 万元。另外,建筑物可租赁给另一家餐厅,每年可收入 50 万元。什么是做资本预算决定时应考虑的现

The FCF is therefore a measure of the after-tax cash flows from operations over and above what is necessary to make any required investments. The idea that we can evaluate the cash flows from a project independently is known as the stand-alone principle. It is another way of saying that we can treat the project as if it is a stand-alone firm that has its own revenue, expenses, and investment requirements. Then the projects can easily be assessed.

The incremental cash flow from operations (CF Opns), equals the incremental net operating profits after tax (NOPAT) plus the incremental depreciation and amortization (D&A) associated with the project. We exclude interest expenses when calculating NOPAT because the cost of financing a project is reflected in the discount rate that is used in the NPV calculation. We use the firm's marginal tax rate (t) to calculate NOPAT because the profits from a project are assumed to be incremental to the firm. We add incremental depreciation and amortization (D&A) to NOPAT when calculating CF Opns because, as in the accounting statement of cash flows, D&A represents a noncash charge that reduces the firm's tax obligation. However, since D&A is a noncash charge, we have to add it back to NOPAT in order to get the cash flow from operations right.

Once we have estimated CF Opns, we simply substract cash flows associated with required investment to obtain FCF for a project in a particular period. Investments can be required to purchase long-term tangible assets and intangible assets, or to fund current assets.

2. Estimating cash flows in practical capital budgeting

There are five general rules for incremental cash flow calculations: (1) Include cash flows and only cash flows in calculations. Do not include allocated costs or overhead unless they reflect cash flows. (2) Include the impact of the project on cash flows from other projects. If other projects are expected to cannibalize or boost sales of the concerned project, we must include the expected impact of the new project on the cash flows from the other project in the analysis. (3) Include all opportunity costs. By opportunity costs, we mean the cost of giving up another opportunity. (4) Forget sunk costs. Sunk costs are costs that have already been incurred, but all that matters when you evaluate a project at a particular point in time is how much you have to invest in the future and what you could expect to receive in return for that investment; this means that past investments are irrelevant. (5) Include only after-tax cash flows in the cash flow calculations. The incremental pretax earnings of a project only matter to the extent that they affect the after-tax cash flows that the firm's investors receive.

Example 10 – 1   A budget hotel group plan to have a new branch in a new location. The projected sales for a new service are 4,000,000 yuan per year, although it is estimated that 750,000 yuan of these sales are from current customers that will switch from one of the group's other hotels. What is the correct incremental revenue from the new hotel that should be used in the capital budgeting decision? The new hotel mentioned above owns a building that is not currently offering services. The original cost

金流量？新酒店对建筑物的检测、调查、开发花了 100 万元,以决定是否在新址开设新的酒店。在做资本预算决定时,这 100 万元是否该被列入现金流量的估算？

确保所有的现金流量以名义货币或实质货币计算是非常重要的。名义货币是我们通常所认知的货币。名义货币代表了我们期望一个计划在未来产生的实际金额,不作任何调整。当物价上涨时,给定的名义金额购买力会逐渐降低。实质货币则代表购买力不会随着物价与时间而改变。我们可以将资本成本 k 表示如下：

$$1+k=(1+\Delta P_e)\times(1+r)$$

式中：r 是实质资金成本；ΔP_e 是预期通货膨胀率；r 是实质报酬率。

投资计划在计算各年份的自由现金流量时,最后一年的现金流量通常不予计算。例如,在到了一个计划的最后一年时,计划期间所获得的资产可能已被出售,所投入的营运资金也可能已被回收。

增加的营运资金＝现金与折合现金的改变
　　　　　　　＋应收账款的改变＋投资的改变－应付账款的改变

最后一年 FCF 的计算除了计算销售时受到的公司税的影响,当资产出售将有残值时,我们也必须在资产出售的销售额(计算税后净值)上加入实现的残值。

净现值分析时所预测的 FCF 仅是我们的估算。对于某年的预期的FCF,其计算等于可能的结果(自由现金流量)与这些结果发生概率的乘积总和。

3. 预测自由现金流量

(1) 营运的现金流量

要从营运中预测增量现金流量,我们必须预测计划所产生的增量净收益、营业费用和折旧及摊销,以及公司的边际税率。当预测营业费用时,分析人员往往将费用分成变动成本和固定成本。

(2) 投资现金流量

计算自由现金流时我们必须考虑投资的两大基本分类：增量资本支出和增量营运资金。

(3) 资本支出

在净现值分析中资本支出的预测,反映了计划期间每年所预期的投资额。计划的资本支出通常始于计划的第一年。

of the building was 7,000,000 yuan and its current market value is 12,000,000 yuan. Alternatively, the building could be leased to another restaurant for 500,000 yuan per year. What are the relevant cash flows that should be considered when making the decision? The new hotel has spent 1,000,000 yuan on service testing, surveys, and development and is deciding whether or not to market the new hotel service. Should the 1,000,000 yuan be included in the project cash flow estimation when making the decision?

It is important to make sure that all cash flows are stated in either nominal dollars or real dollars. Nominal dollars are the dollars that we typically think of. They represent the actual dollar amounts that we expect a project to generate in the future, without any adjustments. When prices are going up, a given nominal dollar amount will buy less and less over time. Real dollars represent dollars stated in terms of constant purchasing power. We can write the cost of capital, k, as

$$1 + k = (1 + \Delta P_e)(1 + r)$$

Where: r is the real cost of capital, ΔP_e is the expected rate of inflation, and r is the real rate of return.

The FCF in the last, or terminal, year of a project often includes cash flows that are not typically included in the calculations for other years. For instance, in the final year of a project, the assets acquired during the life of the project may be sold and the working capital that has been invested may be recovered.

Add WC = change in cash and cash equivalents + change in accounts receivable + change in inventories − change in accounts payable

When an asset is expected to have a salvage value, we must include the salvage value realized from the sale (net of any tax consequences) of the asset and the impact of the sale on the firm's taxes in the terminal-year FCF calculations.

We are estimating when we forecast FCF in an NPV analysis. The expected FCF for a particular year equals the sum of the products of the possible outcomes (FCFs) and the probabilities that those outcomes will be realized.

3. Forecasting free cash flows

(1) Cash flows from operations

To forecast incremental cash flows from operations we must forecast the incremental net revenue, operating expenses, and depreciation and amortization associated with the project, as well as the firm's marginal tax rate. When forecasting operating expenses, analysts often distinguish between variable costs and fixed costs.

(2) Investment cash flows

We must consider two general classes of investments when calculating FCF: incremental capital expenditures and incremental additions to working capital.

(3) Capital expenditures

Capital expenditure forecasts in an NPV analysis reflect the expected level of

（4）营运资金

在净现值分析中,现金流量预测包含四个营运资金项目：1) 现金和折合现金；2) 应收账款；3) 存货；4) 应付账款。

10.3　特定情形

1. 计划有不同的期间

这情形往往涉及资本预算中两个互斥投资计划的问题,主要是两个投资计划有不同的投资期间。在这样的情况下,我们可以假设两个计划重复投资,直到期间相同,然后比较它们的净现值。这个问题的处理可以用一个既方便且更有用的方法,就是计算年当量成本（EAC）。EAC 计算公式如下：

$$EAC_i = k\,NPV_i\left[\frac{(1+k)^t}{(1+k)^t-1}\right]$$

式中：k 为资金的机会成本；NPV_i 是投资 i 的名义 NPV；t 是计划的期间。

EAC 只是反映投资计划的 $\Delta FCFs$ 在我们考虑投资期间的年金具有相同的现值。

2. 何时回收资产

最佳的回收时间是在该时间点上现金流量的增加率不再大于资本成本。该时间点就成为最佳的回收点,同时再持续进行投资大于资金机会成本的计划。

3. 何时替换现有资产

有两个基本问题：置换的现有资产利益是否超过了成本？如果没有,什么时候可以超过？要解决这个问题,可以简单地用 EAC 计算新资产,并将其与旧资产的年度现金流相比较。

4. 使用现有资产的成本

计算增量税后现金流量的第四个规则是包含所有无法直接观察到的机会成本。有时,必须首先搞清楚一组给定的现金流的 EAC,如果 EAC 不是以现值的方式呈现,再以适当的折现率和期间来调整 EAC 的计算。

investment during each year of the project's life. Capital expenditures are typically required at the beginning of a project.

(4) Working Capital

Cash flow forecasts in an NPV analysis include four working capital items: 1)cash and cash equivalents, 2) accounts receivable, 3) inventories, and 4) accounts payable.

10.3 Special Cases

1. Projects with different lives

A problem that arises quite often in capital budgeting involves choosing between two mutually exclusive investments where the investments have different lives. In a situation like this, we can effectively make the lives of the mowers the same by assuming repeated investments over some identical period and then comparing the NPV of their costs. A less cumbersome and more powerful method to handle the problem is to compute the equivalent annual cost (EAC). The EAC can be calculated as follows:

$$EAC_i = k\,NPV_i \left[\frac{(1+k)^t}{(1+k)^t - 1} \right]$$

Where: k is the opportunity cost of capital; NPV_i is the normal NPV of the investment i; t is the life of the investment; EAC simply reflects the annuity that has the same present value as the ΔFCFs of an investment over the investment period we are considering.

2. When to harvest an asset

The optimal time to harvest is the point in time at which the rate of increase in cash flows, from period to period, is no longer greater than the cost of capital. At this point in time, it becomes optimal to harvest the trees and invest the proceeds in alternative investments that yield the opportunity cost of capital.

3. When to replace an existing asset

Two fundamental questions: Do the benefits of replacing the existing asset exceed the costs, and, if they do not now, when will they? Solving this problem is simply a matter of computing the EAC for the new asset and comparing it with the annual cash inflows from the old asset.

4. The cost of using an existing asset

The fourth rule of calculating incremental after-tax cash flows is to include all opportunity costs that are not always directly observable. Sometimes we have to compute it by first figuring the EAC for a given set of cash flows and then adjusting the EAC by the appropriate discount rate and time, if the EAC is not in present value form.

第11章 资本预算决策方法

- 了解资本预算的评估程序
- 了解资本预算的决策方法与优缺点
- 了解资本预算的决策准则

如前章所述,资本预算探讨酒店在固定资产上所做的投资决策,是长期发展不可或缺的关键因素,其目标是酒店价值的最大化,有严谨的决策程序。依据投资计划的特性,有适用的决策方法与各方法决定投资与否的决策准则。当然,各种决策方法的优缺点就有赖财务经理人的判断与取舍了。

本章的学习架构如图 11 – 1 所示。

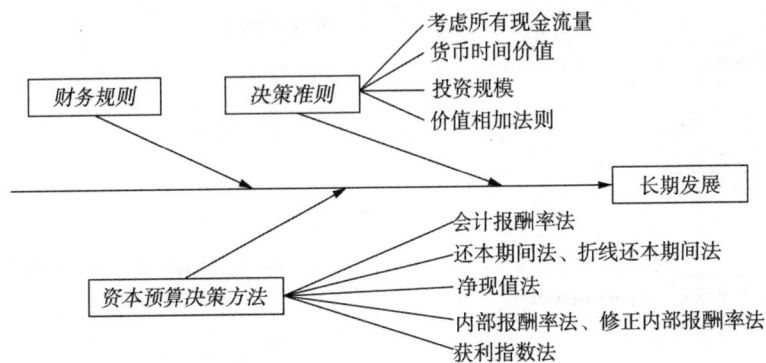

图 11 – 1 本章学习架构

11.1 资本预算的投资领域与评估程序

资本预算事关公司长期发展。公司的投资决策主要集中于三个领域:

(1) 维持公司营运及降低成本的资产重置。

(2) 扩充现有产品或市场的资产投资。

Chapter 11　Capital Budgeting Decision Methods

![Learning Outcomes icon] Learning Outcomes

- Understand capital budget assessment procedure
- Understand methods as well as pros and cons of capital budgeting decisions
- Understand capital budgeting decision criteria

As we mentioned in the previous chapter, capital budgeting is for hotels to make decisions in investing fixed assets which is a key factor for long-term development. The goal of capital budgeting is to maximize the value of the hotel with rigorous decision-making process. Capital budgeting has different methods with their suitable decision criteria according to the characteristics of investment projects. Financial manager is responsible for decision making of capital budgeting among different methods along with their pros and cons.

The learning framework of this chapter is shown in Figure 11 − 1.

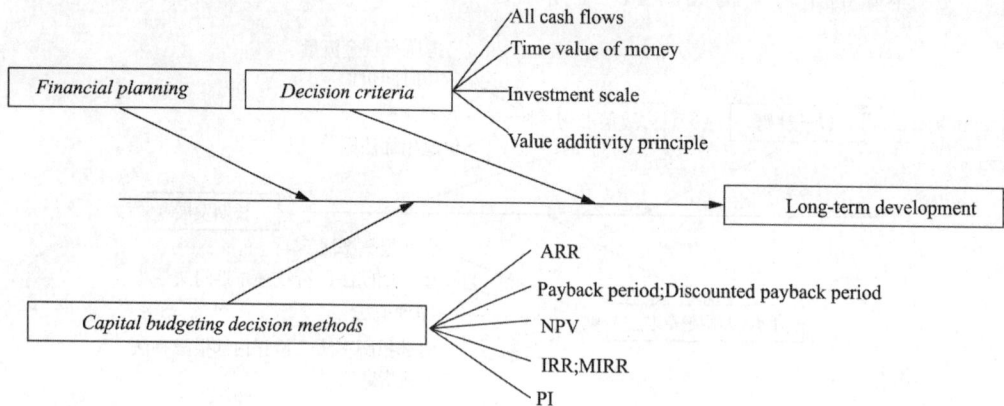

Figure 11 − 1　Learning framework

11.1　Capital Budgeting Fields and Assessment Procedure

Capital budgeting concerns about company's long-term development. Decisions of capital budgeting is involved mainly in three main areas:

(1) Asset replacement of company's operation and cost cutting.

(2) Asset investment of expansions of products or markets.

（3）安全的投资计划。

资本预算是一套系统化的决策过程，其步骤为：

（1）决定投资计划的成本。

（2）估计投资计划的预期现金流量。

投资计划的预期现金流量估计项目包括：

1）需求预测——估计未来企业产品的销售量、价格。

2）成本预测——估计营运成本、存货成本、折旧、销管费用、税捐等费用。

3）资金成本预估——用加权平均资金成本来做估算。

（3）预测并评估各计划中现金流量的风险。

（4）依据目标及可接受的准则，选择最佳投资计划。

（5）控制并监督计划的执行。

资本预算的目的是综合公司各部门的资源，对未来投资计划达成共识，并经由各部门的合作了解未来公司的可能获利机会。

11.2 资本预算评估方法

一般常用资本预算评估方法如下。

1. 平均会计报酬率法

平均会计报酬率（AAR）指投资方案平均每年税后净利除以平均投资金额，并假设期末方案的价值为零。AAR 的公式如下：

$$AAR = \frac{投资期间的每期平均净利}{投资期间的每期平均投资金额}$$

例 11-1 大院酒店的投资计划如表 11-1 所示，计算平均会计报酬率。

表 11-1 大院酒店的投资计划

单位：千美元

项目	年度				
	0	1	2	3	4
投资金额	(4000)				
收入		5000	6000	4000	3000
成本		(3000)	(3600)	(2400)	(1800)
折旧		(1000)	(1000)	(1000)	(1000)
税前盈余		1000	1400	600	200
所得税		(250)	(350)	(150)	(50)
净利		750	1050	450	150

(3) Safety investment plan.

The capital budget is a systematic process of decision-making, the steps are:

(1) Determine the cost of investment plan.

(2) Estimate the expected cash flows of investment plan.

Expected cash flow includes:

1) Demand forecasting —Forcast sales and price of product.

2) Cost forecasting —Estimate expenses of operating costs, inventory costs, depreciation, sales and management expenses, taxes, and etc.

3) Capital cost estimating: Apply the perspective of WACC.

(3) Forecast and evaluate the risk of cash flow in investment plan.

(4) Select the best investment plan according to the objectives and criteria of capital budgeting.

(5) Control and monitor the implementation of capital budgeting.

Capital budgeting is to integrate resources among departments, to get consensus on the future investment plans, and to make profit through cooperations among various sectors of a company.

11.2 Capital Budgeting Methods

The common methods of capital budgeting are as follows.

1. Average accounting return (AAR)

Average accounting return is the average annual net income divided by the average amount of investment with assuming that the final value of the programme is zero. AAR formula is as follows:

$$AAR = \frac{\text{Annual net income}}{\text{Average amount of investment}}$$

Example 11 - 1   The investment plan of Dayuan hotel is as Table 11 - 1. Calculate AAR.

Table 11 - 1   The investment plan of Dayuan hotel

unit: thousand USA dollars

Items	Year				
	0	1	2	3	4
investment	(4,000)				
revenue		5,000	6,000	4,000	3,000
cost		(3,000)	(3,600)	(2,400)	(1,800)
depreciation		(1,000)	(1,000)	(1,000)	(1,000)
EBT		1,000	1,400	600	200
tax		(250)	(350)	(150)	(50)
net income		750	1,050	450	150

解　$\text{AAR} = \dfrac{投资期间的每期平均净利}{投资期间的每期平均投资金额}$

$$= \dfrac{\dfrac{750+1050+450+150}{4}}{\dfrac{4000+3000+2000+1000+0}{5}} = \dfrac{600}{2000} = 30\%$$

平均会计报酬率法的决策准则是：选择会计报酬率较高的计划投资。

优点：

(1) 易懂易用。

(2) 会计资料容易获取并且完整。

缺点：

(1) 以会计所得做基础，并非真实的报酬率。

(2) 未考虑未来现金流量的波动。

(3) 忽略货币时间价值(由于采用简单账目平均报酬率，所以远期的现金流量被给予太大的比重)。

(4) 计划的选择无一定的标准。

平均会计报酬率法最大的问题是得到的数字取决于会计人员如何决定成本。例如：就我们所知，折旧并非是一项有实际现金流出的成本，但是会计人员将之计为成本。相似地，一些被资本化的项目及其他根据非经济原则所决定的费用亦然。因此最后所算出的利润数据会因为现金流量的种类不同而有误差。

2. 还本期间法

还本期间指公司从投资计划的现金流量中收回期初投资的资金所需的时间。评估的标准是接受能在一定期间内回收原始成本的计划，且回收期间越短越好。公式如下：

$$\sum_{t=1}^{n} \text{CF}_t > I$$

式中：CF_t 表示各年底现金流量；I 表示原始投资金额。

还本期间法的决策准则：选择回收期间最短的投资计划。

优点：

(1) 简单，容易计算，可用来评估计划的风险与流动性(计划期间愈短，风险愈小、流动性愈好)。

(2) 不考虑未来的不确定性。

(3) 着重于流动性。

Solution

$$AAR = \frac{\text{Annual net income}}{\text{Average amount of investment}}$$

$$= \frac{\dfrac{750 + 1050 + 450 + 150}{4}}{\dfrac{4000 + 3000 + 2000 + 1000 + 0}{5}} = \frac{600}{2000} = 30\%$$

Decision criteria: Invest on projects with higher AAR.

Advantages:

(1) Easy.

(2) Accounting data is accessible and complete.

Disadvantages:

(1) Accounting base is not the real rate of return.

(2) Ignore fluctuations in future cash flows.

(3) Ignore the time value of money (Adopt simple accounting rate of return on average, weighted too much on the long-term cash flows).

(4) There is no standard for decision-making.

The biggest problem of AAR is the results depending on how accountants decide costs. For example, depreciation is not a cost that actual cash outflow, but accountants counts depreciation as cost item; Similarly, expenses from other capitals and non-economic principles also have the same problem. Consequently, errors happened when cost items are treated by different perspectives to compute real cash flow and profits.

2. Payback period method

Payback period means the period of cash flow that can cover the initial amount of investment. Assessment criteria is the amount of investment can be collected within a specific period of time. The shorter the period, the better the investment project. The formula is as follows:

$$\sum_{t=1}^{n} CF_t > I$$

Where: CF_t is cash flow at the end of each year; I is the initial amount of investment.

Decision criteria: Select an investment project with the shortest period.

Advantages:

(1) This method is simple and easy for calculation. It can be used to assess risk and liquidity of a project (plan period shorter, less affected by the period).

(2) There is no need to consider the uncertainty of the future.

(3) Focus on liquidity.

缺点：

（1）未考虑还本期后的现金流量。

（2）忽略货币时间价值。

（3）未考虑投资方案所使用资金的机会成本。

（4）不符合价值附加性原则。

（5）不适合评估长期计划。

还本期间法的回收期间计算公式为

$$回收期间 = \frac{完全回收前的年数 + 尚未收回的投资余额}{回收年度现金流量}$$

例 11 - 2 表 11 - 2 给出的两个投资方案，依还本期间法计算应采用哪个方案？

表 11 - 2 两个投资方案

单位：千美元

方案	年度				
	0	1	2	3	4
甲	−6000	2500	4000	3000	1000
乙	−6000	2500	3000	5000	500

解 甲方案 1.875 年回收，即第 2 年回收；乙方案 2.2 年回收，即第 3 年回收。比较甲方案与乙方案的回收期间，甲方案的回收期间较短，故应选择甲方案。

例 11 - 3 钱柜企业投资海外子公司方案见表 11 - 3，问其还本期间为多久？

表 11 - 3 钱柜企业投资方案

单位：千美元

原始投资	年度			
	2005 年	2006 年	2007 年	2008 年
−27603	10251	13056	294924	3470

解 钱柜企业投资海外子公司的回收期间为

$$2 + \frac{252724}{294924} = 2 + 0.856 = 2.856$$

所以钱柜企业投资海外子公司第三年回收。

3. 折现还本期间法

还本期间法最大的漏洞就是忽略了"货币的时间价值"。"折现还本期间

Disadvantages:

(1) Ignore cash flows after the payback period.

(2) Ignore the time value of money.

(3) Ignore the cost of opportunity of the capital in investment projects.

(4) The mothod doesnot comply with the value additivity principle.

(5) The method is not suitable for assessing long-term projects.

The formula of the payback period is as

$$\text{payback period} = \frac{\text{years before payback} + \text{residuals of payback amount}}{\text{cash flow at payback year}}$$

Example 11 - 2   What project should be adopted between the following two investment projects based on the method of payback period (see Table 11 - 2)?

Table 11 - 2   Two investment projects

unit: thousand USA dollars

Case	Year				
	0	1	2	3	4
A	− 6,000	2,500	4,000	3,000	1,000
B	− 6,000	2,500	3,000	5,000	500

Solution

Case A: Payback period is 1.875 years. The initial amount of investment can be covered in 2 years.

Case B: Payback period is 2.2 years. The initial amount of investment can be covered in 3 years.

It is supposed to choose case A because the payback period is shorter.

Example 11 - 3   What is the payback period of Cash Box's oversea investment (see Table 11 - 3)?

Table 11 - 3   Cash Box's investment project

unit: thousand USA dollars

Initial Investment	Year			
	2005	2006	2007	2008
− 276,031	10,251	13,056	294,924	3,470

Solution   The payback period of Cash Box's oversea investment is

$$2 + \frac{252,724}{294,924} = 2 + 0.856 = 2.856$$

The payback period is 3 years.

3. Discounted payback period method

The major problem of payback period method is to ignore the time value of money. Discounted payback period method improves the payback period method that pays attention to

法"即为修正后的还本期间法,重视折现后的累积现金流量,并要求在一定期间内的现金流量超过其原始投资。此方法考虑到了截止期限内现金流量的时间价值。尽管如此,还本期间法与折现还本期间法最严重的缺失在于"忽略了还本期间后的现金流量"。

折现还本期间法是将各期现金流量先折算现值,再找出现值还本期限。公式如下:

$$\sum_{t=1}^{n} \frac{CF_t}{(1+r)^t} > I$$

折现还本期间法的决策准则:选择回收期间最短的投资计划。

优点:

(1) 易懂易用。

(2) 考虑了货币的时间价值。

(3) 不会有选择具有负的 NPV(净现值)的投资计划。

缺点:

(1) 忽视了取舍点之后的现金流量。

(2) 取舍点的选取无一定标准。

折现还本期间法的回收期计算公式为

$$折现后的回收期间 = 完全回收前的年数 + \frac{尚未收回的投资余额}{回收年度现金流量现值}$$

例 11 - 4　同例题 11 - 2 方案(见表 11 - 2),请问折现还本期间为多少(折现率为 10%)?

解　上述现金流量折现后的各年度现金流量如表 11 - 4 所示。

表 11 - 4　折现后各年度现金流量 CF_t

单位:万美元

方案	年度				
	0	1	2	3	4
甲	−600.0	227.3	330.6	225.5	68.3
乙	−600.0	227.3	247.9	375.6	34.1

甲方案折现还本期间为 3.19 年,乙方案折现还本期间为 3.33 年,故甲、乙方案回收期间相同,择一即可。

例 11 - 5　钱柜企业投资表格见表 11 - 5,假使折现率为 5%,计算其折现后的回收期。

表 11 - 5　钱柜企业投资表

单位:万美元

钱柜企业	原始投资	第 1 年	第 2 年	第 3 年	第 4 年
原值	−27603.1	1025.1	1305.6	29492.4	347.0
折现后现值	−27603.1	976.3	1184.2	25476.6	285.5

cumulative discounted cash flow to cover the initial amount of investment. This method considers the time value of money within the payback period. There exists another big problem that is this method ignores cash flows after the payback period.

The discounted payback period method discounted each cash flow to the present value at each period, then find the payback period through accumulative present value of cash flows. The formula is as follows:

$$\sum_{t=1}^{n} \frac{CF_t}{(1+r)^t} > I$$

Decision criteria: Select an investment project with the shortest period.

Advantages:

(1) This method is simple and easy for calculation.

(2) The time value of money is taken into consideration.

(3) We won't choose a project with negative net present value (NPV).

Disadvantages:

(1) Ignore cash flows after the payback period.

(2) There is no standard for decision-making.

The formula is as follows:

$$\text{Discounted payback period} = \text{Years before payback} + \frac{\text{Residuals of payback amount}}{\text{Cash flow payback year}}$$

Example 11 - 4   Follow the example 11 - 2 (see Table 11 - 2), what is the discounted payback period (the discount rate is 10%)?

Solution   Discounted cash flow of investment plans is shown in Table 11 - 4.

Table 11 - 4   Discounted cash flow CF_t of investment plans

unit: thousand USA dollars

Case	Year				
	0	1	2	3	4
A	- 6,000	2,273	3,306	2,255	683
BC	- 6,000	2,273	2,479	3,756	341

The discounted payback period is 3.19 years for case A whereas case B is 3.33 years. Either is fine for decision-making because of the same payback period.

Example 11 - 5   Cash Box oversea investment is shown in Table 11 - 5. What is the discounted payback period (the discount rate is 5%)?

Table 11 - 5   Cash Box discounted cash flow of investment plans

unit: thousand USA dollars

Cash Box Inc.	Initial investment	Year 1	Year 2	Year 3	Year 4
initial value	- 276,031	10,251	13,056	294,924	3,470
discounted value	- 276,031	9,763	11,842	254,766	2855

解　折现后的回收期为

$$T = 2 + \frac{254766 - 340}{254766}（第 3 年尚有 340 千美元未回收）$$

$$= 2 + \frac{254426}{254766} = 2 + 0.999 = 2.999（即为第 3 年回收）$$

4. 净现值法

净现值法（NPV）指将投资方案每期所可能产生的净现金流量以资金成本或必要报酬率作为折现率加以折现后加总,计算的金额即为该方案的净现值。只要净现值大于等于零,该方案就值得投资。公式如下:

$$NPV = -I + \sum_{t=1}^{n} \frac{CF_t}{(1+r)^t}$$

式中：CF_t 为各期的现金流量的净现金流入 $(t = 1, 2, \cdots, n)$；I 为投资方案的原始投资金额。

计算净现值的概念可以用图 11-2 所示的时间线表示。

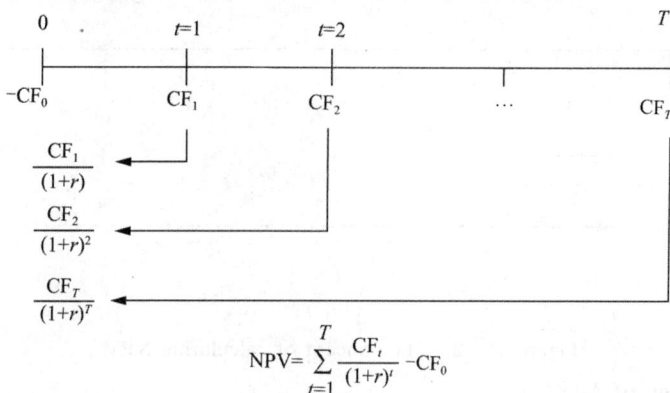

$$NPV = \sum_{t=1}^{T} \frac{CF_t}{(1+r)^t} - CF_0$$

图 11-2　计算净现值的概念

净现值法的优点:

(1) 能显示出投资计划所能带给公司股东的利益。

(2) 考虑了货币的时间价值。

(3) 符合价值相加原则,即计划价值具有累加性。例如:有计划 A 与计划 B 两个计划,则 NPV(A&B) = NPV(A) + NPV(B)。

(4) 考虑计划所能带来的最大利润。

净现值法的缺点:

(1) 未能提供投资资本的风险信息。

(2) 计划中的现金流量都是预期未来会发生的,具不确定性。

(3) 需要一个适当的折现率,但这个折现率具有不确定性。

当同时评估多个计划且只能选择其中一个执行时,也就是选择互斥方案时,最好的方式为先计算个别计划的 NPV,再选择其中具最大 NPV 的计划执行。如果同时可以执行多项计划,这些计划的综合 NPV 就是个别计划 NPV 之和。

Solution

Discounted payback period

$$= 2 + \frac{254766 - 340}{254766} \text{(there lacks 340 thousand dollars to payback at the end of year 3)}$$

$$= 2 + \frac{254426}{254766} = 2 + 0.999 = 2.999 \text{ (the payback period is 3 years)}$$

4. Net Present Value (NPV)

NPV accumulate the discounted cash flows with discount rate of WACC or other required return rate in an investment project. A project is worth of investing as long as NPV is greater than zero. The formula is as follows:

$$\text{NPV} = -I + \sum_{t=1}^{n} \frac{CF_t}{(1+r)^t};$$

Where: CF_t is the net cash flow per period ($t = 1, 2, \cdots, n$); I is the initial amount of investment.

To calculate NPV, it is good to express as timeline in Figure 11 - 2.

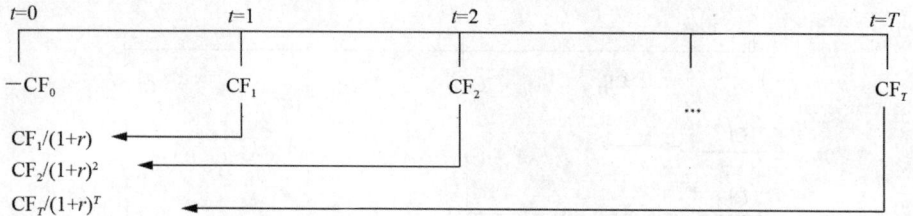

$$\text{NPV} = \sum_{t=1}^{T} \frac{CF_t}{(1+r)^t} - CF_0;$$

Figure 11 - 2   The concept of calculating NPV

The advantage of NPV:

(1) NPV method can reveal profits of shareholders from investment projects.

(2) NPV method take the value of time into consideration.

(3) NPV method meets the principle of value additivity, which means values of project can be added directly. For example, NPV of two projects of A and B is as the formula: NPV(A&B) = NPV(A) + NPV(B).

(4) NPV method considers the profit maximization.

The disadvantage of NPV:

(1) NPV method doesn't reveal the risk of capital budgeting.

(2) The method is uncertainty because cash flows are all happen in the future.

(3) Discount rate is essential, which is uncertain.

The best way of applying NPV method is calculating each NPV of each project and choose the biggest NPV if projects are mutual excluded. If projects are not mutual excluded, which means we can choose all projects that NPV is larger than zero, the total NPV is the sum of each NPV per project.

例 11-6 钱柜企业投资表格见表 11-6,假使市场折现率为 5%,计算其净现值。

表 11-6 钱柜企业投资表

单位:千美元

原始投资	第 1 年	第 2 年	第 3 年	第 4 年
-276031	10251	13056	294924	3470

解

$$\text{NPV} = -I_0 + \sum_{t=1}^{T} \frac{\text{CF}_t}{(1+r)^t}$$

$$= -276031 + \frac{10251}{(1+5\%)} + \frac{13056}{(1+5\%)^2}$$

$$+ \frac{294924}{(1+5\%)^3} + \frac{3470}{(1+5\%)^4}$$

$$= 3043(\text{千美元})$$

净现值大于 0,是个值得投资的方案。

若公司用于投资的资本额有所限制,则无法接纳所有 NPV 大于零的方案,此时即产生所谓资本配额问题。在此情况下,公司只能在有限的资本配额内,选择能够提供最大利润的投资计划组合。

若投资计划都相互独立,选择最佳方案的准则是:

(1) 将所有 NPV 大于零的投资计划按净现值高低排序。

(2) 由净现值最高者往下选,直至预算用完为止。

5. 内部报酬率法

投资计划的内部报酬率(IRR)即使现金流入现值等于现金流出现值的折现率,亦即使得净现值等于零的折现率。公式如下:

$$\text{NPV} = -I + \sum_{t=1}^{n} \frac{\text{CF}_t}{(1+\text{IRR})^t} = 0$$

实际上,IRR 即 NPV=0 时不赚不赔的内部报酬率。

简单地说,内部报酬率就是"损益两平"的概念,若方案未来现金流量使用 IRR 折现,恰等于原始投入的成本,代表方案刚好不赚不赔。若 IRR 大于决策者预期的报酬率,代表该方案损益两平时的报酬率已超过必要报酬率了,决策者可以采用该方案;反之则否。

决策准则:选择 IRR 较高的投资计划。在采用内部报酬率法时只要 IRR 大于公司必要报酬率,该计划便值得执行。但若存在两种互斥的投资计划,则须选择 IRR 较高且大于公司必要报酬率的计划。

Example 11 – 6　Table 11 – 6 shows Cash Box's investment project. Assume the discount rate is 5%. Calculate the NPV of the investment project.

Table 11 – 6　Cash Box's investment project

unit: thousand USA dollars

Initial investment	Year 1	Year 2	Year 3	Year 4
– 276,031	10,251	13,056	294,924	3,470

Solution

$$NPV = -I_0 + \sum_{t=1}^{T} \frac{CF_t}{(1+r)^t}$$

$$= -276031 + \frac{10251}{(1+5\%)} + \frac{13056}{(1+5\%)^2} + \frac{294924}{(1+5\%)^3} + \frac{3470}{(1+5\%)^4}$$

$$= 3043 (\text{thousand dollars})$$

NPV is larger than 0, it is worth to invest this project.

Capital quota happens when a company has budget limits of capital budgeting, a company will be constrained to receive all the projects of NPV greater than zero. In such case, a company can only choose the projects combination that can generate a maximum profit within the budget limits.

If investment projects are mutual independent, the criteria for selecting an investment portfolio are:

(1) Rank all projects of NPV greater than zero.

(2) Choose projects from the highest NPV until the budget is used up.

5. Internal rate of return (IRR)

IRR is the internal return rate that the present value of cash inflows equal to the present value of cash outflows. That is a discount rate to make NPV equal to zero. Formula is as follows:

$$NPV = -I + \sum_{t=1}^{n} \frac{CF_t}{(1+IRR)^t} = 0$$

IRR can be got when NPV = 0.

In short, IRR is a "break even" concept. If a project can be broke even using IRR as discount rate, it nepresents the internal return rate can make the present value of cash inflows equal to the present value of cash outflows. When IRR of a project is greater than the expected return rate of policy makers, it means the discount rate of break even has exceeded the required return rate of decision makers. The project is worth of investing.

Decision criteria: Choose the higher IRR investment project. Project is worth to be invested if IRR is greater than the required return of a company. However, if projects are mutually exclusive, we need to choose the higher IRR one.

内部报酬率的计算方法：可利用试误法求解内部报酬率。

内部报酬率的优点：

提供安全边际或投资资本风险的讯息。

内部报酬率的缺点：

以 IRR 作为再投资的报酬率会有多重解的现象，选择互斥方案时会有矛盾产生。

例 11 - 7　钱柜企业投资表格见表 11 - 6。假设市场折现率为 5%，计算其内部报酬率。

解
$$NPV = -I_0 + \sum_{t=1}^{T} \frac{CF_t}{(1+IRR)^t}$$

$$= -276031 + \frac{10251}{(1+IRR)} + \frac{13056}{(1+IRR)^2}$$

$$+ \frac{294924}{(1+IRR)^3} + \frac{3470}{(1+IRR)^4} = 0$$

$IRR = 5.481\%$，内部报酬率大于市场折现率，可投资本方案。

IRR、NPV 法的比较：评估独立投资方案时，两方法对计划是否可以接受的结论相同。然而，在评估互斥方案时，IRR 和 NPV 对投资方案的决策就可能有所不同。例如在图 11 - 3 中，若用 IRR 法评估方案，我们将会接受 S 方案，因为 $IRR_S > IRR_L$，若用 NPV 法评估方案，当折现率小于转折点 8.7% 时我们会接受 L 方案，因为 $NPV_L > NPV_S$

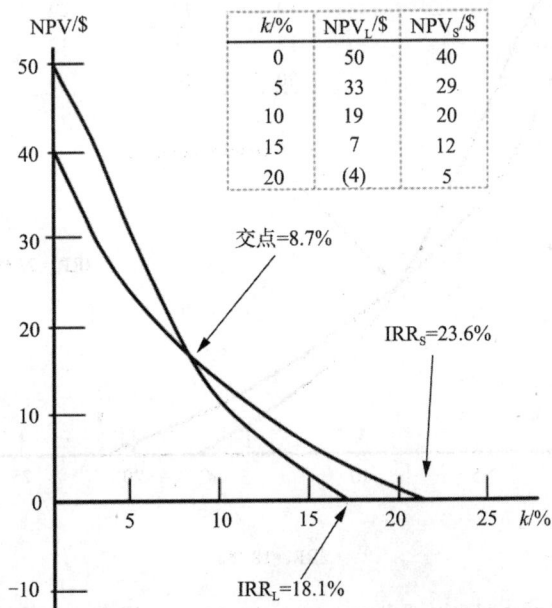

$k/\%$	$NPV_L/\$$	$NPV_S/\$$
0	50	40
5	33	29
10	19	20
15	7	12
20	(4)	5

图 11 - 3　IRR 法和 NPV 法的比较示例

Calculation method: Use trial and error to calculate IRR, or use computer simulation to get IRR.

Advantages: IRR method provides a risk perspective of capital budgeting.

Disadvantages: Multiple solutions or decision contraditions might happen when using IRR as a reinvestment rate.

Example 11 - 7   Table 11 - 6 shows Cash Box's investment project. Assume the discount rate is 5%, calculate the internal rate of return.

Solution

$$NVP = -I_0 + \sum_{t=1}^{T} \frac{CF_t}{(1 + IRR)^t}$$

$$= -276031 + \frac{10251}{(1 + IRR)} + \frac{13056}{(1 + IRR)^2} + \frac{294924}{(1 + IRR)^3} + \frac{3470}{(1 + IRR)^4} = 0$$

IRR is 5.418%, the IRR is larger than the discount rate, so Cash Box can invest this project.

Comparison of IRR and NPV: When evaluate independent investment projects, both of IRR and NPV methods get the same decision of acceptance on a given plan. However, when evaluate mutual exclusive investment projects, IRR and NPV methods might have different decision of acceptance on a given plan. For example: In Figure 11 - 3, we will choose project S using IRR method because $IRR_S > IRR_L$. We will choose project L when discount rate is less than crossover point, 8.7%, because $NPV_L > NPV_S$.

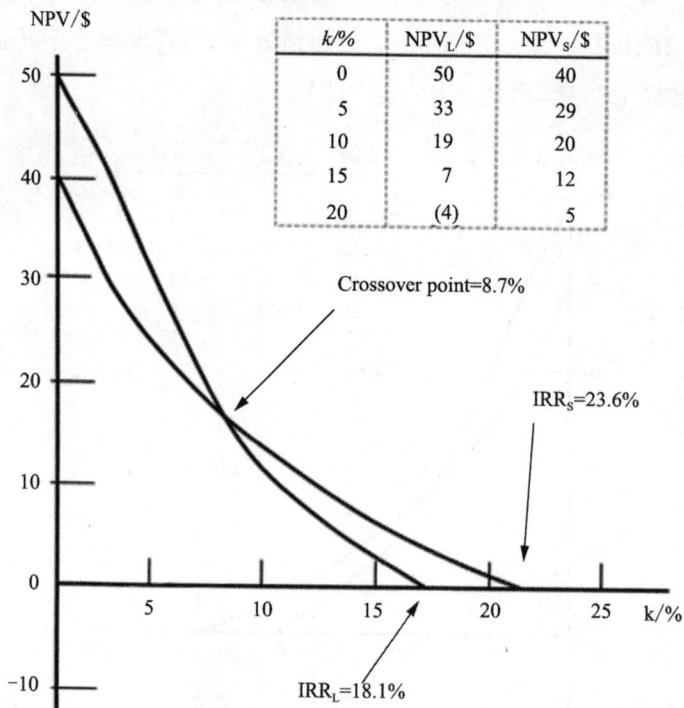

k/%	NPV_L/\$	NPV_S/\$
0	50	40
5	33	29
10	19	20
15	7	12
20	(4)	5

Figure 11 - 3   Example of comparison of IRR and NPV

若两个计划的原始投资规模相同,但现金流量产生的时间不同亦会造成两方法的结论的不同。造成两者冲突的原因在于,两者对于再投资报酬率假设的差异。IRR 法假设公司以内部报酬率作为现金流入再投资的报酬率;而 NPV 法假设公司以资金成本作为现金流入再投资的报酬率。

NPV 法优于 IRR 法,但因 IRR 法以计算机处理后较易做决策,实务上亦常用 IRR 法做投资决策。若第一期后发生负的现金流量,则会产生多重 IRR,导致无法判断投资决策。

例 11-8 多重 IRR 示例。以表 11-7 所示的数据计算 IRR 和 NPV。

表 11-7 多重 IRR 的个案

单位:万元

年度	0	1	2
CF_t	−500	1000	−200

解 $$NPV = I_0 + \sum_{t=1}^{T} \frac{CF_t}{(1+IRR)^t}$$

$$= -500 + \frac{1000}{(1+IRR)^1} + \frac{-200}{(1+IRR)^2} = 0$$

$$IRR = \pm\sqrt{300}$$

IRR 数据多重,无法判断投资决策。

6. 修正内部报酬率法

如果有前述 IRR 多重报酬率的问题,可用修正内部报酬率法 MIRR 予以解决。所谓 MIRR 是指整个投资期间的折现率,此折现率使投资计划成本现值等于投资计划现金流入量终值的现值,现值的计算则以资金成本作为折现率。公式如下:

$$\sum_{t=0}^{n} \frac{COF_t}{(1+r)^t} = \sum_{t=1}^{n} \frac{\sum_{t=0}^{n} CIF_t (1+r)^{n-t}}{(1+IRR)^t}$$

例 11-9 现金流如表 11-8 所示,计算修正内部报酬率。

表 11-8 投资计划的现金流

单位:元

年份	0	1	2	3	4	IRR
现金流	−5000000	3000000	−2000000	4000000	2000000	IRR=13.7%

Another situation that makes different decision between IRR and NPV is cash inflow at different time even the initial amounts of two projects are the same. The contradiction is resulting from differnt assumptions of reinvestment rates of cash inflow of investment project. IRR method assume the internal rate of return as the reinvestment rate of cash inflow of investment project. NPV method assume the cost of capital as the reinvestment cash inflow of investment project.

NPV is better than IRR method. But IRR method is easy for decision making when IRR is calculated by computer. In practice, IRR method is used frequently for capital budgeting.

The question of IRR is that if negative cash flow generated after the first period, multiple IRR might happen to cause the difficulty of decision making on investment.

Example 11 - 8 The calculation of multiple IRR is as Table 11 - 7.

Table11 - 7 The case of multiple IRR

unit: ten thousand yuan

Year	0	1	2
CF_t	-500	1,000	-200

Solution

$$NPV = -I_0 + \sum_{t=1}^{T} \frac{CF_t}{(1+IRR)^t} = -500 + \frac{1000}{(1+IRR)} + \frac{-200}{(1+IRR)^2} = 0$$

$$IRR = \pm \sqrt{300}$$

6. Modify internal rate of return (MIRR)

If suffering from a question of multiple IRR, MIRR can be a way to offer a solution. The MIRR means a discount rate that makes the present value of investment cost equal to the present value of the final value of cash flows of investment project. Where the calculation of present value uses the cost of capital as the discount rate. The formula is as follows:

$$\sum_{t=0}^{n} \frac{COF_t}{(1+r)^t} = \sum_{t=1}^{n} \frac{\sum_{t=0}^{n} CIF_t (1+r)^{n-t}}{(1+IRR)^t}$$

Example 11 - 9 Given the cash flow of investment project as Table 11 - 8. Calculate the MIRR.

Table 11 - 8 Cash flow of investment project

unit: yuan

Year	0	1	2	3	4	IRR
Cash flow	$-5,000,000$	3,000,000	$-2,000,000$	4,000,000	2,000,000	IRR = 13.7%

解　计算过程如下：

资金成本 k=10%	$t=0$	$t=1$	$t=2$	$t=3$	$t=4$
现金流	-5000000	3000000	-2000000	4000000	2000000
现金流出现值	-1650000		$1/(1+10\%)^2$	$(1+10\%)$	4400000
	-6650000				3393000
		$(1+10\%)^3$			
现金流入现值					103393000
NPV	6650000			$1/(1+\text{MIRR})^4$	
	0				

$$5000000 + \frac{2000000}{(1+10\%)^2} = \frac{3000000 \times (1+10\%)^2 + 4000000(1+10\%) + 2000000}{(1+\text{MIRR})^4}$$

$$\text{MIRR} = 111.8\%$$

MIRR 法较优于一般 IRR 法，因为 MIRR 法假设投资计划的所有现金流量均以资金成本再投资；而一般 IRR 法系假设投资计划的现金流量均以 IRR 再投资，因为以资金成本再投资的假设较合理，MIRR 法同时解决了 IRR 法多重解的问题。

7. 获利指数法

获利指数（PI）法以投资计划预期现金流量的现值除以期初投资额，形成获利指数，分母为成本，分子为收益，凸显了成本效益的观念。获利指数法考量了货币时间价值及报酬率，但无法如 NPV 法那样直接呈现投资方案的具体价值。

获利指数法的决策原则：接受利润指数大于 1 的计划，拒绝指数小于 1 的计划。

公式如下：

$$\frac{\sum_{t=1}^{n} \dfrac{\text{CF}_t}{(1+r)^t}}{I} = \frac{\text{NPV}+I}{I}$$

例 11-10　钱柜的投资计划如表 11-6 所示，假设折现率为 5%，对该计划进行评估。

解

$$\text{PI} = \frac{\sum_{t=1}^{n} \dfrac{\text{CF}_t}{(1+r)^t}}{I_0} = \frac{\dfrac{10251}{(1+5\%)^1} + \dfrac{13056}{(1+5\%)^2} + \dfrac{294924}{(1+5\%)^3} + \dfrac{3470}{(1+5\%)^4}}{276031}$$

Solution

$$5000000 + \frac{2000000}{(1+10\%)^2}$$

$$= \frac{3000000 \times (1+10\%)^2 + 4000000(1+10\%) + 2000000}{(1+MRR)^4}$$

$$MIRR = 111.8\%$$

MIRR method is better than IRR method because MIRR method assumes the cost of capital as the reinvestment rate of cash flow of a project; IRR method assumes the internal rate of return as the reinvestment rate of cash flow of a project. The cost of capital as the reinvestment rate is reasonable, thus MIRR method is better than IRR method. MIRR method also solves the problem of multiple IRR.

7. Profit index (PI)

PI is formed by the present value of expected cash flows divided by the initial investment amount, the denominator is the cost and the numerator is the revenue of a project that highlights the cost-benefit concept. Profit Index takes into account of the time value of money and rate of return, but cannot demonstrate its investment value directly as NPV method.

Decision criteria: Accept projects when PI is greater than one. Reject projects when PI is less than one.

The formula is as follows:

$$\frac{\sum_{t=1}^{n} \frac{CF_t}{(1+r)^t}}{I} = \frac{NPV + I}{I}$$

Example 11 - 10   Given Cash Box's investment project as Table 11 - 6, assume the discount rate is 5%. Calculate the PI of investment project.

Solution

$$PI = \frac{\sum_{t=1}^{n} \frac{CF_t}{(1+r)^t}}{I_0}$$

$$= \frac{\frac{10251}{(1+5\%)^1} + \frac{13056}{(1+5\%)^2} + \frac{29424}{(1+5\%)^3} + \frac{3470}{(1+5\%)^4}}{276031}$$

$$=\frac{279074}{276031}=1.01$$

由于 PI 大于 1,此方案值得投资。

获利指数法与净现值法的差异是:净现值法是以现金流量现值和减去投入成本,所表达的是总量的概念。而获利指数法是以现金流量现值除以投入成本,表达的是"报酬率"的概念。

8. 资本预算各种方法的比较

表 11-9 汇总了本章介绍的资本预算的各种方法。

表 11-9　资本预算的各种方法汇总

方法	决策准则			
	货币时间价值	所有现金流量	投资规模	价值相加原则
平均会计报酬率法(AAR)			√	
还本期间法			√	
折现还本期间法	√		√	
净现值法(NPV)	√	√	√	√
内部报酬率法(IRR)	√	√	√	
修正内部报酬率法(MIRR)	√	√	√	
获利指数法(PI)	√	√		

各种方法比较如下:

平均会计报酬率法(AAR),资料容易取得,简单易用。从大院酒店的例子可以看出,只要简单知道净利、投资金额以及折旧,就可以轻松算出 AAR。但是本方法无法看出现金流量的波动以及货币的时间价值。最主要的问题在于 ARR 所使用的会计成本和资本预算使用经济成本的原则有所差异。然而,这种会计投资报酬分析在投资方案需要快速分析时仍具有一定的参考价值。

还本期间法,容易计算,且清楚知道何时可以回收初期投资资金,时间越短风险越小。但还完本期后面的现金流量未纳入考虑。而货币的时间价值也被忽略。适合用来决定短期计划。从钱柜投资的个案可以很快地计算其回收投资资本的时间与所承担的风险。

折现还本期间法与还本期间法唯一的差别在于加入了现金流量折现的观念,但对于还本期间后的现金流量仍然有所忽略。

净现值法(NPV),因考虑了资本预算大部分的决策准则而优于其他的方法。唯一的疑虑是预期未来现金流量所造成的不确定性因素。

$$=\frac{279074}{276031}=1.01$$

PI is larger than 1, it is worth to invest this project.

The difference between profit index method and net present value method is that net present value is the present value of cash inflows deducts cash outflows to demonstrate a total amount, and profit index method is based on the present value of cash inflows divided by cash outflows to present a concept of "rate of return".

8. Comparisons of methods of capital budgeting

Table 11 - 9 shows the summary of methods of capital budgeting in this chapter.

Table 11 - 9   Summary of methods of capital budgeting

Methods	Decision criteria			
	Time value of money	All cash flows	Investment scale	Value additivity principle
AAR			√	
payback period			√	
discounted payback period	√		√	
NPV	√	√	√	√
IRR	√	√	√	
MIRR	√	√	√	
PI	√	√		

The comparison of the methods is as following.

The average accounting return method (AAR): This method is easy to get accounting data, and is easy to be applied to assess investment project. We can easily calculate the AAR when we get the data of net income, the amount of investment and depreciation from the example of Dayuan hotel.However, this method can not evaluate fluctuation of cash flows, the time value of money is also ignored. The major issue is that this method uses accounting cost, which is different from economic cost for capital budgeting. However, this method still has its reference value when a quick assessment of investment projects is needed.

Payback period method: This method is easy to calculate the payback period, which means when can we get back the initial amount of investment. However, this method does not evaluate cash flows after payback period, the time value of money is also ignored.This method is suitable to evaluate short-term investment projects. From the case of Cash Box Inc., we can calculate the payback period easily and realize the risk of the project.

Discounted payback period method: The only difference from payback period method is the addition of discounted cash flows. However, this method still does not take into account of cash flows after payback period.

Net present value (NPV) method: Superior to other methods, this method takes into account most of the criteria in capital budgeting. The only concern is the uncertain risk

内部报酬率法(IRR),提供了 NPV 所不具备的安全边际或投资资本风险的信息。虽不如 NPV 符合大部分的决策准则,但通过百分比表示必要收益的方法,可以简单地做资本预算的判断。

修正 IRR 法(MIRR),基本上是 IRR 的修订方法,考虑了现金流量再投资时的观点,以资金成本再投资的假设亦比较合理。因再投资率假设中不会产生 IRR 多重解的问题,这使 MIRR 法优于 IRR 法。

获利指数法(PI),NPV 表达的是总量,也就是显示了投资规模,而 PI 主要表达的是报酬率。只是一个通过与原来投入成本比较计算出的一个比较值。

comes from the expectation of future cash flows.

Internal rate of return method (IRR): This method provides a margin of investment rate, or the information of investment risk that NPV method can not provide. Although this method doesn't fit all decision criteria as NPV, it is easy for decision making of capital budgeting using a perspective of required rate of return.

Modified IRR method (MIRR): Modified from IRR method, this method takes into account the reinvestment of cash flows of a project, it is reasonable to use cost of capital as the reinvestment rate. MIRR method is better than IRR method because of the assumption of reinvestment rate without multiple solutions as IRR method.

Profit index (PI): NPV express a total amount of an investment project, which shows the scale of investment. PI expresses a rate of return, which forms from the ratio of the present value of cash inflows over the initial amount of investment.

第 12 章　营运资金管理

学习目标

- 了解营运资金的重要性
- 了解营运资金政策与管理
- 管理流动资产与流动负债

12.1　营运资金与管理

1. 营运资金决策

营运资金包括所有流动资产,如现金、有价证券、应收账款、存货等,以及流动负债,如应付账款、银行短期融资、商业本票、应付薪资等。营运资金管理就是管理流动资产与流动负债,在流动性(安全性)和获利性之间取得平衡。

营运资金管理包括下列决策:

(1) 应持有多少现金与有价证券?

(2) 应保有多少存货以支应生产与销售?

(3) 应给予客户多少信用额度(应收账款)?

(4) 应保有多少短期融资及融资方法的选择?

我们常看到公司在下列两种情形下会面临营运资金不足的困境:

(1) 付款太快

公司购货后,未能充分应用供应商所给予的信用宽限期,过早付款,以至于造成营运资金缺乏,没有足够的资金支付其他款项。

(2) 扩张太快

公司在面临市场荣景时,会积极追求快速成长,但此时往往是最容易发生风险的时刻。为了市场的扩张,公司必须投入大量的营运资金来购置存货,增加广告行销费用,提供给顾客较好的信用条件等,这些都会导致营运资

Chapter 12   Working Capital Management

Learning Outcomes

- Understand the importance of working capital
- Understand the working capital policy and management
- Learn to manage current assets and current debts

12.1   *Working Captial and Management*

1. Working Capital Decisions

Working capital includes all current assets such as cash, securities, accounts receivable, inventory, and current liabilities such as accounts payable, bank short-term debt, commercial paper, accounts payable. Working capital management is the management of current assets and current liabilities that can make a balance between profitability and liquidity.

Working capital management includes the following decisions:

(1) How much cash and securities?

(2) How much inventories to cover production and sales?

(3) How much accounts receivable?

(4) How much short-term debt and what are the financing methods?

Working capital is insufficient mainly becaue of the following circumstances:

(1) Pay too quick

A company pays too quick after a purchase that fails to use credit from supplier.This results in insufficient working capital to pay for other items.

(2) Expand too fast

A company will pursue rapid growth when economic boom. However, this is time for higher risk derived from market expansion, which need to spend more money to buy inventory, to increase marketing budget, and to provide customers with better credit conditions. These will cause operations difficulties because of insufficient working capital.

金的短缺而造成营运上的困难。

案例 ▶▶▶▶▶▶

佳姿与亚力山大健身中心

佳姿与亚力山大健身中心无法继续经营的最大原因,主要是企业扩张过速。以佳姿为例,该公司斥巨额投资位于台北的 101 大楼,打造顶级健身俱乐部,后来因为 101 大楼招商缓慢,会员招收不如预期,大笔投入的资金无法回收,资金出现巨大缺口而倒闭。亚力山大也快速扩张事业版图,除了在台湾快速展店,也在大陆开设数家分店,投资过速使得营运资金不足从而产生经营危机。

2. 现金转换循环

现金转换循环指公司实际上从以现金支付各种和生产有关的费用开始,一直到公司将产品卖出并且收到现金为止所需的时间(如图 12-1 所示)。

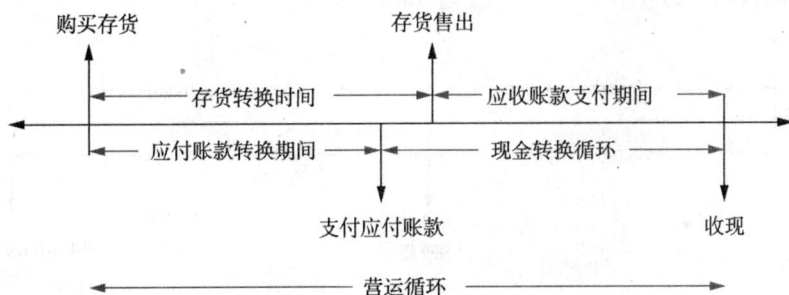

图 12-1　现金转换循环

其公式为

$$现金转换循环＝存货转换期间＋应收账款转换期间$$
$$－应付账款支付期间$$

式中:存货转换期间指公司将原料转换为制成品到卖出所需的平均时间;应收账款转换期间指公司将应收账款转换成现金所需的平均时间;应付账款支付期间指公司以赊购的方式取得原料后到期将应付账款还清所需的平均时间。

现金转换循环的意义:现金转换循环的期间越长,公司的外来融资需求越大,而公司必须付出相当成本才能取得此种融资,故如果能缩短现金转换循环的期间,利润将会因此提高。

缩短现金转换循环的方法如下:

Case ▶▶▶▶▶▶

Wincare and Alexander Fitness Center

The main reason that Wincare and Alexander Fitness Center can not continue to operate is their expansion were too fast.For example，Wincare spent huge amount of investment to build the Taipei 101 branch for top tier fitness club，but cash inflows from membership were insufficient because enterprise-establishing in Taipei 101 is slow.The huge investment can not be paid back. A significant shortfall in working capital made Wincare go bankrupt. Alexander is also a case of expanding too fast. In addition to expand its business territory in Taiwan，Alexander also ran a number of branches in Mainland. The rapid expanding ran out of its money that made Alexander go bankrupt as well.

2. Cash conversion cycle

The cash conversion cycle means a period of time from a company pay the cash to suppliers to collect cash from customers(see Figure 12 - 1).

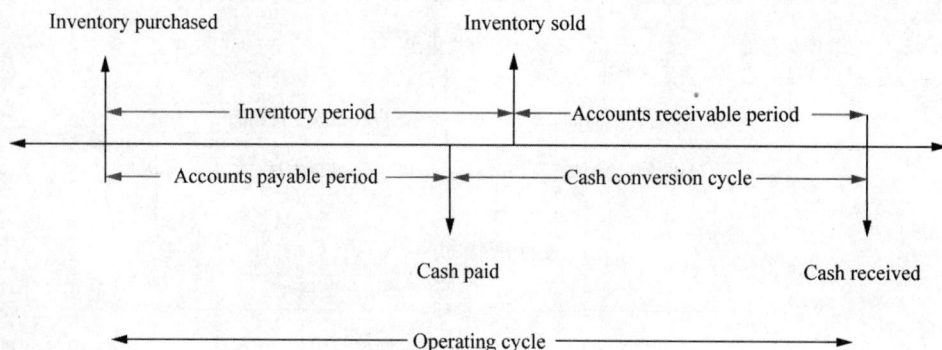

Figure 12 - 1　Cash conversion cycle

The formula is

$$\text{Cash conversion cycle} = \text{Inventory period} + \text{Accounts receivable period} - \text{Accounts payable period}$$

Where inventory period is the period that a company uses raw materials to produce goods and sell them in market；Accounts receivable period is the period that a company collects cash from the beginning of accounts receivable to cash received；Accounts payable period is the period that a company acquired raw materials on credit to the date cash paid for accounts payable.

The meaning of cash conversion cycle：The longer the cash conversion cycle，the more demanding of external financing，the higher cost to obtain such financing. Thus，if a company can shorten the period of the cash conversion cycle，more profit can be made.

Ways to shorten the cash conversion cycle are to：

（1）使存货周转率加快；

（2）应收账款回收要有效率；

（3）应付账款递延天数要拉长。

3. 营运资金政策

营运资金决策系一种权衡风险与报酬的决策。例如：若公司握有较多流动资产，资金流动性较高，短期偿债能力较强，则公司安全性较高，但相对的投资报酬会较低；相反地，若公司流动资产较少，大部分资金投资于固定资产，虽可提高营业报酬，但公司的资金流动性会较低、风险较大。合适的营运资金水准取决于以下因素：

（1）短期资产与短期负债的期间结构。

（2）短期资产的流动性。

（3）短期负债的适合性。

（4）短期资产的收益。

（5）短期负债的成本。

（6）企业能够承担的风险。

（7）经营者的风险偏好。

12.2　营运资金投资政策

根据企业所持有的流动资产的多寡，可分为宽松、适中、紧缩三种营运资金投资政策。宽松政策意味着，公司持有相当多的现金、有价证券、存货以及应收账款，为了提高销售额，公司还采用了可使客户享受到优惠的融资保证的信用政策。相反地，若公司使用紧缩政策，则公司会将现金、有价证券、存货以及应收账款维持在相当低的水准。营运资金投资政策如图 12-2 所示。

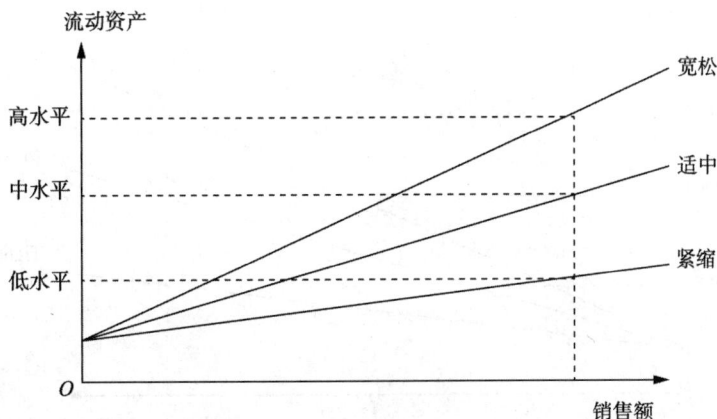

图 12-2　营运资金投资政策

(1) accelerate inventory turnover rate;

(2) collect accounts receivable efficiently;

(3) defer accounts payable days.

3. Working Capital Policy

Working capital decision is a trade-off decision between risk and return. For example: The higher level of current assets, the higher liquidity of assets, the higher short-term debt-paying ability, the higher security of a company. On the other hand, the lower level of current assets, the higher ratio of fixed assets, the higher returns on operations, the lower liability of assets, the higher risk of a company. An appropriate level of working capital depends on:

(1) Maturity structure of short-term assets and short-term debts.

(2) Liquidity of short-term assets.

(3) Suitability of short-term debts.

(4) Revenue of short-term assets.

(5) Cost of short-term debts.

(6) Risk that a company can afford.

(7) Risk preference of business operators.

12.2 Working Capital Investment Policy

Working capital investment policy can be divided into three types, which are easy, medium, tighten policies according to the amount of current assets held by a company. Easy policy means that a company holds high levels of cash, securities, inventories, and accounts receivable. A company will also adopt credit policy of allowing customers' financing guarantee to boost sales. Conversely, a tighten policy means a company holds low levels of cash, securities, inventories, and accounts receivable at a low level. Working capital investment policy can be shown as Figure 12 − 2.

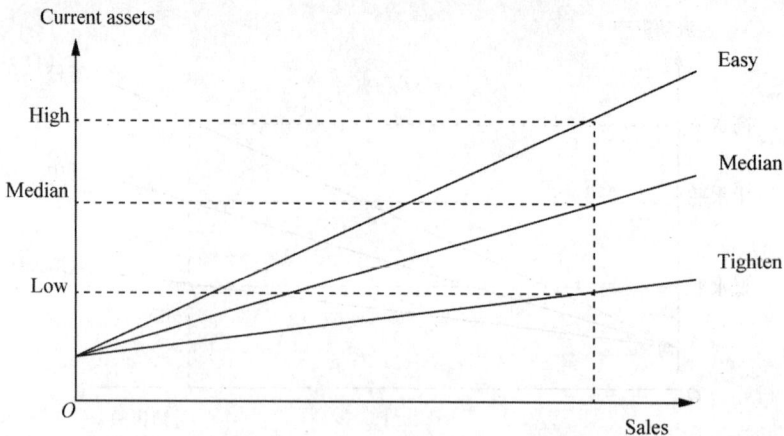

Figure 12 − 2 Working capital investment policy

资金规划应考虑长、短期资金的特性,分别做有效的资金规划。

（1）长期资金需求

根据公司未来营运目标,决定产能扩增的适当条件,计算长期的资金需求。

（2）短期资金需求

公司短期资金主要投资于存货及应收账款,而此种资金需求又常以应付账款来支应。当公司经由营业循环增加企业的营运资金,经由良好的营运资金控制产生更多利润,便会有剩余的营运资金可投资于短期的有价证券;有些企业亦会因短期季节性因素提早收款,降低存货,推迟付款以增加更多的营运资金。当存货与应收账款的加总大于应付账款时,便有多余的营运资金可以运用;反之,若存货与应收账款的加总小于应付账款,则代表企业须向外融资,以取得额外的资金。所以,公司在营运资金不足或过多时应有适当的对应策略。

公司在制定融资策略之前,应预先掌握每个月的资金需求,并依据目前的营运状况,考虑销货、进货及各项费用付款的时间,编制现金预算表,以了解公司每月的资金是否有余额或缺口,才能尽早规划调度必要的营运资金,以避免公司资金左支右绌,暴露于周转失灵的风险中,从而可以积极地抓住短期资产的投资机会,提高现金的管理效率。

案例 ▶▶▶▶▶

亚力山大健身中心

亚力山大健身中心最大的问题在于缺乏整体的财务规划。虽然其积极招揽会员,并向旧会员争取续约,但会员费与其他相关的资金又不断被投资到新的项目,导致营运资金不足,员工薪资、会馆或健身中心日常营运所需要的保养维持费用持续缺乏,因此财务黑洞越来越大。

本个案是典型的扩张太快导致破产的企业经营个案。其破产的主要原因如下:

（1）错估形势,扩张太快,导致每月现金流量不足。

（2）盲目扩点,导致营运资金不足,无法支应每月营运费用。

（3）管理混乱及内部财务账目不明,导致最后公司无法营运。

营运资金的流动性风险并非表示企业机构或市场没有获利,它是比企业

Financial planning should take into account the characteristics of short-term and long-term funding for financial effectiveness:

(1) Long term capital

Long-term capital requirements are determined by appropriate conditions of company's future operating goals for capacity expansion.

(2) Short-term capital

A Company's short-term capital mainly invests in accounts receivable and inventory. The demand for such funding usually comes from accounts payable. A company can increase working capital through operating cycle that can generate profits be invested in short-term securities through well control of working capital. Some companies might cash accounts receivable, reduce inventory level, and postpone accounts payable due to seasonal factors to have more working capital. There is surplus working capital for short-term investment when the sum of inventory and accounts receivable is greater than accounts payable. On the other hand, a company need to obtain additional funding if the sum of inventory and accounts receivable less than accounts payable. A company should have appropriate strategies to cope with conditions of short or surplus of working capital.

A company's financing strategy should consider the monthly funding requirements according to the current operations, sales, purchase and the timing of payment. A cash flow statement can help understand the company's monthly funds with balance or gap to dispatch the necessary working capital for operations. Thus risks of capital inadequacy and loss of liquidity can be avoided. Effective cash management can create extra opportunity of short-term assets investment.

Case ▶▶▶▶▶▶

Alexander Health World (AHW)

AHW's biggest problem is lack of financial planning. Although AHW made big efforts to recruit new memberships and to renew the old memberships, the membership incomes and other related funding kept investing in new projects that led to lack of working capital, which was insufficient to pay employees's salaries and maintenance cost of clubhouse or fitness center. Financial black hole was growing because of insufficient working capital.

This is a typical case of expansion too fast that leads to bankruptcy. Main reasons that cause bankruptcy are as follows:

(1) Expanding too quickly causes insufficient monthly cash flow due to misprediction of the economy.

(2) The expansion in China led to insufficient working capital for monthly operations.

(3) Bad management and internal financial control led to bankruptcy.

The liquidity risk of working capital, which is a survival issue serious than financial loss, does not mean that a company is not profitable. A company may go bankrupt due to cash flow

亏损还严重的存亡问题,一个企业即使账面上有盈余也可能因周转不灵而倒闭。当出现流动性陷阱时,任何账面有盈余的公司,不论是知名的品牌企业,还是资深的经营者,都将陷在资金不流动的泥沼中,等着被其他公司接收或看管。因此流动性停滞的问题远远比营运亏损还严重。

1. 各项流动资产管理原则

(1) 现金管理

现金管理的重要工作包括以下方面。

1) 现金需求预测

好的现金管理需要经常做现金需求预测。信息化作业系统可以有效地帮助做好现金需求预测。

2) 账户平衡管理

账户平衡管理也就是在取得现金与支付现金之间取得良好的平衡。公司必须能准确判断,何时会有现金不足的情形,需要向外界融资取得平衡,何时公司内会有多余的现金,可作短期投资而加以应用。

公司的现金管理基本上着重于加速现金的收回并延缓现金的支付,另持有现金应适当利用再投资。现金的成本包括持有成本和交易成本(见图 12 - 3)。

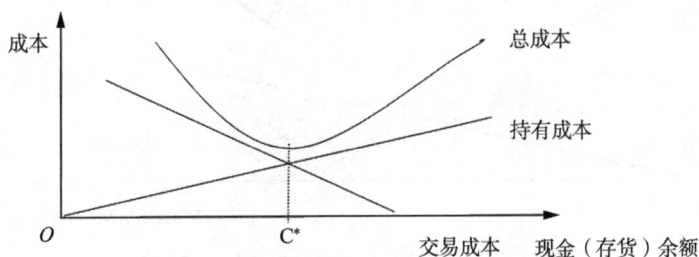

图 12 - 3　最适现金(存货)成本

持有成本指牺牲其他短期投资机会(如有价证券)的报酬。

交易成本指短期投资转换为现金的成本(如手续费)。

$$C^* = \sqrt{\frac{2bT}{i}}$$

式中:b 为每次交易成本;T 为期间内现金总需求量;i 为现金的持有成本。

例 12 - 1　假设文山公司持有满足交易性需求所需的现金总额,$T = 2140$ 万元,而持有现金的机会成本 $i = 12\%$,举债时公司所负担的交易成本 $b = 2000$ 元,计算文山公司的最适现金持有金额。

problems even it is profitable. When the liquidity trap occurs，any company with a surplus no matter it is a well-known brand，or it has a well-known operators，will be trapped in the financial crisis of liquidity risk waiting to be fail in operations. Thus the problem of liquidity trap is serious than the operating loss.

1. The principles of current assets management

（1）Cash management

The important tasks of cash management include：

1) Cash demand forecasting

Good cash management needs to do cash demand forecasting constantly. Information system can help forecast cash demand.

2) Cash balance management

Make a balance between cash inflows and cash outflows. A company needs to predict when there will be cash shortage and to make a balance from outside financing. In contrast，a company can make short-term investments when there is extra cash.

Basically，a company's cash management focus on accelerate cash income and defer cash outcome. A company should reinvest cash in short-term assets if there is extra cash. The costs of holding cash include(see Figure 12 – 3).

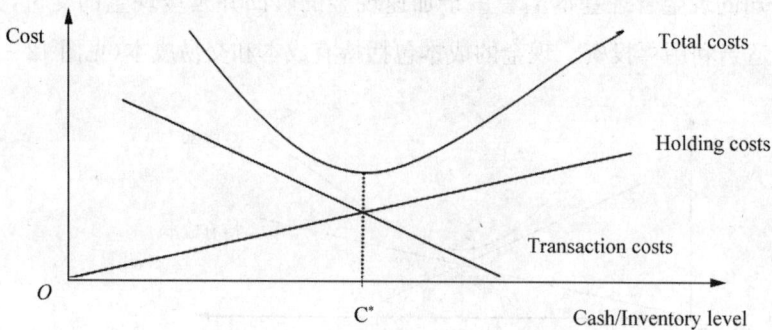

Figure 12 – 3　The optimal amount of cash

Holding costs：It refers to the cost of opportunity of losing returns from other short-term assets when holding cash.

Transaction costs：the cost of converting short-term investments into cash（such as transaction fees）.

The optimal amount of cash is

$$C^* = \sqrt{\frac{2bT}{i}}$$

Where：b is the transaction costs；T is a total amount of cash during a period；i is the holding costs.

Example 12 – 1　Assume Wenshan company holds an amount of cash for transactions. $T = 21,400,000$，the cost of opportunity of holding cash $i = 12\%$，the transaction cost $b = 2,000$.

解

$$C^* = \sqrt{\frac{2bT}{i}} = 844590.63$$

由于现金管理对风险控制有较高要求，因此现金管理中主要的投资标的系选择风险低、流通性高的短期有价证券，如国债、商务票据、银行定期存单、政府短期债券，企业债券等。目前企业可以通过金融机构投资的现金管理投资标的有：国债回购、短期拆借和政府短期债券等。

国债回购交易是一种以国债为抵押品拆借资金的信用行为。国债回购分交易所和银行间两个市场，银行间交易市场仅限于银行和有资格的非银行金融机构参与，交易所市场则允许机构投资者通过在证券公司开立法人账户的方式参与交易。

短期拆借是指银行间的拆借市场，是在金融机构、有资格的非银行金融机构间进行的信用交易行为，可作为短期投资的工具。由于国债回购，短期拆借受市场资金供需直接影响，波动较大，收益也较大，企业如能适时进行这类短期投资，将获得比银行存款利息更高的收益。

（2）存货管理

存货管理的概念如图 12 - 1 所示。在存货持有成本与交易/订购成本取舍间计算最低总成本以求取经济订购量（EOQ）。有公式：

$$EOQ = \sqrt{\frac{2KS}{H}}$$

式中：K 为交易成本；S 为每期存货总需求量；H 为持有成本。

存货管理的重要原则是，公司须维持适当存货量以降低成本，若公司存货管理不当，持有过多或过少的存货，则会产生额外成本或招致损失。

（3）有价证券管理

公司持有有价证券的理由如下：

1）因有价证券变现性较好，仅次于现金，所以有价证券可成为现金的代替品。

2）以有价证券为短期投资标的。

有价证券管理原则：

1）有价证券的流动性较高，获利性则较低，因此需要权衡流动性与获利性。

What is the optimal amount of cash?

Solution

$$C^* = \sqrt{\frac{2bT}{i}} = 844590.63$$

Cash management needs higher standard of risk control, so the major investment targets are short-term securities with low-risk and high-liquidity, such as bonds, commercial bills, bank certificates of deposit, short-term government bonds, corporate bonds. Currently the targets of investment that companies can invest through financial institutions are treasury repurchase, short-term lending and short-term government bonds.

Treasury repurchase transaction is a credit behavior targeted to the treasury as collateral lending funds. Treasury repurchase transactions are operating in two markets, which are exchange market and banking market. The transactions in interbank market is limited to banks and non-bank financial institutions. The exchange market allows institutional investors with a legal person account to make transactions of treasury repurchase.

Short-term loan within banking refers to the inter-bank lending market. This is the credit transactions among financial institutions and eligible non-banking financial institutions that can be a short-term investment tool. Treasury repurchase and short-term loan within banking are affected by the demand and supply inmonetary market with higher fluctuation and returns. A company can invest in these kinds of short-term financial tool to obtain higher returns.

(2) Inventory management

The concept of inventory management can be shown in Figure 12 − 1. A company can calculate the lowest cost between inventory holding costs and ordering costs to obtain economic order quantity (economic order quantity, EOQ):

$$\text{EOQ} = \sqrt{\frac{2KS}{H}}$$

Where: K is transaction costs; S is total demand of inventory; and H is holding costs.

An important principle of inventory management is that a company should maintain an appropriate inventory level for cost reduction. If a company doesn't manage inventory properly, either holds too much or too little inventory, it will raise additional costs or incur shortage losses.

(3) Securities management

Reasons of holding securities:

1) Securities have high liquidity similar to cash. It can be a substitution of cash.

2) Securities can be short-term investment targets.

Principles of securities management:

1) Securities have higher liquidity, but the return is lower. Thus holding of securities need to balance the liquidity and profit.

2）常用于短期投资的有价证券有定期存单、商业本票、国库券、银行承兑汇票等。

（4）应收账款管理

应收账款管理的指标主要是应收账款收现天数。过长的天数表示公司必须要长时间才能收回账款，资金成本压力大；相对地，低应收账款收现天数表示公司未能给予客户宽松的信用政策，客户的购买意愿会降低，公司的销售收入也将因而减少。因此应收账款管理的重点是要在权衡加速应收账款收现及放宽信用政策增加销货收入之间取得平衡。应收账款政策说明如下。

1）信用政策

制定信用标准与设定信用条件如 $2/7,n/20$ 为 7 天内付款享 2% 折扣，20 天为付款期限。

2）收账政策

即应收账款的收现政策。收账政策弹性宽松较易创造营收，但现金收现情形较差；相反地，收账政策保守严格，较易影响营收，但现金收现情形较佳。

为了作好应收账款管理，售货后的各项策略有：

（1）要求业务单位必须负责将货款收回。

（2）做账龄分析，将可能的坏账列出追踪，分析判断和认列坏账。

（3）阐明延迟付款的处理程序。

（4）寄发延迟付款通知。

（5）取消客户的购货权利。

（6）找收账公司帮忙处理。

（7）采取法律行动。

应收账款太多会引起公司的营运问题。首先是资金成本，如果公司提供客户信用额度或放宽信用政策，公司本身必须有能力取得相当数额的现金以支应营运所需，然而这些资金必须付出成本。此外，坏账也可能因此增加。

案例 ▶▶▶▶▶▶

远东航空应收账款不正常增加

应收账款如果管理不当将直接影响现金流量。远东航空的应收款项从 2005 年的 2.32 亿元增加至 2006 年的 6.07 亿元，再剧增到 2007 年第三季度的 13.39 亿元，同时期的营业收入却未等幅度增加，如 2005—2007 年第三季

2) The commonly used securities are certificates of deposit, commercial paper, treasury bills, and banker's acceptance.

(4) Accounts receivable management

The main indicator of accounts receivable management is days sales outstanding. Long days mean that a company needs a long time to recover the balance, the cost of capital is high. However, short days mean that a company failed to give customers easy credit policy, incentives of customers' consumptions will be reduced to influence the company's sales revenues. Therefore, accounts receivable management need to balance between accelerating cash of accounts receivable and easy credit policy for sales.Accounts receivable policies are as follows:

1) Credit policy

A set of credit standards and credit conditions are set as 2/7, n / 20 to enjoy a 2% discount payment within 7 days, payment period is 20 days.

2) Collection policy

This policy is about cashing accounts receivable. An easy collections policy can increase sales to create more revenue, but to obtain less cash; on the contrary, the conservative strict collections policy will cause less sales to influence revenue, but will have more cash inflows.

In order to have a well management of accounts receivable, the process after sales are to:

(1) ask sales unit to be responsible for cash collections;

(2) analyze the aging of accounts receivable. A process of aging analysis is to list, analyze, judge and recognize bad debts;

(3) clarify the process when there is delayed payment;

(4) send the notification for delayed payment;

(5) cancel the rights of new purchase;

(6) find a collections company to help collections of cash;

(7) take legal actions.

Too much accounts receivable can cause operation problems. First, if a company provides customer credit or easy credit policy, the company must have the capacity to obtain extra required cash for operations.However, the extra funds come with higher costs. Second, the cost of bad debts might be higher.

Case ▶▶▶▶▶▶

Abnormal of accounts receivable of Far Eastern Air Transport (FEA)

Accounts receivables influence cash flows directly.FEA's accounts receivables had increased from 0.232 billion in 2005 to 0.607 billion in 2006, the increasing was even more to the amount of 1.339 billion in 3Q 2007. However, operating income, 2005—2007/3Q was

度分别为 72.4 亿、79.8 亿、59.7 亿元,导致了远东航空大量应收账款无法及时收现。应收账款太多常常是财务危机的温床,这从远航应收账款非常态增加(即收现天数大幅拉长)中得以验证。

12.3   营运资金融资政策

企业的季节性变化或短期的投资应以短期负债来融资;而长期资产及永久性短期资产的投资,则应以长期资金融通。亦即每一种资产应以相似到期年限的融资工具来支付,根据此原则,企业的营运资金融资政策有下列三种。

1. 中庸融资政策(长支长,以短支短)

中庸融资政策是指短期资金需求(季节性及永久性流动资产)以短期融资方式调度。永久性的资金需求(固定资产)则以长期融资方式配合。采用中庸政策可使公司得以降低其无法偿还将到期负债的风险(见图 12-4)。

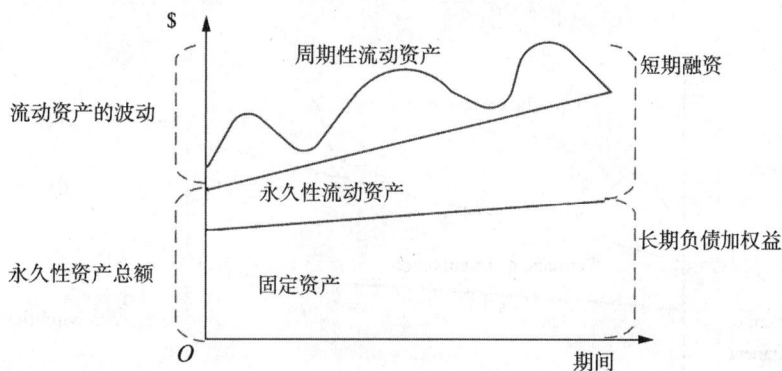

图 12-4   中庸型营运资金融资政策

图 12-4 中,永久性流动资产指在公司的营运循环跌至谷底时,公司依旧持有的流动资产。周期性流动资产指随着营运循环中季节性或循环性波动而变动的流动资产。

案例 ▶▶▶▶▶▶

亚都丽致大饭店股份有限公司

表 12-1 所示为亚都丽致大饭店股份有限公司的简易资产负债表。其中的流动资产从 2004 年度 23024 万美元成长到 2005 年度的 34302 万美元,对应到流动负债由 8390 万美元增加到 14604 万美元,表明该公司是以短期

7.24,7.98, and 5.97 billion respectively, did not increase as the same pace during the period. Financial crises come along with large amount of accounts receivable which can be seen from the case of FEA.

12.3 Working Capital Financing Policy

Seasonal variations or short-term investment should be financing by short-term loan; Investment in long-term assets and permanent short-term assets should be financing by long-term debt. That means each of the assets should be financing by similar maturity of liabilities. According to this matching principle, a company's working capital financing policy has the following three ways:

1. Moderate financing policy (Financing sources match with financing period)

Short-term funding needs (e. g. seasonal and permanent current assets) are financing by short-term loans. Permanent funding needs (e. g. fixed assets) are financing by long-term debts. Moderation financing policy can reduce the risk of unpaid debts(see Figure 12 - 4).

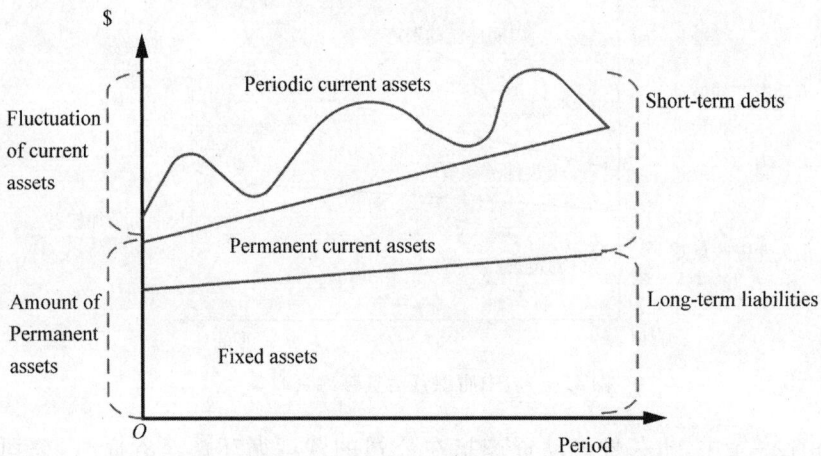

Figure 12 - 4   Moderate financing policy of working capital

In Figure 12 - 4, permanent current assets are current assets held when operating cycle is at bottom. Periodic Current assets are current assets variate with seasonal fluctuations in operating cycle.

Case ▶▶▶▶▶▶

The Landis Hotel Co., Ltd.

As shown in Table 12 - 1, the current assets of Landis Hotel Co.grew from $230,241,000 in 2004 to $343,022,000 in 2005, the current liabilities increased from $83,899,000 to $146,038,000. This case showed that short-term liabilities were balanced with short-term

融资方式来支应短期的现金与资产的需求。

从固定资产的方面来观察,2004 年度的固定资产为 77290 万美元,略为减少至 2005 年的 71128 万美元,而特别的是亚都丽致的长期融资方式并不倚赖一般负债,而着重于其他的融资工具,由 27387 万美元缩减到 17308 万美元,下降的幅度大于固定资产减少的幅度,意即其固定资产偿还负债的能力优良。

表 12 - 1　亚都丽致简易资产负债表

单位:万美元

项目	2005 年	2004 年
流动资产	34302.2	23024.1
基金与投资	16757.0	17527.1
固定资产	71127.5	72290.4
其他资产	9614.6	11521.9
资产合计	131801.3	124363.5
流动负债	14603.8	8389.9
长期负债	0.0	0.0
其他负债	17307.8	27387.4
负债合计	31911.6	35777.3
股本	70239.6	70239.6
股东权益合计	99889.7	88586.2

2. 保守融资政策(以长支短)

保守融资政策是指,公司不但以永久资金融通永久性资产,且以永久性资金满足因季节性或循环性波动而产生的暂时性资金需求(见图 12 -5)。采用保守融资政策可使公司增加资产的流动性,风险较低。

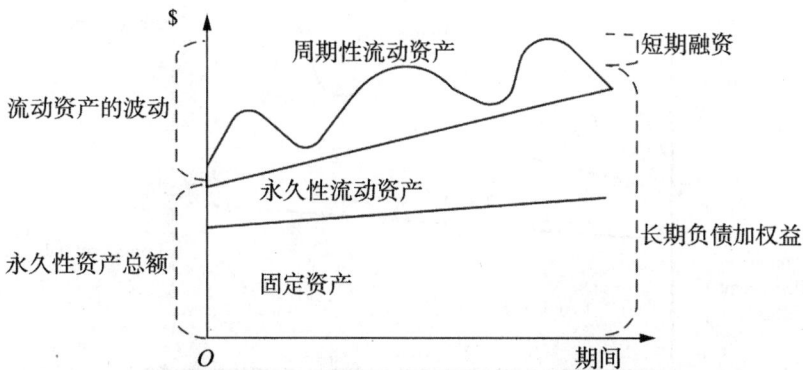

图 12 - 5　保守型营运资金融资政策

assets.

Fixed assets of Landis Hotel Co. were reduced from $772,904,000 in 2004 to $711,275,000 in 2005. In particular, the long-term financing of Landis hotel did not rely on general long-term debts. Other debts were reduced from $273,874,000 to $173,078,000. The decrease of debts was greater than the reduction in fixed assets, which meant superior ability to repay long-term debts by fixed assets.

Table 12 – 1   Balance sheet of Landis hotel

unit: thousand USA dollars

Items	Year 2005	Year 2004
Current assets	343,022	230,241
Funding and investment	167,570	175,271
Fixed assets	711,275	722,904
Other assets	96,146	115,219
Total Assets	1,318,013	1,243,635
Current debts	146,038	83,899
Long-term debts	0	0
Other debts	173,078	273,874
Total debts	319,116	357,773
Capital	702,396	702,396
Total equity	998,897	885,862

2. Conservative financing policy

Conservative financing policy means that a company not only uses permanent financing for permanent assets but also for periodic assets (see Figure 12-5). Conservative financing policy increases assets liquidity, reduce the unpaid risk.

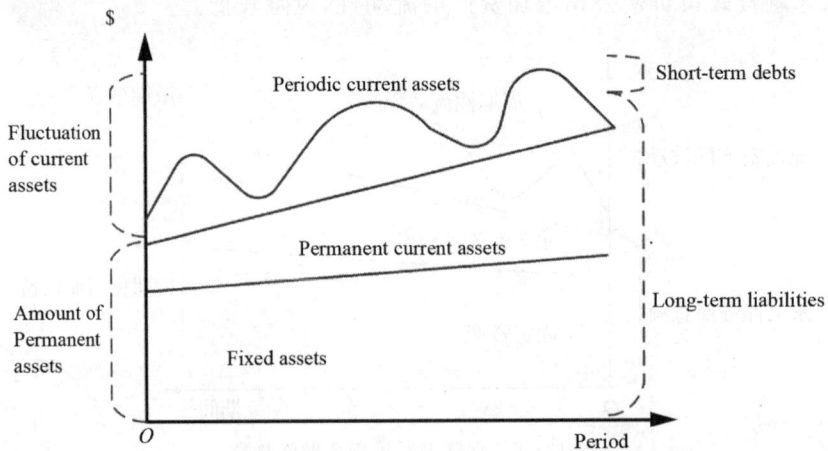

Figure 12 – 5   Conservative financing policy of working capital

案例 ▶▶▶▶▶▶

凯萨饭店

由表 12-2 可知,凯萨饭店的流动资产从 2006 年的 13497.0 万元新台币
增加至 2007 年的 16244.4 万元新台币;流动负债则由 2006 年的 20433.5 万
元新台币减少至 2007 年的 13587.7 万元新台币;且长期负债由 2006 年的
2725.0 万元新台币减少为 2007 年的 1409.0 万元新台币。流动资产增加反
映了以永久性资金满足循环性波动的需求,可推知凯萨饭店采取保守性融资
政策。

表 12-2　凯萨饭店简易资产负债表

日 期	2007 年 12 月 31 日		2006 年 12 月 31 日	
会计科目	金额(万元新台币)	%	金额(万元新台币)	%
流动资产	16244.4	22.52	13497.0	17.30
基金及投资	0	0.00	559.9	0.71
固定资产净额	55197.3	76.54	62732.0	80.41
其他资产合计	672.9	0.93	1217.4	1.56
资产总计	72114.6	100.00	78006.3	100.00
流动负债	13587.7	18.84	20433.5	26.19
长期负债	1409.0	1.95	2725.0	3.49
其他负债合计	1426.8	1.97	1358.5	1.74
负债总计	16423.5	22.77	24517.0	31.42
保留盈余合计	−8615.1	−11.94	−10816.9	−13.86
股东权益总计	55691.1	77.22	53489.3	68.57

3. 扩张型融资方式(以短支长)

公司通常以长期负债和权益等长期资金融通固定资产,短期负债融通流
动资产,但采用扩张型融资方式的公司却额外使用短期融资来筹措永久性流
动资产和部分固定资产所需的资金。此政策会造成公司须不断举新短债还
旧短债,以支付庞大的长期资产(见图 12-6)。愈扩张的融资政策,依赖短期
负债的程度愈高,容易造成公司现金不足无法偿还负债的风险。

Case ▶▶▶▶▶▶

Caesar Hotel

Table 12 - 2 showed that Caesar hotel's current assets increased from NT $134,970,000 in 2006 to NT $162,444,000 in 2007. Current debts decreased from NT $204,335,000 in 2006 to NT $135,877,000 in 2007.Long-term debts decreased from NT $27,250,000 in 2006 to NT $14,090,000 in 2007. The increase of current assets showed that Caesar hotel used permanent funding to pay for periodic fluctuation of assets. This presented that Caesar applied conservative financing policy.

Table 12 - 2　Balance sheet of Caesar Hotel

unit: thousand NT dollars

Date	Dec. 31, 2007		Dec. 31, 2006	
Accounting items	Amount	%	Amount	%
Current assets	162,444	22.52	134,970	17.30
Funding and investment	0	0.00	5,599	0.71
Fixed assets	551,973	76.54	627,320	80.41
Other assets	6,729	0.93	12,174	1.56
Total assets	721,146	100.00	780,063	100.00
Current debts	135,877	18.84	204,335	26.19
Long-term debts	14,090	1.95	27,250	3.49
Other debts	14,268	1.97	13,585	1.74
Total debts	164,235	22.77	245,170	31.42
Retained earnings	- 86,151	- 11.94	- 108,169	- 13.86
Total equity	556,911	77.22	534,893	68.57

3. Aggressive financing policy

A company usually uses long-term liabilities to finance fixed assets and uses short-term debts to finance current assets. The aggressive financing policy will use some of short-term debts to finance permanent current assets and fixed assets. This policy will result in keeping financing new short-term debts to repay old short-term debts to cover long-term assets(see Figure 12 - 6). The more aggressive financing policy, the higher the dependence on short-term debts. It is likely to cause risk of unpaid debts.

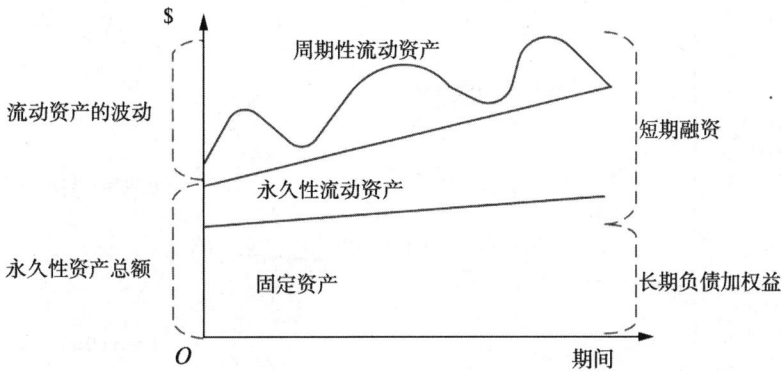

图 12 - 6　积极型营运资金融资政策

案例 ▶▶▶▶▶▶

美利达酒店有限公司

表 12 - 3 所示为美利达酒店简易资产负债表,其中的流动资产从 2006 年的 263241.4 万美元成长到 2007 年的 358610.6 万美元,对应到流动负债由 228360.8 万元增加到 308831.7 万美元,显示出其在营收成长上的积极尝试。

该公司 2006 年与 2007 年的流动负债差额为 80470.9 万美元,其他负债 15099.3 万美元,合计 95570.2 万美元,大于流动资产与固定资产增值的总额,故美利达酒店在扩充资产时运用了大量的流动负债与其他负债,其他剩余部分运用在基金与投资上,融资的风险相当高。

表 12 - 3　美利达酒店资产负债表

单位:万美元

项目	2007 年	2006 年
流动资产	358610.6	263241.4
基金与投资	440908.7	351091.2
固定资产	87569.7	86731.1
其他资产	461.1	831.1
资产合计	890440.6	705212.8
流动负债	308831.7	228360.8
长期负债	0.0	0.0
其他负债	86328.8	71239.5
负债合计	395160.5	299590.3
股本	215309.2	215309.2
股东权益合计	495280.1	405622.5

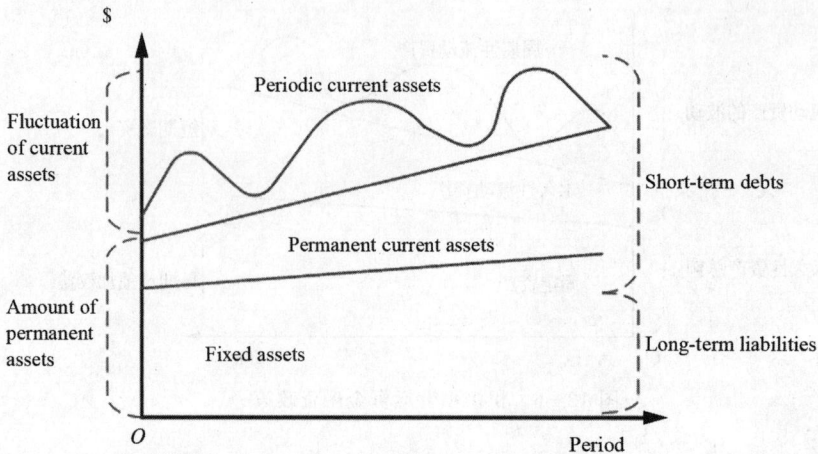

Figure 12 - 6 Aggressive financing policy of working capital

Case ▶▶▶▶▶▶

Merida Hotels Ltd.

Table 12 - 3 showed that Current assets of Merida hotel grow from $2,632,414,000 in 2006 to $3,586,106,000 in 2007. Current debts increased from $2,283,608,000 in 2006 to 3,088,317,000 in 2007. The statements showed Merida hotel's aggressive attemption on revenue growth.

The current debt difference is $804,709 between 2006 and 2007 and other debts $150,993,000is total amount of $955,702,000. This total amount is greater than the total amount of current assets and fixed assets increment. It showed that Merida hotel uses large amount of current debts and other debts for financing assets and other investments.The unpaid risk of Merida hotel is quite high.

Table 12 - 3 **Balance Sheet of Merida Hotel**

unit：thousand USA dollars

Items	Year 2007	Year 2006
Current assets	3,586,106	2,632,414
Funds and investments	4,409,087	3,510,912
Fixed assets	875,597	867,311
Other assets	4,611	8,311
Total assets	8,904,406	7,052,128
Current debts	3,088,317	2,283,608
Long-term debts	0	0
Other debts	863,288	712,295
Total debts	3,951,605	2,995,903
Capital	2,153,092	2,153,092
Total equity	4,952,801	4,056,225

4. 企业短期融资工具

（1）商业本票

商业本票（CP）指由大公司所发行的无担保短期本票，到期期间为两个月到六个月，利率略低于基本利率。

（2）向银行短期融资

向银行短期融资成本即银行所收利率，有公式：

$$简单利率 = \frac{每年利息费用}{借款人所收到贷款额}$$

如果简单利率贷款的到期期间不到一年，则它的有效利率将比名义利率高。在贷款期间低于一年时，由于银行收到利息的时间会比贷款的到期期间早，故银行实际上能享受到较高的有效利率，亦即借款人须付较高的利率。

例 12 - 2　假定某人向银行借到一笔面值为 1 万美元、利率等于 12%、90 天后到期的贷款，则有效利率为多少？

解　有效利率 $= \left(1+\dfrac{k}{n}\right)^n = \left(1+\dfrac{12\%}{4}\right)^4 - 1 = 12.55\%$

式中：k 代表名义利率；n 代表每年的贷款次数。

（3）应付账款资金成本

应付账款是伴随着交易产生的，因此属于自发性融资。应付账款的资金成本（APC）很高，故当公司有足够的资金来源时，应于折扣期间付款，以便享受现金折扣。有公式：

$$APC = \frac{折扣率}{100\% - 折扣率} \times \frac{365}{最后到期日 - 折扣期间}$$

（4）应付费用

应付费用会随着公司营运的扩充而自动增加，但不会给公司带来外在的利息负担，故乃是一种可供公司利用的免费短期负债。

4. Short-term financing instruments

(1) Commercial paper(CP)

Commercial paper is issued by large companies which is notes of short-term loans without collateral. The period ranges from two months to six months. The interest rate is slightly lower than the base rate.

(2) Short-term bank financing costs

Bank interest rates have formula as

$$\text{Simple interest rate} = \frac{\text{Annual interest}}{\text{Principal}}$$

If the maturity of a simple interest loan is less than one year, the effective interest rate is higher than nominal interest rates. A bank can receive higher interest, which means a company needs to pay higher cost, if a loan maturity is less than a year.

Example 12 - 2 Suppose a person borrow a loan with principal of $10,000 from a bank, the interest rate is equal to 12 %, the maturity is ninety days. What is the effective interest rate?

Solution

$$\text{Effective interest rate} = \left(1 + \frac{k}{n}\right)^n - 1 = \left(1 + \frac{12\%}{4}\right)^4 - 1 = 12.55\%$$

Where: k represents the nominal interest rate; n is the times of loans for a year.

(3) Account payment cost (APC)

Accounts payable comes along with transactions. It is a spontaneous financing instrument. The cost of capital is high for APC. If a company has enough funding sources, it should pay the accounts payable for a cash discount in the discount period.

$$\text{APC} = \frac{\text{Discount rate}}{100\% - \text{Discount rate}} \times \frac{365}{\text{Maturity} - \text{Discount rate period}}$$

(4) Accrued expenses payable

Accrued expenses payable is increasing with the expansion of a company. It will not bring extra interest to the company, thus it is a free financing instrument of the company's short-term debt.

第 13 章　红利政策

学习目标

- 了解影响红利政策的因素
- 了解红利政策相关理论
- 了解红利政策实务

红利政策为公司重要的财务决策,系指企业在经营过程中所赚取的利润,应于何时发放、按多少比例发放以及以何种方式(现金红利、股票红利)分配的决策。红利政策所涉及的决策包括:盈余部分有多少当作红利发放给股东;有多少应保留下来当作再投资用。最佳红利政策就是能够在红利支付与未来成长间做权衡,使公司的股价最大化的红利政策。

戈登成长模式:

$$P_0 = \frac{D_1}{K_s - g}$$

式中:g 为红利预期成长率;P_0 为特别股市价;D_1 为第一年红利;K_s 为特别股必要报酬率。

$D_1 \uparrow \rightarrow P_0 \uparrow$;$D_1 \downarrow \rightarrow g \uparrow \rightarrow P_0$?

13.1　影响红利政策的因素

1. 法律规定

公司法对红利分配的规定:

(1) 公司在弥补亏损及提出法定盈余公积后,才可以分派股息红利。

(2) 公司无盈余时,不得分派股息及红利。

法律规定的目的是保障债权人的权益,防止股东以红利方式收回其股本。

Chapter 13   Dividend Policy

Learning Outcomes

- Understand factors that influence dividend policy
- Understand the relation between dividend policy and stock price
- Understand practices of dividend policy

Dividend policy is an important financial decisions of a company. The policy decides when, how much, and what form to distribute dividends when a company has made its profit. The decisions of dividend policy involved: How much percentage of surplus as dividends to pay stockholders? How much percentage of surplus should be retained for reinvestment? The best dividend policy is to maximize company's stock price by trade-off between the dividend payment and retained earning for future growth.

Gordon Growth Model:

$$P_0 = \frac{D_1}{K_s - g}$$

Where: g is the expected dividend growth rate; P_0 is the preferred stock price; D_1 is the first year dividend; K_s is the return rate of preferred stock.

$D_1 \uparrow \rightarrow P_0 \uparrow$; $D_1 \downarrow \rightarrow g \uparrow \rightarrow P_0$?

13.1   Factors that Influence Dividend Policy

1. Regulation of law

Laws on dividend distribution are:

(1) Dividends can be dispatched after covering the deficit and legal reserve.

(2) Dividends and bonuses can not be distributed to stockholder without earnings.

The purpose of the laws is to protect the interests of creditors, to prevent shareholders recover their capital by payment of dividend.

案例 ▶▶▶▶▶▶

六福酒店

由表13-1和表13-2可知,六福公司从1996年开始盈利逐年下降,股东权益报酬率亦逐年减少,红利和股票账面价值成正比。2000年由盈转亏,但一直到2007年营运都不见好转,根据法律规定,不得发放股东红利及员工红利。

表13-1 六福酒店红利情况

单位:美元/股

项目	年度					
	1996	1997	1998	1999	2000	2001—2007
现金红利	1.00	1.00	1.00	0.50	0.00	0.00
盈余配股	1.05	0.00	0.00	0.00	0.00	0.00
公积配股	1.50	2.00	1.11	0.50	0.50	0.00
股票红利	2.55	2.00	1.11	0.50	0.50	0.00
合计	3.55	3.00	2.11	1.00	0.50	0.00

表13-2 六福酒店获利与红利关系

单位:%

项目	年度							
	1996	1997	1998	1999	2000	2005	2006	2007
资产报酬率	7.38	5.56	0.38	-0.22	-10.59	-0.20	11.43	-2.36
股东权益报酬率	9.64	7.28	0.39	-1.26	-17.09	-0.75	14.59	-4.52
营业利益占实收资本比率	27.79	18.86	1.37	-2.41	-25.29	-1.09	46.23	-6.94
税前纯益占实收资本比率	28.60	19.38	1.44	-3.37	-32.80	-1.35	49.79	-9.08
纯益率	19.92	17.02	1.11	-3.37	-2.54	-0.11	27.52	-0.68
每股盈余(元)	2.15	1.48	0.08	-0.25	-2.95	-1.49	3.80	-6.98

2. 税法上强制归户限制

所得税法为避免股东将盈余保留在公司以逃漏个人所得税,设有未分配盈余强制归户的规定。

Case ▶▶▶▶▶

Luk Fook Hotel

Table 13 - 1 and Table 13 - 2 presented that Luk Fook hotel's profits and return on equity had decreased year by year since 1996. Dividend is proportional to book value. Deficit had happened from 2000 to 2007. The operations had not improved until 2007. According to the regulation of the law, dividends can not be paid to stockholders and bonuses can not be paid to the employees.

Table 13 - 1   The dividends of Luk Fook Hotel

unit：USA dollars/share

Items	Year 1996	Year 1997	Year 1998	Year 1999	Year 2000	Year 2001—2007
Cash dividend	1.00	1.00	1.00	0.50	0.00	0.00
Stock dividend from retained earnings	1.05	0.00	0.00	0.00	0.00	0.00
Stock dividend from capital reserve	1.50	2.00	1.11	0.50	0.50	0.00
Stock dividend	2.55	2.00	1.11	0.50	0.50	0.00
Total	3.55	3.00	2.11	1.00	0.50	0.00

Table 13 - 2   Relationship of profit and dividend of Luk Fook Hotel

Unit：%

Items	Year 1996	Year 1997	Year 1998	Year 1999	Year 2000	Year 2005	Year 2006	Year 2007
ROA	7.38	5.56	0.38	− 0.22	− 10.59	− 0.20	11.43	− 2.36
ROE	9.64	7.28	0.39	− 1.26	− 17.09	− 0.75	14.59	− 4.52
Operating income to capital stock	27.79	18.86	1.37	− 2.41	− 25.29	− 1.09	46.23	− 6.94
Income before tax to capital stock	28.60	19.38	1.44	− 3.37	− 32.80	− 1.35	49.79	− 9.08
Net profit margin	19.92	7.02	1.11	− 3.37	− 2.54	− 0.11	27.52	− 0.68
EPS	2.15	1.48	0.08	− 0.25	− 2.95	− 1.49	3.80	− 6.98

2. Restrictions of tax law

Income tax law has restriction of retained earnings to prevent tax avoidance of stockholders by retaining money in a company. The tax law has regulations of paying dividends from retained earning to stockholder's personal property.

3. 债务契约的限制

债务契约中常限制公司红利的发放以保护债权人的权利,因此公司红利会受到债务契约的影响。

4. 现金状况

现金红利只能以现金发放,若公司现金短缺会限制公司现金红利的发放。

5. 投资计划

若公司想要急速扩充或实施有获利机会的投资计划,则公司将会减少现金红利的发放而将盈余保留在公司内,以应对未来发展所需。

6. 股东的税率

若公司大部分股东的税率都很高,那么公司会保留较多的盈余,减少红利发放,这可降低股东的税赋。

7. 资金取得难易

信誉较佳的公司因资金取得较容易,不必保留过多的盈余,因此发放红利的金额会较高。反之,规模小的公司因资金取得较困难,发放红利的机会较少。

8. 红利所提供的资讯内涵

外部投资人通常对公司的获利能力不甚了解,公司的管理部门可用红利发放的多寡来将公司的经营绩效及未来愿景传达给投资者。公司减少红利发放,则投资人可能会认为这是管理部门预测未来盈余不佳而须预留资金的讯息。反之,则代表公司对未来盈余有良好的预期。因此红利宣告隐含着公司经营的资讯,需要仔细推敲。

13.2　红利政策与公司股价的关系

对于红利政策是否影响公司股价,学术界有不同的看法(见图 13 - 1)。

1. Gordon 与 Linter 的"一鸟在手"理论

"一鸟在手"理论主张企业应该发放红利以吸引更多投资人买进股票,红利发得越多,股价就越高。

3. Limits from debt covenants

Debt covenants usually restrict the payment of dividend to protect creditor. The dividend of a company will be affected by the debt covenants.

4. Cash amount

Cash dividend can only be paid in cash. If there is cash shortage, there is limitation of cash dividend.

5. Investment plan

If a company has plans of aggressive expansion or has profitable opportunities of investments, the company will reduce the cash dividend payment and remain retained earnings in the company for future investment.

6. Tax rate of stockholders

If the tax rates of majority of stockholders are high, then the company will remain more retained earnings to reduce dividend payments, which can reduce stockholders' tax.

7. Funding

A reputational company is easy to get funding that doesn't need to keep too much of operations surplus, therefore the amount of dividends payment will be higher. On the other hand, a smaller company is difficult to obtain funding that need to keep more operations surplus, thus dividends payment will be reduced.

8. Signal from dividends

Investors usually do not get a company's inner information of profitability. The management authority of a company can use the amount of dividends to release the signal of the company's operating performance and future vision to investors. If a company reduce dividends, investors may guess that the dividend reduction means the company's future vision is not well and it needs more retained earnings for operations. In contrast, it represents the company's future is well and less retained earnings is needed. Therefore, a company need to be cautious of declaration of dividend payment because it implies information of company's operations.

13.2 The Relationship of Dividend Policy and Stock Price

The academia has different opinions of dividend policy as shown in Figure 13 - 1.

1. Gordon and Linter's Bird-in-the-hand theory

The bird-in-the-hand theory claims that a company should pay high dividends in

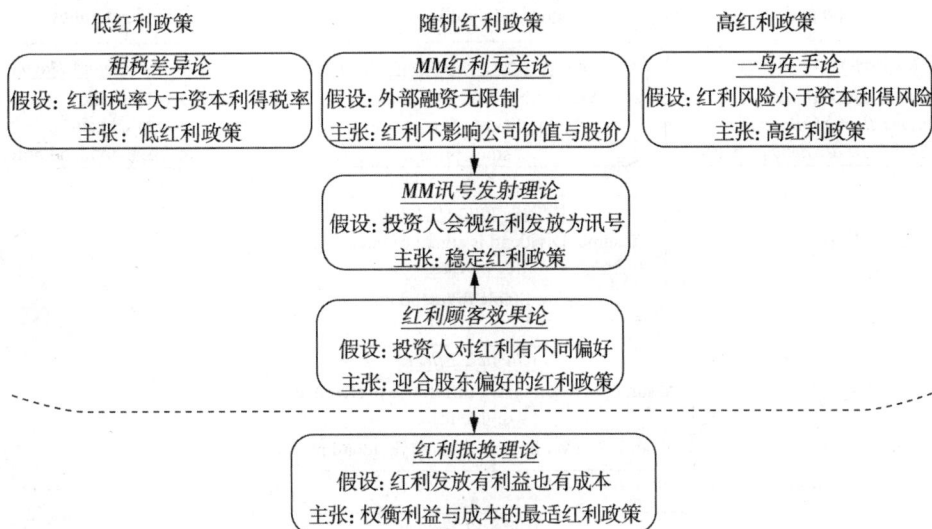

图 13-1 红利政策理论

以戈登模型说明：

$$K_s = \frac{D_1}{p_0} + g$$

式中：K_s 为股东收益率；P_0 为期初股价；D_1 为第一期红利；g 为资本利得收益率。

（1）红利收益率（D_1/P_0）风险较小。

（2）资本利得收益率（g）风险较大，须待公司成长，股价上涨，才有资本利得。

（3）投资人较喜欢红利，而非资本利得。

Modigliani 和 Miller（M&M）两位学者批评此学说是"一鸟在手"的谬论。M&M 认为，即使是投资者今日把钱拿回来了，还是得做下一个新的投资，投资仍然具有风险。

2. M&M 的红利无关论

红利无关论认为，红利与股价相互独立，没有关系。以戈登模型说明：

$$K_s = \frac{D_1}{p_0} + g$$

式中：K_s 为常数。

（1）股息政策不会影响公司股价。

（2）公司股价取决于公司创造盈余的能力与本身的风险。

红利无关论无法解释实务上红利政策与股价表现之间的关系。M&M

Low dividend policy   Contingent dividend policy   High dividend policy

Tax Preference Theory
Assume:Dividend tax rate is
higher than capital gain
Claim:Low dividend policy

MM Dividend Irrelevance Theory
Assume:No limit for financing
Claim:Dividend are irrelevance to
stock price

Bird-in-the-hand Theory
Assume:Dividend risk is lower than
capital gain
Claim: High dividend policy

MM Signaling Hypothesis
Assume: Dividend is signal of operations
for investor
Claim: Stable dividend policy

Clientele Effect
Assume: Investors have difference preference of
dividend
Claim: Stocker holder-oriented dividend policy

Trade-off Theory
Assume: Pros and cons of dividend
Claim: The best dividend policy after trading off pros
and cons of dividend

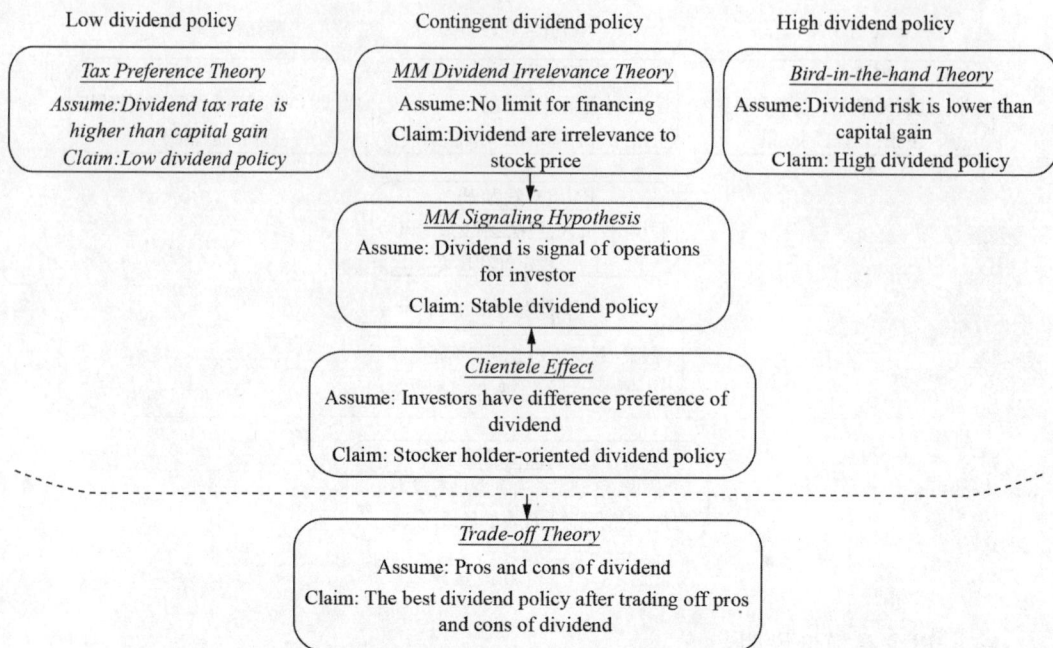

Figure 13 - 1   Dividend policy

order to attract investors to buy stocks. The more dividends, the higher stock price.

Explain by Gordon model as follows:

$$K_s = \frac{D_1}{p_0} + g$$

Where K_s is stockholder's return rate; P_0 is beginning stock price; D_1 is dividend at the first period; g is capital gain.

(1) Dividend yield (D_1/P_0) has lower risk.

(2) Capital gains (g) have greater risk because capital gains got from the rise of stock price after a company's development form capital budgeting.

(3) Investors prefer dividends rather than capital gains.

M & M criticized this theory that suffered from a bird-in-the-hand fallacy. M & M argued that even investors get their money back from dividends; they still need to do new investments along with risk.

2. M & M dividend irrelevance theory

Dividend and stock price is independent. Explain by Gordon model as follows:

$$K_s = \frac{D_1}{p_0} + g$$

Where: K_s is a constant.

(1) The dividend policy will not affect the company's stock price.

(2) The stock price determines by a company's profitable ability with its own risks.

In practice the dividend irrelevance theory can not explain the real relationship

提出红利政策无关论,乃基于下列严谨的假设:

(1) 没有税,没有交易成本,即资本市场是"完美的市场"。

(2) 所有投资者对于公司未来的投资、利润及红利皆有"相同的预期"。

(3) 公司的投资政策已定,不会受到红利政策的影响。

实务上值得注意的是:"红利政策与公司价值没有太大的关系,但红利却与公司价值有关。"

案例 ▶▶▶▶▶▶

国宾饭店

国宾饭店处于稳定成长阶段,考虑到饭店未来的资金需求,并满足股东对现金的需求,饭店于年度结算后若有盈余,一部分作公司资本预算,并发放一定比例的现金红利满足股东现金需求(见表 13-3)。只有当未来年度的盈余及资金较为充裕时,才提高发放比例。

表 13-3　国宾饭店红利分发表

红利年度	现金红利		董监酬劳(美元)
	股东红利(美元/股)	员工红利总金额(美元)	
2007	0.68	24341307	12170653
2006	0.80	27359220	13679610
2005	0.70	13878238	13878238
2004	0.30	4394774	4394774

饭店 2007 年度现金红利经 2008 年股东大会通过,决议每股配发 0.7 元,因公司一些可转换公司债的债权人申请转换普通股,故现金红利调整为每股配发0.68元。从资料来看,国宾饭店是个稳定发展的企业,虽然 2007 年盈余稍微下滑,但并不影响其红利政策,由此判断,国宾饭店采用红利无关政策;实务上则采用稳定的现金红利政策。

3. 租税差异论(低红利政策)

(1) 现金红利的税率比资本利得的税率高,故公司不该发放过多红利,

between the dividend policy and stock price. M & M's dividend irrelevant theory is based on the following stringent assumptions:

(1) There are no taxes, no transaction costs, and the capital market is "perfect market".

(2) All investors have the same expectations for the company's future investments, profits and dividends.

(3) Company's investment policy has been esttle that will not be influenced by dividend policy.

However, it should be noted that in practice the dividend policy does not influence the company's value, but the dividend has influence on the company's value.

Case ▷▷▷▷▷▷▷

The Ambassador Hotel

The Ambassador Hotel is at a stable growth stage. Considering hotel's future demand of capital budgeting and stockholders' needs for cash, the hotel saved part of the revenue margin for its capital budgeting and a certain percentage of cash dividends for shareholders' cash demand(see Table 13 – 3). When there is more revenue surplus, the hotel increased the proportion of dividends payment.

The cash dividends in 2007 has been set in the 2008 regular stockholders' meeting. The decision of stockholder's dividends is 0.7 per share. Because some of the convertible bonds are converted into common stocks, the cash dividend was adjusted to 0.68 per. Table 13 – 1 showed that the Ambassador hotel is a steady development enterprise. Although a slight decline in earnings in 2007, it does not influence hotel's dividend policy. We can tell that the Ambassador Hotel was holding dividend irrelevant policy. In practice hotel was adopting a stable cash dividend policy.

Table 13 – 3   The Dividends of the Ambassador Hotel

Year	Cash dividends		Directors' remuneration (dollars)
	Stockholder's dividends (dollars/share)	Amount of employee's bonus (dollars)	
2007	0.68	24,341,307	12,170,653
2006	0.80	27,359,220	13,679,610
2005	0.70	13,878,238	13,878,238
2004	0.30	4,394,774	4,394,774

3. Tax preference theory (Low dividend policy)

(1) Cash dividend tax rate is higher than the capital gains tax rate. A company

以免投资人缴较高的税。

（2）公司应尽可能地少发红利，保留现金用于再投资。

（3）管理者有动力去寻找降低红利的资金（例如保留盈余）用于投资。

4. M&M 信息发射理论

（1）红利代表公司经营的信息，股价对红利所传递的信息会有所反应。

（2）红利隐含的重要信息：红利增加超过投资人预期，表示管理者预期未来盈余将改善；股息减少超过投资人预期，表示管理者预期未来盈余将变差。

5. 红利顾客效果论

（1）喜欢高红利的投资人，会选择高红利股票投资。喜欢低红利的投资人，会选择低红利股票投资。

（2）因此，公司应建立股东导向红利政策，以吸引其目标顾客群。

（3）公司一旦制定好红利政策后，不应经常改变。

在顾客效果假说下，企业倾向于发放红利以留住原有股东，并吸引更多的投资人购买股票，以利于稳定企业股价。

6. 红利抵换理论

Rozeff（1982）提出红利支付会有成本与利益，最合适的红利政策为成本与利益权衡抵换而得。

13.3　红利政策实务

1. 剩余红利政策

剩余红利政策系指公司的盈余要等资本预算所需资金决定后，剩余的盈余再发放红利。"剩余红利政策"的好处在于，公司先用内部资金来支应投资所需，可降低资金成本。而坏处就是，红利金额每年会变动，易让投资人觉得公司风险较大。依此方式所引申的红利政策为，当公司面对好的投资机会时，会多使用保留盈余而采取低红利政策；而面对较差的投资机会时，则采取高现金红利政策。问题是，投资机会总是随产业环境变化有波动，依此方式分派红利将使公司的红利分派比率波动极大，会使投资人有较高的风险预

should not pay high dividends to make investors pay high taxes.

(2) The company shall issue less dividends to preserve cash for reinvestment.

(3) Managers have incentives to find funding to lower dividends payment (e.g. retained earnings) for investment.

4. M & M signaling hypothesis

(1) Dividends imply the signal of operations of a company. The stock price will response the signal of dividends.

(2) The signal of dividends: Dividends increase more than investors' expectations which imply managers'expectations of future earnings will improve. Dividends reduce more than investors' expectations which imply managers'expectations of future earnings will be worse.

5. Clientele effect

(1) Investors like high dividend will choose high-dividend stocks. Investors like low dividend will choose low-dividend stocks.

(2) A company should establish a stockholder-oriented dividend policy to attract its target market.

(3) The dividend policy should be stable once it has been settle.

A company tends to pay dividends to retain the existing shareholders and attract more investors to buy stocks that can keep the level of its stock price.

6. Dividend trade off theory

Rozeff (1982) advocated dividend payment came with costs and benefits. The optimal dividend policy is to trade off between costs and benefits of dividend payment.

13.3 Practical Dividend Policy

1. Residual dividend policy

Residual dividend policy means earnings of a company needed to allocate to capital budgeting first, the remaining to pay dividends. The benefit of residual dividend policy is that the cost of capital is low becase of funding comes from inner capital with low cost. The disadvantage is that the dividend amount will change each year, so that investors would sense the higher risk of a company. The practical implication of residual dividend policy is that a company will use more retained earnings, less dividends payment,when a company has good investment; in contrast to a company that doesn't have good investment opportunities, it will have high dividends payment. The problem is that the investment opportunities vary with industry environment all the time, the way of distributing dividends will make dividend payout ratio fluctuate with risk.This will affect

期,从而影响其投资意愿。

2. 固定红利政策

固定红利政策指公司每年支付固定金额的红利加上对应通货膨胀的红利成长率,红利成长率则依每年的公司成长率发放。此政策适合需要稳定现金收入的投资机构及个人。该政策的优点在于公司可提前规划红利的发放,该红利的现金流量固定,容易做好公司整体的财务规划。企业生命周期正值"成熟期"、投资报酬率相对稳定的公司较适合采取此红利政策。对需要稳定现金收入的机构投资人(如退休基金)而言,此类公司为有利的投资标的。

3. 固定发放率政策

固定发放率政策指红利发放为盈余的固定百分比,如红利发放为盈余的50%。每年红利发放率随公司成长率以固定或递增的成长率增加,只是采用该项红利政策的公司,每年必须有稳定增长的现金流入。此政策适用于企业生命周期正值"成长期"的公司。

4. 低正常红利再加红利

公司平时发放一定金额的红利,当经济形势好时,加发红利。每年至少发放少量的现金红利,当公司有较多的盈余或资金充足时,则提高红利发放比率。此红利政策适用于企业生命周期处于"创业期"及"成长期"的公司,该类公司虽仍待资金投入作资本预算,但为了满足股东对现金收入的需求,所以采用这种红利政策。

5. 稳定成长的现金红利政策

公司每年的现金流量呈现稳定成长,红利支付率也随之每年稳定增加。

6. 红利政策的实证研究

65岁以上的投资人喜好投资高红利的公司,其中已退休者更明显,他们的股票组合有80%以上都是发放高红利的股票。相反的,45岁以下的投资人持有发放高红利的股票只占其股票投资的65%。

the willingness to invest in the company's stock because of the higher risk expectation.

2. Fixed dividend policy

Fixed dividend policy means a company pays a fixed amount of annual dividends, in addition, the annual growth rate of dividends followed the growth rate of the company will be paid to cope with the inflation. This policy is suitable for institutional and individual investors who need stable cash income. The advantage of this policy is that a company can plan its distribution of dividends. The cash flow of dividends is settle that make the company's overall financial planning easier. This policy is suitable for companies which are at the "mature" phase of enterprise lifecycle. It is also good for those companies with stable ROI. Companies that apply the fixed dividend policy are good investment targets for institutional investors (such as pension funds).

3. Fixed payout ratio policy

Fixed payout ratio policy refers to a fixed percentage of the earnings as dividend payout ratio. For example, dividend payment is 50% of earnings. The dividend payout ratio is increasing by a fixed rate or an increasing rate followed with the growth rate of a company. However, companies need to have steady growth of cash inflows to adapt this policy, which is at the "growing" phase of enterprise life cycle.

4. Low dividends with bonuses

This policy means that a company pays a certain amount of dividends with bonus when economy is good. A small amount of cash dividends will be paid each year, in addition, bonuses will be added when the company has earnings or sufficient funding. This dividend policy is suitable for the "startup" or "growing" phase of enterprise life cycle. Even fundings of capital budgeting for company to grow up is important, cash inflows of dividends for stockholders is also essential.

5. Steady growth of cash dividend

Dividend payout ratio increases steadily every year when cash inflows of a company increases steadily.

6. Empirical studies of dividend policy

Investors over 65 years old, especially for retirees, prefer to invest in high dividend stocks. Their stock portfolio had more than 80% on high dividend stocks. On the contrary, investors under 45 years old hold high dividends stocks in their portfolio was only 65%.

案例 ▷▷▷▷▷▷

只是规划公司

只是规划公司提供的餐饮业及 Makasete 网络的 ASP 服务,用于销售、采购、职工考勤管理等功能。其红利政策采用固定红利政策,同时仍确保内部储备资金处于适当水平,以资助未来业务拓展和加强业务基础。公司的固定红利保持在每股 18 元左右,2014 年为每股 20 元系因纪念公司成立 20 周年。红利支付率反映了上下波动的情形(见图 13-2)。

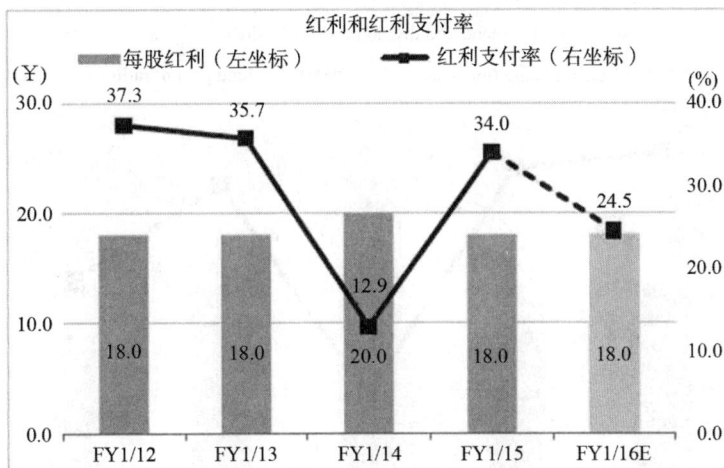

图 13-2 只是规划公司的红利发放

Case ▶▶▶▶▶▶

Just Planning Inc.

Just planning Inc. provided the catering service for food industry and ASP service for Makasete network. Services are for companies' sales，purchasing，employee attendance management and other functions. Just Planning Inc. adopted fixed dividend policy，while still ensuring an promotion level of internal reserves for capital budgeting of future business expansion and promotion of business sales. The company maintained a fixed dividend of 18 yuan per share，20 yuan per share in 2014 is to commemorate the company's 20th anniversary．Dividend payout ratio presented a fluctuating condition（see Figure 13 - 2）.

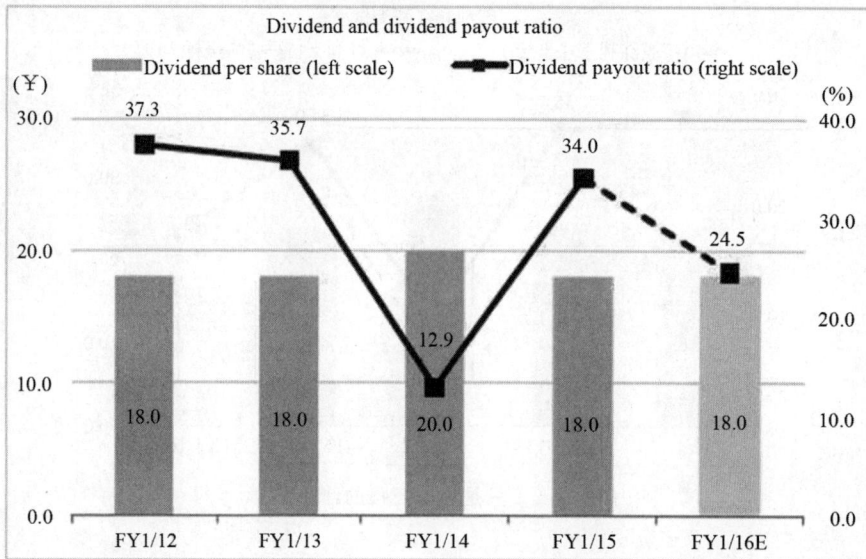

Figure 13 - 2　The dividend payment of Just Planning Inc.

第 14 章　酒店估值

学习目标

- 了解酒店估值的概念
- 能定义不同类型的价值
- 应用三种不同的酒店估值方法

14.1　引　言

由于酒店企业需要在建筑、家具、固定装置和设备(FF&E)甚至有时候在土地购置上投入巨额的投资,所以酒店企业属于资本密集型企业。虽然酒店有其独特的为顾客提供临时住宿和食品饮料产品和服务的行业本质,然而从房地产的角度来看,它和商业地产如写字楼有一些共同点:两者皆旨在可用和有限的空间上尽可能产生最高的盈利。如果酒店无法像写字楼那样在每平方米的基础上产生相匹配的利润或至少能给业主提供等额的价值,业主就可能需要考虑在与现有的酒店管理公司合作的基础上是否继续持有该酒店所有权,或者更换现有的管理公司、关闭酒店改造物业、更好地利用物业,甚至干脆变卖酒店物业。

或者,酒店业主为求进一步发展的机会会向债权人融资,寻求财政支持,银行考虑贷款申请的时候会想了解酒店物业作为贷款抵押品的价值的多寡。酒店估值在出售酒店物业或者申请银行贷款的情况下至关重要,因为其评价过程和结果会清清楚楚地向业主和潜在买家/债权人提供酒店的实际价值。但应该指出的是,价值评估是一个相当主观的过程,最终酒店物业能否出售或者贷款是否获批则取决于卖方和买方/债权人能否就某一交易金额达成共识。

Chapter 14　Hotel Valuation

Learning Outcomes

- Understand the concept of hotel valuation
- Be able to define various types of values
- Apply the three approaches to hotel valuation

14.1　Introduction

Hotel businesses are capital-intensive as they require significant amount of fixed asset investments in hotel buildings, furniture, fixture and equipment (FF&E) and sometimes land purchase. While the nature of hotel business is rather unique in providing transient accommodation and food and beverage products and services to customers, from a real estate perspective it has shared certain commonality with commercial properties such as office buildings as both aim to generate highest possible income from available and limited space. If a hotel is not able to generate as much profit per square meter as compared to an office building or offer at least equivalent amounts of value to the owners, owners may need to consider whether or not continuing its ownership with the existing hotel management company, replacing the existing management company, closing down the hotel and transforming the building for better use or simply selling off the hotel property.

Or, when hotel owners seek financial support from creditors for further growth opportunities, banks will want to know how much a hotel property is worth in terms of it being used as a collateral in considering a loan application. In the case where a sale of hotel property or a bank loan is involved, hotel valuation is of critical importance as such valuation process and result shall provide owners and potential buyers/creditors with a clear picture of how much the hotel is worth. However, it should be noted that valuation is a rather subjective process, in which a final sale or granted loan is only possible when the seller and the buyer/creditor both agree upon the amount of the deal.

14.2　不同类型价值的定义

价值评估时会因为估值目的不同而存在很多不同的价值定义,描述如下。

1. 市场价值

海因斯将市场价值定义为:"一个物业在具有公平销售条件的竞争市场中所反映出来的价钱,而这个价钱来自于买卖双方在知情和没有不当压力的情况下谨慎行事的谈判结果。"而国际估价准则委员会则定义市场价值为:"经由适当的营销而且买卖双方在知情、谨慎和未受强迫的情况下各自采取行动,于估值日期在公平交易的情况下,买卖双方自愿交换的资产或负债的估计金额。"因此,在考虑一个目标的市场价值时应该系统性地评估及考虑所有可能的影响因素之后的基本价值。

应当注意的是,市场价值与市场价格是不同的概念,尽管它们的数值有时可能是相同的。市场价值应该反映理论上推导出的估价,而市场价格是实际交易金额。

2. 账面价值

账面价值一般是指企业账簿上(资产负债表)所示的资产价值。换句话说,资产的账面价值等于其购置成本减去资产的折旧、摊销和减值费用。此外,企业的账面价值也等于将总资产减去总负债之后的股东权益金额。企业的账面价值与市场价值之间没有明确的关系,市场价值有时候可能会高于或低于账面价值。

3. 评估价值

评估价值指的是以物业税收为目的的指定价值,往往是基于市场价值来定义的。通常,评估价值评估的不仅包括土地而且还包括地上改良物。有时候评估价值会低于其市场价值。

4. 保险价值

保险价值指的是根据物业的重置成本所指定的价值,该价值等于酒店物业的市场价值减去土地价值。重置成本是利用替代资产将物业恢复到损失前状态的实际成本估算。

14.2   Define Various Types of Values

As valuation varies with the purpose of valuation, there exist many definitions of value, which will be described as follows:

1. Market value

Hines defines market value as "the dollar amount a property should bring in a competitive market under conditions requisite to a fair sale, which would result from negotiations between a buyer and seller, each acting prudently with knowledge and without undue pressure." According to the International Valuation Standards Council, market value is "the estimated amount for which an asset or liability should exchange on the valuation date between a willing buyer and a willing seller in an arm's length transaction, after proper marketing and where the parties had each acted knowledgeably, prudently and without compulsion." Therefore, the market value of a subject under consideration should reflect the subject's underlying value after a systematic assessment with due considerations on all possible influential factors.

It should be noted that market value is different from market price, albeit they sometimes could be the same. While market value should reflect theoretically derived assessment of a subject, market price is the amount of transaction taken place.

2. Book value

Book value generally refers the value of an asset shown on a firm's books (the balance sheet). In other words, book value of an asset is equal to its acquisition costs minus any depreciation, amortization or impairment costs for the asset. In addition, book value of a firm can also be referred to as the amount of stockholder equity, which is equal to total assets minus total liabilities. There is no definite relationship between a firm's book value and market value; sometimes the market value could be higher or lower than the book value.

3. Assessed value

Assessed value refers to value assigned to property for tax purposes and is often defined in terms of market value. Normally assessed value will include value appraised for not only land but also improvements. It is not unusual that assessed value of a property is less than its market value.

4. Insurable value

Insurable value is the value assigned to a subject based on its replacement cost, which is equal to market value of a hotel property minus the land value. Replacement cost is the actual cost estimate to replace assets and restore them to a pre-loss condition.

5. 清算价值

清算价值是业主被迫接受强制或快速出售物业的价值。在因为破产而须清算销售的情况下，业主可能会被迫以低于市场价值的价格在很短的时间内卖掉他们的资产，以期望能偿还债务。

6. 修订价值

修订价值是指业主在其投资持有期期末时酒店物业的市场价值。当业主购买酒店物业时，他们的目标之一可能是改造酒店，并通过资产管理公司的协助在运营三至五年后，提高该酒店对其他买家的吸引力和自身价值，并通过出售酒店物业来实现资本收益。

应当注意的是，上述关于价值的定义并不详尽，还有更多类型的价值存在。就算以同一个价值名称称呼，它们的含义也因它们被提到的上下文而有所不同。但是，当就不同目的进行酒店估价时，使用适当的术语是很重要的。

14.3　三种不同的酒店估价方法

无论酒店物业是因为出售或用作贷款申请抵押或其他目的，极有可能通过估价师来评估其价值。估价师在评价结果中将针对财产目标在某一时间点的价值给出意见。价值评估的过程是相当复杂的。步骤之一是应用适当的估值方法来进行价值评估。酒店估值是一个相当主观的过程和课题，在实践中有多达九种不同的估值方法。在本节中，我们将介绍其中三种方法，包括成本法、销售比较法和收益资本化法。

1. 成本法

成本法的实质是估计需要花费多少钱来重建具有相同条件的物业。对于一个典型的酒店物业，主要成本组成为土地、家具、装置和设备以及建筑物本身，而它们在酒店估价时皆单独考虑。应用成本法的步骤如下。

步骤一：估计土地价值。

步骤二：估计家具，装置和设备价值。

步骤三：决定净再生产成本。

步骤四：将所估的土地价值、家具、装置和设备价值加到净再生产成本，得出所估的目标价值。

5. Liquidation value

Liquidation value is the value an owner is compelled to accept for a property in a forced or quick sale. In the case of a bankruptcy sale, the owners may be forced to sell off their assets at lower than market value in a very short period of time so as to hopefully cover their debt obligations.

6. Revision value

Revision value refers to the market value of a hotel property to the owner at the end of an investment holding period. When owners purchase hotel real estate, one of their goals may be to revamp the hotel and operate it for three to five years through the assistance of an asset manager in a hope to enhance its value and appeal to other buyers and realize capital gains from such investment via a sale.

It should be noted that the above definitions of values are not exhaustive nor exclusive and there are many more types of values. Even if they are of the same name, their meanings may be different depending on the context in which they are mentioned. However, it is important to use the right terminologies when hotel properties are being valued for different purposes.

14.3　Three Approaches to Hotel Valuation

Whether a hotel property is being valued for the purpose of a sale or being used as a collateral for loan considerations, among others, it most likely will be to be assessed for its value by an appraiser. An appraisal will be produced to show the opinion of the appraiser on the value of the subject property at a certain point in time. The process of conducting an appraisal is rather complicated; one of the steps in conducting an appraisal is to apply appropriate approaches to valuation. While hotel valuation is a rather subjective matter, in practice there are as many as nine different valuation techniques. In this section we will introduce three techniques including the cost approach, the sales comparison approach and the income capitalization approach.

1. The cost approach

The essence of the cost approach is to estimate how much it would cost to rebuild the subject property to the same condition at the time of valuation. For a typical hotel property, the major cost components are land, FF&E and the building itself and they are considered individually in valuating the hotel. The steps in applying the cost approach are as follows.

Step one: estimate land value.

Step two: estimate value of FF&E.

Step three: determine the net reproduction cost.

Step four: add land value, FF&E value to the net reproduction cost to derive an estimated value of the subject property.

假设我们为在香港拥有 300 间客房和 3 间餐厅并有 500 个餐位、于 2010年开业、有 25 年预期寿命的 X 酒店进行估值,业主在 2015 年时考虑出售该酒店。

步骤一:经过调查后,据估计这块面积 4 万平方英尺的土地价值 4 亿港元。

步骤二:家具、装置和设备的原始成本为 2.5000 亿港元,目前大约值原始成本的 70%,或 1.75 亿港元。

步骤三:在测算净再生产成本时,我们首先考虑酒店开业当年以及进行估值时的建筑工程指数,再来估计再生产成本。假设当初酒店工程成本为 8 亿港元,2010 年和 2016 年香港的建筑工程投标价格指数(即工程指数)分别为 1266 和 1777。然后,我们可以应用以下公式来估算该酒店的再生产成本:

$$估计的再生产成本 = 原始成本 \times \frac{现年工程指数}{当年工程指数}$$

$$= 8 \times \frac{1777}{1266} \approx 11.2(亿港元)$$

然而,作为固定资产其账面价值会随着多年的运营而折旧,我们可以通过使用直线折旧法计算累计折旧:

$$累计折旧 = 再生产成本 \times 剩余使用寿命比率$$

$$= 11.2 \times \frac{5}{25}$$

$$= 2.24(亿港元)$$

这样一来,我们就可以通过将再生产成本减去累计折旧而得出净再生产成本如下:

$$11.2 - 2.24 \approx 9(亿港元)$$

步骤四:我们加总土地价值、家具、装置和设备价值和净再生产成本得出评估值 14.75 亿港元(即 4 亿港元 + 1.75 亿港元 + 9 亿港元)。

成本法对酒店物业进行的估值完全基于其原始成本,然而这种方法并没有考虑酒店的创收能力。虽然这种方法因为建筑价格上涨在估值过程中做了一些调整,但它可能还是比较适合应用在新一点的酒店物业上。

2. 销售比较法

一个相对可靠的评估酒店物业价值的方法是对比其他具有可比特征的

Suppose we are appraising Hotel X in Hong Kong with 300 guestrooms and three restaurants with a total seating capacity of 500 guests, which was opened in 2010 with an estimated lifespan of 25 years that the owners are considering for sale in 2015.

Step one: after some surveying it is estimated that the piece of land is worth HK$400 million with an area of 40,000 square feet.

Step two: the original cost of FF&E was HK$250,000,000 and currently is worth about 70% of the original cost, or HK$175,000,000.

Step three: in finding the net reproduction cost, we will first estimate the reproduction cost by taking into consideration of building construction indices in the years when the hotel was open and the year of valuation. Suppose that original cost of construing the hotel was HK$800,000,000 and the Building Works Tender Price Index (i.e., construction indices) were 1,266 in 2010 and 1,777 in 2016, respectively. We can then estimate that the reproduction cost of the hotel property is applying the following formula:

$$\text{Estimated reproduction cost} = \text{Original cost} \times \frac{\text{Current construction index}}{\text{Original construction}}$$

$$= \text{HK}\$800000000 \times \frac{1777}{1266} = \text{HK}\$1122906793$$

However, as fixed assets would have been depreciated along the years of operations, we can calculate accrued depreciation by using a straight-line depreciation method as follows:

$$\text{Accrued depreciation} = \text{Reproduction cost} \times \text{Percentage of remaining lifespan}$$

$$= \text{HK}\$1122906793 \times \frac{5}{25}$$

$$= \text{HK}\$224581359$$

As a result, we can then determine the net reproduction cost by subtracting accrued depreciation from the reproduction cost as follows:

$$\text{HK}\$1122906793 - \text{HK}\$224581359 = \text{HK}\$898325434$$

Step four: we sum up the land value, FF&B value and the net reproduction cost as the appraised value HK$1.473 billion (i.e., HK$400000000 + HK$175000000 + HK$898325434).

As the cost approach value a hotel property purely based on its original cost, albeit some adjustment was done in accounting for construction price increase, it may be suitable for hotel properties of relatively young history as this approach doesn't take the hotel's income generation ability into valuation consideration.

2. Sales comparison approach

A relatively reliable way of valuating a hotel property is to see how much other hotels of comparable characteristics were/are being sold for. From a buyer's perspective, he would not want to pay more than other buyers who have bought other similar types of

酒店是以多少价钱卖出或放售的。从买方的角度来看,买方不想比购买其他类似类型酒店的买家付出更多的钱;从卖方的角度来看,卖方也不希望以低于该物业可以卖出的售价出售物业。因此,销售比较方法在估值酒店物业方面有其优势。采用销售比较法的步骤如下。

步骤一:收集可靠的近期/当前类似的酒店物业销售信息。

步骤二:决定要比较的销售酒店数。

步骤三:将目标酒店与酒店对比并做出调整。

步骤四:确定评估价值。

假设我们使用销售比较法对同一家 X 酒店进行估值,在步骤一和步骤二我们收集并确定了最近的两个不同年份的酒店(Rikko 酒店及派拉蒙酒店)的销售信息(见表 14 - 1)。

表 14 - 1　两个不同年份的酒店的销售信息

项目	X 酒店	Rikko 酒店	派拉蒙酒店
售价	?	16 亿港元	18 亿港元
出售日期	—	2015 年 7 月 1 日	2010 年 4 月 1 日
客房数	300	464	570
餐饮设施	3 间餐厅,500 个餐位	5 间餐厅,650 个餐位	5 间餐厅,700 个餐位

在步骤三,我们可以通过对比目标酒店与 Rikko 酒店和派拉蒙酒店的特征而调整销售价格(见表 14 - 2)。

表 14 - 2　调整销售价格

项目	X 酒店	Rikko 酒店	派拉蒙酒店
售价	?	16 亿港元	18 亿港元
调整*:			
时间因素	—	2000 万港元	15000 万港元
餐饮设施	—	(1600 万港元)	(2000 万港元)
客房数	300	464	570
调整后价格	—	16.04 亿港元	19.3 亿港元
调整后每个客房价格	346 万港元	339 万港元	

*假设变动调整的百分比是经由调查房地产升值数据及实地考察得出。括号表示扣除项。

从上面的步骤中我们了解到,通过比较和调整 Rikko 酒店及派拉蒙酒店的销售信息,每个客房销售价格为 339 万~346 万港元。步骤四在确定

hotels; from a seller's perspective, he would not want to sell the property for less then what it could have been sold. Therefore, the sales comparison approach has its advantage in valuing a hotel property. The steps in applying the sales comparison approach are as follows.

Step one: collect reliable most recent/current sales information of similar hotel properties.

Step two: determine the number of units of comparison.

Step three: compare subject property against other comparing ones and make adjustments.

Step four: determine an appraised value.

Suppose we are appraising the same Hotel X in Hong Kong using the sales comparison approach and in steps one and two we have collected and determined two recent hotel sales (Rikko Hotel and Paramount Hotel) in Hong Kong at different years as Table 14 - 1.

Table 14 - 1 Hotels' sales at different years

Items	Hotel X	Rikko Hotel	Paramount Hotel
Sales price	?	HK$1.6 billion	HK$1.8 billion
Date of sale	—	July 1, 2015	April 1, 2010
No. of rooms	300	464	570
Food service outlets	3 restaurants, 500 seats	5 restaurants, 650 seats	5 restaurants, 700 seats

In step three, we can adjust the sales price by comparing Rikko Hotel and Paramount Hotel property attributes against our subject hotel, Hotel X, as Table 14 - 2:

Table 14 - 2 Adjustment of the sales of Rikko Hotel and Paramount Hotel

Items	Hotel X	Rikko Hotel	Paramount Hotel
Sales price	?	HK$ 1.6 billion	HK$ 1.8 billion
Adjustments *:			
Time factor	—	HK$ 20 million	HK$ 150 million
Food service outlets	—	(HK$ 16 million)	(HK$ 20 million)
No. of rooms	300	464	570
Adjusted price		HK$ 1.604 billion	HK$ 1.93 billion
Adjusted price per room		HK$ 3.46 million	HK$ 3.39 million

* Assuming percentage changes in adjustments were made after surveying real estate appreciation statistics and field visits. Parenthesis represents deduction.

From the above step we learn that by comparing sales information of Rikko Hotel and Paramount Hotel with adjustments, adjusted sales price per room ranges from

X 酒店的评估价值时,我们可以将经调整后的每间客房销售价取平均值作为 X 酒店的建议售价,再将该平均价格乘以客房数得出评估价值如下:

$$X 酒店的估值 = \left(\frac{339 \text{ 万港元} + 346 \text{ 万港元}}{2}\right) \times 300$$

$$= 10.3 \text{ 亿港元}$$

只要能够找出相关和可比的销售信息,销售比较法是相当简单的。然而,售价调整过程的考虑是相当主观的,毕竟每个酒店物业的地理位置、品牌价值、提供的服务等都具有其独特性。因此,相比于住宅地产,此方法应用在酒店行业是相当受限的。

3. 收益资本化法

由于酒店企业在日常运营过程中会产生收益,所以收益资本化法应该是较适合应用于酒店估值的方法。假设有两家类似的酒店,两者唯一的区别是它们不同的创收能力——一家强一些,另一家弱一些,很明显,具有较强创收能力的酒店物业可以比另一家酒店以更高的价格出售。因此,在评估酒店价值时考虑其创收能力更符合逻辑。换句话说,收益资本化法通过资本化(即贴现)酒店未来的收益流来决定酒店物业的市场价值。应用收益资本化法的步骤如下。

步骤一:估计酒店物业在其经济寿命内的收益流。

步骤二:估算一个合适的资本化比率(资本化率)。

步骤三:以资本化率折现收益流。

假设我们使用收益资本化法来对同一家 X 酒店进行估价。在步骤一估计酒店的收益流时,我们用销售收益减去运营费用(除了折旧和利息费用之外)。然而,应该指出的是,酒店每年的收益流并不是一个常数;它可能每年都会受到许多因素,如新的竞争酒店、管理能力、市场状况等的影响。此外,估算的收益流应该在考虑通货膨胀后以已计通胀收益表示。最后,酒店物业的生命周期(成长、壮大或衰退)和它的经济寿命也应一并考虑。通常情况下,收益流应该按物业的剩余寿命估算(X 酒店是 20 年),然而在估计更长年份收益时通常涉及更多的不确定性。为了便于说明,我们假设业主打算在 5 年内出售财产,所以我们估计酒店 5 年收益流如表 14 - 3 所示。

HK $ 3.46 million to HK $ 3.39 million. In step four in determining an appraised value for Hotel X, we can take the average of the adjust sales price per room to derive a suggested sales price per room for Hotel X, and then derive an appraised value by multiplying the average price by the number of rooms as follows.

$$\text{Appraised value of Hotel X} = \left(\frac{\text{HK \$ 3.39 million} + \text{HK \$ 3.46 million}}{2}\right) \times 300$$
$$= \text{HK 1.03 billion}$$

The sales comparison approach seems to be rather straightforward as long as relevant and comparable sales information can be identified. However, the adjustment consideration is rather subjective and each hotel property is unique in its geographical location, brand equity, service provisions, and etc. Therefore, compared to residential real estate, the method's application to the hotel industry is rather limited.

3. Income capitalization approach

The income capitalization approach is likely a more suitable way in valuing a hotel property's market value as hotel businesses are generating incomes from their normal course of business operations. If there are two identical hotels with the only difference being their different income generation abilities: one stronger and the other weaker, it is rather obvious that the hotel property with stronger income generating ability will sell for a higher price than the other one. Therefore, it sounds more logical to consider a hotel property's income generation ability in its valuation. In other words, the income capitalization approach is applied to determine the market value of a hotel property by capitalizing (i.e., discounting) its future income stream. The steps in applying the income capitalization approach are as follows.

Step one: project the hotel property's income stream over its life.

Step two: derive an appropriate capitalization rate (capitalization rate).

Step three: discount the income streams by the capitalization rate.

Suppose we are appraising the same Hotel X in Hong Kong using the income capitalization approach. In step one in projecting the hotel's income stream, we can subtract operating expenses (except for depreciation and interest expense) from revenues. However, it should be noted that a hotel's income stream is not a constant; it may be affected by many factors such as new competitions, management competency, market conditions... etc from year to year. Besides, the income stream should be stated in inflated dollars taking inflation into consideration. Lastly, the life cycle of the property (growing, peak or declining) and its lifespan should also be considered. Normally the income stream should be projected for the remaining life of the property (for Hotel X is 20 years); however, it involves many more uncertainties when projecting longer years' income. For illustration purposes we assume the owners plan to sell the property in five years so we project five years of income stream as Table 14 - 3.

表 14 - 3　酒店 5 年收益流估计

年份	收益流（港币）
1	130000000
2	136500000
3	143325000
4	150491250
5	158015813

在步骤二决定资本化率时有几种方法，在此我们介绍一个较实际的方法——投资组合法，这个方法考虑到现实中大多数酒店物业都是同时由债务和权益融资的。

$$总资本比率＝DF\%×MC＋EF\%×ER$$

式中：DF 是债务融资占总融资的比例；EF 是股权融资占总融资的比例；MC 是抵押贷款常数；ER 是必需的股本回报率。

由于债务和股权是企业融资方案的两个组成部分，股权融资占总融资的比例 EF% 也就是（1－DF%）。抵押贷款常数 MC 基本上是债务的资本化率。然而在测算资本化率时债务融资的利息税盾被忽略，同时假设该笔债务是永久的。抵押贷款常数 MC 可以计算如下：

$$抵押贷款常数＝\frac{每年本金和利息费用}{初始贷款额}$$

假设 X 酒店 70% 的资产是以 25 年、5% 利率的贷款融资，其业主的要求回报率是 12%，换句话说，初始贷款金额为 8 亿港元×70%，而每年偿还的贷款总额是每月偿还额乘以 12，也就是 40197341 港元。因此，抵押贷款常数为 7.18%。总资本化率可以如下计算得出：

$$总资本比率＝70\%×7.18\%＋30\%×12\%＝8.63\%$$

我们可以利用测算出的资本化率来折现 5 年的估计收益流，以确定 X 酒店的市场价值（如表 14 - 4 所示）。

表 14 - 4　X 酒店 5 年的估计收益流

年份	收益流（港币）	折现因子（8.63%）	折现收益流（港币）
1	130000000	0.9205	119665000
2	136500000	0.8474	115670100
3	143325000	0.7801	111807833
4	150491250	0.7181	108067767

Table 14 - 3   Hotel's five years' income stream

Year	Income stream (HK$)
1	130,000,000
2	136,500,000
3	143,325,000
4	150,491,250
5	158,015,813

In step two for determining a capitalization rate, out of a number available methods, we introduce a more practical one—the band of investment method, which considers the reality that most properties are financed with both debt and equity component as follows.

$$\text{Overall cap rate} = DF\% \times MC + EF\% \times ER$$

Where: DF is debt financing as a percentage of total financing; EF is equity financing as a percentage of total financing; MC is mortgage constant; and ER is required equity return rate.

As debt and equity are two components in firms' financing options, the proportion of equity financing to total financing EF% is then (1—DF%). MC is essentially the capitalization rate for debt however in the calculation of cap rate the interest tax shield from debt financing is ignored and an assumption of perpetual debt is made. MC can be calculated as follows.

$$\text{Mortgage constant} = \frac{\text{Annual payment of principal and interest expense}}{\text{Original loan amount}}$$

Assuming Hotel X financed its assets with 70% of debt with a 5% interest rate for 25 years; its owners' required return is 12%. In other words, the original loan amount is HK$800,000,000 × 70% and the annual loan payment is monthly payment times 12, which is HK$40,197,341. Therefore, the mortgage constant is then 7.18%. The capitalization rate is then determined as follows.

$$\text{Overall capitalization rate} = 70\% \times 7.18 + 30\% \times 12\% = 8.63\%$$

With the calculated capitalization rate, we can then use it to discount the projected income stream of five years to determine a market value for Hotel X as shown in Table 14 - 4.

Table 14 - 4   Hotel X five years' projected income stream

Year	Income stream(HK$)	Discount factor at 8.63%	Discounted income stream (HK$)
1	130,000,000	0.9205	119,665,000
2	136,500,000	0.8474	115,670,100
3	143,325,000	0.7801	111,807,833
4	150,491,250	0.7181	108,067,767
5	158,015,813	0.6611	104,464,254
6	1,831,005,944	0.6611	1,210,478,030
Total value			1,770,152,894

年份	收益流（港币）	折现因子（8.63%）	折现收益流（港币）
5	158015813	0.6611	104464254
6	1831005944	0.6611	1210478030
总值			1770152894

　　由于假设 X 酒店的业主计划在 5 年后出售酒店物业，除了之前预测 5 年的收益流之外，同时应该预估出售物业时所产生的一笔末期收益。酒店物业出售价钱可以将第 5 年的收益 158015813 港元除以资本化率 8.63% 而得出 1831005944 港元。这个估算的出售价钱是基于第 6 年之后的年收益额将等于第 5 年的收益额的假设，对于一家正步入稳定成熟期的酒店来说这应该算是一个合理的假设。通过加总贴现收益流和预计第五年年末的销售价格，从收益资本化法得出 X 酒店的市场价值为 1770152894 港元。

As we assume that the owners of Hotel X plan to sell the property at the end of Year 5, in addition to the previously projected five years' income stream, a terminal income generated from the sale of the property should be projected as well. The sales price can be determined by dividing Year 5's income of HK$158,015,813 by the capitalization rate of 8.63%, which is equivalent to HK$1,831,005,944. This projected sales amount is estimated based on the assumption that the annual income after Year 5 will be a constant at an amount as Year 5's, which is a fair guestimate if the hotel is growing into a stable and mature stage. By summing up the discounted income stream plus projected sales price, the market value of Hotel X derived from the income capitalization approach is HK$1,770,152,894.

参考文献
References

Andrew，W. P.，Damitio，J. W.，& Schmidgall，R. S. （2007）. *Financial management for the hospitality industry*. New Jersey，USA：Pearson Prentice Hall.

Berle，A. A.，& Means，G. C. （1932）. *The modern corporation and private property*. New York：The Macmillan Company.

Bucknall，R. L. （2016）. HongKong report：Quarterly construction cost update. from https：//www.rlb. com

Chatfield，R. E.，& Dalbor，M. C. （2005）. *Hospitality financial management*. Upper Saddle Rever，New Jersey：Pearson/Prentice Hall.

de Roos，J.，& Rushmore，S. （2016）. Hotel valuation techniques. from http：// www. HVS. com/library

Donaldson，G.，& Fox，B. （2000）. *Corporate debt capacity：A study of corporate debt policy and the determination of corporate debt capacity*. Beard Books.

Fama，E.F.，& French，K，R. （1992）. The cross-section of expected stock returns. *Journal of Finance*，47(2)，427 – 465.

Gu，Z. （2000）. *Perceived risk and foreign investment in encyclopedia of tourism* (J. Jafari Ed.). London，United Kingdom：Routledge Limited.

Hilton-hotel. （2014）. *Hilton worldwide* 2014 *annual report*. McLean，VA：Hilton Worldwide Holdings，Inc.

Hines，M. A. （1981）. *Real estate appraisal*. New York：Macmillan.

Jensen，M. C. （1998）. *Self-interest，altruism，incentives，& agency*. Cambridge， MA：Harvard University Press.

Kraus，A.，& Litzenberger，R. H. （1973）. A state-preference model of optimal financial leverage. *Journal of Finance*，28(4)，911 – 922.

Modigliani，F.，& Miller，M. （1958）. The cost of capital，corporation finance and the theory of investment. *The American Economic Review*，48(3)，261 – 297.

Myers，S. C. (1984). The capital structure puzzle. *Journal of Finance*，39(3)，911 – 922.

Schmidgall，R. (2006). *Hospitality industry managerial accounting* (6th ed.). Lansing，MI：The Educational Institute of the American Hotel & Lodging Association.

USALI. (2014). *Uniform systems of accounts for the lodging industry*. Lansing，MI：American Hotel & Lodging Educational Institute.

Zhou，B. W. (2015). Guided prices for hotels in Sanya：RMB5,000 per day for a standard room during the Chinese New Year. from